SHAPING FLEXIBILITY IN VOCATIONAL EDUCATION AND TRAINING

Shaping Flexibility in Vocational Education and Training

Institutional, curricular and professional conditions

Edited by

Wim J. Nijhof

University of Twente,
The Netherlands

Anja Heikkinen

University of Jyväskylä,
Finland

and

Loek F.M. Nieuwenhuis

Stoas Research,
Wageningen, The Netherlands

KLUWER ACADEMIC PUBLISHERS

DORDRECHT / BOSTON / LONDON

A C.I.P. Catalogue record for this book is available from the Library of Congress.

ISBN 1-4020-1145-8 (HB)
ISBN 1-4020-1146-6 (PB)

Published by Kluwer Academic Publishers,
P.O. Box 17, 3300 AA Dordrecht, The Netherlands.

Sold and distributed in North, Central and South America
by Kluwer Academic Publishers,
101 Philip Drive, Norwell, MA 02061, U.S.A.

In all other countries, sold and distributed
by Kluwer Academic Publishers,
P.O. Box 322, 3300 AH Dordrecht, The Netherlands.

Printed on acid-free paper

Printed in the Netherlands.

TABLE OF CONTENTS

LIST OF FIGURES

LIST OF TABLES

LIST OF CONTRIBUTORS

Alan Brown is a Principal Research Fellow at the Institute for Employment Research at the University of Warwick. His principal research interests are in the fields of vocational education and training; identity formation; and the use of IT to support continuing professional development.

Geoff Chivers holds the Chair of Risk and Professional Development in the Business School at Loughborough University. He is the Director of the Centre for Hazard and Risk Management and researches in this field, as well as in the fields of continuing professional development, adult vocational learning and HRD. Prior to taking up this appointment Geoff was, for fifteen years, Professor of Continuing Education at the University of Sheffield. He has published and taught widely in the fields of adult learning, gender and science and technology, and organisational risk management. Professor Chivers has a strong interest in international comparative adult learning research and professional development.

Jos Geerligs –jog@stoas.nl- holds a MSc in plant pathology and a PhD of Twente University. He spent 12 years in general and vocational education in the Netherlands and Zambia. He was an inspector for vocational education and a senior staff officer for knowledge policy for another 12 years. At present he is a researcher and knowledge engineer for Stoas Education in Wageningen. His focus is on studying the linkage of working and learning in complex systems e.g. education and policy development.

Anja Heikkinen is a professor of adult education in the Department of Education at University of Jyväskylä. Her research interests and publications focus on cultural - historical, sociological and philosophical - and gender aspects of vocational education. She has for years been active in European research networks and projects promoting cross-cultural approaches in adult education and VET research, university studies and practices. More information at website http://www.jyu.fi/~hoanhe/

Phil Hodkinson is Professor of Lifelong Learning and Director of the Lifelong Learning Institute, in the University of Leeds, England. He has researched and written widely on vocational education and training, and on transitions from education into work. He is currently researching into informal and formal learning in the workplace, and in English Further Education Colleges, examining the interactions between organisational and individual backgrounds and characteristics, in relation to wider social, political and economic contexts.

Leif Hommen is an associate professor with the Department of Technology and Social Change, Linköping University (Sweden). He received his PhD in educational studies from the University of British Columbia (Vancouver, Canada) in 1994. His research has focused on relations between innovation and employment and has addressed both 'labour market' policies and 'innovation' policies. Recent publications include "Systems of innovation: Theory and policy for the demand side", with C. Edquist, in *Technology In Society* 1999, and "Innovation and qualification: Institutional challenges," in Kurt Mayer (ed.), *Approaching a learning economy: Innovation, qualification and employment in a new policy framework*, 2002 – forthcoming.

Cathy Howieson is currently a Senior Research Fellow at the Centre for Educational Sociology where she has worked since 1986. Her research interests include post-compulsory education and training systems with a particular interest in the relationship between academic and vocational learning; and young people's transitions through education, training and the labour market and the role of guidance in this process.

Tuija Hytönen is a project manager in the Vantaa Institute for Continuing Education in the University of Helsinki. Before moving to the University of Helsinki she worked in the Department of Education at University of Jyväskylä and as an adult educator in the Open University in the University of Jyväskylä. She researches and teaches about human resource development, professional development of HRD practitioners, professional expertise, learning at the workplace and adult learning. Her PhD study "Exploring the practice human resource development as a field of professional expertise" was published in August 2002.

Lorenz Lassnigg, is Head of the research group EQUI (Employment - Qualification - Innovation), at the IHS Sociology department (www.equi.at) in Vienna (Austria). He received a PhD from the University of Vienna (pedagogy, political science). Since 1985 he is leading research projects about labour market policy, education policy, and innovation policy. He works as an expert for the European Commission (European Social Fund; 1997-99) and for the OECD (youth labour market and transition from education to work; 1997-99).

Fernando Marhuenda, Associate Professor at the University of València, in Spain, in the Department of curriculum studies and educational policy. He has taken part in a 4th FP TSER on Work experience as well as in a Leonardo project on post-16 strategies and enhancing vocational education and he is currently taking part in a 5th FP on Vocational identities. He has also coordinated two research projects on vocational training for youth at risk in the region of Comunidad Valenciana, in Spain. His areas of interest are those of vocational education and training as well as education and social justice.

Kurt Mayer is a senior researcher at the Institute for Advanced Studies (IHS) in Vienna. He graduated in 1995 in political science, then he completed a two years postgraduate-programme in sociology at the IHS. He has been involved in various research projects in the areas of labour market evaluation, education and training policy and the social and economic preconditions of innovation.

Loek Nieuwenhuis is senior researcher at Stoas Research in Wageningen, the Netherlands. He is co-ordinator of the labour market research programme for agricultural education. Before he worked at Groningen University and Erasmus University Rotterdam on institutional and learning aspects in VET. At Groningen University, 1991, he finished his PhD study on complex learning situations in school and enterprise. Together with Twente University, he is recently working on a new research program "The Learning Potential of the Workplace", granted by NWO (Dutch Science Foundation).

Wim Nijhof is professor of Education, University of Twente, The Netherlands. His research interests are curriculum theory and design, implementation and evaluation in vocational and adult education, and corporate training. Focus of recent studies is on competencies, informal and formal learning at work, design and effects of information technology on work, and studies on effectiveness and transfer in corporate training. He is chairing a group of researchers in a new research program "The Learning Potential of the workplace" (NWO grant, 2001-2006).

Rob F. Poell is a lecturer in Human Resource Development and Vocational Education at Nijmegen University, The Netherlands. He researches and teaches about workplace learning, project-based learning, and strategies of workers, managers and HRD practitioners in creating learning programmes. His 1998 PhD thesis "Organising Work-Related Learning Projects: A Network Approach" was granted the Malcolm Knowles Dissertation of the Year Award by the Academy of Human Resource Development.

David Raffe is Professor of Sociology of Education at the University of Edinburgh, where he directed the Centre for Educational Sociology until September 2001. He has research interests in secondary and post-secondary education, education-work transitions, the relation of vocational to academic learning and the comparative analysis of education systems. He has conducted several comparative studies among European and OECD countries and within the UK.

Luisa Ribolzi is professor of Sociology of Education at the Faculty of Educational Science, University of Genova (Italy): she co-ordinates the research group of Italian Sociologists of education. Her scientific interests are mainly on institutional aspects of education, as organisational models, teachers, and assessment. She worked on transition from education to job, as a consultant for the Italian Entrepreneurs Association, ISFOL, Unioncamere, researching on career guidance, stages, competencies and industries' educational needs.

Gerald A. Straka, Ph.D., Professor of education with special reference to empirical learning-teaching and evaluation research at Bremen University, Faculty of Education and Institute of Technology & Education; chairperson of the Research Group Learning, Organised & Self-Directed. His research areas are: conceptualisation, identification and promotion of self-directed learning in business and industry, development and application of theoretically grounded learning-teaching concepts, assessment of vocational competencies. http:///www.los-research.de, email: straka@uni-bremen.de.

Teresa Tinklin has been a Research Fellow in the Centre for Educational Sociology since 1998. She is an experienced educational researcher, with an interest in issues of inequality in education. Recent and current work includes research into the participation and experiences of disabled students in higher education and gender and pupil performance in schools.

David Tuohy is the director of Masters Programmes in the Education Department of the National University of Ireland, Galway. He has written extensively on leadership, school culture and staff development for schools as learning organisations.

László Zachár, (Hungary) Mechanical engineer teacher, associate professor at the Budapest University of Technical/Economical Sciences (BUTES). His teaching area is the "world of work" including job orientation, labour market training, training for disadvantage people. His special research area is the theory and practice of the adult vocational training particularly the structures of skills and methodology. He co-ordinated the Phare-project for renovation the technical teacher education at the BUTES in 1996-98.

PREFACE

This book is based on the enthusiastic, competent, and intensive work of members of Working Group 4 of the COST Project A 11: Vocational Education in the years 1998-2002. Flexibility, Transferability, and Mobility were the key concepts, as well as the key targets to be covered by the whole COST Project. More than 200 researchers from 16 countries were involved in this unique project in the area of vocational education in Europe. While the other working groups were focused on policy-making processes, teaching and learning environments, transfer, evaluation and assessment, the focus of Working Group 4 was on the systems' level of Vocational Education and Training systems. The study of shaping conditions for a flexible VET was, from the start, the most hybrid, complex and rather broad topic to be covered. It was especially at the beginning of the work that this generated long discussions, not only on the concepts and definitions of flexibility, but even more on the context, history, culture, and traditions of VET systems and their consequences. Of course, combining researchers from different countries, with totally different VET systems, disciplines, and research traditions, yields contrasting and competing views on values, norms, politics, the labour market, and education. Working Group 4 opted to work, on a comprehensive and comparative basis, on flexibility, and divided this topic into three subthemes: institutional and organisational conditions; curriculum conditions, pathways, and assessment; conditions for and of VET professionals.

The outcomes of the work are presented in this volume. It was agreed that the cross-cultural nature of social-scientific research should be given attention, first and foremost to understand the culturally embedded and rooted meanings of the phenomena and categories that each of the researchers hold. This is a sociopsychological process, with its own logic. Secondly, we have progressed into debating and learning from each other by better understanding interpretations and visions, all of which come from different cultures and research traditions.

We learned during the project that VET systems and VET research are now high on the political agenda of the EU and of most countries in the world. We learned too that flexibility is a really controversial issue, which cannot be solved by single technological strategies, master plans, or curriculum designs. But we have seen a series of solutions, critical studies - quantitative as well as qualitative - and reviews, which better help us to understand the complexities of actor systems, institutions, organisations, and people who have to work in practice: professionals.

VET has regained prestige and status in the past decade; it shows not only the important economic function of skilling for the labour market, but also the pedagogical and social function of educating human beings with their responsibilities for a future that will never be known. Transferability, as a personal attribute, and flexibility, as an institutional condition, prove to be crucial concepts for designing lifelong learning systems - public as well as private - and for creating opportunities for employability.

Without the expertise and friendship of the members of the COST group, this volume would not have come into existence. We should like to thank all our colleagues for their support and the authors for their efforts and collaboration in the editorial work. Our thanks also go to the reviewers, Leif Hommen, Fernando Marhuenda, and Phil Hodkinson, for their excellent work, especially where the cultural diversity and scientific controversy related to flexibility is so evident.

We have the best of reminiscences of the plenary discussions at Newcastle, Göttingen, and Gothenburg, as major events of the whole COST Project at which to present our work, and as wise lessons to review our conclusions. We also enjoyed the working group meetings in Twente, Genova, Jyväskylä, Vienna, and Wageningen, where hospitality and professional work were combined in a productive way. The formula of COST has proved to be successful in bringing together researchers from all over Europe.

We are very grateful indeed to the Dutch Science Foundation (NWO-COST) for its financial support in preparing this book. Many thanks to Gay Howells and Janice Collins, who used their language competence elegantly to allow people to say what they really think, and who helped us to produce a consistent book. Monique Kole did the layout and all the necessary correspondence, and supported the authors and editors.

We hope this book will be seen as a major contribution for promoting VET and VET research, and as a real help for policy-makers, practitioners, teachers, students, researchers, and governmental institutions for thinking ahead on the flexible future of VET within their cultures and traditions, to give meaning to the demands of the economy, society, and the individual. VET is education par excellence.

Enschede, Summer 2002
Wim J. Nijhof, Anja Heikkinen and Loek Nieuwenhuis

SECTION I

INTRODUCTION

CHAPTER 1

Shaping conditions for a flexible VET

LOEK F.M. NIEUWENHUIS, WIM. J. NIJHOF AND ANJA HEIKKINEN

1.1 Flexibility: a systems' view

FLEXIBILITY SEEMS TO BE THE CORE CONCEPT of economic and educational change in our time. The promise of solutions to many problems at the individual, institutional, and national level evokes as much controversy as acclaim. This might be related to the different perspectives of actors and researchers involved in problem-solving in VET, where, on the one hand, solutions to VET should be sought in key qualifications and transferability, in changing teaching and learning processes, while, on the other hand, political, institutional, organisational, and professional conditions are seen as the key interventions to build a responsive workforce on the basis of a re-engineered VET system. Consequently, flexibility in connection with vocational education and training (VET) and the labour market has several divergent connotations. In this volume, we treat flexibility as a system characteristic of VET. Flexibility in this sense is an input/throughput factor for the delivery of required competencies to respond to social and economic demands in the various economies in the European community. Nijhof & Streumer (1994) present a cognitive map of flexibility in VET, in which three types of flexibility are presented, corresponding to the input, throughput, and output of VET. Input flexibility concerns the responsiveness of VET systems to changing skill demands, e.g. as a consequence of the emerging knowledge economy. Throughput flexibility concerns the capacity of VET systems to deal with individual differences amongst students, e.g. by designing different pathways to becoming skilled. Output flexibility refers to the transferability of skills and the mobility of trainees. Raffe (1994) presents four types of flexibility: curricular flexibility (comparable to input), flexibility of delivery and pathways (comparable to throughput), and individual flexibility (or transferability and mobility). Especially this last form of flexibility has elicited a major political debate on social equality and exclusion, as reported by Coffield (2002), referring to the undesirable effects of the flexibilisation of VET on social equality and the division of labour. Felstead, Ashton & Green (2001) report a direct relation between labour market flexibility and skill development. The skills of part-timers and flexible workers have deteriorated, compared to those working full-time. Felstead (in press) also reports the development of regional skill differences, related to regional economic development. In the UK debate, flexibility is contested with labour political issues, especially around individual flexibility. In the Dutch context, Hartog (1996) refers to the same debate, stating that "... the new economic order asks for an increased flexibility of workers on the one hand (higher skills, life long learning), but on the other hand for job security. Flexibility should be translated in trainability and learning skills and not in external flexibility."

Transferability and mobility (individual flexibility) can be seen as outcomes of educational investments: transferability refers to the cognitive results for students,

3

W. J. Nijhof et al. (eds.), Shaping Flexibility in Vocational Education and Training, 3-14.
© 2002 *Kluwer Academic Publishers. Printed in the Netherlands.*

in terms of sustainable competencies and skills, which equip students well for lifelong learning and working. Mobility refers to the socio-economic results for students, in terms of gateways and passports to a labour market where lifetime employment is exchanged for lifetime employability. Both transferability and mobility have acquired new meaning in the light of an emerging knowledge-based economy, in which changing skill requirements and changing market conditions are the only certainties left (Nijhof, Kieft & Van Woerkom, 2001). To prepare students for the future, European VET and VET systems should be responsive and proactive towards future developments. This requires an enormous curricular and throughput flexibility or adaptability at all levels in the different VET systems.

Systemic flexibility is the main subject of this book. In order to deliver transferable skills and foster students' mobility in a knowledge-based economy, VET is in search of new ways of political governance, institutional set ups, organisational and curriculum designs in all European countries. However, we do not expect to end up in one European VET system. The national systems are deeply rooted in cultural, political, educational, and socio-economic traditions and institutions. These systems are quite diverse, and the expectations of stakeholder groups like students, parents, teachers, employers, and politicians are closely connected to these traditions and institutions, resulting in country-bound public and private skilling systems, although migration and immigration in Europe is putting great pressure on the current ideologies, politics, and pathways to skill formation. These insights outline the playing field for the present book.

Shaping flexibility in VET means analysing the conditions and implications to be found in the institutional and political context of VET systems, in the socioeconomic expectations of stakeholders, reified in regular pathways to the labour market, in the organisational design of VET inside colleges and companies, in the educational tools, such as pathways, curricula, learning materials and assessment procedures, and, last but certainly not least, in the professional expectations and ambitions of teachers and trainers. These conditions form the context for powerful teaching and learning environments in which the formal and non-formal skilling processes will take place. Learning is context-bound and, while VET systems are designed to skill people in context, these three groups of conditions seem to be essential for shaping flexibility (see Figure 1.1.).

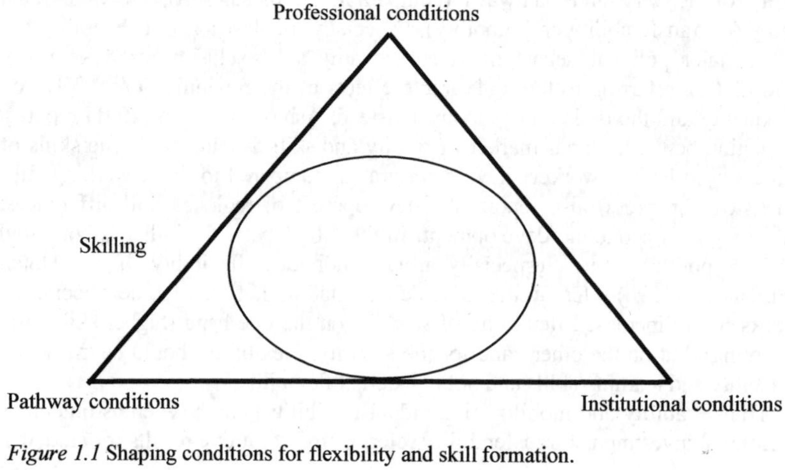

Figure 1.1 Shaping conditions for flexibility and skill formation.

This overview of themes forms the problem definition of and the challenge for this book. For such a complex social system as VET, a wide variety of conditions have to be met, to reach the systemic flexibility needed in the near future. To organise this variety, the book is divided into three main parts. After this introductory section, the second section deals with the changing economic conditions that VET is confronted with, and the consequences it will have on the institutional and organisational conditions of a flexible VET. The third section deals with pathways and curriculum designs, evaluation, and assessment as a means to respond to the economic challenges through flexibility (Nijhof, Kieft & Van Woerkom, 2001; Raffe, 1994); in this section, particular attention is given to system change in some specific European countries. The fourth section is focused on the roles, tasks, and future demands of VET professionals, and the challenges they are confronted with. Before going in depth into the different sections and individual contributions, a framework is presented to analyse in greater depth connections between the various sections and conditions involved.

1.2 Governance of change in VET

In this section, an analytical frame (see Figure 1.2.) will be presented for the governance of change in vocational education and training. The basic perspective is the idea that changing complex social systems need coherent, persistent, and consistent political actions at all levels of the systems, e.g. political debate and legislation, institutional setup, organisational and financial conditions, and the design of skilling systems and processes should be in line with each other. In order to realise system flexibility, change is needed at all system levels.

VET is a rather complex social system, because it is located on the edge of two basic human activities: learning and working (Ellström, 1999). For both activities, systems have to be built at local, national, and European levels. Within VET, these systems are intertwined in many ways. Changing VET is thus a long-lasting enterprise, requiring interactions and debates inside and between the different interest groups of the system. In this section, these ideas and models are built into a comprehensive model for changing VET systems, to prepare them for the emerging learning society. According to Edquist and Johnson (1997), social systems are specific set ups of institutions and organisations. Social systems are designed incrementally to reach societal goals:

- Institutions can be defined as sets of common habits, routines, rules, or laws that regulate the relations and interactions between individuals and groups. Functions of institutions are, for example, the provision of information and the reduction of uncertainty; managing conflicts and cooperation; the provision of incentives; the channelling of resources;
- Organisations are formal structures with an explicit purpose; they are consciously created and they are players and actors in the system.

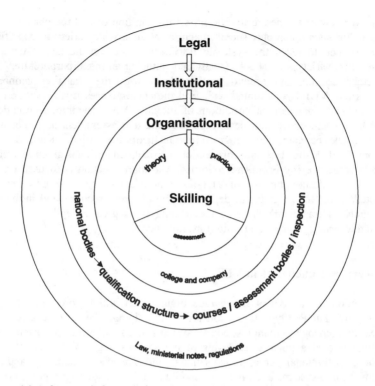

Figure 1.2 A framework for analysing educational change in skilling systems (adapted from Nieuwenhuis, Mulder, Jellema & Van Berkel, 2001).

VET is a social system for which in each country and/or economic sector a specific set of institutions and organisations has been developed over time. Governments, business and industry, unions, and educational organisations have built an institutional setup for VET, which is deeply rooted in social, cultural, and economic patterns. Because of these roots, VET institutions are difficult to change, and are sometimes even obstacles to innovation of the system. Changing VET is not only a matter of the educational system, but also of the socioeconomic system and of cultural traditions. Examples of VET institutions are: laws on education and labour; public-private arrangements; training funds; collective labour agreements; pathways to becoming skilled; qualifications and wages; occupational identity; training traditions.

In theory, organisations are much easier to change than institutions, but organisations depend on the institutional set up. Thus, technical-rational arguments (e.g. instructional science for VET) for a systems' change are not convincing if they are not compatible with the institutional set up. This is an important observation for understanding the design and restructuring of VET systems. Changing VET and its evaluation has to be directed simultaneously at all the levels involved. Policy, intermediary structures, colleges, companies, and teachers should interact in the change process; managing this process is like directing a large orchestra: if one party is out of tune, the whole performance is endangered.

In Europe, all states are seeking to flexibilise their VET systems. Old systems were built on stable economies and labour market institutions (e.g. Germany and the Netherlands) or were built on a low-skill equilibrium (e.g. UK; see Finegold, 1991). In both cases, powerful economic forces urge the upgrading and flexibilisation of VET systems: globalisation of markets, high-speed technological innovation, and ICT development are examples of these forces. The permanent development of and change in the NVQ system in England, the reform of the dual system in Germany, shaping and reshaping of VET in Eastern European countries, new legislation in the Netherlands, and changes in the Italian VET system: there is no VET system which is not under revision. This revision is not only a technical debate: societal and political issues are at stake (cf. Coffield, 2002; Nijhof, 2001). In all VET systems the search is on for new equilibria:

- Between initial VET and lifelong learning: the old infrastructure is built on the delivery of initial VET; the new one should be able to deliver support for lifelong learning;
- Between traditional occupations and flexible qualifications: old-fashioned occupations are slowly disappearing, but the institutions are still built on the traditional occupational structure; there is no room in the arena for new occupations;
- Between school-based learning and qualification through work experience: learning steered by attainment targets is to be replaced by learning within changing communities of practice; on the other hand, instruction and training is a proven, very powerful educational tool;
- Between social demands and economic markets: should the student be adapted to labour market demands or can the worker shape his own economical context?
- Between employment and entrepreneurship: is the 'new economy' for employed workers or for entrepreneurial workers?

Policy-makers and other stakeholders try to formulate new balances on those dimensions, but in each case, the institutional setup of VET is at stake. The old regulations and appointments and the social-economic meaning of VET are changing. Stakeholders (like community colleges, employers, trade-unions and the government) should reposition themselves towards the newly developing VET systems.

Crouch, Finegold and Sako (1999) offer a sceptical view of the feasibility of a high-skills strategy in western economies. Analysing skill creation systems in seven OECD countries, they conclude that both state-based and market-oriented strategies are doomed to failure. State-based VET will suffer from low responsiveness and innovativeness, whereas market-led VET will not be able to upskill the majority of the workforce. Thus, each country should reconsider these outcomes, and rearrange their VET system. Crouch et al. (1999) do not believe in a single best solution at system level: copying best practices from elsewhere needs careful planning and consideration of the institutional history of both source and receiving system.

The learning culture in colleges and companies and the professional ambitions of teachers and trainers are connected to institutional views on knowledge, skills, and values. The teaching-learning arrangements offered to the students depend on these cultural and professional conditions. The learning processes in the VET system, developed in the industrial economy of the 20th century, are different from the learning processes within innovating companies (Hoeve & Nieuwenhuis, 2002). These differences in learning processes cause different professional profiles for teachers and educators on the one hand and for professionals in companies on the other. The work culture and the incentive structures also differ greatly for professionals and managers in companies and colleges. The design of a flexible VET for the knowledge economy involves not only reorganisation of the course supply but also a redesign of the fundamental processes and culture (Lassnigg, 2001). Industrial VET is targeted at codified knowledge and skills: methods, books, and curricula form an intermediary between learners and practice. According to Wenger (1998), codification has its costs and returns: it facilitates the entrance to new knowledge, but hinders the giving of meaning to that knowledge through participation. The exchange value of competencies is connected to codification, whereas the use value refers more to participation (Tomassini, 2000; Sfard, 1998). In such a practice, teachers have little chance of developing their expertise and identity as participants in innovative processes, and are no longer strong role models for their students. Colleges should offer teachers more opportunities for authentic participation in economic activities. Getting in touch with the uncertainties of innovative activities, they might experience the tacit aspects of competencies, the trial-and-error aspects of innovation, and the uncertainty of innovative learning processes. Through the authentic participation of teachers, both students and teachers can act as full participants in the VET community of learning for working.

Changing VET systems can be seen as a kind of governmental learning, depending on the specific problem definition and the specific configuration of institutional and organisational actors and their stakes, policy strategies, and targets of systems change should be defined. There is no one right way for VET, although a European approach suggests a convergence of targets and goals. There are no safe recipes for countries to reach these goals and targets. VET policy is a matter of chaos and complexity: each country has to examine its own 'setup'; examples from other countries can be used as good practice, but should be adapted to one's own national situation. (See for instance Resnick & Wirt, 1996). One important lesson for systems' innovations is that the learning and experimentation should be coherent and compatible at all systems' levels: from law, through institutions and organisations, up to teaching-learning processes.

1.3 Rationale of the book

In this volume, different research traditions in the field of VET are presented. To study the complexity of VET as a social system, and the conditions to be met, and to reach systemic flexibility, many disciplines of social sciences have potential contributions. Outside the German-speaking countries, VET hardly has a research tradition. Since the start of the COST Action 11 programme on Flexibility, Transferability, and Mobility in Vocational Education (Achtenhagen, Nijhof & Raffe, 1995), a research capacity in Europe is growing, and lines to common frames of interest in VET research are imminent. Parallel to the development of the importance of learning within and for economic development, the research community in the area of work and learning has become increasingly professional and coherent (Nieuwenhuis & Nijhof, 2001). Before 1980, consistent research on VET was rare in social sciences, except for the economic-based research (Wirtschaftspädagogik) in Germany. Since that time, research has become increasingly focused on the socio-economic function of VET. In this volume, studies from the three perspectives will be presented on shaping flexibility in VET systems in three sections.

Section II: Institutional and Organisational Conditions
This section starts with three chapters on the relation between developments in the economic context of VET on the one hand and the organisational and institutional design of VET on the other. The transition of Western economies from industrial to knowledge-based working processes has major consequences for the design of VET systems and the organisation of VET colleges. Kurt Mayer describes in Chapter 2 the transition to a learning economy and its consequences for innovation and learning at the company level. He describes the changes in learning and working processes that are happening within innovative firms. Mayer highlights the growing apart of experiential learning processes accompanying innovation processes and codified learning processes within educational settings. He stresses the importance of the context of application, as offered by innovating firms, for the acquisition of transferable skills and competencies, which should lead to a new division of tasks in vocational training between the public VET sector and private firms. In Chapter 3, Loek Nieuwenhuis describes the difficulties VET colleges are confronted with, while changing towards responsive organisations for VET delivery. The managements of VET colleges, both in the Netherlands and in Europe, are aware of the urgency of changing their organisations into learning colleges. However, the external incentive structure and the internal organisational tools do not support this change. Institutional and organisational conditions are locking VET colleges into the routines of an industrial training paradigm, and they need support from other actors and levels in the system to escape. This requires innovative action at systems' level. Leif Hommen reviews in Chapter 4 the two contributions from an institutional-economic perspective. He perceives VET as a social construction, and, to this end, points to the role of social actors in the construction process. From that perspective, economic and societal stakes become closer and are no longer seen as opposed constructs. Hommen perceives educational organisations as loose coupling entities, which tend to 'decouple' internal processes from external incentive structures. This makes these organisations resistant to external influences, but, at the same time, offers opportunities to establish innovative internal processes. From that perspective, Hommen points to the contribution to the institutional setup from bottom-up processes out of component organisations within social systems. Bottom-up perspectives form a welcome complement to top-down views on institutional and organisational change in social systems.

Section III: Educational tools and resources for flexibility
In this section, the perspective changes towards educational tools and resources for the flexibility of delivery and pathways at national level. In this section, some national systems will be described in the perspective of a system change towards flexibility. Each chapter show the particularities and set ups of VET systems, and will indicate the problems, perspectives, conditions, and effects being confronted with flexibility.

Education can be flexible at the micro, meso, and macro-level, when it is designed in such a way that it can be adapted to different circumstances. In fact, the concept of differentiation is used, taking measures on the basis of the educational functions in society in such a way that differences emerge in the structures, grouping, contents, processes, goals, time, and characteristics of the givers and receivers of education

(Nijhof, 1978). Internal flexibility of VET is a complex phenomenon, in which context factors play a dominant role in pushing the system forward into a pro-active institution. In this section of the book, the focus is on the macro-level of the system, but with pure intentions to relate flexibility designs and effects.

Two contributions focus on the systems' level responses to the demand for flexibility in VET delivery. In Chapter 5, Cathy Howieson, David Raffe & Teresa Tinklin describe the introduction of a unified educational system for post-16 in Scotland. The first experiences with and results of VET within that unified system are presented. Luisa Ribolzi presents in Chapter 6 a comparable movement towards flexibility in the Italian VET system. In Chapters 7 and 8, system presentations are offered. For the Hungarian VET system by Laszlo Zachar, going into a new era of democracy and economy, and for the Irish VET system by David Tuohy. Geerligs and Nijhof present in Chapter 9 the design and effects of a system tool to establish flexibility in the Dutch agricultural VET system. A qualification structure is presented as a carrier (and codification) for flexibility, and it is shown that these kinds of tools are necessary for professionals to deal with the required flexibility and to establish efficiency, at least in terms of learning time. Finally, Gerald Straka analyses in Chapter 10 the conceptual, institutional and implementation consequences of new instruments for assessing competencies, based on experiential learning. Fernando Marhuenda concludes this section with a critical review of the six contributions. He argues that the systems' perspective is only a condition for teaching practices, where the 'proof of the pudding' is to be found. He states firmly that effective comparative research in and for VET should be conducted in multidisciplinary teams of researchers, in order to establish a genuine research approach to VET.

Section IV: Professional Conditions
The shared aim of the authors in section IV is to discuss the potential of VET professionals as promoters of flexibility, mobility, and transferability in the framework of a common educational core in their work. In sections II and III, the initial conditions for flexibility in VET are primarily discussed from a systems' perspective. The main challenge for VET systems is their "responsiveness" to the changing employment systems, influenced by societal, economic, and organisational megatrends. Their main implication is the flexible utilisation of human labour. Flexibility in VET refers to the characteristics of the learning processes, the curriculum, and of VET institutions, which constitute the VET system. In this framework, VET professionals could be seen as part of VET institutions, managing, steering, or coordinating the adjustment of the VET system to the employment system. VET professionals are by no means merely technicians, but rather, crucial actors in the definition and constitution of VET. Nor is the reduction of VET work into job profiles and roles in training courses or curricula enough for understanding its dynamic complexity. Therefore, flexibility, mobility and transferability as targets of the VET systems must also be analysed as *transforming* categories, connected to the constitution of VET professionals themselves. Crucial enabling and impeding factors, tendencies and challenges are identified, instead of exhaustive descriptions and analyses at member state and European level. The variety of VET professionals is an outcome of transforming patterns of negotiation about the division of VET work and the ways of becoming a VET professional. What kinds of transformations underlie the emergence of the new VET professional, faced with the challenge of flexibility? The following chapters exemplify the complexities and controversies of

VET work both in terms of its functions and its cultural embeddedness. Lorenz Lassnigg (Chapter 12) elaborates the transforming division of VET work in the European landscape. He discusses the problems and possibilities of professionalisation as the solution to the challenge of flexible interaction between VET and employment. Anja Heikkinen attempts to historicise VET work in general and shows the need for its cultural contextualisation in the case of Finland. Tuija Hytönen, Rob Poell and Geoff Chivers highlight in Chapter 14 the diffuse and unestablished area of Human Resource Development work, reminding us about the limits of mobilising its actors into anything like a shared professional project. On the other hand, actors in this field are most interestingly representing the imperatives of flexibility, mobility, and transferability in their own risky positions, struggling between autonomy and subordination to management. Alan Brown stresses in Chapter 15 the interdependence between the functions and actors of VET, especially from the perspective of occupational practice in health care. The parallel reduction of practical and experiential learning in formal education and the intensification of work processes leads to growing demands for employees to include training and education functions in their job profile: collective negotiations about this seem to be marginal, however. In the concluding chapter, Phil Hodkinson shows the limits on the part of VET teachers and trainers to take a lead in the professionalisation of VET work. Even if the context is the UK, the auditing culture is generally strengthening in European policy (EU). The educational professionalisation of VET work is impossible without recognition and support from other players who influence the future development of European societies, economies, and conditions of work and education.

1.4 What did we learn? Towards a research agenda

In this volume, systemic flexibility is seen as a promising educational answer to hyperinnovation and changing economic conditions in the emerging knowledge-based economy. Individuals, local communities, and VET systems should be able to adapt effectively to changing conditions in society, work, and labour markets. Community colleges, training firms, and teachers should be able to support that adaptation. On the other hand, it is argued that the institutions and traditions in VET are deeply rooted in local and national cultures, and thus difficult to change. In the case of pathway flexibility, Raffe (2002) argues that the impact of flexibility depends on 'institutional logic' (inside the world of work). The study of flexibility therefore needs to be grounded in the social, economic, and organisational context of each country. Conditions for flexibility do not have their own intrinsic logic, but should be studied in the context of cultural and institutional differences, connected to national and local histories. Bringing in the perspective of teachers and VET professionals, this argument counts twice, caused by the historical embeddedness of teacher training and teachers' professionalism. Researching conditions for a flexible VET should not be restricted to educational-technical issues, but should be embedded in cultural and institutional issues of local and national systems.

Hommen argues that social systems should be seen as social constructions. VET is not a static physical relic, but a cristallisation of appointments and agreements between social actors, reified in institutions. By neglecting the constructive character of social systems, both actors and construction processes can be hidden in the actual political discourse. Doing that, the debate on VET could be reduced to a technical discussion, ruled by economic arguments, and the role of VET could be reduced to learning at the workplace. By stressing the constructive character of VET as a social system, the political and pedagogical debate can come to the fore, giving emphasis to cultural and traditional differences in the various countries and regions within the European community.

Not only education, but also the labour market and the economic sphere, can be considered as socially constructed. Markets are not opposed to, but integrally part of, society and institutions form the fundament for market functioning. By emphasising the connections between society, economy, and education, the debate on flexibility can avoid the pitfall of short-term adaptations to the short-sighted needs of firms: flexibility and responsiveness should be considered in longer-term perspectives as lifelong learning and employability and in creating an adaptive labour force with a high transferability potential. Flexibility should be translated into trainability and learning skills and learning strategies to prepare people for the future.

The strategic behaviour of VET colleges is a last point added to the future research agenda by Hommen: he observes a precarious equilibrium between the autistic behaviour of schools on the one hand and externally detemined behaviour on the other. A carefully decoupling strategy, in which internal work processes and external structures are loosely coupled, can have positive effects on the innovative capacity of schools. Decoupling creates space for innovation.

Marhuenda also argues in favour of a VET system which is not only steered and developed in a rather technical way. Flexibilisation is on many occasions related to the modularisation of the curriculum and to the fragmentation and deconstruction of knowledge into skills and competencies. Policies to deliver a flexible workforce are often based on strict regulations for colleges. These policies reject, rather than devolve, power and autonomy to colleges in the name of flexibility. This tendency can be counterproductive, when related to the expectations of young people, whereas, on the other hand, the flexibility of pathways and delivery can keep education up to date and motivate students. It is the democratic embeddedness of measures for a flexible VET which makes them socially interesting and appealing and connected to the individual pathways to develop their vocational and personal identities. Thus, also at the level of resources for flexibility, the assessment of tools and instruments is embedded in an institutional frame, the utility of flexibility and the main stakeholders in this argumentation are essential to understanding how tools, pathways, and instruments work. Comparative research could help to understand better how these tools and systems work under different cultural conditions and traditions. But traditions themselves are answers to problems of the past, and should be assessed in the light of the new demands. Traditions can also serve as blocking mechanisms, to prevent adaptation to modern times, as much as they can help us to overcome overly hasty changeovers that deteriorate personal interests, equity, equality, and other important values and norms. Assessment of prior experiential learning in a diploma society has untied many people from institutional pathways to become accredited and create opportunities for employability.

Hodkinson adds to this view the perspective of an emerging body for VET professionals, influencing the working conditions for teachers and HRD professionals. His conclusion is that VET professionals will not have a great influence on the conditions within VET and training inside companies, just because of the many stakeholders and institutional frames around VET. The impact of 'others' is more powerful on the design of flexible VET than the impact of VET professionals themselves. A balance should be sought between external specifications and professional design by teachers themselves to create an innovative sphere inside VET colleges. With that argument, Hodkinson ends the circle started by Hommen that VET is socially constructed by many players in the field. Researching the conditions for flexible VET implies a research programme directed at the embeddedness of VET systems in local and national institutional setups of the systems for work and education. As Raffe (2002) states, the study of flexibility (of VET) needs to be grounded in the social, economic, and organisational context of each country. The impact of flexibility depends on the institutional logic within each national system for learning and work, and our understanding of that logic not to block innovations, but to find conditions and actor systems to become innovative. Working together in Europe on a comparative base can help open the windows for understanding cultural diversity, and promote systemic flexibility in learning and work settings for the good of the individual and of society.

References

Achtenhagen, F., Nijhof, W.J., & Raffe, D. (1995). *Feasability Study: Research Scope for Vocational Education in the framework of Cost Social Science.* Luxembourg: Office of Official Publications of the EU.

Coffield, F. (2002). *Will Cinderella go to the ball?* Key note speech for the COST A11 conference, June 2002 Gothenburg. Newcastle upon Tyne: University of Newcastle.

Crouch, C., Finegold, D., & Sako, M.(1999). *Are skills the answer? The political economy of skill creation in advanced industrial countries.* New York: Oxford University Press.

Edquist, C., & Johnson, B. (1997). Institutions and organisations in systems of innovation. In C. Edquist (Ed.), *Systems of Innovation. Technologies, institutions and organisations* (pp. 41-63). London: Pinter.

Ellström, P.E. (1999). The role of Labour Market Programmes in Skill Formation: The Case of Sweden. In W.J. Nijhof &. J. Brandsma (Eds.), *Bridging the Skills Gap between Work and Education* (pp. 55-69). Dordrecht/Boston/London: Kluwer Academic Publishers.

Felstead, A., Ashton, D., & Green, F. (2001). Paying the price for flexibility? Training, skills and non-standard jobs in Britain. *International Journal of Employment Studies, 9,* (1), 25-52.

Felstead, A. (in press). Putting skills in their place: the regional pattern of work skills in late twentieth century Britain. In K. Evans, P. Hodkinson & L. Unwin (Eds.), *Learning and the workplace.* London: Kogan Page.

Finegold, D. (1991) Institutional incentives and skill creation; preconditions for a high skill equilibrium. In P. Ryan (Ed.), *International comparisons of vocational education and training for intermediate skills* (pp 93-116). London: the Falmer Press..

Hartog, J. (1996). Kennis van de toekomst. In *Bouwstenen voor het kennisdebat* (pp.49-85). Zoetermeer: ministerie van OC&W.

Hoeve, A., & L. Nieuwenhuis (2002). *Learning in innovation processes.* Paper for the Dutch/Vlamish educational research conference in Antwerp. Wageningen: Stoas Research.

Lassnigg, L. (2001). The Learning oriented company and policy perspectives for VET and HRD. In L.F.M. Nieuwenhuis & W.J. Nijhof (Eds.), *The dynamics of VET and HRD Systems* (pp. 35-59). Enschede: Twente University Press.

Nieuwenhuis, L., Mulder, R., Jellema, M., & Berkel, H. van (2001). Tussen voorschrift en autonomie: het organiseren van attractief beroepsonderwijs [Organising attractive VET]. *Pedagogische Studien, 78,* (6), 412-424.

Nieuwenhuis, L.F.M., & Nijhof, W.J. (2001). Emerging research approaches in the European Vet and HRD agenda. In L.F.M. Nieuwenhuis & W.J. Nijhof (Eds.), *The dynamics of VET and HRD systems* (pp 1-11). Enschede: Twente University Press.

Nijhof, W.J. (1978). *Interne differentiatie als een Innovatie*. Den Haag: SVO (Intra class room grouping as an Innovation).

Nijhof, W.J. (2001). The VET system between private demands and public interests; the Dutch Challenge. In L.F.M. Nieuwenhuis & W.J. Nijhof (Eds.), *The dynamics of VET and HRD systems* (pp. 11-24). Enschede: Twente University Press.

Nijhof, W.J., & Streumer, J.N. (1994). Flexibility in vocational education and training: an introduction. In W.J. Nijhof & J.N. Streumer (Eds.), *Flexibility in training and vocational education* (pp. 1-12). Utrecht: Lemma.

Nijhof, W.J., Kieft, M., & Woerkom, M. van (2001). *Reviewing Flexibility*. Luxembourg: Office for Official Publications of the European Communities. ISBN 92-894-1482-0.

Raffe, D. (1994). The new flexibility in vocational education. In W.J. Nijhof & J.N. Streumer (Eds.), *Flexibility in training and vocational education* (pp. 13-33). Utrecht: Lemma..

Raffe, D. (2002). *Flexibility of pathways*. Keynote address for the Gothenburg conference of COST A11. Edinburgh: University of Edinburgh.

Resnick, L.B., & Wirt, J.G. (1996). *Linking School and Work*. San Francisco: Jossey Bass Publishers.

Sfard, A. (1998). On Two Metaphors for Learning and the Danger of Just Choosing One. *Educational Researcher, 27*, (2), 4-13.

Tomassini, M. (2000). Knowledge dynamics, communities of practice: emerging perspectives on training. *European journal on vocational training, 19*, 38-47. Thessaloniki: Cedefop.

Wenger, E. (1998). *Communities of practice; learning, meaning and identity*. Cambridge: University Press.

SECTION II

INSTITUTIONAL AND ORGANISATIONAL ASPECTS OF

FLEXIBILITY

CHAPTER 2

Vocational education and training in transition:
from Fordism to a learning economy

KURT MAYER

2.1 Introduction

DURING THE PAST TWO DECADES, in highly industrialised western countries, systems of vocational education and training (VET) have been increasingly challenged by a major shift in the techno-economic paradigm. The Fordist industrial paradigm, which was the predominant mode of development from the middle of the former century until the 1980s, based on nation states, Tayloristic work organisation, and assembly line techniques was increasingly sliding into a crisis. In parallel with this decline, the outlines of a new techno-economic paradigm became apparent, characterised by information and communication technologies (ICTs), an increased orientation towards global markets, flat hierarchies in work processes, and lifelong learning. Some authors refer to the new paradigm as a learning economy (Lundvall & Johnson, 1994; Archibugi & Lundvall, 2001). Given this transition, the main argument of this chapter highlights the organisational and institutional challenges deriving from a new interplay between Vocational Education and Training (VET) and innovation, the core process of the learning economy.

Section 2.2 discusses the patterns of VET delivery in the Fordist industrial paradigm; section 2.3 analyses the broader political and societal context of VET, deriving from a newly emerging nexus between innovation and learning in the framework of a learning economy. This macro-level analysis is complemented by a closer look at the micro-level in section 2.4. Two alternative models, reflecting the interplay between VET and innovation at the organisation level are contrasted: the *social organisation of innovation,* based on cooperation, networking and an extensive development of human resources, is contrasted to an alternative trajectory of *technical organisation of innovation,* based rather on a reduction in product costs, by deepening the division of labour and tightening discipline in the factory. We will argue that both models are founded on their own idea of flexibility. Nevertheless, only the flexibility concept of the social organisation of innovation is compatible with the learning economy paradigm, and points to new requirements for VET. Section 2.5 is particularly focused on these new requirements and corresponding VET policies in a learning economy.

17

W. J. Nijhof et al. (eds.), Shaping Flexibility in Vocational Education and Training, 17-33.
© 2002 *Kluwer Academic Publishers. Printed in the Netherlands.*

2.2 VET in the Fordist[1] industrial paradigm

Despite the dramatic changes we are facing in the fundamental patterns of the economy and employment, the traditional Fordist industrial paradigm is still deeply rooted in our concepts and institutions of work, industry, education and social policy (Carnoy & Castells, 1997). A gap can be observed between the real changes and dynamics in the business processes and re-engineering strategies of companies, with crucial repercussions *for VET* on the one hand and rather traditional institutional set-ups and organisational rationales *in VET* on the other.

In this first part, we try to analyse the role of VET in the Fordist period, taking the Fordist/Tayloristic employment model as a starting point. As a result, we discover a predominantly hierarchical and polarised labour market paradigm related to a skill-producing system, which predominantly released companies from responsibility, and produced only a few transferable and rather poor technical skills (Boyer & Caroli, 1993).

2.2.1 The employment model of the Fordist industrial paradigm

In the Fordist/Tayloristic paradigm, work followed two fundamental principles: functional specialisation and hierarchical integration (Schienstock, 2000), pointing to hierarchical chains of command, narrow divisions of tasks and a large component of unskilled labour. As the core of the Fordist economy, large corporations have been structured on the principles of vertical integration and the institutionalised social and technical division of labour (Castells, 1996). The information flow in these companies typically contained channels in which only a vertical flow of information was possible, and through which the performance of hierarchically-arranged units was controlled. Management as a practice has been about being in control, exercising specific expertise, and maintaining clear lines of responsibility (Kelleher & Cressey, 2000). The Tayloristic organisation of labour had a tendency towards the separation of the conception and execution of work processes, and hence towards "the systematic incorporation of the know-how of technical workers in the automatic operations of machines" (Lipietz, 1994). The Tayloristic paradigm broadly excluded the direct producers from any involvement in the intellectual aspect of labour, hence industrial relations have been restricted to issues of wages, working time, and industrial safety. The hierarchical character of the Tayloristic division of labour has never been in doubt, nor has training been perceived as an issue for trade unions (Mayer, 1999).

At the macro-level, this paradigm was based on *"productivity gains obtained by economies of scale in an assembly-line based, mechanized process of production of a standardized product, under the conditions of control of a large market"* (Castells, 1996).

---

[1]   In contrast to Bell's general definition of the industrial society, characterised by the coordination of workers and machines for the production of goods (1973), the concept of Fordism – pioneered by the French Regulation Approach in the late 1970s and refined in the 1980s (cf. Aglietta, 1979; Boyer, 1992; Jessop, 1986; Lipietz, 1997) – is used to denote the specific phase of capitalist industrial development between the 1930s and the 1970s, reflecting *"loosely the pioneering mass production methods and rules of management applied by Henry Ford in his car factories during the 1920s and 1930s."* (Amin, 1994).

2.2.2 The skill-production model of the Fordist industrial paradigm

This work paradigm emerged in co-evolution with Fordist institutional set-ups like full-time employment, clear occupational assignments, and a well-established career pattern over the worker's lifespan, corresponding to the concept of a guaranteed "job for life". It was possible to work in a specific occupation for a lifetime, and requirements hardly changed: young people went to school, got a job and often did that job for much of the rest of their lives. Learning was clearly localised at the start of life; after initial education, training was seldom needed (Carnoy & Castells, 1997). Because of the stability on the labour market, the educational supply could continue to exist for a long period of time. Hence, education was designed within a context of certainty: the knowledge was judged as true and objective, and the instructional techniques were authoritarian, receptive, and nonparticipative.

Within this context, VET could be developed in an industrial way within the framework of the *adaptation approach*. Technological developments were assumed to be *automatic*, hence the requirements of the production process and the features of occupations just had to be anticipated, codified, and translated into different educational steps, qualification standards, and examination demands. In this process of *backward mapping* on the one hand, occupational analyses played an important role. On the other hand, the development of skill definitions and appropriate technical and vocational courses has often been controlled by professional groups at national level[2]. The resulting job structures and function profiles had the status of true canons (cf. Brown & Duguid, 1996) of the future demand for workers and skills, although the definition of these profiles is abstract and the result of a compromise, with a conservative flavour.

The Fordist mode of labour organisation, separating conception and execution, has been mirrored in the separation of general and vocational education, and the corresponding low prestige of vocational and occupational education compared to general academic education. *"Whilst vocational education might offer entry into occupational communities of practice, it was restricted in that the general education required for career progression or for dealing with the growing complexity in industry and commerce was not provided." "And universities have increasingly been seen as offering a better opportunity for career development"* (Attwell & Hughes, 2001). The tasks of vocational colleges in this paradigm were restricted to the implementation of prescribed criteria. Consequently, the student has been *put through*' the educational process: once chosen for a specific part (course) of the system, the educational process - well defined from start to finish - had to be consumed (Nieuwenhuis & Smulders, forthcoming).

In terms of further training, classical, continuing vocational training in companies (internal and external courses and seminars) has been important only for the upper segment of the labour market (management and engineers) and for individual workers who wanted to climb the promotion ladder. For the majority of employees in companies and organisations, classical on-the-job training (vocational adjustment training) was sufficient, and continuing training for the unemployed was not important either.

---

[2]   Trade unions and employers' organisations especially played their roles in the definition of vocational courses in the German and Dutch apprenticeship systems and in the formulation of national vocational qualification standards in the UK system (Nieuwenhuis & Smulders, forthcoming).

2.3 Towards a learning economy

Since the 1970s, and especially in the 1980s and 1990s, processes of structural change and the emergence of new socio-economic forces and political interests - strategies of internationalisation, the impressive development of Information and Communication Technology (ICT), the emergence of an information economy, and the struggle for flexibility, deregulation and market liberalisation - modified the time and space dimensions of economic activities, and hence substantially changed the rules for company behaviour. This had fundamental implications for the meaning of education, training, and learning in the industrial and in the broader societal context too. In the following part we first analyse the forces of change and second we try to relate these arguments to the new paradigm of a learning econmy.

2.3.1 The forces of change

Increased Competition
Globalisation, ICT and the neoliberal policies of deregulation tremendously increased the pressure of global market competition. The number of competitors in a certain area increased. The fields of market competition increased as well, since companies had recently been competing not only for customers, but also for network partners and human resources.

Economies of scope: competition becomes increasingly information-based
Nevertheless, market competition has not only increased, it has also changed its mode, as it is increasingly based on information. Due to the rapid progress of ICT, information has become increasingly important for competition, since data, information, and codified knowledge can a) be easily stored in information infrastructures, b) spread rapidly over the whole economy, and c) be easily accessed. As a consequence, information has become an economic good, it can be bought and sold on the marketplace, and it is also an important factor in knowledge acquisition and technology dissemination.

These new opportunities to access information are challenging the traditional competitive advantages of companies, regions, and nations. Within advanced industrialised economies, they have the tendency to trigger a shift from the search for economies of scale to economies of scope. Economies of scope derive from the ability of companies to configure available information in novel ways, and to use this information for creating new production processes and new products.

Innovation
This competence in innovation gives companies a comparative advantage over those that simply adopt and adapt production processes in low-wage economies. Consequently, in their seminal report *The globalising learning economy,* Lundvall & Borrás (1999) draw the far-reaching conclusion that *"Innovation is not a marginal phenomenon in the economy - it is central to the industrial dynamics and growth of regions and nations".*

Competence-building and learning
As the importance of innovation has increased, the rate of change has speeded up significantly in the past two decades. This is mirrored to a considerable extent in the

area of competence and skill requirements[3]. As a consequence, Lundvall points out that change and innovation in the economy *and* learning are two sides of the same coin, since the acceleration in the rate of change confronts *"agents and organisations with new problems and to tackle the new problems requires new skills"* (Lundvall, 1999). Innovative companies select more learning-oriented employees, and the market selects more change-oriented companies. Hence, according to Lundvall (1999), *"the new economy is characterised by a process of 'circular cumulative causation' between innovation and learning."*

2.3.2 The learning economy

The arguments above reflect fundamental shifts in the way knowledge is produced, organised, and utilised in the Post-Fordist economy. The high rate of change and the new pressures of market competition are forcing companies to build an ability to configure information resources in novel ways which cannot be easily imitated or replaced by competitors (Lam, 2001). Since ICT make a vast amount of data and information available and easily accessible, the problem of information-based competitive advantages is to continually innovate and stay one step ahead.

As a consequence, the learning economy concept has at its core the basic distinction between information as a commodity of increasing importance in the globalising information society *and* the complex social and technical processes that are a precondition for making the new amount of information useful. This difference is analysed by the concepts of *codified knowledge* and *tacit knowledge*.

Codified knowledge or information can be obtained through reading books, attending lectures, and accessing databases. Due to the improvement in ICT, codified knowledge can be packaged, bought, and sold in ways and to an extent never seen before. It is treated like a commodity, and can be accessed by an economic transaction and/or an appropriate ICT infrastructure.

The economic value of these transactions - of patents, investments in formal R&D, qualifications, papers published and cited - has traditionally been well recognised by standard economics, which assumed that rational agents make choices on the basis of a given amount of information. In this line of argument, the access of agents to new information sets triggers the economic value of knowledge.

Looking at the nature of the innovation process, we have to point out that innovation involves strong elements that cannot be planned. If *"innovation concerns the search for, and the discovery, experimentation, development, imitation, and adoption of new products, new production processes and new organisational set-ups"* (Dosi, 1988), then the dimensions of complexity, uncertainty, cumulativeness, interactivity, acting collectively, and learning play a major role in the innovation process. Hence, in terms of innovation, it seems to be knowledge at the top end which is not yet well defined and is hard to transfer in a routine manner that *"provides the 'competitive edge' for firms which are trying to stay ahead of the pack"* (Ducatel, 1998). Drawing on a concept of Polanyi (1958), this top-end knowledge is referred to as 'tacit knowledge,' in contrast to 'codified knowledge' or

---

[3]   In the European Commission's Green Paper on Partnership for a new Organisation of Work, it is pointed out that 80 per cent of the process technologies used today will become obsolete within a decade (quoted in: Lundvall & Borrás, 1999). A Human Resource Director in the telecommunications industry estimated that eighty per cent of current jobs would be obsolete even within five years (Kelleher & Cressey, 2000).

mere information. *"Tacit knowledge is personal, context specific and therefore hard to formalize and communicate."* (Nonaka & Takeuchi, 1995). It refers to the observation: *"We know more than we can tell"* (Polanyi, 1958). Being ´tacit´[4] means that this knowledge is not migratory, because it is deeply embedded in complex social interactions and relationships within organisations (Lassnigg, 1998). Since tacit knowledge resides in the skills, shared experiences and behaviour of groups and individuals, it cannot be easily acquired or bought in the marketplace. This is the main difference from codified knowledge that can typically be accessed. Tacit knowledge on the other hand is rooted in practical experience and social interaction. Since tacit knowledge is socially-constructed knowledge, it can only be appropriated in a social context by interactivity and social interaction. It will typically be learnt (Lundvall, 1996).

The acceleration in processes of creation and use of codified knowledge via ICT is intrinsically related to the increasing importance of tacit knowledge, enabling information to be used. Tacit knowledge in terms of the processing of information comes to the fore, which is needed to effectively acquire, select, and use data and information created within the company and elsewhere (Soete, 2000). Hence, *"codified and tacit knowledge are complementary and co-exist in time"* (Lundvall & Borrás, 1999), and tacit knowledge seems to have the role of defining how to use explicit knowledge.

Against this background, Nonaka & Takeuchi (1995) argue that only *"when tacit and explicit knowledge interact (...) an innovation emerges"*. Their dynamic model of 'knowledge conversion' *"is anchored to a critical assumption that human knowledge is created and expanded through social interaction between tacit knowledge and explicit knowledge"* (ibid). In this line of reasoning, the sources of innovation multiply *"when organizations are able to establish bridges to transfer tacit into explicit knowledge, explicit into tacit knowledge, tacit into tacit, and explicit into explicit"* (Castells, 1996).

Until now, the learning economy paradigm has had a rather unbalanced focus on the company as a knowledge-building organisation. Nevertheless, given the aforementioned significance of tacit knowledge issues, it becomes evident that the learning economy paradigm also raises salient questions about the content of vocational education and training, the forms and channels for its provision, and its timing over the worker's lifespan. These questions are rather different from the ones raised in the Fordist industrial paradigm, where VET systems provided initial training of different kinds, giving access to specific professional trajectories determined from the start (Soete, 2000a).

In this section, we want to link the level of firm organisation and company behaviour to the role played by the wider institutional arrangements and trajectories of VET systems. Hence, in the next section, we will contrast two alternative models of linking innovation to flexibility at the company level. Both models correspond to

---

[4]   Tacit knowledge has two dimensions: the ´cognitive´ and the ´technical´ elements (Nonaka & Takeuchi, 1995). The cognitive elements focus on ´mental models´ (schemata, paradigms, perspectives, beliefs, and viewpoints) in which human beings create working models of the world by making and manipulating analogies in their minds. These cognitive elements, which help individuals to perceive and define their world, refer *"to an individual´s images of reality and visions for the future, that is ´what is´ and ´what ought to be´.* The technical elements include know-how, crafts and skills. Both dimensions of tacit knowledge suggest that tacit knowledge defines how to use codified knowledge or, even clearer: tacit knowledge is a precondition for making use of codified knowledge.

different challenges for the tasks and functions of VET institutions and VET organisations. This will be the background to raise in section 2.5 the question: How can the VET system - which is still largely rooted in the Fordist industrial paradigm - be redesigned so that it corresponds to the challenges of a learning economy?

2.4 Innovation and flexibility at company level

With respect to the new challenges of globalisation, ICT and a new mode of competition, firm behaviour is changing at three different levels: a) within companies, b) in the interaction with other companies (competitors, users, suppliers) and other institutions (universities, technical societies etc.), and c) in the interaction with a recently emerging KIBS (Knowledge Intensive Business Services) sector. Nevertheless, as Castells (1996) argues *"what emerges from the observation of major organizational changes in the last two decades of the century is not a new, 'one best way' of production (...). A variety of models and organisational arrangements emerged from that crisis"*. Some companies are failing completely to establish new knowledge-sourcing strategies, and most of them will drop out of the market. Other companies, in turn, are installing strategies aimed at reducing product costs, by deepening the division of labour and tightening discipline in the factory, whilst a third category of companies, in turn, are reorganising themselves by reducing levels of hierarchy, delegating responsibilities, and enhancing collaboration and interaction between departments and with other companies.

Based on empirical evidence[5] and a literature study[6], we have been developing two ideal typical models of firm behaviour, dealing with the challenges of globalisation, new IC potentials, and innovation as a core of the economy. These are the concepts of 1) a social organisation of innovation, and 2) a technical organisation of innovation. Both models challenge the roles and functions of VET in different ways.

2.4.1 The social organisation of innovation

The trajectory of a *social organisation of innovation* comprises a broad approach to innovation, aimed especially at product innovation and organisational innovation, and not exclusively at technological process innovation. As a result, labour cuts, driven by technological process innovations, are balanced by new labour needs, driven by product innovations. Product innovations will open new markets, with few competitors and high added value, thereby initiating a new cycle of growth and expansion. The revenues are largely used to invest in education, new organisational set-ups for human resource development (HRD), and research and technological development (RTD) to make the growth path sustainable. Furthermore, organisational innovations like project teams and work groups within the company, and technological partnerships with customers, or research networks with suppliers and universities will strengthen the knowledge-sourcing capacities, and hence innovativeness, quality of products, and technological leadership. *"Thus, the actual opera-*

---

[5]   We carried out 25 qualitative expert interviews with management staff and six in-depth company case studies in the course of a European TSER project in the 4th framework programme (http://www.univ-aix.fr/lest/sesiweb/).

[6]   Brödner, 1999; Castells, 1996; Lundvall & Borrás, 1999; Schienstock, 2000.

ting unit becomes the business project, enacted by a network, rather than individual companies or formal groupings of companies. Information circulates through networks: networks between companies, networks within companies, personal networks, and computer network. New information technologies are decisive in allowing such a flexible, adaptive model to actually work" (Castells 1996). The implementation of ICT is explicitly dedicated to supporting work processes, enhancing transparency, and enabling and assisting cooperation.

Moreover, elaborated knowledge management and communication strategies are assisted by organisational and technological knowledge from outside, provided by the new KIBS. Within the company, communication between hierarchies, which may have been reduced, and also between departments will be enhanced, to simplify the ´knowledge and competence puzzle´ as the precondition for innovation and integrated product development. This, in turn, is complemented by lifelong learning and HRD strategies for the whole workforce, since, according to the principles of a learning organisation, *"inventing knowledge is not a specialised activity.(...) it is a way of behaving in which everyone is a knowledge worker"* (Nonaka, 1991).

The major competitive advantage of a firm approaching the path of a social organisation of innovation does not principally lie *"in enlarging the pool of proprietary knowledge which is subject to imitation as it is utilised, but the ability to access a wide spectrum of knowledge resources and configure them in unique ways"* (Lam, 2000). This wide spectrum of knowledge resources is configured in new products and new technologies that enable the company to compete in new, high value-added markets.

2.4.2 The technical organisation of innovation

The trajectory of a *technical organisation of innovation* comprises a rather narrow concept of innovation, pointing particularly to technological process innovation. Consequently, strategies to survive in market competition mainly consist of retrenchment, rationalisation, and the implementation of a strict control of all work processes. The focus is on a reduction of product costs, by deepening the division of labour and tightening discipline in the factory. The implementation of an IT infrastructure is primarily dedicated to supporting central planning, supporting efficient supply chain logistics (Brödner, 1999), and to reinforcing control over the employees, to meet the goal of tightening discipline. HRD and training strategies are not available to the whole workforce, but restricted to a minor part of management and leading scientists and engineers. As a result, there is a divide between a smaller group of highly educated and well-paid, long-term employees on the one hand and a huge section of a low-wage and low-skilled, flexibly-employed labour force, on the other. However, in this trajectory, the incentives for employees to develop their own initiative to optimise the production processes are rather low, since new organisational forms of work are traditionally used to cut costs and reduce employment (Brödner, 1999). If cooperation does happen, it is primarily directed at the goal of making the supply chain as cost efficient as possible, i.e. of refining and accelerating supply chain management, just-in-time production, and outsourcing. Very often this kind of cooperation is accompanied by specific power structures, mirroring predominance and supplier selection, via tough cost competition (Brödner, 1999).

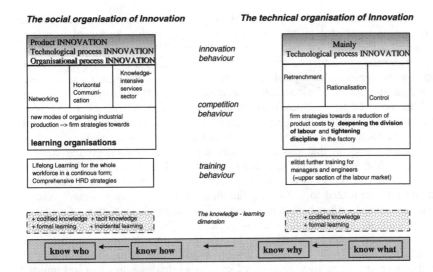

Figure 2.1 Two ideal typical trajectories.

2.4.3 Different concepts of flexibility interact with the VET system

The two ideal-typical models of innovation at company level are related to different concepts of flexibility. In the case of the *technical organisation of innovation,* flexibility is an individualised and reactive concept, anchored rather in the process, not in the product. Individuals, groups, and organisations are conceptualised as flexible by their reaction to price movements. Given this rationale, the flexible company is directed towards removing ´rigidities´ that hamper the reactive qualities of the internal and external labour markets to use the time of individual employees as efficiently as possible. The tightening of discipline and control, used as instruments to balance varieties of demand by the flexible use (and payment) of the labour force, is combined with rationalisation and retrenchment, based on a narrow focus on price competition.

Flexibility in this model can be characterised as a passive and reactive approach, aimed at adapting the use of a given set of unchangeable skills of individuals (that are defined by functions and units) as exactly as possible to varieties in an unchangeable demand. In terms of skills, flexibility in this model means the upgrading of skills in accordance with the deployment of new and more efficient technologies and machinery (corresponding to technological process innovation), which basically stands for adaptation to new codified knowledge. Nevertheless, for the most part, flexibility is related to the working hours of individual employees.

In this concept, new technologies and skills are in principle a force originating from outside the economic system, and people will have to adjust to a future determined by the ´external´ force of technological change. We can state here that the concept of flexibility applied still corresponds in principle to the traditional Fordist industrial paradigm, keeping and even strengthening the same Tayloristic principles in a regime of diversified and IT-based mass production (the only exception being that flexibility is emphasised much more). Hence, a VET system meeting the challenges of the ´technical organisation of innovation´ can still be rooted in its traditional pillars: the ´adaptation appproach´, ´backward mapping´ vocational adjustment training, etc.. Flexibility in VET would mean at best the implementation of continuing courses and seminars for most of the labour force, to cope with new technological processes and new equipment. Given the socioeconomic forces of globalisation, increased competition, and the resources of ICT, the model of the ´technical organisation of innovation´ reflects a certain type of company behaviour that meets challenges by using ICT mainly for rationalisation and retrenchment, for deepening the division of labour and for tightening discipline. Companies based on that model innovate step by step, by integrating codified knowledge from outside aimed at making technological processes more efficient.

In the opposite model of a *social organisation of innovation,* a large part of the activities are dedicated to connecting the different actors in the economic process (firm departments, firm hierarchies, companies, suppliers, customer, universities, communities etc.) to enable the establishment of a rather ***collective tacit knowledge base***. As a consequence of sharing the knowledge in intra and inter-firm networks, knowledge is principally accessible, flexibly available and dynamically developed. Furthermore, the interactive processes of knowledge sharing imply that instrumental behaviour will become mixed with 'communicative rationality', where the common goal is for the partners involved to understand better what the problems are, and what solutions can be developed. In this respect, interactivity, shared experiences, and learning stimulate the development and appropriation of shared beliefs and common interpretations of the social context (Lundvall & Borrás, 1999).

Enhanced communication between hierarchies, which may have been reduced, and between departments is intended to simplify the 'knowledge and competence puzzle' as the precondition for innovation. These strategies of social interaction are complemented by lifelong learning and HRD strategies for the whole workforce (Schein, 1992).

Flexibility in this model can be characterised as a proactive approach, aimed at building capacities to flexibly access the appropriate knowledge - just in time - if the need arises. According to the commitment to product innovation, process innovation, and organisational innovation, all employees are involved in problem-defining and problem-solving processes, and need flexibility in terms of trainability and learning skills on the one hand and flexible access to codified knowledge bases (ICT infrastructure, seminars and courses) and to tacit knowledge bases (informal networks, participative practice) on the other, to be able to meet the challenges of ´knowledge working´. This kind of flexibility also allows for agent behaviour, which is independent of price signals, but derives instead from the creative imagination of individual and collective agents. In contrast to the flexibility concept, related to the technical organisation of innovation, it is not labour time, but the building of knowledge and competences that is at the core of flexibility.

2.5 VET in the learning economy

In sum, the new firm behaviour of learning organisations points to an increasing need for skills that can be learned mainly through work experience, and that reflect a shift in the focus from education and training to learning. In the Fordist industrial paradigm, the main task of the VET system was to provide students with ´true´

codified knowledge that had been ´deduced´ from the production process. While being put through the VET system, students ´accessed´ and acquired mainly codified knowledge. The certificate resulting from this ´learning process´ was the entry card to the labour market.

In an ICT-based world with plentiful accessible information, the learning process is increasingly shifting to a new „*competence in innovation (defined) in terms of the ability to solve problems by selecting relevant data and skills and organise them appropriately (...) by arranging what exists in novel ways*" (Gibbons, Limoges, Nowotny, Schwartzman, Scott, & Trow, 1994). Processes of problem definition, problem solution, and innovation point to knowledge creation and learning in a context of application, requiring the use of the noncodifiable, nonformal, and tacit elements of knowledge.

Whilst the traditional concept of VET is associated with training that can be planned and is predictable, the new learning culture in a learning organisation is characterised particularly by the extension, and in some cases, replacement of traditional instructional learning with constructivist and experience-based learning forms based on a concept of flexibility related to trainability and ´just-in-time´ knowledge sourcing. The focus is on the learner as an active and reflecting subject, and teaching is conceived and conducted rather as a supervisory and monitoring process (Dehnbostel, forthcoming).

In this respect, many of the studies in the field of education and learning have tended to concentrate on human resource development and on the implications of new forms of work organisations for management development (Attwell, Jennes & Tomassini, 1997). Less attention has, however, been paid to the comprehensive role of VET facing the new challenges of tacit knowledge and informal learning. In essence, there seems to be a major contrast between concepts of the 'learning organisation', which is dynamic in attending to corporate change, and VET, which tends towards stability of competence and skill creation. Given this contradiction, we argue that a redesign of the fundamental processes and culture of VET is needed. This will have major consequences for the basic rationale of VET and for the role of colleges, teachers, and students. Hence, new policies will have to foster in a purposeful way the new forms of knowledge and learning, which will enable the requisite adaptability, flexibility, and creativity at individual and collective levels. (Gavigan, Ottitsch & Mahroum, 1999).

In the event that the VET system fails to appropriately respond to these challenges, this could be an incentive for companies to be caught in the trajectory of a technical organisation of innovation. Hence, in the last part, we will discuss in six points institutional and organisational directions of change in the VET system that are explicitly connected to the learning economy paradigm.

1. A new rationale: from the ´adaptation approach´ to the ´shaping principle´
In the learning economy paradigm, lifelong learning is not the requirement of realising economic pressures, but the result and prerequisite of permanent innovation and nonformal learning at the workplace. It is not technical skills and domain-specific knowledge that are the crucial assets of competitiveness, but learning skills, which are not in constant danger of obsolescence. The focus on tacit knowledge and learning skills is directly in opposition to the traditional ´adaptation approach´ in the VET development process (see section 2.2.2).

An alternative concept is the *'shaping principle'*, arguing that - in contrast to mere adaptation - people should acquire competencies not just to adapt and to cope, but to shape their processes of work and technology implementation. Consequently, at the centre of the concept is the task of fostering the ability of workers to do their work *self-reliantly, independently, using creativity and communication skills* (Heidegger, 1997). Taking the concept of a social organisation of innovation, and its consequences for learning seriously, it is complementary and coexists in time with the shaping principle, which is based on a proactive and innovation-oriented idea of flexibility.

2. *Integrating general education and VET on the basis of broader occupational profiles*

According to the Tayloristic separation of conception and execution of work processes, VET in the Fordist industrial paradigm was broadly divided into general education with a high reputation and VET with rather low prestige. Against the background of tacit knowledge as the most powerful tool for innovation in learning organisations, the clear-cut divide in the building of rather theoretical *'planning'* competences on the one hand and the applied execution of assignments on the other will be a barrier to innovation.

If general academic schools and universities fail to provide attendees with the applied work process knowledge, which is the foundation of Mode 2 of knowledge production (Gibbons, Limoges, Nowotny, Schwartzman, Scott, & Trow, 1994), and the VET system fails to provide students with broader theoretical knowledge, the necessary *'bridges'* for permanent knowledge conversion will be too fragile, and companies will run the risk of being locked into the trajectory of a technical organisation of innovation. Hence, VET reform has to integrate general and vocational education at the curricular level on the one hand and develop broader occupational profiles, including *"wider skills and knowledge of an occupation over and above the immediate application of occupational skills in a particular workplace and the process or core skills needed for updating that skills and knowledge base"* on the other (Attwell & Hughes, 2001). Broader profiles will allow occupational knowledge to develop over time, as the content of jobs changes, or 'neighbouring' occupations provide new opportunities for employment, and thus increase the flexibility and mobility of the whole system and the avoidance of one-way VET tracks.

3. *Permeability and Modularisation of VET Systems*

The development of newly integrated curricula and broad profiles, providing the basis for movement within and between competence profiles (vertical flexibility), has to be combined with the design of an open system of VET that defines clear chart progression routes from the occupationally-skilled worker to the managerial post (horizontal flexibility). Access has to be provided from basic VET modules to a university degree. Such a design is appropriate to increase the motivation of employees to upgrade their skills on the one hand and to make the VET system more efficient and responsive, corresponding to a flexibility concept based on trainability and *'just-in-time'* knowledge sourcing on the other.

The development of core and modular occupational learning programmes can be a major pillar in allowing flexibility and customisation to meet changing needs and the requirements of individual employers. The core modules provide the basis for entry into the work process, whilst further modules, which may be optional, enable specialisation in particular areas. The provision of optional modules can also allow for subject updating and for the provision of continuing vocational education (Attwell & Hughes, 2001).

4. *A continuum of learning: integrating initial VET (IVT) and continuous VET (CVT)*

Continuous innovation and speed require lifelong and life-wide learning processes to counteract the rapid obsolescence of traditional initial qualifications, even if these are based on broad occupational profiles. Nevertheless, although a variety of regulations exist for IVT (training content, place and time of learning, learning outcomes, and evaluation, etc.), little attention has been paid to regulating CVT (Attwell & Hughes, 2001). The aforementioned development of modular programs offers the opportunity to design a continuum of learning - based on broad occupational profiles - which resolves the contradiction between IVT and CVT in a learning economy. In contrast to the industrial society, where the VET system corresponded to segmented and hierarchical promotion ladders, the whole VET system rather has the form of a web, in which each learner designs his own self-controlled learning process and career path. The continuum of learning consists of continuously changing periods of intentional learning in schools, colleges and/or via ICT and books, and informal learning and expertise in work processes and communities of practice. As Attwell & Hughes (2001) put it, *"Periods of work based learning can be provided in alternance with school based learning for adults as well as young people. Adults may also be provided with time for autonomous learning in school or company training centres. The major point is the need to develop new mixes of learning and working opportunities for the entire workforce."*

5. *Coordinating VET policies with other policies influencing firm behaviour*

The different company trajectories of the technical organisation of innovation and the social organisation of innovation exhibit a new area of political reflection in terms of VET: the organisational pathways and the dynamic efficiency of private companies. A comprehensive strategy of VET in the learning economy has to support the building of learning organisations and integrating strategies of competence-building at the level of the company. As a consequence, VET policies have to be coordinated with other policies that influence the innovation trajectory of the company, especially labour market policies, competition, and industrial policies and innovation policies.

The 'Mattheus syndrome' (Lundvall, 2000) as an example illustrates this point. In most companies, it is primarily those with extensive training that are offered even more training within companies. It is tempting for companies to focus skill upgrading on those who are rapid learners, and leave the rest to public training programmes. Public policies should focus on the establishment of incentives to counteract these tendencies, by creating multidimensional policy tools, probably consisting of tax incentives, and/or promotion schemes, and/or incentives for the establishment of cooperative regional training associations of SMEs and/or an instrument to support the establishment of benchmarking instruments for companies that stimulate reflection and knowledge conversion (Lundvall, 2000, 21)[7]. In terms of social integration and the avoidance of segmented labour markets, the policy mix will be effective if many instruments of different policy areas are combined in a coordinated way, to stimulate companies to go a way towards learning organisations. It will be less effective if the VET system just takes over what the companies themselves are not prepared to do.

6. Accreditating informal/prior learning

As argued (see section 2.3), the speed of knowledge advancement triggers the limitations of traditional institutional signals (e.g. occupational certifications) and exposes codification as a process too slow for the transmission of rapidly evolving tacit knowledge. On the other hand, work-related knowledge is increasingly being acquired outside VET schools and colleges in nonformal learning processes in a context of application. The establishment of systems of accreditation of informal/prior learning - parallel to the formal VET systems - may be an appropriate pathway to recognise the labour market and everyday work as an area of learning and competence-building.

This process will undoubtedly lead to the codification of some areas of practical knowledge but - since accreditation is based on the judgement of assessors, rather than on formal tests - it will also extend our ablility to map the immeasurable area of tacit knowledge (see Ducatel, 1998).

2.6 Conclusion

We are very aware that our six points do not cover the whole spectrum of institutional and organisational dimensions of change in the VET system, which correspond to the new socioeconomic paradigm of a learning economy. The role of colleges (see Nieuwenhuis, this volume), the identity of teachers (see Heikkinen, this volume), and a new design of the teaching-learning process - besides a series of other points - would, without doubt, extend the list of key aspects.

Nevertheless, our main argument is to show the mutual interdependence between a mode of socio-economic paradigm, its employment model, the predominant innovative behaviour of companies and VET institutions, and forms of skill provision. We tried to show that the concrete form of an information-based economy has a great potential to become a learning economy connected to the predominant innovation strategies of learning organisations and to a concept of flexibility, based on trainability and 'just-in-time' knowledge sourcing. But the information age can as well take a different form of a rather neoliberal and neo-Tayloristic economy based on the strategies of a technical organisation of innovation and a passive, reactive and adaptive flexibility concept. We further argued that the forms and design of VET

---

[7]   While benchmarking in the strict sense may be based on crude assumptions, a broadly defined process of 'learning by comparing' is a useful activity. Confronting what you are doing and the institutional context within which you operate with what others are doing in different contexts, you are forced to reflect on your own practice. And reflection is a key element in learning. Taking a step back and thinking about the possibility of doing things differently enhances the results of learning by doing, and it may be a way of making tacit knowledge more explicit. So, while naïve ideas about benchmarking may give negative results, 'learning by comparing' in order to enhance performance is both a legitimate and useful activity (Lundvall, 2000).

institutions and VET organisations play a role in shaping the new techno-economic paradigm, and hence we tried in the last step to derive six crucial dimensions of VET reform, corresponding to the learning economy paradigm. Further research should go a way to systematically linking the dimensions of the VET system to that paradigm.

References

Amin, A. (1994). Post-Fordism: Models, Fantasies and Phantoms of Transition. In A. Amin (Ed.), *Post-Fordism. A reader (pp. 1-40)*. Oxford: Blackwell.

Aglietta, M. (1979). *A Theory of Capitalist Regulation: The US-Experience*. London: NLB.

Attwell, G., & Hughes, J. (2001). *Developing Social Identities in a period of change: A Forum policy document*. Paper presented at the FORUM Workshop on Occupational Identities. Rome, 22nd – 25th February 2001.

Attwell, G., Jennes, A., & Tomassini, M. (1997). Work-related knowledge and work process knowledge. In A. Brown (Ed.), *Promoting Vocational Education and Training: European Perspectives* (pp. 69-80). Hämeenlinna: Tampere University Press.

Bell, D. (1973). *The Coming of a Post-Industrial Society*. New York: Basic Books.

Boyer, R. (1992). Neue Richtungen von Managementpraktiken und Arbeitsorganisation. Allgemeine Prinzipien und nationale Entwicklungspfade. In A. Demirovic, H.-P. Krebs & T. Sablowski (Eds.), *Hegemonie und Staat. Kapitalistische Regulation als Projekt und Prozeß*. (pp. 55-103). Münster: Westfälisches Dampfboot.

Boyer, R., & Caroli, E. (1993). *Production regimes, education and training system: From complementary to mismatch?* Paper presented for the RAND conference on Human Capital and Economic Performance. Santa Barbara, 17th November 1993.

Brödner P. (1999). Innovationsfähigkeit – unternehmerische Grundlage der Vorauswirtschaft. In P. Brödner, E. Helmstädter & B. Widmaier (Eds.), *Wissensteilung. Zur Dynamik von Innovation und kollektivem Lernen* (pp. 147-170). München: Rainer Hampp Verlag.

Brown, J.S., & P. Duguid (1996). Organisational learning and communities of practice: towards a unified view of working, learning and innovation. In M.D.Cohen & L.S.Sproull (Eds.). *Organisational learning (pp. 58-82)*. London: Sage.

Carnoy, M. & Castells, M. (1997). *Sustainable Flexibility. A Prospective Study on Work, Family and Society in the Information Age*. Paris: OECD.

Castells, M. (1996). *The Rise of the Network Society*, Oxford: Blackwell.

Cohen, W.M. & Levinthal, D.A. (1990). Absorptive Capacity. A New Perspective on Learning and Innovation. *Administrative Science Quarterly, 35,* 128-152.

Dehnbostel, P. (forthcoming). Innovation and learning strategies in learning companies. In K. Mayer & L. Lassnigg (Eds.), *Building Competences for the Learning Economy*. Heidelberg: Springer.

Dosi, G. (1988). The nature of the innovative process. In G. Dosi, C. Freeman, R. Nelson, G. Silverberg, & L. Soete (Eds.), *Technical Change and Economic Theory* (pp. 221-238). London: Pinter Publishers.

Ducatel, K. (1998). *Learning and Skills in the Knowledge Economy*. Aalborg: DRUID Working Paper No. 98-2.

Gavigan, J.P., Ottitsch, M, & Mahroum, S. (1999). *The Futures Project: Knowledge and Learning: Towards a Learning Europe*. Seville: European Commission, Institute for Prospective Technological Studies.

Gibbons, M., Limoges, C., Nowotny, H., Schwartzman, S., Scott, P., & Trow, M. (1994). *The new production of knowledge: The dynamics of science and research in contemporary societies*. London: Sage.

Heidegger, G. (1997). Key considerations in the education of vocational education and training professionals. In A. Brown (Ed.), *Promoting Vocational Education and Training: European Perspectives* (pp. 13-24). Hämeenlinna: Tampere University Press.

Jessop, B. (1986). Der Wohlfahrtsstaat im Übergang vom Fordismus zum Postfordismus [The Welfare State in the Transition from Fordism to Post-Fordism]. *Prokla 65/ Dezember*; 4-33.

Kelleher M., & Cressey P. (2000). *The active roles of learning and social dialogue for organisational change*. Paper presented at the FORUM Workshop on Learning in Learning Organisations & VET Culture. Wageningen, 23rd – 25th November 2000.

Lam, A. (2000). *Skill formation in the knowledge based economy: transformation pressures in European High technology industries*. Paper prepared for the Plenary Session 'Exploring Trends in Employment Relations and New Approaches to Work in the 21st Century' in the IIRA 12th World Congress. Tokyo, May 29th -June 2nd 2000.

Lam, A. (2001). *Changing R&D Organization and Innovation: Developing the New Generation of R&D Knowledge Workers*. Paper prepared for the international conference 'The Contribution of European Socio-Economic Research to the Benchmarking of RTD Policies in Europe', European Commission, Directorate General for Research, Albert Borschette Conference Centre, Brussels, March 15-16, 2001.

Lassnigg, L. (1998). Qualifizierungspolitik, Innovationssystem und Beschäftigung - Herkömmliche und neue Perspektiven. In Zukunfts- und Kulturwerkstätte (Ed.), *Re-engineering der österreichischen Industriepolitik* (pp. 76-132). Wien: Zukunfts- und Kulturwerkstätte.

Lipietz A. (1994). Post-Fordism and Democracy. In A. Amin (Ed.), *Post-Fordism. A reader* (pp. 338-358). Oxford/UK: Blackwell.

Lipietz, A. (1997). Die Welt des Postfordismus (The World of Postfordism). In Forschungsgruppe Europäische Gemeinschaften (Ed.), *Labour Markets and Employment Policy in the European Union* (pp. 9-48), Marburg: FEG Study Nr.10.

Lundvall, B.-Å. (1996). *The Social Dimension of the Learning Economy*, Kopenhagen: Danish Research Unit for Industrial Dynamics (DRUID).

Lundvall, B.-Å. (1999). *From Fordism to the Globalising Learning Economy - implications for innovation policy*. Paper presented for the International seminar on Learning Economy: Innovation - Qualification – Employment. Vienna, Renner Institut, June 21st 1999.

Lundvall, B.-Å (2000). *Innovation policy and knowledge management in the learning economy*. Paper presented for the 4th International Conference on Technology Policy and Innovation, Curitiba, Brazil, August 28th – 31st 2000.

Lundvall, B.-Å., & Johnson, B. (1994). The learning economy. *Journal of Industrial Studies*, Vol. 1, no 2, 23-42.

Lundvall, B.-Å., & Borras S. (1999). *The Globalising Learning Economy; Challenges for Innovation Policy (Report based on contributions from 7 projects under the TSER programme)*. Brussels: DG XII.

Lundvall, B.A., & Archibugi, D. (2001). Introduction: Europe and the Learning Economy. In D. Archibugi & B.A. Lundvall. (Eds.), *The Globalizing Learning Economy: Major Socio-Economic Trends and European Innovation Policy* (pp. 1-20). Oxford/ UK: Oxford University Press.

Mayer, K. (1999). Auf dem Weg zum Postfordismus. Bemerkungen über das Verhältnis von Ökonomie und Politik in der Formierung von „Globalisierung", „Standortkonkurrenz" und neoliberaler Hegemonie [Approaching Postfordism. Some remarks concerning the relationship of economy and policy under conditions of globalisation, competition of industrial locations and neoliberal hegemony]. In K. Althaler (Ed.), *Primat der Ökonomie? Über Handlungsspielräume sozialer Politik im Zeichen der Globalisierung* [Economy first? Scopes of social policy under conditions of globalisation] (pp. 133-168). Marburg: Metropolis.

Nieuwenhuis, L. (forthcoming). Learning Colleges within Learning Regions. In K. Mayer & L. Lassnigg (Eds.), *Building Competences for the Learning Economy*. Heidelberg: Springer.

Nieuwenhuis, L., & Smulders, H. (forthcoming). Organisational strategies of Dutch VET-colleges in linking education and labour. In L. Lassnigg, J. Brandsma, A. Dietzen & K. Mayer (Eds.), *Beyond Bureaucracy and the Market – New Perspectives on Coordination of Education, Training and Employment*. Dordrecht: Kluwer Academic Publishers.

Nonaka, I. (1991). The Knowledge-Creating Company. *Harvard Business Review*, November-December, 96-104.

Nonaka, I., & Takeuchi, H. (1995). *The Knowledge-Creating Company: How Japanese Companies Create the Dynamics of Innovation*. New York: Oxford University Press.

Polanyi, M. (1958/ 1978). *Personal Knowledge*. London: Routledge and Kegan.

Schein, E.H. (1992). *Organizational culture and leadership*. San Francisco: Jossey Bass.

Schienstock, G. (2000). *Towards a Reflexive Organisation in the Global Information Economy?*. Paper prepared for the Conference "Towards a Learning Society. Innovation and Competence Building with Social Cohesion for Europe". Lisboa, Quinta da Marinha, Guincho, May 28th –30th.

Soete, L. (2000). The challenges and the potential of the knowledge based economy in a globalised world. Contribution to the background paper for the Portuguese Presidency of the European Union: action line *employment, economic reforms and social cohesion – for a Europe of innovation and knowledge*. Lisbon: Portuguese Presidency.

Soete, L. (2000a). *Towards a European Learning Society*. Paper prepared for the Conference "Towards a Learning Society. Innovation and Competence Building with Social Cohesion for Europe". Lisboa, Quinta da Marinha, Guincho, May 28th –30th.

CHAPTER 3

Learning organisations for VET

3.1 Introduction

THIS CHAPTER DISCUSSES THE POSITION OF VOCATIONAL AND TECHNICAL COLLEGES within regional economies. An analysis of developments in the knowledge-based economy leads to the conclusion that VET colleges should develop into recognised players in regional innovative networks of companies. Based on case studies from a regional and intraorganisational perspective, the conclusion is drawn that VET colleges in Europe have not yet attained such a position.

The case studies were taken from studies of the Dutch context in metal engineering and agriculture. The results of these studies were the impetus for a European project on comparable issues; the results of this project are presented too.

The colleges in these projects were aware of the urgency of developing new tasks in the regional economy, but have not as yet developed operational strategies, although some good practices are found as benchmarks. Learning cultures inside companies, on the one hand, and inside colleges, on the other, are growing apart: educational learning processes are characterised by certainty and codification, whereas innovative learning processes within companies are typified by uncertainty and participation. College managements should reorganise learning and working inside colleges in interaction with working and learning in society and the regional economy.

Section 3.2 of this chapter discusses the new challenges for VET as a consequence of the emerging knowledge based economy. Learning and innovation are seen as two sides of the same coin, taking place in networked companies. VET colleges have to join these networks to be able to respond to social and economic skill demands. Section 3.3 presents two case studies from the Dutch VET context analysing the strategic behaviour of VET colleges and section 3.4 presents the results of a European survey amongst VET colleges in six European countries. Section 3.5 concludes that VET colleges are locked up in an industrial learning paradigm, which is no longer compatible with the knowledge based economy. To prepare VET for the challenges of the new economy, VET management has to reorganise the colleges into 'learning organisations', closely connected to regional innovation networks.

3.2 Education and training in the new economy

The western economy is developing rapidly towards becoming a dynamic knowledge-based economy. Work processes will become increasingly knowledge-intensive, and the dynamics of knowledge development will increase too. Innovation and technological development will have a major impact on work at all levels of the

35

W. J. Nijhof et al. (eds.), Shaping Flexibility in Vocational Education and Training, 35-52.
© 2002 *Kluwer Academic Publishers. Printed in the Netherlands.*

economy. Economic activity in Western society is only sustainable if economic policy is based on dynamics and knowledge development. Innovation is vital for the competitive strength of western companies. Mayer describes this development more extensively in Chapter 2.

Dynamics in knowledge development will lead to rapid changes in production processes and connected tasks and functions. The rate of change in functions and occupations will increase, as will qualifications and competence requirements. The qualitative demand for the labour force will show an analogous shift on the labour market, and in the process, vocational and technical education will be confronted with large shifts in the demand for new graduates and for maintaining the competencies of the workforce. The product definitions for VET, as specified in qualification structures and in requirements for company training, will show great dynamics and changes. VET colleges will be forced into enormous flexibility and external orientation, in order to be able to adapt their services to changing external demands.

Flexibility in VET may take different shapes and forms: at the level of course supply (e.g. modularisation of courses, different market strategies), as well at the level of services (other supporting services besides course supply), and at the level of 'deliveries' (distinct levels of knowledge and skills, e.g. connecting tacit and codified knowledge). Legislation at the level of educational systems should support the development of such flexibility.

The emergence of a knowledge-based economy presents VET with a great challenge. The OECD (2001) states that individual learning, supported by colleges, must be combined with organisational learning inside firms, to enhance regional development towards the 'new learning economy'. The OECD is strongly in favour of new forms of production and a regional organisation of the economy, with major consequences for learning and education. Keep and Brown (2000), on the other hand, are more sceptical about the emergence of the new economy; they argue that traditional 'tayloristic' production models are still operational in the majority of UK firms. With this sceptical warning in mind, we elaborate in the next sections on innovation as the driving force behind the emergence of the new economy. In the knowledge-based economy, producers can no longer rely on established routines. As a result of global information flows and an emerging global market - meaning worldwide competition, cycles of product innovation shorten. Production then becomes synonymous with innovation. During the 1990s, there was growing attention to the concept of the learning organisation: learning was no longer perceived as an individual activity isolated from daily work tasks, but an activity that needed to be embedded in the organisation to ensure the effective, efficient, and innovative performance of that organisation. The organisation, in turn, is embedded in an economic context, so a network approach is needed to understand learning and innovation processes at the organisational level.

3.2.1 Understanding innovation

Innovation is essential for the competitiveness of companies and industrial sectors, regions, and local communities. Innovation and technological development is the main tool to survive the economic process of creative destruction (cf. Schumpeter in Kleinknecht, 1994). Protection of 'old' companies hinders the process of creative destruction, which will lead to underinvestment in innovation. Innovative companies are more resistant to economic crises. Dosi (1988) describes the microeconomic processes of innovation. Innovation is, according to Dosi, problem-solving: ill-defined technical problems have to be solved through creative 'learning', based on formal and tacit knowledge. Tacit knowledge is important in relation to the appropriateness of innovations: the comparative advantage depends on it. Innovations are cumulative; they are built on former activities and in-company knowledge, which hinders the imitation of innovation by competitors. Company-internal knowledge and routines lead to a preference for the company's internal innovation. Even in the case of purchasing new tools, internal capacity is needed to implement the new knowledge. Innovative companies are built on their own core competence (Hamel & Prahalad, 1992). The embeddedness of innovations within this core competence and internal learning processes is the best protection against imitation. Innovation leads to company-specific knowledge (tacit knowledge; see Dosi, 1988; Nonaka & Takeuchi, 1995), which strengthens the 'forward' position of innovative companies. Tacit knowledge depends on people: it is important to have long-running contracts with the core of the employees. Hartog (1996) states that the new economic order demands increased flexibility of the workers on the one hand (higher skills, life long learning), and job security on the other. Flexibility should be translated into trainability and learning skills, and not into labour market mobility.

Problem-solving and innovation by trial-and-error processes are part of informal learning processes, in which social networks play an important role. Workers learn by sharing knowledge in the working team, and employers learn by creating networks of colleagues and advisers. Research studies of innovation (see Coehoorn, 1995; Engel, 1995; Röling, 1992) show that linear models for knowledge transfer should be replaced by or combined with interactive models, in which trial-and-error processes on the shop floor are interrelated with the existing knowledge base and research infrastructures. Detecting and using external knowledge sources, combined with the organisation of internal learning processes, is a central aspect of modern management. Oerlemans (1997) regards innovation as an embedded process within a broader knowledge context, in which the exchange of learning and technical sources is elemental, especially for SMEs. Economic networks are crucial to transform heterogeneous knowledge sources into useful *"neue Kombinationen"*. According to Oerlemans, companies are embedded in a heterogeneous knowledge context. Innovation is an embedded process; knowledge and technology are exchanged within networks of collaborative companies and institutions. The innovative process can be characterised as rearranging existing knowledge into new combinatory knowledge. To organise this combinatory process, companies need to collaborate with other companies and knowledge institutes. This is especially the case for small and medium-sized companies, because they do not possess large internal knowledge sources or research potential. For effective innovation, small and medium-sized companies have thus to use external knowledge sources. Public agencies and innovation centres at the sectoral and regional level, technical colleges and universities may play this important role of back-up service for SMEs. In addition, industrial, local, and regional networks are necessary for the transformation of knowledge into new innovative combinations and products.

The external knowledge context is complex for SMEs. The entrepreneur or the employer, with his skilled employees, is continuously involved in problem-solving and innovative processes (Nieuwenhuis, 2001). In the first instance, he looks for internal solutions, but soon the use of external sources will become a necessity.

Professional journals, financial advisers, suppliers, and customers will bring in new knowledge, deliberately or accidentally. An interactive exchange of knowledge will thus develop around internal company processes and their external relations. The company is embedded within an expanding knowledge context. This context is multidimensional: at least three dimensions can be discerned:

- The production chain, in which knowledge and innovation 'accompany' the product through different firms on its journey from raw material to end-users;
- The professional sector, in which craftsmen and professionals exchange standards, new methods, and innovative knowledge;
- The socioeconomic region, in which local processes enhance the exchange of knowledge between firms and knowledge institutes.

Depending on socioeconomic preconditions, strategic decisions have to be taken in all three dimensions; the balance between common interests and competitive advantage depends on many variables. In the next sections, these three dimensions will be elaborated on.

Chained knowledge or knowledge chains?
Companies exist within interfirm product chains. They need raw materials, tools, and machinery to be able to produce their products and services, which, in turn, should be tuned to the specific needs and requirements of their customers. Interfirm chain management is an important new field of business management, targeted at intercompany relations: product accountability, quality information exchange, logistics for transportation, and stockkeeping are major subjects in this field. Knowledge development and collaborative innovation should be part of this chain management. Sources for innovative activities are, however, not always located inside the innovating company. According to Von Hippel (1988), the source of innovation is located within the supplier-producer-user chain, depending on the expected benefits and the required innovative resources. As a result of the tacit aspects of innovation, the partial appropriateness of new technologies, and the cumulative character of innovation (cf. Dosi, 1988), companies are developing differently or in different directions. If the introduction of new products has been successful, innovative companies are often able to define the economic rules for their competitors. Innovation leads to comparative advantages; imitation and diffusion lead to convergency. Depending on market figures and chain-dependency, companies are increasingly pleading for a kind of 'collaborative innovation'. Within supplier-dominated chains, collaboration is easier to realise.

Interfirm production chains are important units for analysing innovation processes and related skill developments. Joint innovative activities are often based on a chain of linked relations between companies, but skill developments are not yet related to chain developments. However, whereas interfirm production chains have a great potential for new economic and innovative perspectives, this is an interesting new area for developing VET strategies: the focus within VET on single occupations and firms blinker it to 'in-between' developments, as happen in chains.

The sectoral dimension
Industrial sectors and branches have their own possibilities for scaffolding innovative activities within SMEs. According to Finegold (1991), industrial sectors should look for ways to facilitate cooperation and common activities between companies, to enhance investments in training and innovation. Prisoners' dilemmas

are setting up low-skill traps: individual companies will decrease their investments in human resources if they are endangered by the poaching behaviour of their competitors. Industrial sectors thus have to look for policies which will support cooperative behaviour in training and innovation; trade unions can play a facilitating role here. Industrial sectors establish sectoral infrastructures for the transfer of technology and for training policies, fitting into sector-specific technological regimes (cf. Pavitt, in Breschi & Malerba, 1997). In order to scaffold these sectoral policies, systems are needed for the monitoring of future technological developments; the results of monitoring activities can be translated into transfer-supporting measures and skill-requirement forecasts. Sectoral challenges to facilitate innovation and learning processes are: establishing preconditions for collaboration between competitive companies in the field of training and innovation; building future-oriented monitoring systems for technological development; building support systems for company-bound innovation and training; defining key competencies for skilled workers and entrepreneurs; and creating sectoral ownership for vocational education and training systems.

The regional dimension
Morgan (1997) stresses the importance of the network paradigm in understanding regional development strategies. He emphasises the importance of creating learning regions, analogous to the concept of learning organisations, such as building up collective learning capacities between geographically-related companies and regional infrastructural provisions/opportunities. Strong industrial districts are to be characterised by learning interrelationships between companies (OECD, 2001). Italian industrial regions and districts are characterised by their monostructures, in terms of products and services: each district is famous for a single set of products (cf. Dondi, 1999). Learning and the exchange of expertise is essential to keep the quality of this set at a guaranteed level. Other emerging regions are characterised by chain relations: the exchange of innovation and information is related to purchasing and selling activities. These kinds of learning networks are strong, because of their hedging impact on economic activities (cf. Cooke, Boekholt & Tödtling, 2000). In less developed regions, these kinds of learning networks are weaker or nonexistent, because of a lack of economic activities and infrastructure. The challenge for regional and local authorities is to establish education, training, and labour market policies which will lead to a high level of learning potential and the emergence of networks for the support of SMEs and starting entrepreneurs, as a part of their economic policy (cf. OECD, 2001). Innovative VET provisions could lead to a substantial improvement in the innovative capacity within regional economies (see Morgan, 1997) and give decisive impulses to regional and local economic development. One of the challenges is thus to improve these provisions. To reach that target, regional VET provisions should act in alliance with other knowledge provisions, like innovation centres and sectoral knowledge centres. Regional policies which serve to enhance industrial innovation and learning processes are in the main: learning networks of companies; facilitating infrastructures for technology transfer; educating and training a highly skilled labour force. Meeting these challenges is one major condition for stimulating regional economic development. Regional and national governments, however, have restricted options for facilitating knowledge networks: establishing intermediate organisations, enhancing fundamen-

tal research and development, and maintaining vocational education and training are
mentioned as the main governmental instruments in this respect (see OECD, 2001).

3.2.2 VET as part of the knowledge context

In the above sections, the knowledge context for innovating firms is sketched
roughly, based on three dimensions (chain, sector, and region). The support of
innovation and economic developments demand an adaptive delivery of required
skills. VET can be a major player in this field, but is often not seen as such. In the
production chain dimension especially, the importance of VET supply is scarcely
mentioned. VET is an important actor in the sectoral dimension, but often in a
traditional way: vocational courses and qualifications play an important role in the
hedging of economic activities through the establishment of an occupational identity
(see De Bruyn & Nieuwenhuis, 1994). Trade unions and employer organisations are
playing their role in defining vocational courses in German and Dutch
apprenticeship systems and in formulating national vocational qualification
standards in the UK system. VET is delivering and developing occupational
standards, in interaction with the professional sectors.

For building competitive regional economies, VET can be a major player, as shown
by Rosenfeld (1998). In addition to the supply and maintenance of a skilled labour
force, a new task is indicated for technical colleges: brokering new and existing
knowledge towards the local economy. This implies regional strategies for economic
development, of which VET should increasingly be an integral part. Cooke,
Boekholt & Tödtling (2000), on the other hand, state that VET is seen as an
externality: in regional development projects, VET is seen as a given, delivering the
necessary labour force. In order to enhance knowledge transfer processes, vocational
education, training and further or continuing education and training should play four
important roles (Rosenfeld, 1998):
• The education and training of new employees and employers to scaffold the
  knowledge base in companies;
• The supply of up-to-date information and training facilities to update the
  knowledge and skills of the workforce;
• The facilitation of adaptation to new technologies;
• The organisation of active networks of companies to facilitate interactive
  learning and innovation processes.
Technical colleges and training institutes should accept the challenge of
improving in-company industrial learning by ensuring a high degree of
responsiveness to the results of research/science and technological and other
developments. Regional training colleges, supported by sectoral innovation centres,
have the opportunity to play a pivotal role in the learning networks of small and
medium-sized companies, by incorporating innovative knowledge from the R&D
infrastructure into their course supply, and linking more closely to local networks
and companies. Central to the model are intermediate structures established by
economic and industrial sectors, to enhance communication between R&D and VET
systems. These intermediate structures depend on the features of both the sectoral
training system and the innovation system.

VET is at the crossroads of regional and sectoral policies: labour markets are regionally defined, and the supply and demand of employment is spatially bound, because of mobility limits. Craftsmanship, on the other hand, is highly sectorally bound, because of the intertwining of occupational domains and economic activities. Educational policies in VET are more or less connected to sectoral policies, depending on national VET systems and socioeconomic constraints. VET institutions have to build on both sectoral and regional networks to operate effectively in supplying a well-qualified labour force, prepared for permanent innovation within the new economy. From the literature on economic and regional development policy (cf. Cooke, Boekholt & Tödtling, 2000), a rather pessimistic view emerges of the flexibility of VET in the face of these new challenges. In order to shed more light on the institutional and organisational flexibility of VET, the next sections present data from case studies and surveys of the role of VET in Dutch and European regional developments.

3.3 Dutch case studies of regional VET strategies

During the late 90s, several case studies were undertaken of the role of VET in a variety of Dutch industrial sectors containing a large proportion of SMEs (Grooters & Nieuwenhuis, 1996; Nieuwenhuis, Gielen & Lokman, 2000). The intermediate knowledge infrastructure in several industrial sectors was studied, and comparative analyses were made of the role of vocational education and training in facilitating innovations in companies. Elsewhere, we have described these case studies more extensively (Nieuwenhuis, 1999). In installation engineering, VET is used for the sectoral hedging of economic activities by connecting licences to qualifications; in the bakery sector, a sectoral technology hub is serving as intermediary between the innovating supplying industry and the traditional craftsmen, by delivering an informative journal and a physical exposition of new technologies. In environmental engineering, a linear approach to technology diffusion is described as failing.

As a conclusion, out of these case studies, a sectoral-regional innovation model has been built, in which four actors play a major role: SMEs, R&D infrastructure, sectoral innovation agencies, and VET institutes. In this model, SMEs are the innovative players, improving their competitiveness. They use knowledge from different sources, but they also produce new knowledge, as a result of their innovative activities. Institutes for research and development produce a lot of new knowledge, but they meet problems in disseminating and, even more so, in introducing that knowledge to SMEs. In several industrial sectors, innovation centres have been established and targeted at the translation of innovative knowledge to the sector-bound companies. Not only were public funds made available, but the social partners also play an important role in the funding of these centres. Regional innovation centres play a facilitating role in disseminating innovative knowledge. VET provisions have the opportunity to contribute to regional networks, by educating youngsters, training adult workers, and organising learning networks of companies.

For this chapter, we have opted to describe the results of two cases more extensively in the next two sections: regional networking in the metal industry and the regional strategies of VET colleges in agriculture. By 'region' we are not referring to global regions like Southeast Asia or Western Europe, but to mobility-bound regions, in which people are used to travelling to work and school. 'Regional' and 'local' are interchangeable terms. Labour market mobility at secondary level, at least in the Netherlands, is bound to such regions, as is student mobility for VET attendance. By 'region' we thus mean entities like South Wales, Luxembourg or Eastern Brabant. In such regions, Rosenfeld's challenges can become concrete and tangible for VET colleges.

3.3.1 Regional networking in the engineering and toolmaking industries

The regional economy around the city of Eindhoven, Eastern Brabant, in the southern part of the Netherlands, is strongly based on the engineering industry. Out of 8,000 Dutch companies in this sector, 1,100 are located in the region of Eindhoven, including large ones, such as Philips (electronics), DAF (trucks) and Océ (copying machinery). Most of these engineering companies, however, are small in size: 75% have 10 employees or less. The small companies play a supplying role for the larger ones. The Eindhoven region is known as highly innovative: 50% of the national R&D budget is spent in this region, notably by larger companies, and about 11% of employees in the Eindhoven region are involved in R&D activities.

In the late eighties, Eastern Brabant was confronted with an economic crisis, but with the help of European and national funds, the region recovered and built a strong regional structure of networks and chains of companies. Regional intermediary organisations, such as the innovation centre and a regional promotion institute, played an important role in this structure, as did sectoral organisations of the engineering industry sector, organised at national level.

In the Eindhoven region, a number of large knowledge-creating, treating and disseminating institutes are located, including the Technical University of Eindhoven, TNO industry (one of the largest private-public R&D organisations), Fontys Technical College (delivering professional courses), and two regional colleges for vocational education and training (at secondary level). The metal industry has its own institute for adult technical courses and Fontys houses the Micro-Centre (a laboratory for microtechnology). The large companies have their own R&D labs (like the famous Natlab at Philips).

In the nineties, engineering in the region became very prosperous, but a shortage of skilled workers is nowadays an ever-greater threat. Skill shortages will be the problem for the next decade, because of a lack of interest amongst youngsters in technical and engineering occupations and professions. Employers in the region are therefore increasingly cooperating in promoting activities jointly with technical colleges, in order to attract new students to technical courses, natural sciences, and engineering disciplines.

Within this dynamic region, the Eindhoven regional college (ROC Eindhoven) was established in 1996, based on a merger of several vocational and technical institutes, both apprenticeship courses and full-time vocational education. This ROC has 16,000 younger or primary students, 8,000 adult students, 1,400 employees, and around 20 buildings in the region. About 10% of the turnover is generated by specific contractual courses and activities. The innovative mission of the ROC is based on a network strategy: partnerships, collaboration with other regional knowledge institutes, and cooperative courses in joint ventures with companies. ICT-based courses and individual pathways are the main characteristics of the course supply of the ROC Eindhoven. The ROC aims to be an open institute with a regional function. Its core competence is restricted to the delivery and maintenance of skilled and highly skilled craftsmanship in the region. Facilitating innovation is not a part of the core activities of the ROC; networking and connecting companies and knowledge institutions, however, is the strategy for scaffolding innovation. Delivering skills and qualifications in terms of craftsmanship involves all kinds of regular courses, and takes into account individual pathways in cooperation with companies or the regional labour supply offices. The ROC Eindhoven made a clear choice only to play a restricted role within the region. Within these restrictions, its core competence is elaborated in an excellent manner.

According to Rosenfeld's model, the ROC Eindhoven delivers a good practice of a networking technical college, sustaining local development and innovation. As a gateway to the labour market, it delivers support for technical branches to attract scarce personnel through innovative programmes. The maintenance of the skills of the labour force is in good hands with the ROC, and it plays a brokering role for those companies requiring specialists' support in technical fields. The ROC is seen by the local economic community as a valuable partner in technical networks.

3.3.2 College management strategies within regional agricultural networks

Greenhouse farming is a rather prosperous sector of Dutch agriculture. Vegetables, flowers, and plants are exported all over the world. Today, however, greenhouse farming is confronted with large shifts in its economic fundament. The Dutch government is stepping aside from its leading role in agricultural policy. Economic developments on the global food market will be steering impulses for the agricultural sector, both positive and negative. Competition will increase. This shift has been reinforced by a new policy of the European Union. A major economic tendency is the shift of power in the different food chains. Supported by the European policy, the suppliers in the food chain had for several decades had the major say. In the past decade, however, the balance of power has swung in favour of the other side of the chain, i.e. the consumers, represented in the main by the supermarkets. Because of this shift, traditional cooperative structures are breaking down, and will be replaced by structures which are better prepared for competition on the international scale.

These structural changes are having an impact on the agricultural knowledge system. This knowledge system has traditionally been oriented towards the farmer. Employees in the sector are usually low-educated/trained. Most greenhouse farmers are at the forefront of interactive innovative processes; they are involved in collective study clubs, in which practical knowledge is exchanged, based on a reciprocal agreement. This knowledge is used for investment in new equipment, and often these farmers experiment with plant material and/or the automation of their greenhouses. Through formal and informal contacts, individual farmers or networks of farmers have an influence on the research and development programmes of the institutes for applied agricultural research, while the results of research are directly available to the farmers through evening courses and extension programmes. The economic shifts affect the way the knowledge system operates. Recently, groups of farmers have built competitive hedges, and consequently, cooperation in the knowledge system has been basically affected. Around the turn of the millennium, agricultural organisations are looking for new ways to promote the knowledge transfer between research institutes, intermediate organisations, and farmers/ companies (Nieuwenhuis, Hoeve & Verhaar, 2002).

Within the Dutch agricultural knowledge system, the role of agricultural education and training has been in danger of a certain degree of marginalisation. Vocational education is still seen as the major supplier of future farmers, although the role of education/training within the innovation processes in the sector is decreasing. Agricultural education is experiencing difficulties, especially at the national level, in obtaining the necessary information to respond adequately to innovation, and at regional level, the educational institutes are not playing an important role in the innovation networks of the greenhouse farmers. The commitment of the sector to education and training is declining and, therefore, the responsiveness of the whole agricultural education and training provision to this vastly changing and very open-minded sector seems to be decreasing.

In 1998, schools for agricultural education were studied as regards their management strategies as regional innovation centres. All 18[1] Dutch agricultural colleges were involved in an interview survey, based on the Rosenfeld model. The most striking and paradoxical result of this survey is that all schools agreed about the necessity of developing new regional networking strategies, because of losing contacts with their 'natural' partner firms, but only one of these schools is, in fact, involved in regional innovation networks. Regional networking is ranked very high on the priority list for school management, but the operational tools have yet to be developed.

The reasons mentioned for underlining the need for new networking strategies and innovative course supply are: the fall of demand within traditional occupations, the rise of new occupations (e.g. environmental care; green amenities in urban regions), and the declining demand from agricultural companies for the support of innovative processes by the agricultural colleges. One general reason for these processes is the pace of technological development, which is causing the obsolescence of technical knowledge to spread rapidly and speed up. The traditionally slow development process for new courses for VET is hindering responsiveness, and should be replaced by a flexible and tailor-made course supply. In order to improve the responsiveness of colleges and training centres, it is crucial to play a role within innovative networks. Colleges are aware of the danger of not being involved in such a network-building process; they are conscious that they may run the risk of losing their supplying role for skilled craftsmanship, and of being increasingly limited to the delivery of courses for the low-skilled, for disadvantaged young people, and unemployed adults to be retrained.

Against this backdrop, the agricultural schools and colleges are nowadays starting to develop strategies to regain their position in regional networks, and to improve the innovativeness of their course supply. One major obstacle they mention is linked to staff development problems. Teachers for vocational education and training are educated as generalists, whereas operating in innovative networks demands specialist competencies. The new networking needs and strategies imply double qualifications for teachers, trainers, tutors, and supervisors: both general didactics and specific technologies/competencies should be part of their qualification.

---

[1] Since this survey, further mergers between colleges have taken place: in 2002, there are 12 agricultural colleges left.

Transforming VET institutions into network players requires major investment in the further education and training of the teaching and training staff themselves. This is an urgent need.

Whereas the Eindhoven case in the above section (3.3.1) displays a good practice of a responsive VET college, the survey of agricultural colleges shows the difficulties and pitfalls developing in that direction. Colleges are caught in organisational traditions and institutional constraints, resulting in a long developmental route towards responsiveness. It requires a clear management strategy within the VET colleges and a reshaping of the incentive structures of VET systems to support colleges developing responsiveness on a scale which exceeds the individual involvement of the Eindhoven good practice.

3.4 European views and perspectives

Based on Dutch experiences as described in section 3.3, a Leonardo da Vinci project, called Spidervet (contract number NL/97/1/34038) has been targeted at skill and competence needs and the role of VET within the innovative processes of early and late adopting SMEs. The increasingly rapid pace of innovations is forcing VET to develop new strategies to deliver and maintain skilled craftsmanship for the local, regional, and sectoral labour market. The traditional target for initial, regular course delivery should be combined with new targets, tasks, and strategies for adult courses and activities which aim at accompanying and facilitating innovations, as stated by Rosenfeld (1998; see section 3.2.2). Organisations for VET can no longer act as stand-alone institutions, but should develop network-oriented strategies. VET colleges should define their own specific role within 'learning SME networks' and should look for strategic alliances with other knowledge institutions within their regional context.

In the Spidervet project, the research model is built on insights from the Dutch case studies. Based on the four new fields of tasks for VET colleges (Rosenfeld, 1998: gateway to the labour market, maintenance of workers' competencies, technology adaptation, and creation of innovative networks), the Spidervet project stresses the need for VET colleges to change and become recognised players in regional and sectoral innovation networks. The Spidervet project focused on testing this network model, using a sectoral-regional perspective on the one hand, and an organisational perspective on the other.

The Spidervet project was carried out in six European countries, in which particular regional-sectoral combinations were selected:

- In the Netherlands, the nursing and care sector at national level;
- In Germany, metal engineering in the Bremen area;
- In Finland, forestry at national level;
- In the UK, rural and agritourism in Wales;
- In France, the plastics industry in Rhone-Alpes;
- In Portugal, the ornamental rocks sector in Alentejo.

The first stage of the project was to carry out a case study for each country, in which the socioeconomic position of the sector, its knowledge requirements and its training infrastructure were analysed. This included descriptions of how the system was organised, what kind of institutions had developed over time, and what position was taken by the vocational and technical colleges involved. At this stage, the focus is on sectoral and regional aspects of the Spidervet model.

The second and third stages of the project focus on organisational aspects within VET colleges. Using a benchmarking approach, attempts were made to identify successful examples of "spider colleges", from which successful strategies for transforming colleges into regional-sectoral knowledge hubs could be derived, and inhibiting factors identified. Using a survey approach, which involved interviewing 66 colleges (6 to 15 in each country), the extent to which the information is generalisable was analysed as well.

Table 3.1 *Spidervet results from six European countries (all scales from 1 to 10).*

	Portugal (n=6)	France (n=12)	Netherlands (n=13)	Germany (n=11)	Finland (n=15)	Wales (n=9)
1. Antenna function	8.13	8.31	8.27	8.77	5.95	6.66
2. Interpretation external information	6.50	6.50	5.15	6.45	8.20	8.61
3. Internal-external orientation	7.38	7.56	7.06	7.55	6.40	5.33
4. Mission	7.75	6.13	6.08	6.18	5.70	--
5. Innovative role	8.13	8.13	5.33	5.70	4.90	7.11
6. Internal communication	3.63	4.56	8.00	3.25	4.00	7.33
7. No personnel problems	6.00	7.00	6.31	8.36	6.60	9.26
8. No constraints	7.30	7.55	7.00	7.41	8.40	5.19
9. Access IVET	6.40	4.60	6.70	6.89	3.28	8.51
10. Market-orientation IVET	7.25	4.00	8.00	7.68	4.40	6.48
11. Flexibility IVET	2.30	3.50	4.44	2.95	4.38	7.47
12. Accessibility CVET	4.75	4.38	6.06	5.09	5.35	8.89
13. Turnover CVET	6.00	5.00	1.25	3.73	2.93	--
14. Flexibility CVET	4.00	3.00	3.83	4.95	3.60	6.67
15. Technology intermediary	5.00	3.86	1.23	5.23	3.80	4.26
16. Network alliances	7.02	4.76	5.77	3.15	3.78	4.48

Table 3.1 presents the main results of the Spidervet project: based on Rosenfeld, 16 dimensions are discerned, on which the information from the managements of VET colleges is scored. In each country 6 (Portugal) to 15 (Finland), colleges were interviewed. The average results for each dimension are interpreted briefly:
1. Most of the colleges have an information structure, with external partners used for strategic information; focus on the region is expressed by contacts with other colleges and knowledge institutes;
2. Colleges show major differences in interpreting the innovativeness of their sector: some colleges do not see any innovations, while others in the same sector do, and try to react;
3. Mission statements are strongly externally-oriented, targeted at both social goals and the labour market. The economic development of the region is scarcely mentioned;

4. In the mission statements, the characteristics of the responsive college are mentioned, but not systematically. Short courses are seen as the main way to deliver college knowledge to the regional economy. Some colleges do not deliver any courses, but most of them are active in this market.
5. Colleges see themselves as adaptors to sectoral innovation, and see a role for themselves in knowledge transfer;
6. College managers score high on internal communication efforts and knowledge management;
7. They consider their staff as professionals and experts for new knowledge development;
8. They do not mention lots of obstacles and constraints (like lack of information, financial and legal constraints, etc.);
9. Colleges are active in enhancing the enrolment of students, considering labour market shortages;
10. Colleges mention many activities to link course content to the needs of local companies;
11. The curriculum is, however, not very flexible for a variety of career patterns (self-directed learning; exemptions, short courses, free choices, tailor-made);
12. The colleges offer only a few short courses for post-initial training;
13. The turnover in continuing VET is only 10% of total turnover;
14. Courses for continuing VET are rarely tailor-made;
15. Adaptation to new technology is not seen as a regular task for colleges;
16. The colleges are not very active in regional networks; if they participate in regional networks, their target is to obtain information for their curriculum development; participation in innovation is hardly mentioned. Half of the colleges undertake no action in that direction.

The main conclusion is that, although VET colleges in Europe are aware of the urgency of developing new ways of VET delivery, they have trouble in turning this awareness into practice. The first eight dimensions, expressing management visions, all score rather high, whereas the last eight, expressing actions in practice, systematically score substantially lower. We can thus conclude that VET colleges agree that there is a need for change towards responsive VET, but do not yet have the right instruments for realising this perspective. VET colleges function as loosely coupled systems: management and 'production' are organised separately.

The knowledge economy demands a redefinition of educational goals and learning trajectories: the equilibrium between reified and experiential learning (through participation) should be balanced back to lively learning. This means for colleges and teachers that they should fundamentally redefine the educational enterprise. Lifelong programmes mean an end to anchor points like exams, stable length of courses, the certainty of academic knowledge, etc. The Spidervet model assumes that colleges have a clear idea of this new enterprise; if not, they will not be able to join innovative networks of companies, and they will not be able to have an adequate supply of worker-oriented courses and support. The results of the Spidervet project should thus be interpreted in this light: colleges have great trouble implementing a new educational enterprise, despite being aware of the urgency of redesigning.

3.5 Locked up in codification

Evidently, it is not easy for VET colleges to take up a new task, as sketched by Rosenfeld. Lifelong learning, the facilitation of technology adaptation, and the supporting of innovative networks seem to be mentally understood by the colleges, but, in practice, rarely put into action. This is the case in all the European VET colleges investigated.

The development of a system for lifelong learning in a dynamic knowledge-based economy is not simply a supplement to the education and training programmes on offer by the colleges; lifelong learning implies a fundamental change of work for the colleges. The learning process in the traditional VET system, developed for the industrial economy of the 20th century, is different from the innovative learning processes within knowledge-intensive companies (cf. Hoeve & Nieuwenhuis, 2002). These differences in learning processes produce different professional profiles for teachers and educators on the one hand, and professionals in companies on the other. The work culture and incentive structures also differ greatly for professionals and managers in companies and colleges. The design of VET for the knowledge economy involves not only the reorganisation of the course supply, but also a redesign of the fundamental processes and culture.

In the traditional theory of the development of human capital, knowledge and skills are seen as individual aspects. Hommen (1997) argues in favour of the social aspects of learning and skill development: knowledge is a collective commodity, developed in social and economic communities (communities of practice: see Wenger, 1998). Knowledge is developed in the complexity of work; skills are not bound to individuals or positions, but are spread over a group of workers. This vision is compatible with the evolutionary theory of innovation: innovation is an interactive process of problem-solving between workers and companies.

Stasz (2000) postulates two perspectives to analyse work competencies: the economic perspective, in which the human capital approach fits, and the sociocultural perspective, in which the social and cognitive context plays a major role. In traditional educational policy and course design, the economic perspective has played the most important role. Berryman and Bailey (1992) show for the US that the existing educational system fits perfectly into the traditional industrial workplace. Taylor's workplace is not designed for knowledge development and innovation, so traditional vocational education has the same reproductive characteristics.

Traditionally, education is designed within a context of certainty: the knowledge is judged as true and objective, and the instructional techniques are authoritarian, receptive, and nonparticipative. VET is designed from the same perspective; Tomassini (2000) explains the power of this perspective, with the distinction between the exchange value and the use value of competencies. The institutional demands on the labour market focus on the exchange value of competencies (accreditation and acknowledgement of labour rights), which causes the importance of the use value of competencies (what to do at the workplace) to decline. The use value of competencies should be developed at the workplace after finishing initial VET. The exchange value of competencies is deeply rooted in the VET structure; both employers and trade unions support this value strongly. For employers, the exchange value implies certainty in hiring processes, while for workers the exchange value forms a guarantee for their labour market position. The exchange value of competencies is thus an unavoidable aspect, but Tomassini argues that the disequilibrium between use and exchange value should be reconsidered.

In the actual VET system, colleges get their returns from efficiency in the industrial paradigm: participatory goals are addressed at the workplace, and by doing that, the college and teachers can concentrate on the codified part of the curriculum. According to Wenger (1998), codification has its costs and benefits: it facilitates entrance to new knowledge, but it hinders the giving of meaning to that knowledge through participation. In traditional VET, the equilibrium between codification and participation has disappeared. The actual noncompetitive position on the 'student market' does not force colleges to invest in adult education; noninitial education takes only 5%-10% of the turnover of colleges, and the course supply in adult education is restricted to routine content. As a result of the traditional incentive structure, colleges are not interested in innovation of the learning processes and the organisational visions behind this. Most of the discussion is directed at adapting external developments into the codified educational paradigm. Without a systemic debate and a paradigm shift at all levels in the educational system, the margins for innovative policies at college level will remain restricted. Colleges are aware of the urgency of a repositioning in the local economy, but they lack the instruments and the vision for claiming new roles. Moreover, teachers are locked into the traditional paradigm of VET, which results in professional resistance to uncertainty in participatory adventures with professionals from outside school.

Within Spidervet some good practices are found as benchmarks for new educational policy, but they should be considered as frontrunners and innovators, for which no institutional and organisational set-up exists inside the educational system. An educational system, supporting innovation and learning within economic practices, is not only a matter for the colleges, but requires strategic design at all levels of the system: legislation, institutional set-up, organisational design, and the constraints and redesign of the learning process itself.

3.6 Organising regional communities of learning and working

A pivotal role for VET colleges in the regional knowledge-based economy requires a coherent vision at the level of the organisation, through which the college internally and externally gives a clear statement on the social demand for vocational qualifications and the economic demand for an innovative labour force. This vision has to be developed in interaction with the social and economic environment. At the organisational level, this should be supported by a targeted human resources development policy: the expertise of the teachers is at this moment one of the larger bottlenecks holding up the realisation of an open, externally-oriented VET college. The innovative college organisation should be supported by professional teachers, who are externally recognised as partners in technology adaptation and organisational change. At the level of the learning process, great flexibility and responsiveness should be developed, both in the variety of course supply and supporting services, and in the design of attractive teaching-learning arrangements and assessment procedures. This implies reconsideration of the professional profile of the teacher: it seems impossible for a single teacher to achieve all the expertise needed to support the learn-and-work communities in the college. Differentiation of tasks and specialisation is needed, implying that arranging learning processes will become more and more teamwork. Domain specialists, assessors, coaches, test developers, and developers of learning materials and environments: each teacher has to define and develop his or her own specialty.

Teachers are both important actors and resources in the design of learning communities. A teacher's identity, based on codified knowledge in sterile contexts, gives few opportunities to develop an identity as a participant in regional and sectoral communities of practice. This makes them an ineffective role model for their students, in preparing them for participation in the local economy. Colleges should organise ways for the authentic participation of their teachers, in order to encourage students and teachers to participate in the community of learning and working at the college. The identity of the teachers is a major resource for the educational enterprise.

Organising the college as a configuration of sectoral learning and working communities, with continuous border-crossing contacts to the local community, is an exciting prospect. Lots of innovation takes place inside economic communities of practice, whereas VET colleges, through their multisectoral organisation, have an ideal position for connecting local communities. Effective connecting and networking requires, on the one hand, a solid position within local networks and, on the other, a well-developed antenna for 'neue Combinationen' of knowledge and skills, which can be used as new impulses for economic development. Neither requirement is being fulfilled within VET colleges at this moment. VET colleges find themselves in a difficult dilemma, from which they can only escape in cooperation with actors at the institutional level of the VET system. They can start redesigning the internal organisation structure of the college towards the perspective of the responsive school, consisting of sectoral, learning communities of teachers with strong links to innovative processes in their region.

Participation in regional and sectoral knowledge networks by VET colleges requires a new vision of the role of VET for the local economy: colleges should use every effort to develop an attractive supply of labour-oriented courses for the regional market. This supply should be embedded in and fostered by a flexible supply of services for the maintenance of skills in the labour force and for technology adaptation processes. This requires a coherent vision at the level of college management, a targeted HRD strategy inside the colleges, and the development of attractive teaching-learning arrangements and assessments. The challenge for VET colleges is to develop into innovative, learning organisations, welcomed by the local economic community as partners in technological development and innovation.

References

Berryman, S.E., & Bailey, T.R. (1992). *The double helix of education and the economy*. New York: Institute on education and the economy/Columbia University.

Breschi, S., & Malerba, F. (1997). Sectoral innovation systems: technological regimes, Schupeterian dynamics and spatial boundaries. In C. Edquist (Ed.), *Systems of innovation; technologies, organisations and institutions* (pp. 130-156). London: Pinter.

Coehoorn, C.A. (1995). *The Dutch innovation centres: implementation of technology policy or facilitating of small enterprises?* PhD-study; University of Groningen.

Cooke, P., Boekholt, P., & Tödtling, F. (2000). *The governance of innovation in Europe. Regional perspectives on global competitiveness*. London: Pinter.

De Bruyn, E., & Nieuwenhuis, L.F.M. (1994) The development of vocational education; industry and service compared. In W.J. Nijhof & J. Streumer (Eds.), *Flexibility in training and vocational education* (pp. 109-132). Utrecht: Lemma.

Dondi, C. (1999). A regional innovation programme in Emilia-Romagna, Italy. In B. Nyhan, G. Attwell & L. Deitmer (Eds.), *Towards the learning region; education and regional innovation in the European Union and the United States* (pp. 151-154). Thessaloniki: Cedefop.

Dosi, G. (1988). Sources, procedures and micro-economic effects of innovation. *Journal of economic literature, 26*, 1120-1171.

Engel, P. (1995). *Facilitating innovation. An action oriented approach*. Wageningen: Wageningen University.

Feldmann, M.P. (1994). Knowledge complementarity and innovation. In *Small Business Economics, 6*, 363-372.

Finegold, D. (1991) Institutional incentives and skill creation; preconditions for a high skill equilibrium. In P. Ryan (Ed.), *International comparisons of vocational education and training for intermediate skills* (pp. 93-116). London: the Falmer Press.

Grooters, J.W., & Nieuwenhuis, A.F.M. (1996). *Beroepsonderwijs in de kennisinfrastructuur*. Amsterdam: Max Goote Kenniscentrum BVE.

Hamel, G., & Prahalad, C.K. (1995). *Competing the future*. Oxford/New York: Oxford University Press.

Hartog, J. (1996). Kennis van de toekomst. In *Bouwstenen voor het kennisdebat* (pp. 49-85). Zoetermeer: Ministerie van OC&W.

Hippel, K. von. (1988). *Sources of innovation*. Oxford/New York: Oxford University Press.

Hoeve, A., & Nieuwenhuis, L.F.M. (2002). *Learning in innovation processes*. Paper for the Dutch/Flemish educational research conference in Antwerp. Wageningen: Stoas Research.

Hommen, L. (1997). Conceptualising the learning dimension of innovation in small firms: arguments for an "institutional" approach. *Studies in the education of adults, 29*, no. 2.

Keep, E., & Brown, A. (2000). *Review of vocational education and training research in the UK*. Luxemburg: COST A11.

Kleinknecht, A. (1994). Heeft Nederland een loongolf nodig? In *Tijdschrift voor politieke economie, jrg. 17, No. 2.*

Morgan, K. (1997). The learning region: institutions, innovation and regional renewal. In *Regional Studies, 31.*

Nieuwenhuis, L.F.M. (1999). New developments in qualifying strategies for sectoral and regional innovation. In B. Sellin (Ed.), *European trends in the development of occupations and qualifications* (pp. 243-257). Thessaloniki: Cedefop.

Nieuwenhuis, L.F.M., Gielen, P.M., & Lokman, A.H. (2000). *Sector, regio en kennisorganisatie; kennisnetwerken rond het beroepsonderwijs*. Amsterdam: Max Goote Kenniscentrum BVE.

Nieuwenhuis, L.F.M. (2001). Innovation and learning in small companies. In L.F.M. Nieuwenhuis & W.J. Nijhof (Eds), *The dynamics of VET and HRD systems* (pp. 125-140). Enschede: Twente University Press.

Nieuwenhuis, L.F.M., Hoeve, A., & Verhaar, C. (2002). Networking between economy and education; regional knowledge transfer in Dutch agriculture. In F. Boekema, E. Kuijpers &

R. Rutten (Eds.), *Economic geography of higher education*. Cheltenham: Edward Elgar Publishing.

Nonaka, I., & Takeuchi, H. (1995). *The knowledge creating company; how Japanese companies create the dynamics of innovation.* Oxford/New York: Oxford University Press.

OECD (2001). *Cities and regions in the new learning economy.* Paris: OECD-publications.

Oerlemans, L. (1997). *De ingebedde onderneming: innoveren in industriële netwerken.* Tilburg: University Press.

Röling, N. (1992). The emergence of knowledge systems' thinking. In *Knowledge and policy, 5.*

Rosenfeld, S. (1998). Stock taking paper for the workshop *'Technical colleges, technology deployment and regional development'.* OECD international conference Modena on 'building competitive regional economies'.

Stasz, C. (2000). *Assessing skills for work: two perspectives.* Paper for the conference "skills measurement and economic analysis". Canterbury UK. Santa Monica, CA: RAND.

Tomassini, M. (2000). Knowledge dynamics, communities of practice: emerging perspectives on training. *European journal on vocational training, 19,* 38-46. Thessaloniki: Cedefop.

Wenger, E. (1998). *Communities of practice; learning, meaning and identity.* Cambridge: University Press.

CHAPTER 4

Perspectives on institutional and organisational flexibility in VET

4.1 Introduction

GIVEN THE THEME OF THIS SECTION, it is appropriate to begin by reflecting briefly on the terms 'institution' and 'organisation'. Although these words are sometimes used interchangeably, it can be useful to make a clear distinction between them. Such a distinction is implied, for example, when we refer to institutions in the sense of 'rules'.

The economic historian Douglass North has used a sports analogy in order to distinguish between institutions as "the rules of the game" and organisations as its "players" (North, 1990: 5). This distinction provides the basis for a now widely accepted definition of institutions as "sets of common habits, routines, established practices, rules or laws that regulate the relations and interactions between individuals and groups" (Edquist & Johnson, 1997: 46), and of organisations as "formal structures with an explicit purpose [that are] consciously created" (ibid.: 47). But these terms of definition are not altogether mutually exclusive, since organisational forms, if not actual organisations, can still be thought of as institutions – i.e., as 'rules' that establish the identities of the players. Hence, some sociologists are reluctant to adopt North's distinction completely. Richard Scott (1994), for example, recognises that "organisations incorporate, perhaps even better, instantiate institutional elements," although he also calls attention to "the effects of wider institutional systems on organisational forms" (ibid.: 70). He therefore incorporates an addendum into his account of institutions as representational constitutive, and normative rules, together with enforcement mechanisms. "Institutions," he writes, "operate at a variety of levels and their elements can be embodied in and carried by cultures, by regimes and by formal organisations" (ibid.).

Each of the contributors to this section draws attention to one or another of the various levels at which institutions exist and operate, as well as reflecting on the interplay between institutions and organisations. Kurt Mayer addresses historical changes in advanced capitalism's mode of regulation, a term which encompasses a complex and multi-dimensioned structure of institutions and organisations. He concentrates, however, on the "skill-labour nexus" of institutionalised relations between the skill producing system and the wage relation (referring to both external and internal labour markets) and develops an even more specific focus on changes in the firm as a "specific organisational form." Similarly, Loek Nieuwenhuis begins with broad institutional changes, both in the economy and in European Union and national policy, but he develops a dual organisational focus on VET colleges and

53

W. J. Nijhof et al. (eds.), Shaping Flexibility in Vocational Education and Training, 53-63.
© 2002 *Kluwer Academic Publishers. Printed in the Netherlands.*

firms. His contribution emphasises the creation and transmission of knowledge within and among organisations, and draws attention to different institutional contexts for this activity: "product chains," "sectors," and "regions." Both authors elaborate policy implications that focus on changes to VET policy, primarily at the regional and national levels, but with ramifications for the international or supra-national level of the European Union. Mayer's discussion of existing and emergent policy regimes – such as the different 'models' of VET that can be identified with alternative forms of firm-level adaptation to 'post-Fordist' economic conditions – points to the importance of formally regulated relations among organisations of different kinds. He contends that "a redesign of the fundamental processes and culture of VET" can enable VET to influence "the shaping ...of the new techno-economic paradigm" – i.e., to help define a new mode of regulation consistent with the principles of a 'learning economy'. Similarly, Nieuwenhuis relates the choices now facing VET organisations to the growing economic importance 'networks of innovation', discussing several key dimensions. "Organisations for VET," he argues, cannot act anymore as stand alone institutions, but should develop network oriented strategies."

Flexibility is, of course, another key word for this section, as it is for this entire volume. As those familiar with the debate on labour market and firm flexibility that began in the 1980s and persisted into the 1990s will be aware, there are different institutional varieties of flexibility and each is realised through different processes and mechanisms. In his chapter, Kurt Mayer outlines fundamentally different kinds of firm-level flexibility and innovation that are possible under 'post-Fordist' conditions. Similarly, Lundvall and Archibugi (2001), in their recent discussion of 'Europe and the learning economy' are careful to point out that "Flexible labour markets may be at the core of adaptation in some innovation systems while others adapt more through functional flexibility within organisations" (ibid.: 7). With specific reference to the strategies of firms, they identify at least two 'best practice' models, each of which depends for its success on the institutional set-up of training and labour market institutions. One model is the "internal competence building" strategy preferred by Japanese firms and some large US corporations. The other is the strategy of "networking among firms and high mobility in the labour market" that is typical of 'industrial districts' in places as different as Denmark and California's Silicon Valley. (Ibid.: 12)

This section's contributors address flexibility in a number of different ways. For VET colleges, Loek Nieuwenhuis identifies flexibility with "external orientation", "responsiveness," and the principle that "linear models for knowledge transfer should be replaced by interactive models." He concludes with recommendations for VET colleges to develop a combined strategy of – to use Lundvall and Archibugi's terms -- 'functional flexibility' and 'networking'. Kurt Mayer discusses flexibility as a necessary response to the economic problems created by the rigidities of Fordism. But, as he indicates, the neo-liberal remedy of developing greater reliance on markets has hardly proved to be a complete solution. The practical shortcomings of this strategy, Mayer suggests, have provided the starting points for a new economic policy, which will both influence and incorporate new firm strategies. In his account, then, there is now an opening for political and strategic choices between alternative forms of flexibility. Loek Nieuwenhuis, however, indicates that such choices may not be easily accomplished. Contradictions in educational reform can stem from overt conflicts among the identifiable policy alternatives. For example, VET organisations appear, on one hand, to have adopted an orientation towards labour force flexibility based on a more theoretical, and thus broader, conception of learning – but, on the other hand, they are evidently locked-in to purveying "codified knowledge" that meets the short-term interests of firms but neglects their longer-term interests. Responsiveness to market forces may thus undermine reforms that are vital to the creation of a more adaptive labour force and more adequate forms of VET. This implies a need for strong market regulation, based on negotiation and social partnership, which are essential foundations for ensuring functional flexibility.

4.2 The skeptical view: raising critical challenges

The contributors to this section deal with broad patterns of institutional change and their implications for VET organisations. While they agree, at least in general terms, on the broad outlines of the new institutional landscape and the situation of VET within it, their perspectives remain somewhat different. Kurt Mayer takes the long view. He examines different possible solutions to the crisis of Fordism and emphasises that the outcomes are not yet decided. Loek Nieuwenhuis adopts a more immediate and pragmatic perspective. Taking the new demands of the labour market and public policy as given, he concentrates on the question of how VET providers can best respond to them.

What both these authors have in common is that they offer positive visions of the future, based on a constructive analysis and interpretation of present trends. In this respect, they are perhaps vulnerable to the charge of optimism. It may be helpful, therefore, to consider their contributions from a more sceptical standpoint – from which, for example, it might be argued that the future of VET entails few real opportunities or choices for any actors other than economic and political elites. Some critics might react to terms such as 'innovation' and 'the learning economy' with deep suspicion. Similarly, they might regard the term 'evolution' as a code-word for the notion of one – and the only – path of development, even though they are also sceptical about the emergence of any alternative paths.

Critical scepticism of this kind raises some very fundamental institutional challenges concerning the future of VET. It can be illuminating to consider how such challenges are dealt with by the contributors to this section, since this is a means by which it is possible to generate 'new combinations' of perspective, in addition to testing perspectives against one another. The remaining part of this discussion therefore proceeds by elaborating two broad critical themes, then exploring how these themes are dealt with in the contributions of Kurt Mayer and Loek Nieuwenhuis. Although several other selections were certainly possible, the two themes that have been chosen for this purpose are 'markets versus society' and 'innovation as elitism'.

4.3 Markets versus Society?

From a critical perspective it can be argued that instead of seeing VET as a 'system', we should view it as something socially constructed by actors. Yet both actors and processes of social construction, the argument might continue, are effectively hidden by the current policy discourse on VET. In this discourse, which takes 'the market' as its basic frame of reference, the distinction between something mediated by society, e.g., qualifications or skills, and something tied to a concrete labour process, e.g., competence, is obscured. In fact, even the idea of education as something more than 'learning in the workplace' begins to disappear. Here, as elsewhere, the market is equated with the needs of individual companies. Even EU political discourse can be seen to be strongly influenced by the 'vision' of major European corporations interested in creating a global free market through liberalisation and deregulation. Hence, firms can be readily identified as some of the main actors engaged in the redefinition of VET as a project of 'social construction'. It requires only a short, though rather reductionistic, step to see them as the *only* actors, and to argue on this basis that public discussion and policy-making now focus not on the needs of people but on those of companies, an orientation for which the EU's emphasis on regions is a merely convenient euphemism.

This is a compelling argument, not least because it relies on a cogent account of organisations as 'carriers' of institutions. However, to be entirely consistent, this kind of argument must also devote its attention to considering markets as institutions and reflecting on how they are socially constructed. As many have observed, there is a wide variety of 'national' capitalisms. Each of the main models that can be identified has very different implications for the organisation and practice of VET. Thus, one comparison of British, German and Italian patterns of labour market regulation and their effects on the form and content of VET concludes that "Regulatory systems are not portable structures, achieving similar results wherever they are deployed, but are in fact deeply rooted in local social structures" (Peck, 1994: 169). If important institutional differences like these can persist at the national level, even in an era of globalisation, it may be somewhat problematic to assume that local and regional markets are in reality one and the same thing as the world market.

Loek Nieuwenhuis evidently does not subscribe to this last-mentioned proposition. He argues that regional training colleges have "the opportunity to become a pivotal pole in the learning networks of small and medium enterprises". This potential depends not only on their possibilities to make connections between "geographically related enterprises and regional infrastructural provisions / opportunities" but also, and perhaps more importantly, on their ability to build upon local institutional structures. The most important of these structures for VET are "learning networks" among firms, which can take various forms – e.g., the "mono-structures in terms of products and services" that characterise Italian industrial districts, or the "chain relations" that are found in other emerging regions. These institutional features are, of course, precisely what distinguishes local and regional markets from 'the market' in general -- and what provides them with sources of competitive advantage within the world market. This is the case, not only for regions dominated by SMEs but also for those that depend on large 'hub' firms. One example of the latter type that is discussed by Nieuwenhuis is the district of Eindhoven, where large firms such as Philips Electronics have come to depend critically upon a dense and elaborate network of "knowledge creating, treating, and disseminating institutes".

Kurt Mayer elaborates the logic of regional institutional variation in his remarks on globalisation. He recognises that one result of recent steps toward internationalisation through deregulation and the deactivation of transnational trade restrictions has been to narrow dramatically the scope for national autonomy in general economic policy. At the same time, however, this development has been accompanied by an increased importance of not only supra-national (e.g., EU-level) policy, but also labour market policies, social policies, education policies, R&D policies and innovation policies at the national and regional level. Hence, globalisation does not necessarily imply homogenisation, given the considerable – and arguably increased – possibility for institutional diversity, particularly at the regional level. And, so far as companies are concerned, such differences can be of decisive importance. As Mayer states, "The fields of market competition [have] increased as well since firms recently not only compete for customers but as well for network partners and human resources".

Nieuwenhuis's example of Eindhoven illustrates that not only 'home countries' but also 'home regions' can remain vitally important, even for 'globalised' multinational enterprises (MNEs), precisely because of the unique institutional features of these locations. The core R&D of a native MNE such as Philips has remained 'at home' partly due to the importance of localised 'tacit knowledge' (Boekholt & van der Weele, 1998). Not only the institutional set-up of R&D is important in this respect, but also "higher education structures, institutional arrangements for knowledge transfer and the workings of labour markets for highly qualified technical specialists" (Mason & Wagner, 1998: 17). Inter-organisational mobility of scientific and technical personnel may be more easily accomplished with close spatial proximity (Breschi & Malerba, 1997).

If there is a high degree of institutional variation in markets, it follows that this should also be the case with firms. This point, however, is not very well captured by a simple equation of 'the market' with 'the needs of companies'. This formulation is also somewhat misleading in that it presents firms as the 'carriers' of only one kind of social institution – i.e., the market. In reality, however, firms operate within and internalise or embody much more complex institutional frameworks that are made up of varied sets of institutions. W.W. Powell (1991), a leading institutionalist in sociology, has enumerated many examples, including "pressures from various regulatory bodies and consumer groups to conform to procedural requirements", "government regulation [that] protects many organisations from competitive pressures", "socially constructed beliefs" influencing market demand and consumption patterns, the crucial role played by governments in "creation of the corporate form" of business organisation, and the activity of organised professions, which – together with the state – "have become the great rationalisers of this century" (ibid.: 187–188).

Kurt Mayer recognises the institutional complexity of the firm when he refers, in his remarks on 'industrial paradigms', to co-evolution between organisations and institutions. He raises the question of whether relatively persistent differences in enterprise governance are linked to wider national institutional arrangements and in particular to labour markets and vocational training systems. Mayer provides an affirmative response by discussing the mutual interdependence of VET provision, corporate governance mechanisms and labour market institutions, during both the Fordist period and afterwards. With regard to the micro-level of the firm during the present period of transition, he points out that the new firm strategies are concerned with connecting different categories of economic actors (many of which occupy very different institutional environments) in "interactive processes of knowledge sharing". In this connection, "interactivity, shared experiences and learning stimulate the development and appropriation of shared beliefs and common interpretations of the social context" as a precondition for intelligent communication and hence problem-solving. As Mayer emphasises, though, the requirement for a common institutional framework within which learning can occur could be met through very different kinds of organisational strategies, each of which would have very different implications for VET.

Loek Nieuwenhuis adds to and broadens this perspective by examining the different kinds of 'knowledge contexts' within which firms are situated and in relation to which they orient their innovative activities. In addition to the regional context (already discussed in some detail), he also discusses the contexts of "product chains" and "sectors". Product chains are characterised by various kinds of user-producer relationships, which provide the basis for interactive learning. However, as Nieuwenhuis demonstrates with his case of greenhouse farming in the Netherlands, shifts in these relationships involve the disruption of established 'knowledge systems' and require the creation of new ones. The recent emergence of a 'supermarket-led' system of innovation in food production has brought about a situation in which "the role of agricultural education and training has been in danger of a certain marginalisation." With respect to the sectoral context, Nieuwenhuis emphasises the key roles that can be played by trade unions and professional organisations in developing institutional frameworks for co-operative behaviour in areas such as technology monitoring and skill development. He identifies a successful model of this kind of practice in the case of Intechnium, an innovation and training centre recently established for the installation engineering sector. As Nieuwenhuis also points out in relation to the sectoral level, however, "technical and vocational courses and curricula based on skill definitions from a specific professional / occupational group .... sometimes ... do not coincide with larger socio-economic needs."

On the whole, what emerges from both Loek Nieuwenhuis's and Kurt Mayer's contributions is a highly nuanced picture of institutional complexity and variation among firms and markets. Given the extent to which market relations and market processes, including processes of technical innovation, are 'institutionalised', it may be more meaningful to think in terms of socially constructed markets than to oppose markets and market actors to society and social interests.

4.4 Innovation as elitism?

Another critical challenge for VET can be found in the conception of innovation as an inherently elitist form of activity. Here, Schumpeter, the 'father' of modern theories of innovation, provides a central point of reference. To Schumpeter and Schumpeterians, it might be argued, distinctions between Capitalism and Socialism are ideological and irrelevant, since politics in either type of system ends up being left to a political elite. It might be possible to take issue with some aspects of this critical interpretation of Schumpeter – for example, some have presented him as an enthusiastic capitalist who saw socialism as an inevitable development, though not a welcome one. Moreover, even the staunchest critics of Schumpeter's 'elitist' political theory might conclude from the study of present day politics and policy-making that Schumpeter might have been right, after all, about democracy as a necessarily limited and imperfect form of decision-making.

In any case, Schumpeter was first and foremost an economist, and we are here concerned primarily with his more strictly economic concepts – particularly those related to innovation. In this connection, the entrepreneur was a central social figure for Schumpeter, since it is the entrepreneur who develops new ideas, makes innovations in terms of new products or processes, creates profits, and so forth. Given Schumpeter's allegedly technocratic view of a converging development of industrial society, there is only a short step to be made from entrepreneurialism to elitism. Some critics are therefore quick to identify as Schumpeter's heirs the present-day political and business elites, for whom the analysis of society is all about the evolution of 'systems' and the primary goal of society is maximising economic growth. In discussion and policy-making related to VET, there is moreover, a fairly direct linkage to be made between these expressions of elitism and the neo-liberal discourse of the market, which we have already discussed at some length.

This is a strong polemic, and latter-day Schumpeterians – at least those who do not count themselves among the 'elite' – might want to present a somewhat different account of Schumpeterianism. They might, for example, object that the idea (and ideal) of a 'free' or 'perfect' market properly belongs to neo-classical economics, rather than the Schumpeterian tradition. They might also point out that the 'evolutionary' economics school descended from Schumpeter has devoted much effort to arguments with mainstream economics concerning the existence of significant differences amongst firms and the 'open-ended' character of economic and social development (Nelson & Winter, 1982). However, even if Schumpeterians declined to comment on these points, they would surely want to correct the critics' 'elitist' account of Schumpeter's concept of the entrepreneur.

A distinction between two Schumpeterian models of entrepreneurship is now commonplace in studies of innovation (Malerba & Orsenigo, 1997). One is the 'heroic' model of the individual entrepreneur already alluded to. The other is a more socialised or 'collective' model, in which innovation is presented as a routine activity of large, bureaucratically organised corporations. As one student of Schumpeter's thought has explained, this second model emerged at a later point in Schumpeter's career, "at the same time that he became convinced of a growing obsolescence of the entrepreneurial function" (Elam, 1993: 16). "Thus, while he believed in the coming of a world where individual initiative would increasingly count for nothing, he continued to put forward a programme for studying development in which human agency still makes a difference" (ibid.). On this account, Schumpeter could not, at the very least, be accused of drawing attention away from 'social actors', or of preferring 'systems' over 'people.'

While there are few if any instances in this section where the contributors discuss examples of 'heroic' entrepreneurship and processes of innovation carried out by lone individuals, there are many illustrations of Schumpeter's 'second model'. Loek Nieuwenhuis provides many of these examples. Moreover, he is clear from the very outset that the phenomenon of 'innovation' is very closely tied to that of 'networks'. Thus he writes, with a clear allusion to Schumpeter, that "Economic networks are crucial to transform heterogeneous knowledge sources into useful 'Neue Kombinationen'." Nieuwenhuis identifies a number of concepts that are useful for mapping the different social dimensions of innovation – for example, those of 'paradigm' and 'trajectory', 'problem-solving', 'learning', 'tacit' and 'explicit' knowledge, and so forth. And, without exception, he illustrates them with examples that point to the highly collective and, in this sense, non-elitist, character of modern innovation processes. For instance, he writes that "Workers learn by sharing knowledge in the working team and employers learn by creating networks of colleagues and advisors." Nieuwenhuis also states that "tacit knowledge is depending on people" and therefore insists that "Flexibility should be translated [into] trainability and learning skills, and not [into] external flexibility.

Kurt Mayer also elaborates a highly 'democratic' view of the innovation process. He suggests, for example, that in all the links and relationships triggered by the new strategies, the main focus of the agents is not on hindering others' access to their knowledge but rather to create a relationship that makes interactive learning possible. He insists, moreover, that interactive learning cannot be reduced to a purely technical matter, governed solely by 'instrumental rationality', but instead depends vitally on 'communicative rationality.' Mayer's account of the innovation process is also explicitly linked to the broader concept of a 'learning society', which has been developed in opposition to the lack of attention to concerns of democracy and social welfare that have characterised some alternative visions of the 'New Economy'. This point is made abundantly clear in Mayer's frequent references to B.-Å. Lundvall, the original author of the term 'learning economy'. The learning economy, according to one quote from Lundvall, "does not signal a science-based economy dominated by hi-tech firms and by those who have an academic training." Extending this reasoning further, Kurt Mayer insists that the learning economy approach has "a broader societal perspective". Certainly, learning shapes the life of citizens in many other respects than the professional and business perspective. Moreover, as Mayer argues, the integration of the 'unskilled' and the support of their developmental potential may become one of the key issues of a sustainable and successful transition towards a learning economy.

On balance, it is fair to say that both Loek Nieuwenhuis and Kurt Mayer, despite their exposure to Schumpeterian influences, present highly 'socialised' and 'democratic' views of the innovation process. There is an obvious difference between their accounts of innovation and the identification of innovation with technocratic elitism. But this difference might perhaps be rather easily explained by these authors' strongly empirical bent. While they have concentrated their attention on concrete studies and analyses of actual innovation processes, many critics have instead looked only at the rhetoric of innovation. Further, Nieuwenhuis and Mayer cite authors who are actually engaged in the study of innovation, as well as actual practitioners. In contrast, critics often take their quotations mainly from political and business leaders who talk about innovation without necessarily having any practical experience or theoretical understanding of the phenomenon. With sources such as these it is easy enough to associate innovation with elitism.

Of course, there are good grounds for the concerns expressed by critics. Why else would so much effort have been devoted to making the case that innovation is not an elitist activity, and arguing that the social requirements of interactive learning include both political democracy and social inclusion? As Kurt Mayer points out, one possible path of development that innovative firms may choose is that of the "technical organisation of innovation." This neo-Fordist trajectory implies "a divide between a [minority] of highly educated and well-paid long term employees on the one hand and a [majority] of low wage and low skilled flexibly employed labour on the other hand". Certainly, there are also 'non-elitist' alternatives to this possible future, and VET policy and practice has an important role to play in making these alternatives more viable. As Loek Nieuwenhuis argues, though, fulfilling this promise will require VET, as a 'community of practice' to become actively engaged in processes of innovation. Otherwise, VET will remain "locked in the codified practices of an educational system developed for and in the industrial society of the 20th century." In this connection, and in relation to critical perspectives, it is significant that Nieuwenhuis attributes this 'lock-in' partly to elites and interest groups – "i.e., the important actors in the system, like social partners, government and even students" – that consistently promote the 'exchange values' of the labour market over the 'use values' of innovation processes.

4.5 Concluding remarks: an agenda for future research

As noted at the outset, the contributions to this section have been concerned with the interplay between institutions and organisations in relation to the resolution of key problems in VET, particularly that of 'flexibility'. On the whole, though, more attention has been given to broad institutional changes and their possible implications for VET than to the manner in which VET has responded to these changes at an organisational level. In this regard, Loek Nieuwenhuis has developed the strongest empirical focus on institutional change in VET organisations. It will therefore be appropriate to conclude by relating the results reported by Nieuwenhuis to an agenda for further research. At the same time, it should be stressed that this research agenda is one that responds to the structural dilemma of VET that has been outlined by Kurt Mayer. Mayer points to "a major contrast between concepts of the ´learning organisation´ that is dynamic in attending to corporate change and VET that is tending towards stability of competence and skill creation", resulting from VET's historical role of mediating between public policies, on one hand, and firm strategies, on the other.

Nieuwenhuis, in his account of the results of the 'Spidervet-project', states as a main finding that "VET colleges are aware of the urgency of developing new ways of VET delivery, but ... have trouble in turning this awareness into practice." This finding provides a very clear illustration of 'loose coupling' -- a phenomenon that institutional analysts have long recognised as being very typical of educational organisations. Such organisations normally operate within highly institutionalised environments where they are "rewarded for establishing correct procedures and processes, not for the quantity and quality of their outputs" (Scott, 1987: 126). Consequently, the processes through which they initially respond to important institutional changes are essentially "ceremonial enactments of conformity" to wider institutions (Meyer & Rowan, 1991: 44-45). These responses are superficial, however, and they tend to be accompanied by the 'de-coupling' of internal work processes from external structures. This strategy masks "inconsistencies, irrationalities and inefficiencies," maintains "public faith," secures "commitment on the part of employees," and "allows local input into organisational processes without disrupting outward institutional conformity" (Ingersoll, 1993: 86).

'Loose coupling' is not necessarily a negative or counter-productive feature of organisations. It is too simplistic to view this phenomenon as a purely manipulative form of adaptation to external environments that has only a negative relation to internal organisational efficiency (Powell, 1991: 190). Rather, it must also be considered that internal decoupling constitutes an essential basis for innovative activity in organisations (Lyles & Schwenk, 1992). Among other things, the loose coupling of knowledge structures requires the constant reformulation of unifying "interpretation agreements" and the renewal or expansion of structures and "codes" of communication within organisations (Daft & Weick, 1984; Orton & Weick, 1990). Thus, processes of institutionalisation involving an increasingly tight external coupling with other organisations, together with internal decoupling, can be viewed as crucial to the development of innovative capacity within individual organisations.

Arguably, this institutionalist perspective on loose coupling could provide a starting point for a deeper analysis of the changes that are now under way within the VET colleges that were studied in the Spidervet-project. More generally, this focus could also provide a means of extending the analysis of the broad institutional changes that have been discussed in this section to include the innovative responses of VET organisations. Thereby, it would provide a useful 'bottom-up' complement to the largely 'top-down' perspectives on institutional and organisational change that have been presented here.

References

Boekholt, P., & Weele, E. van der (1998). Southeast Brabant: A regional innovation system in transition. In H.J. Braczyk, P. Cooke, & M. Heidenrich, with G. Krauss (Eds.), *Regional innovation systems: The role of governances in a globalized world* (pp. 48–71). London: UCL Press.

Breschi, S., & Malerba, F. (1997). Sectoral innovation systems, technological regimes, Schumpeterian dynamics and spatial boundaries. In C. Edquist (Ed.), *Systems of innovation: Technologies, organisations and institutions* (pp. 130-156). London: Pinter Publishers/Casell Academic.

Daft, R.L., & Weick, K.E. (1984). Toward a model of organisations as interpretation systems. *Academy of Management Review, 9*, 284-295.

Edquist, C., & Johnson, B. (1997). Institutions and organisations in systems of innovation. In C. Edquist (Ed.), *Systems of innovation: Technologies, organisations and institutions* (pp. 41 - 63). London: Pinter Publishers/Casell Academic.

Elam, M. (1993). *Innovation as the craft of combination: Perspectives on technology and the economy in the spirit of Schumpeter*. Linköping, Sweden: Linköping University, Department of Technology and Social Change.

Ingersoll, R.M. (1993). Loosely coupled organisations revisited. *Research in the Sociology of Organisations, 11*, 81-112.

Lundvall, B.Å., & Archibugi, D. (2001). Europe and the learning economy. In D. Archibugi & B.Å. Lundvall (Eds.), *The globalising learning economy* (pp. 1 - 20). Oxford/New York: Oxford University Press.

Lyles, M.A., & Schwenk, C.R. (1992). Top management, strategy and organizational knowledge structures. *Journal of Management Studies, 29*(2), 155-174.

Malerba, F., & Orsenigo, L. (1997). Schumpeterian patterns of innovation. In D. Archibugi & J. Michie (Eds.), *Technology, globalisation and economic performance* (pp. 241-267). Cambridge: Cambridge University Press.

Mason, G. & Wagner, K. (1998). *High Level Skills and Knowledge Transfer in Britain and Germany: Electronics, Technical Consultancy and Systems Integration*. Paper presented at the Workshop on 'Systems and Services Innovation' at CRIC, University of Manchester, Manchester, U.K., March 17–18.

Meyer, J.W., & Rowan, B. (1991). Institutionalized organisations: Formal structure as myth and ceremony. In P.J. Dimaggio & W.W. Powell (Eds.), *The new institutionalism in organizational analysis* (pp. 41-62). Chicago: The University of Chicago Press.

Nelson, R., & Winter, S. (1982). *An evolutionary theory of economic change*. Boston, Massachusetts: The Bellknap Press of Harvard University Press.

North, D.C. (1990). *Institutions, institutional change and economic performance*. Cambridge,: Cambridge University Press.

Orton, J.D., & Weick, K.E. (1990). Loosely coupled systems: A reconceptualization. *Academy of Management Review, 15*, 203-223.

Peck, J. (1994). Regulating Labour: The social regulation and reproduction of local labour markets. In A. Amin & N. Thrift (Eds.), *Globalization, institutions, and regional development in Europe* (pp. 147-176). Oxford/New York: Oxford University Press.

Powell, W.W. (1991). Expanding the scope of institutional analysis. In P.J. Dimaggio & W.W. Powell (Eds.), *The new institutionalism in organizational analysis* (pp. 183-203). Chicago: The University of Chicago Press.

Scott, W.R. (1987). *Organisations: Rational, natural and open systems*. Englewood Cliffs, New Jersey: Prentice-Hall.

Scott, W.R. (1994). Institutions and organisations: Toward a theoretical synthesis. In W.R. Scott & J.W. Meyer (Eds.), *Institutional environments and organisations: Structral complexity and individualism* (pp. 55-80). Thousand Oaks/London/New Delhi: Sage publications Ltd.

SECTION III

EDUCATIONAL TOOLS AND RESOURCES FOR FLEXIBILITY

CHAPTER 5

Institutional responses to a flexible unified system

CATHY HOWIESON, DAVID RAFFE AND TERESA TINKLIN

THE HIGHER STILL REFORM IS INTRODUCING a flexible unified system of post-16 education in Scotland. The new system will cover nearly all general and vocational education after the end of compulsory school, with the exception of higher education (HE) and Scottish Vocational Qualifications (SVQs) which are designed primarily for workplace training. It will bring different curricula (general and vocational), different institutions, different levels of study and provision for different age groups into a single framework with common design rules for the curriculum, assessment and certification. The reform began in 1999 and is being phased in over a five year period. In this chapter we examine the early progress of the reform in Further Education (FE) colleges, the main public providers of vocational education in Scotland. We start by describing the existing Scottish system and the current reforms; we then introduce our conceptual framework, based on the concepts of unification and flexibility; and we then present some findings of a survey of FE colleges on the progress and impact of the reform.

5.1 The Scottish system

Most young people in Scotland attend comprehensive secondary schools from the age of 12. Full-time education is compulsory to age 16, when young people may stay on, usually at the same school, for one or two years of upper-secondary education. In 1999 just over a quarter (28%) of school leavers left at 16, a quarter (25%) left after one year of upper-secondary school and nearly half (47%) left after two years (Scottish Executive, 2001). Many of those who left at 16 or 17 entered Skillseeker programmes of work-based training leading to occupational SVQs. A small but growing minority of early school leavers continued full-time education at an FE college.

Even before the reform, the curriculum of upper-secondary education in Scotland could be described as flexible. The volume, level, content and duration of study varied from student to student. Unlike most other European countries, Scotland has not required students to complete a specified programme of study in order to 'graduate' from upper-secondary education. Before 1999, the upper-secondary school curriculum was based on 120-hour single-subject courses: Highers, the main qualifications for university entry, and Certificate of Sixth Year Studies (CSYS) courses which were available in the second post-compulsory year for those who had passed at Higher in the relevant subject. Students took up to five courses in a year and filled the gaps with 40-hour National Certificate (NC) modules. The modules covered a range of general and vocational subjects, specified in terms of learning outcomes and internally assessed (that is, assessed by school or college staff). They varied in difficulty but most were less demanding than Highers.

W. J. Nijhof et al. (eds.), Shaping Flexibility in Vocational Education and Training, 67-84.
© 2002 *Kluwer Academic Publishers. Printed in the Netherlands.*

FE colleges offer general as well as vocational courses although, unlike English colleges, they do not usually offer academic courses to young people in competition with secondary schools. The 46 colleges vary widely, but they all subscribe to a mission which emphasises access and social inclusion. They provide a wide range of courses, at all levels, available through full-time or part-time study or by open or distance learning, to students of all ages. Nearly two thirds of students are aged 21 or older. Before Higher Still was introduced NC modules were an important part of college provision. Other college programmes led to SVQs, Highers, Higher National Certificates and Diplomas (HNC/Ds: higher education programmes below degree level with a vocational emphasis) or other vocational and professional qualifications; some programmes did not lead to formal qualifications. Most college programmes were modular or unit-based and most assessment was internal (carried out by college staff).

5.2 The Higher Still reform

In the early 1990s the Scottish system was seen to be failing (SOED, 1992). A growing proportion of 16 year olds with average- and below-average attainments were staying on at school, where they had to choose between modules, often offered in an arbitrary range of subjects depending on school staffing and resources, and Highers which offered a high risk of failure. Many students mixed Highers and modules and had to cope with their different pedagogies and assessment regimes. Modules had low status and often offered limited opportunities for progression; consequently there was pressure to take Highers even for students who had little chance of success. Able students took programmes of Highers which lacked breadth and depth compared to other European qualifications. Employers complained that young workers lacked 'core skills' – formally defined as communication, numeracy, information technology, problem solving and working with others. There were criticisms that standards were too low, that the burden of assessment was excessive and that the system lacked transparency. These weaknesses primarily related to young people and they affected schools more than colleges.

In sum, although the existing system provided considerably flexibility of curriculum and pathways – in the sense that there were few formal restrictions on curriculum choice and students could mix, or move between, the different types of provision – this flexibility was restricted in practice by differences in philosophy, pedagogy and assessment, by obstacles to progression and by the unequal status of different qualifications. The Higher Still reform aimed to rationalise this system and to provide a genuinely seamless and flexible system of pathways. It was announced in 1994 in a document entitled *Higher Still: Opportunity for All* (Scottish Office, 1994). As the existing system of courses and modules covered colleges as well as schools, the reform included colleges even if the main problems it addressed were those of schools (Howieson, Raffe, Spours & Young, 1997).

The architecture of the new unified system is based on 40-hour *units*, which may be combined into 160-hour *courses*; courses and units may be grouped into 640- or 800-hour *Scottish Group Awards* (SGAs). Units, courses and SGAs correspond to modules, courses and group awards in the old system. Each unit, course or SGA is separately certificated. Students can take free-standing units which are not part of courses, or courses which do not contribute to SGAs. Each unit is internally assessed, often using 'NABs' (standard assessments held in a National Assessment Bank). Each course comprises three units, and the remaining 40 of the 160 hours are devoted to induction, remediation, integration and preparation for external assessment. To pass a course a student must pass the internal assessments for each unit and an external assessment (typically an examination or project work, judged by an assessor from outside the school or college) which covers the course as a whole. An SGA consists typically of at least two or three courses and additional units to make up to the total of 640 or 800 hours. To achieve an SGA a student must also show a specified level of attainment in the five core skills. These may be achieved by taking free-standing units, by taking Higher Still courses or units in which particular core skills are deemed to be 'embedded', or on the basis of earlier qualifications.

Higher Still units, courses and SGAs are available at five levels: Access, Intermediate 1, Intermediate 2, Higher and Advanced Higher. The five levels are designed to articulate with compulsory school qualifications, and the top two levels, Higher and Advanced Higher, correspond respectively to Higher and CSYS in the old system. A student may study units or courses at different levels at the same time. A student who has achieved high grades in compulsory school is likely to continue at school and take up to five Highers courses in the first post-compulsory year, perhaps followed by a combination of additional Highers and Advanced Highers in the following year. This represents little change from the previous system: the main differences are that courses now have a unit structure and more internal assessment and there are more Highers in vocational subjects, although these tend to be offered by colleges rather by schools. However weaker students, who previously could either attempt Highers courses with a high risk of failure, and/or take modules whose status and value was doubtful, now have a very different set of opportunities. The unified system allows them to continue in 'mainstream' provision by studying for courses similar to Highers but at a lower level - Intermediate 1 or Intermediate 2 - with the possibility of working up to Highers after one or two years.

The unified system has several implications for colleges. It offers formal parity of esteem: vocational and academic courses are part of the same structure and they are covered by the same certification arrangements. There are now more courses at the Higher level available in vocational subjects than in academic subjects. Many of the design rules of the unified system involve a change from former college practice. The new curriculum architecture means that colleges can organise provision in courses, rather than as programmes of units/modules as in much of their previous provision. The arrangements for assessment are different: unit assessments are more formalised than the old module assessments, and if colleges offer courses rather than just units they must introduce external assessment, whereas formerly nearly all college study was assessed internally. If they offer SGAs they must ensure the provision of core skills, especially those not 'embedded' in regular subjects. Finally, the new Access level, which is intended primarily for students with special needs or for those returning to study after a long break, offers a means for accommodating some of the colleges' less advantaged students within mainstream provision.

5.3 Conceptual framework: unification and flexibility

Our research addresses two current issues in vocational education: unification and flexibility. Higher Still exemplifies a general trend towards the unification of upper-secondary education which affects most European countries (Raffe, 1997; Young, Howieson, Raffe & Spours, 1997; Lasonen & Young, 1998). Unification is a response to global social and economic trends, and to pressures arising from the expansion and greater functional complexity of post-compulsory education systems and the consequent need to increase the coherence of their constituent parts. In an earlier project we developed a conceptual framework which distinguished three types of post-compulsory education and training systems: a *tracked* system, with separate and distinctive tracks; a *linked* system, with features linking the tracks or common properties which underline their similarity or equivalence; and a *unified* system, which brings all provision into a single framework governed by common design rules (Raffe, Howieson, Spours & Young, 1998). These three types are points along a continuum, with tracked systems at one end, unified systems at the other end, and various forms of linked systems in between. Unification is the trend for tracked systems to become linked systems and for linked systems to become unified systems. In practice, of course, each national system is a mixture of the three types: its position on the continuum between tracked and unified systems may vary across different dimensions of system change. Some of the most important dimensions are described in Figure 5.1.

So, although many countries are pursuing unification and some are introducing unified systems, their models of unification vary according to the dimensions along which they unify. The critical dimensions of unification in Higher Still include course structure and pathways, assessment and certification. These are governed by common design rules, which specify the structure of units, courses and SGAs, the five levels and the arrangements for assessment and certification described above. The design rules apply to vocational as well as academic subjects, to colleges as well as schools, and to provision for adults as well as provision for young people.

In contrast to other unified systems, such as those introduced in Sweden and Norway, Higher Still is a *flexible* unified system. An earlier analysis distinguished four aspects of flexibility: *individual* flexibility (an outcome of education, which roughly translates as transferability), *curricular* flexibility, flexibility of *delivery* (in the method, pace and place of learning) and flexibility of *pathways* (Raffe, 1994). These aspects of flexibility can be mapped on to Nijhof and Streumer's (1994) systems framework based on the four levels of context, process, input and output: individual flexibility corresponds to the output level, flexibility of curriculum, delivery and pathways correspond to the process level, and the common design rules of a unified system correspond to the input level. The Higher Still model aims to enhance individual flexibility, through its emphasis on core skills. It also encourages curricular flexibility: there is weak prescription of the content, volume, level and duration of study. It is less strongly associated with flexibility of delivery, as we see below. However, its character as a flexible unified system is defined especially by the flexibility of student pathways. It aims to provide flexible entry points (to cater for students of different abilities), flexible exit points, flexible opportunities for movement within the system, and flexible opportunities for re-entry.

	Tracked system	Linked system	Unified system
CONTENT AND PROCESS			
Purpose and ethos	Distinctive purposes and ethos associated with each track	Purposes and ethos overlap across tracks	Multiple purposes and pluralist ethos
Curriculum	Different content (subjects, areas of study)	Some common elements across tracks	Curriculum reflects student needs and integrates academic and vocational learning
Teaching/learning processes	Different learning processes in different tracks	Different learning processes but some common features	Variation based on student needs and not tied to specific programmes
Assessment	Different assessment methodologies and grading systems	Different methodologies but with level and grade equivalences	Common framework of methodologies including a common grading system
SYSTEM ARCHITECTURE			
Certification	Different certification for each track	Certification frameworks link tracks, eg overarching diplomas, equivalences	A single system of certification
Course structure & pathways	Different course structures and insulated progression pathways	Course structures allow transfer and combinations	Flexible entry points, credit accumulation, and single progression ladder
Progression to higher education	Not possible from some tracks	Conditions of progression vary across tracks	All programmes may lead to HE
DELIVERY			
Local institutions	Different institutions for different tracks	Variable/overlapping relation of track to institution	One type of institution, or choice of institution not constrained by type of programme
Modes of participation	Tracks based on separate modes (academic/FT), vocational/PT)	Tracks partly based on mode	Single system covers different modes
Staff	Different staff for each track, with non-transferable qualifications	Variable/some overlap of staff	Socialisation, qualifications and conditions are consistent for all staff
GOVERNMENT AND REGULATION	Different structures for different tracks	Mixed/variable organisational structure	Single administrative and regulatory system

Source: Raffe, Howieson, Spours & Young (1998).

Figure 5.1 A matrix of unification: types of system and their dimensions.

The design rules described above are intended to support a seamless, unified system of pathways in which students can access education at any level and progress across and between all parts of the system.

The combination of unification with flexibility of curriculum and pathways in the Scottish reforms has implications for:

- *Assessment*. The flexibility of the Scottish system is underpinned by its modularity, and especially by modular assessment and certification. Each unit and course is separately assessed and separately certificated; this leads to a large total volume of assessment.

- *The pervasiveness of the common design rules*. If the main building blocks of a unified system are programmes or group awards, its common design rules have to apply only at this relatively aggregate level. But in a flexible unified system these rules must be applied right down to the level of the unit or course, and their effect is more pervasive.

- *Conflict*. These design rules tend to be the subject of conflict between sectors and interests within education: for example, assessment arrangements which meet the needs of academic education in schools may be seen as less appropriate by those providing vocational education in colleges. The more pervasive the design rules, the greater the scope for conflict. Elsewhere we have documented the conflicts that attended the development and introduction of the Scottish unified system (Raffe & Howieson, 1998; Raffe, Howieson & Tinklin, 2002).

- *Flexibility of delivery*. The design rules which are necessary for flexible pathways may themselves restrict flexibility of delivery. For example, uniform assessment arrangements may restrict possible teaching or learning methods or colleges' ability to vary the time, pace or location of study.

- *Steering mechanisms and empowerment*. A flexible system could potentially empower
    - *individual students*, by giving them more (or more suitable) opportunities to choose from;
    - *end-users (HE, employers)*, who can specify their selection criteria more finely in a system with flexible curricula and exit points;
    - *institutions (colleges and schools)*, which have more discretion over the opportunities which they offer and the way in which these are 'packaged' for students;
    - *government or regulatory bodies*, who may use such instruments as funding mechanisms, regulation or inspection to influence or restrict the ways institutions use this discretion.

A flexible unified system is compatible with different possible structures of control or with different 'information' and 'steering' structures (Geerligs, 1999; Nijhof, Kieft & Woerkom, 1999). It could underpin a market-led system in which the demands of students and end-users are paramount, enable institutions to play a larger role in shaping provision, or provide the means of more detailed central control.

5.4 Research questions and data

In the rest of the chapter we examine survey findings on the implementation of the flexible unified system in Scottish colleges, in order to address the questions:

1. How much support is there for the reform, and how consensual is this support?
2. Does it increase flexibility?
3. What are the implications of changes in assessment?
4. Who is 'empowered' in a flexible unified system?

We use data from a survey of FE colleges carried out in the winter of 2000-01, the second year of the reform, by the Centre for Educational Sociology (CES) and the Scottish Further Education Unit (SFEU). Questionnaires were returned by 40 of the 47 colleges. We also draw on a parallel survey carried out by the CES in secondary schools; we have excluded special schools and independent schools from the responses reported below. From public mainstream (not special) schools we achieved 295 responses, a 76% response rate. In both surveys the returns were usually made by the senior member of staff with lead responsibility for Higher Still in the institution, usually drawing on contributions from other staff.

The questionnaire contained structured questions about the institution's implementation of Higher Still, its attitudes to the reform, the impact to date and the problems that it had encountered. It also invited respondents to amplify their answers through more open-ended comments. Below we draw on the responses to both types of questions.

Table 5.1 *In your view, how important are the following aims of Higher Still to your college/school?*

Aim	% Important	
	Colleges	Schools
Higher attainment:		
To enable all our students to gain marketable qualifications	97	97
To enable all our students to achieve the highest level of attainment of which they are capable	95	99
Flexibility of pathways:		
To offer students a more even progression between different stages	100	98
To enable courses always to be available to students at an appropriate level	95	88
To give our students access to a range of both academic and vocational subjects	81	68
Transferability:		
To develop our students' competence in core skills	90	46
To encourage our students to take a broader curriculum	64	62
Unification:		
To provide a simpler, more efficient system easily understood by students, parents, employers and higher education	90	78
To bring academic and vocational courses into a unified curriculum and assessment system	82	61
To promote parity of esteem of academic and vocational subjects	80	53
n=100%	(39)	(295)

Note: The Table shows the percentage responding in the top two points of a five-point scale from 'very important' to 'not at all important'. Items have been re-ordered. The sub-headings were not shown in the questionnaire.

The surveys are part of a larger project which will also conduct case studies in six institutions and analyse detailed data on student enrolments and attainments held by the Scottish Qualifications Authority (SQA), which awards all Higher Still qualifications. The case studies will collect more data on such issues as the impact on pedagogy, or the implications for staff development, than was possible in the surveys. The surveys will be replicated after two years to show changes during the process of implementation; the case studies and the SQA data will also cover the first four years of the reform. This chapter presents an initial analysis of colleges' responses to Higher Still. In another paper we compare the schools' and colleges' responses and assess the characteristics of the emerging unified system (Tinklin, Howieson & Raffe, 2001).

5.5 College views on Higher Still

The aims of Higher Still received strong support both from colleges and from schools. The items in Table 5.1 are based on the official published aims of Higher Still (Scottish Office 1994). We have grouped them according to our themes of flexibility and unification. The first two aims are about raising attainment, and were strongly supported by both colleges and schools. The next three aims refer to flexibility of pathways, and were also supported by both colleges and schools, although schools – with their predominantly academic curriculum – were less interested in giving students access to a range of academic and vocational subjects. The next two aims correspond loosely to our notion of individual flexibility or transferability. Core skills received strong support from colleges but less support from schools. Finally, aims relating to unification received general support, but once again those concerning the relation of academic to vocational education received stronger support from colleges than from schools. In general, we find broad support from both sectors, but support within schools tended to be more focused on aims relating to raising attainment and to the flexibility of pathways. A further set of questions asked about support for the aims of Higher Still across different categories of staff (table not shown). A majority of all staff were considered to be supportive. Support was strongest among senior management and somewhat less strong among teachers and lecturers; it was stronger among school staff than college staff, although this was primarily due to the larger number of college staff considered 'neutral', possibly because they had had less experience of the reform.

Questions about the specific changes introduced by Higher Still received a rather different response (Table 5.2). There was support – or at least, little opposition – for the general notion of a single curricular framework, and for basing provision on five levels (an important element in the construction of flexible pathways). There was substantial opposition within schools to the emphasis on core skills and to the creation of SGAs. There was least support both in schools and in colleges for the changes to assessment. The volume and organisation of assessment, and the consequences for teaching, learning and staff workload, had been the most contested feature of the earlier modular reforms in Scotland (Howieson, 1992). Higher Still's unified assessment arrangements required colleges to introduce external assessment and schools to increase their internal assessment, and this was resisted on both sides (ADES/ASC/HMI 2001). Assessment became a source of further controversy after the 'exam results crisis' of August 2000, when the volume and complexity of assessment results proved too much for the SQA's systems, and many candidates received inaccurate, incomplete or late results of the qualifications which they had attempted (Raffe *et al.* 2002).

Table 5.2 *In your view, how much support is there in the college/school for the changes introduced by Higher Still in relation to ... (percentages).*

	Support	**Neutral**	**Opposition**	**n=100%**
A single curricular framework for both academic and vocational subjects				
Colleges	68	27	5	(37)
Schools	68	29	3	(265)
Provision based on five levels				
Colleges	46	49	5	(37)
Schools	50	38	12	(258)
The emphasis on core skills				
Colleges	58	35	8	(40)
Schools	11	47	43	(251)
The creation of SGAs				
Colleges	38	58	5	(40)
Schools	6	43	51	(211)
Assessment				
Colleges	28	49	23	(39)
Schools	26	24	51	(285)

Note: 'Support' and 'opposition' refer respectively to the top and bottom two points of a five-point scale from 'strong support' to 'strong opposition'. 'Neutral' describes the middle point. 'Don't know/difficult to say' responses are excluded.

As further evidence of the conflicts aroused by the reform, three quarters of the colleges (30) considered that the Higher Still framework 'responded more to the needs of schools than colleges'; only two felt that it responded more to the needs of colleges and the other eight felt that it achieved a reasonable balance (table not shown). By contrast, only 12% of schools felt that Higher Still responded more to the needs of schools, compared with 28% who said that it responded more to the needs of colleges; the other schools either felt it achieved a reasonable balance or were not sure.

5.6 Implementation

The arrangements for phasing in Higher Still gave priority to Higher courses which replaced existing Highers, referred to as 'phase 1' courses. These tended to be in academic subjects and were offered by schools, but they were also offered in many colleges, mainly to adults or to extend the options for school students. 'Phase 2' Highers in new (typically vocational) subjects, and provision at other levels such as Intermediate 1 and 2, had lower priority. By phasing the reform in this way it was hoped that teachers would become familiar with the new system gradually, starting with the sectors that most resembled the previous system. In any case, materials were slow to become available in some of the Phase 2 courses. As a result, in the first two years Higher Still affected schools more than colleges. In the first year a majority of colleges offered ten or fewer Higher Still courses, mostly in the more academic subjects. Some also offered free-standing units. About two-thirds of FE colleges offered SGAs, but most offered just one or two, as a means of gaining experience of the new system (SFEU/HSDU, 2000). By the second year, when our survey took place, provision had increased, but only modestly. The median college now offered 16 courses and two SGAs, but with a wide variation especially in the number of SGAs. Most of these were provided in the daytime but 18 of the 40 colleges offered Higher Still courses in the evening (usually just two or three courses) and six offered Higher Still courses by open or distance learning. (Two of these offered 19 and 24 courses respectively.) Only in a quarter of colleges were all teaching departments involved: in the median college 70% of departments were involved.

The programmes most likely to be affected by Higher Still included tailored programmes for students with learning difficulties and programmes providing access to higher education for 'less traditional' students. Few tailored programmes for employers had been affected by Higher Still.

Table 5.3 *Percentage of NC programmes (i) fully replaced by Higher Still and (ii) adapted by substituting or adding Higher Still courses and/or units (number of colleges).*

	% Fully replaced						
% Adapted	**None**	**1-10**	**11-25**	**26-50**	**51-75**	**76-100**	**Total**
None	1	1	0	0	1	0	3
1-10%	1	5	1	2	1	0	10
11-25%	1	3	2	1	0	0	7
26-50%	1	4	3	1	0	0	9
51-75%	0	2	1	3	0	0	6
76-100%	0	0	1	1	0	0	2
Total	4	15	8	8	2	0	37

Table 5.3 refers to NC programmes, the largest category of college provision which potentially could be replaced by Higher Still. Only ten colleges had fully replaced as much as a quarter of their NC programmes by Higher Still provision. Rather more colleges had adapted existing programmes by substituting or adding Higher Still courses or units. They thus used Higher Still to extend the menu from which to select units or courses when constructing programmes – as a means of flexibility for colleges if not necessarily for the individual student. Replacement and adaptation were not necessarily alternative strategies: Table 5.3 shows that most colleges did both. Adaptation may have reflected the early stage of implementation, if colleges were converting programmes to the new system in stages. If this were the case we might expect a significant increase in SGAs in future years. However when asked about their plans for next year only 12 colleges expected a moderate or extensive increase in SGAs, compared with 25 and 27 colleges which expected a moderate or extensive increase in Higher Still courses and units respectively. The main reason

for colleges' reluctance to introduce SGAs were that they required external assessment and that they reduced colleges' flexibility, especially in responding to the needs of employers.

Many colleges had links with schools and/or other colleges, and Higher Still had increased these links. For example, 27 colleges offered courses or units to students from schools, and 12 of these colleges reported that their links with schools had increased (table not shown). Many school students who took Highers courses at college took 'new' subjects such as Psychology or Care which had not been available as Highers in the old system. More than half the colleges (24) reported either new or increased planning activities with schools to improve articulation of provision, taking advantage of the fact that they were both offering provision within the Higher Still framework. Only seven colleges reported new or increased articulation arrangements with higher education institutions, whose provision was not covered by Higher Still.

Table 5.4 *To what extent have the following factors influenced your decisions about Higher Still provision to date, including future provision?*

	Very strong influence	Strong	Less strong
Needs or demands of stakeholders:			
Government policies and priorities	8	22	10
The profile of students in the college	13	18	9
The needs of Higher Education institutions	0	8	32
The needs of employers	7	12	21
Local economic trends and conditions	1	10	29
Feedback from students	4	12	24
Resources and practical constraints:			
Existence of appropriate Higher Still provision	26	11	3
Resource issues	12	12	16
Timetabling issues	4	8	31
Single exam diet	4	6	30
Availability of national support materials	17	18	5
Willingness of staff	9	15	16
Readiness of staff	12	18	10
Presence of key individuals in the college	9	14	17
Links with local schools	5	10	23
Programmes offered by other colleges	1	4	35

n=40

Note: The three columns describe the numbers responding in points 1, 2 and 3-5 of a five-point scale from 'very strong influence' to 'no influence at all'. The sub-headings were not shown in the questionnaire.

Colleges were asked about their objectives in the implementation of Higher Still (table not shown). Their four most important objectives related to the flexibility of pathways: improving student progression to HNC/D level, extending the college's provision at particular levels (thus providing more flexible entry points), improving articulation with local schools and improving student progression to employment. However when colleges were asked which factors had most influenced their implementation decisions, the most important factors were the existence of appropriate Higher Still provision and the availability of national support materials; resource and staffing issues were also influential (Table 5.4). The early pattern of implementation thus reflected supply constraints more than colleges' responsiveness to changing contexts or to the needs of clients. The first set of factors in Table 5.4 concern the needs of clients or stakeholders: only the profile of students in the college and government policies and priorities were named as strong or very strong influences by a majority of colleges. The needs of employers, local economic trends and conditions, the needs of higher education institutions, and feedback from students, were less important.

5.7 The impact of the reform

Respondents were asked to describe the impact of Higher Still on aspects of the flexibility of curriculum and pathways (Table 5.5) and of the flexibility of delivery (Table 5.6) in their college. They reported only a modest impact, probably reflecting the early stage of the reform. Colleges which had made more progress towards implementation tended to report more impact.

Table 5.5 *On balance, what impact has Higher Still had on students at your college and on potential students? Has it ...*

	Yes	No change	Not sure	Total
... given students more opportunity to work at a level appropriate to them/their starting point?	23	13	4	(40)
... promoted more mixing of academic and vocational subjects?	9	24	7	(40)
... given students a wider range of subjects to choose from?	14	23	3	(40)
... encouraged high achieving students to take vocational subjects?	4	29	7	(40)

A majority of colleges (23 out of 40) felt that Higher Still had given their students more opportunity to start at an appropriate level (Table 5.5, first item). Colleges were particularly likely to report this if they had used Higher Still to replace or adapt community outreach programmes, pre-entry access programmes or flexible learning programmes, or to replace tailored programmes for students with learning difficulties. The main reason for Higher Still's positive impact arose through the two lowest levels of the framework, Access and Intermediate 1. New units and courses at these levels made it easier for colleges to tailor provision to meet the needs of particular groups, and extended opportunities for accreditation and for progression. The unified system of flexible pathways has thus had some impact on promoting 'opportunity for all'.

However in their open-ended comments colleges identified two more negative issues concerning the Higher Still levels. First, some colleges felt that particular courses or units were too easy or (more commonly) too difficult for the level at which they were nominally set. Usually this seemed to be correctable by fine-tuning, but in some cases it may have reflected a more fundamental issue: that because the unified system was designed to embrace the academic/vocational divide some courses or units were considered to be too 'academic' for traditional vocational students. The second issue concerned progression. The intervals between the five levels of the Higher Still curriculum represent steps in a ladder of educational progression, and in a unified system the steps are of a uniform height. However some students may need to progress up smaller steps than others, and therefor suffer disadvantage. The most important example of this concerned progression to higher education. In principle, an SGA at Higher level leads on to the first year of higher education whether this is for a university degree course or for an HNC/D. However the specification for a Higher SGA corresponds to the traditional entry level for degree courses, whereas most college students who progress to higher education enter HNC/Ds, whose entry requirements are less demanding. The SGA at Higher level represents an unnecessarily high hurdle for them to cross. In principle the flexibility of pathways provides a solution to this, in that colleges can construct programmes whose average level is somewhat lower than the Higher SGA, but this may be at the expense of simplicity or a uniform national currency.

The other three items in Table 5.5 suggest that Higher Still had had less impact (so far) on curriculum choice and even less impact on students' choices of academic and vocational subjects. Colleges commented that the responses of higher education would be influential on choices in the future. A flexible unified system gives more influence to end-users as they have more scope to specify the particular subjects taken by applicants. So far we have little evidence on how they will use this influence; neither universities nor employers had had a strong direct influence on colleges' implementation of Higher Still (see Table 5.3 above), but they were recognised as a potential influence which might constrain its impact in the future.

Table 5.6 *What impact has Higher Still had on the capacity of the college to meet students' needs? To what extent has Higher Still increased or decreased...*

	Strongly increased				Strongly decreased	Don't know	Total
	1	2	3	4	5		
... staff's ability to respond to student needs in the timing of assessments?	0	6	11	15	4	3	(39)
... students' ability to access provision in a flexible way?	0	8	21	5	1	4	(38)
... staff's ability to respond to student needs in their teaching and learning approaches?	0	12	19	9	0	3	(38)

Higher Still's design rules had thus had a positive if modest effect (so far) on the flexibility of student pathways. They had had a less favourable effect on the flexibility of delivery. The most constraining of the design rules, in the view of many college staff, concerned the nature, volume and timing of assessment. Half of the colleges reported a reduction in flexibility in the timing of assessments (Table 5.6). In particular, the fixed annual examination diet, based on the school calendar, inhibited colleges' ability to provide assessment on demand or to offer open and distance learning or 'roll-on roll-off' provision; this reduced their ability to respond to the needs of many adult learners. Eight colleges felt that Higher Still had increased students' ability to access provision in a flexible way, and six colleges felt it had reduced it; the latter group gave assessment as the main reason. Slightly more colleges felt that Higher Still had increased the flexibility in teaching and learning approaches than felt it had been reduced.

There was no strong link between the nature or scale of colleges' Higher Still provision and its reported impact on flexibility of delivery as described in Table 5.6, although colleges offering more courses – whether daytime or evening – were slightly more positive about students' ability to access provision in a flexible way, and the handful of colleges which provided a significant number of SGAs tended to be more positive about all three aspects of flexibility described in Table 5.6. Cause and effect may run in either direction: those colleges which found Higher Still's design rules least constraining, or which found creative solutions to the constraints they imposed, may have been fastest to implement the reform.

In the first year of Higher Still, few colleges had offered Higher Still courses in the evenings because it was difficult to accommodate the increased assessment requirements within a timetable typically based on one evening a week (SFEU/HSDU, 2000). Even in 2000-01, the second year of the reform, only 18 of the 40 colleges offered any Higher Still courses (mainly Highers) in the evenings. They used a variety of approaches to make the time go further: self-study packs (eight colleges), making the sessions longer (five colleges), running the course over two evenings (six colleges), extending the year (four colleges) or adding sessions on Saturday (one college). Nearly half of all colleges had introduced or extended dedicated arrangements for assessment or reassessment in order to manage the new demands of Higher Still. More than a third had introduced or extended diagnostic testing for students entering the college, to help to allocate them to the right Higher Still level. And nearly half of all colleges had introduced or extended flexible learning provision for core skills.

Colleges were asked to what extent Higher Still had affected their capacity to meet the needs of different categories of students. For each category but one, a majority of colleges either gave an intermediate response indicating no net change, or responded 'don't know'. The exception consisted of students with learning difficulties: 21 out of 38 colleges said it had increased their capacity to meet the needs of these students. The other groups, in order of the number of colleges reporting a positive effect, were: disadvantaged students (15 colleges); 16-18 year olds (12 colleges); students on special courses providing access for adults to higher education (eight colleges); students over 18 (seven colleges); students on New Deal (a programme for the unemployed: five colleges); employers (no colleges). In no case did more than three colleges say that Higher Still had reduced their capacity to meet the needs of the group in question.

5.8 Discussion

We summarise our preliminary findings in terms of the four research questions introduced in section 5.4.

1. How much support is there for the reform, and how consensual is this support? There was a high level of support for the aims of Higher Still. This support was broadly consensual in the sense that it was expressed by schools as well as colleges, and it was shared by different staff within institutions, although senior management tended to be the most supportive. However in two respects it was not consensual: there was much less support for some of the specific changes introduced by the reform than for its general aims; and many colleges felt that the reform responded to the needs of schools more than of colleges. These findings endorse our analysis of a flexible unified system. The *aims* of a flexible unified system can easily attract general support: there is little occasion for conflict over the aims and purposes of a system which, almost by definition, allows all purposes to be achieved. However the *means* of creating this system - the common design rules - are more constraining than in other types of system, and they are the object of conflict.

2. Does the reform increase flexibility? The pace of implementation in colleges was slow and any verdict based on the second year of the reform must be tentative. The overall impact was modest. The main benefit for flexibility was in the ability to provide courses or units at the most appropriate level for incoming students, and especially for disadvantaged students and those with learning difficulties. There were, in other words, more flexible entry points. However a potential problem in designing flexible pathways concerned the progression steps between the five levels of Higher Still: if these steps were set at an appropriate height for some students they would not be appropriate for others. This problem is potentially soluble by taking advantage of the modular nature of Higher Still which makes it possible to fine-tune provision by mixing levels and varying the volume of study.

Colleges endorsed Higher Still's aim to promote parity of esteem for vocational and academic subjects, but there was little evidence of impact on curriculum choice or on the propensity to choose vocational subjects. Elsewhere we have contrasted the 'intrinsic logic' of modularisation with the 'institutional logic' of the context within which it is introduced (Raffe, Croxford & Howieson, 1994). The intrinsic logic of Higher Still provides more opportunities for students to mix academic and vocational subjects and for high achievers to increase their vocational focus. However whether or not they respond to these opportunities will depend on the wider institutional logic – in this case, the relative status of academic and vocational subjects, institutional policies, the power relations within the system, and the preferences of universities and employers in selecting applicants.

A reform which aims to increase some aspects of flexibility, such as flexibility of pathways, may undermine others, such as flexibility of delivery. Some colleges found that the design rules of the unified system, in particular its assessment requirements, could make it harder to offer flexible provision. They were slow to implement Higher Still in areas of flexible delivery such as evening classes and open and distance learning. However, several colleges had devised solutions to problems raised by Higher Still, and colleges also reported aspects of flexibility of delivery which had increased as a result of the reform.

3. What are the implications of changes in assessment? There was a tension between the unified design rules for assessment and flexible delivery. Colleges also feared that the increased emphasis on external assessment might discourage adults and 'less traditional' learners.

Assessment was the most controversial issue in colleges - if not as controversial as in schools. Earlier, we suggested that the burden of assessment in Higher Still reflected its nature as a flexible unified system. However this burden was made heavier by an educational agenda which emphasised 'standards' and a lack of trust in the standards represented by qualifications in general and internally-assessed qualifications such as NC modules in particular. Trust may be a precondition of a system of flexible educational pathways which does not impose excessive burdens of assessment and certification.

4. Who is 'empowered' in a flexible unified system? Colleges' implementation of the reform was influenced by relatively short-term practical constraints such as the availability of Higher Still provision, the availability of materials, and staffing. It may be too early to determine the extent to which the reform empowered institutions to pursue their distinctive missions and goals. In the view of colleges, the new provision catered more effectively for particular categories of students, such as disadvantaged students and those with learning difficulties, by offering more differentiated entry points at appropriate levels. However this did not necessarily empower students as clients or consumers more than in the previous system. Greater empowerment would entail, at least, more student input into colleges' planning of provision, greater responsiveness to student demand, and/or a wider range of options from which students could choose as consumers. There was little evidence that end-users directly influenced the implementation of the reform – although employers and (more particularly) higher education were seen to have a powerful future influence through their role in determining the market value of different types of provision. Employer influence was relatively slight and the reform had made little impact on tailored provision for employers. However government policies and priorities were also seen to be influential, reminding us that flexibility may work to increase central power rather than devolve it.

5.9 Wider implications

The experience of Higher Still will have lessons for flexibility of vocational education elsewhere, although at this stage these remain tentative. We provisionally draw five lessons. First, flexibility is multidimensional, and the different types of flexibility may be in tension. We have identified a tension between flexibility of delivery and flexibility of pathways – despite the fact that both are at the same (process) level of Nijhof and Streumer's (1994) framework. Second, the concept of flexibility raises the question: flexibility for whom? More flexible arrangements may redistribute power and control in education, although in the Scottish case it is too early to determine the main beneficiaries. Third, the combination of policies for flexibility with the general trend towards the 'unification' of post-compulsory education and training systems creates specific issues, both for the design of a flexible system and for the process of gaining support for it. Fourth, a system with flexible pathways must be founded on a high level of trust and confidence in the standards achieved across the system, if its flexibility is not to be weighed down by an excessive burden of assessment. Finally, the flexibility inherent in the formal system – its intrinsic logic – may not be reflected in the choices and experiences of students, if these are determined by the stronger constraints of the institutional logic.

Acknowledgements

This chapter is a product of the research project on Introducing a Unified System of Post-Compulsory Education in Scotland, funded by the UK Economic and Social Research Council (R000238420).

References

Association of Directors of Education in Scotland, Association of Scottish Colleges and Her Majesty's Inspectors of Schools (ADES/ASC/HMI) (2001). *National Investigation into the Experience of Higher Still Assessment in Schools and Colleges*. Edinburgh: HMI.
Geerligs, J. (1999). *Design of Responsive Vocational Education and Training: A Reconstruction of a Systems Change in Agricultural Education*. Delft: Eburon.
Howieson, C. (1992). *Modular Approaches to Initial Vocational Education and Training: The Scottish Experience. A Report for the PETRA Research Programme 1991-93*. Centre for Educational Sociology, University of Edinburgh.
Howieson, C., Raffe, D., Spours, K. and Young, M. (1997). Unifying academic and vocational learning: the state of the debate in England and Scotland. *Journal of Education and Work, 10*, (1), 5-35.
Lasonen, J. and Young, M. (Eds.) (1998). *Strategies for Achieving Parity of Esteem in European Upper-Secondary Education*. Institute for Educational Research, University of Jyväskylä.
Nijhof, W. and Streumer, J. (1994). Flexibility in vocational education and training: an introduction. In W. Nijhof and J. Streumer (Eds.), *Flexibility in training and vocational education* (pp. 1-13). Utrecht: Lemma.
Nijhof, W., Kieft, M. and Woerkom, M. van (1999). *Flexibility, transferability and mobility: Mapping the field: Definitions and depositions*. Enschede: University of Twente.
Raffe, D, (1994). The new flexibility in vocational education. In W. Nijhof and J. Streumer (Eds.) *Flexibility in training and vocational education* (pp. 13-33). Utrecht: Lemma.
Raffe, D. (1997). Higher Still in European perspective. *Scottish Educational Review, 29*, (2), 121-133.
Raffe, D. and Howieson, C. (1998). The Higher Still policy process. *Scottish Affairs, 24*, 90-108.
Raffe, D., Croxford, L. and Howieson, C. (1994). The third face of modules: Gendered patterns of participation and progression in Scottish vocational education. *British Journal of Education and Work, 7*, (3), 87-104.
Raffe D., Howieson, C., Spours, K. and Young, M. (1998). The unification of post-compulsory education: Towards a conceptual framework. *British Journal of Educational Studies, 46*, (2), 169-187.
Raffe D., Howieson, C. and Tinklin, T. (2002, in press). The Scottish educational crisis of 2000: an analysis of the policy process of unification. *Journal of Education Policy, 17*.
Scottish Executive (2001). *Scottish School Leavers and their Qualifications*. www.scotland.gov.uk/stats/bulletins/00080-02.asp Downloaded 5.6.01.
Scottish Further Education Unit and Higher Still Development Unit (SFEU/HSDU) (2000). *Higher Still in Practice Survey Report: The first year of the new National Qualifications in FE*. Stirling: SFEU.
Scottish Office (1994). *Higher Still: Opportunity for All*. Edinburgh.

Scottish Office Education Department (SOED) (1992). *Upper Secondary Education in Scotland (Howie Report).* Edinburgh: HMSO.

Tinklin, T., Howieson, C. and Raffe, D. (2001). The emerging model of unified system in Scotland: Evidence from the second year of Higher Still. *IUS Working Paper 4.* Centre for Educational Sociology, University of Edinburgh. www.ed.ac.uk/ces/ius/IUS_-papers.html.

Young, M., Howieson, C., Raffe, D. and Spours, K. (1997). Unifying academic and vocational learning and the idea of a learning society. *Journal of Education Policy, 12,* (6), 527-537.

CHAPTER 6

Demand and supply of qualifications: systems' change towards flexibility

LUISA RIBOLZI

"Education changes mental attitudes of a people, that is the first step towards social change"
(Beeby, 1966).

6.1 Employability and educational structure in Italy

DURING THE PAST SIX YEARS, the Italian school system has been transformed by large and profound reforms, which have overthrown the nature of the system itself:
- a reform of the organisational model, from centralised and bureaucratic to a system of autonomous schools;
- a reform of the pedagogical model, still under debate, but enhancing professional training and education;
- a reform of the system of governing, where the majority of decisions are no longer taken at the central level, but at the regional one ("direzione scolastica regionale"). The Ministry of Education has been completely reorganised, reducing the areas of competencies at the national level. Very recently (October 2001), the Constitution has been modified in order to assign more educational responsibilities to local authorities.

We could emphasise two main purposes of the reforms: to upgrade vocational education, and to introduce elements of flexibility and mobility between general and vocational education (Figure 6.1). In the Italian educational system, the three concepts we are speaking about (flexibility, mobility and transferability) have in the past been brought – and still are being brought – into relation with employability, not education. In my opinion, the reason is that the system itself was entirely school-centred, and school was very rigid, with a highly centralised, standardised curriculum, leading to a legally recognised diploma (*valore legale del titolo di studio*). The incoming reforms and the studies on a competencies-centred curriculum in VET "have imported" into education the concept of flexibility, mainly system flexibility, and the concept of the transferability of competencies. However, the idea of mobility is still firmly linked to the idea of workers' mobility.

As a starting point, we will try to clarify the changes that affect VET, thinking for the first time of school, vocational education and apprenticeship as a system, aimed at realising lifelong education. The main changes have been twofold:
- general and vocational education have more common links, to cope both with the increasing demands of the labour market and with the need to protect workers.
- Production processes require more and more knowledge, and frequent organisational and technical changes need frequent requalifications; workers who have higher qualification levels and are able to update them have greater employability;

85

W. J. Nijhof et al. (eds.), Shaping Flexibility in Vocational Education and Training, 85-102.
© 2002 *Kluwer Academic Publishers. Printed in the Netherlands.*

- after basic education, at 14 young people can choose between school, vocational education and apprenticeship, up to the age of 18. There should be the possibility of using credits to allow change, or to access a different stream. This could be seen as a higher appraisal of vocational education, which until now has received very little praise, and of the extra school or nonformal qualification, including on-the-job training. It also gives better opportunities for flexibility and individualised curricula, more useful than just staying longer at school, particularly for nontraditional or "at risk" students.

In a general sense, the spirit of the reforms is to regard human capital and its changes (to some extent, its maintenance) as the final outcome of the interrelations between personal characteristics and lifelong education (Figure 6.1), to prevent dequalification and educational rigidity. In fact, if the demand for particular skills declines, in a rigid model there could be a negative outcome of educational investments, or so-called "specialised overeducation".

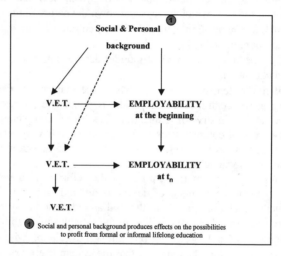

Figure 6.1 Components of employability.

6.2 Models of VET and the dynamics of change

If we want to think about the role and characteristics of education in our knowledge-based economy and society, we should move from the Schumpeterian idea of innovation as the major force of economic dynamics. Empirical analysis has documented, for instance, that investment in knowledge and capabilities is characterised by increasing (rather than decreasing) returns (OECD, 1996). In the global market, developed economies cannot compete by reducing labour costs, but by raising product quality, and "to have quality products and to maintain the products' quality, you need specialised workers" (Dahrendorf, 1995, p. 26), highly educated, able to learn, use and modify new technologies, with the risk of an inflation of credentials, as pointed out by Boudon (1973).

If we take seriously the hypothesis that learning is the main characteristic of social and economic development, what are the implications for the institutional structure of the school system? A modern society cannot develop or remain competitive if its educational policy, particularly for vocational education and training, is inadequate. Classical models of educational policy can be defined as either "redundancy-oriented" or "suitability-oriented" (Regini, 1996)[1]. In the first case, the education system produces overeducation, to have stocks of qualified workers with acquired skills, or it might produce "non embodied knowledge, created and disseminated at a cost, but not inseparably embodied in any particular knowledge carriers or any particular products" (Machlup, 1984). The choice of a model is affected by the speed of change: if it is rapid, a short but suitable qualification is more functional, but it has higher social costs, because workers have rigid competencies, and it is expensive and difficult to modify them in the event of a crisis. If the change is slow, redundant education is better, because workers have general competencies, which can be brushed up or adapted more easily: the transferability of this model is more feasible, but it requires a longer time to be realised (Figure 6.2).

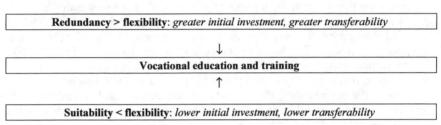

Figure 6.2 Redundancy versus suitability in educational models.

Companies normally prefer specific qualifications, leaving the provision of general education to the State, both because their needs for qualification are often easy to define, and because they want to avoid "poaching", which is frequent and dangerous in the Italian economy. The Italian system consists of SMEs, in which educational investments are very heavy: the risk is that companies that do not invest in qualification could pay more, and "poach" qualified workers, causing the investment to fade. As a matter of fact, there is a "dual enterprise" (Lodigiani, 2000), investing in education for a few stabilised workers, but without any policy for human resources. This kind of policy could be less expensive, but it indirectly damages the so-called "peripheral" workers, who are lacking in education, which works as a shield against the danger of unemployment and as a tool to create a personal path of qualification, employable for any purpose during their working life.

Of course, Rifkin's (Rifkin, 1994) idea of "the end of work" could be discussed, but actually people are facing a constellation of "work opportunities", where for an increasing number of workers, professional careers will probably be mobile and not linear. We can use as an indicator of this trend the number of atypical [2] contracts in new engagements, which are now the majority: 57% of the contracts drawn up between April 1999 and April 2000 were atypical (ISFOL, 2000). Flexibility

---

[1] Of course, we are simplifying matters. The two models could exist simultaneously in different sectors, or for different kinds of workers. It would be better to speak of a "prevalent" model.

[2] Every kind of job differing from a standardised, full-time, permanent one is considered atypical: part-time, job-sharing, temporary job, apprenticeship or youth employment, coordinated workers, who are quasi-professionals.

currently represents the standard attitude in the labour market, and the trend is to transform the stock of employed people. In April 2000, part-time contracts were 1,850,000, or 8.8%; time contracts both full-time and part-time were about 10%, co-ordinated workers were 1,782,507 (about 9%), and temporary workers 200,000. Of the employed stock, flexible forms of occupation were near to 20%, particularly for the traditionally weak groups, such as dropouts, women, and immigrants.

The diffusion of atypical jobs does not influence mobility as a whole, but gives shape in all European countries to a segmented labour market, including, on the one hand, permanent, stable workers and, on the other, mobile and flexible ones. To enhance their employability, new workers need personal abilities to change their own place in the labour market. To avoid obsolescence, and to remain employable in "turbulent markets" (Gallino, 1998), they must update their competencies. Lifelong learning is a personal responsibility, not only a social one[3], even if labour policy must offer opportunities and incentives, reducing the risk of marginalisation (Ambrosini, 2000). In fact, underqualified young people are not excluded from jobs in general; on the contrary, the number of jobs offered to workers with the lowest qualifications is still high. Data from the Excelsior Project[4] show that in 1998-99 industrial companies forecast that they would engage 51.1% of people with compulsory education (58.1% in the no-experience group), 44.2% in 1999/2000 (56.9% without experience), 39.9% in 2001 (54.2% without experience). They do not, however, find a "good" job, with the possibility of a successful career.

Anyway, the opportunities offered to obtain and improve professional skills are very important, but (as in Figure 6.1) they are fragmented and uncoordinated, with a waste of human and financial resources.

Three actors function in VET with different tasks: the State controls schools and universities, setting general norms for public and private bodies; regions and districts run vocational education; the labour market indicates its educational needs (or is expected to do so). Centres for vocational education have to mediate between these actors, and, in addition, the information system on professions is very poor. At the higher education level, the growing knowledge embodied in almost all professions demands greater technological skills: technological and scientific degrees are the most useful to find a job, and graduates have the highest ratio of congruent occupation: the last national survey on graduates (2002) indicates that 67% of graduates on average says that in their job a graduation was necessary, and 33% of them says that it was not, but the variance is very large (Table 6.1). In some way, humanistic and socio-politic degrees are more flexible, because they prepare for a very large, if not qualified, range of jobs. Overeducation would be lower for scientific and technological skilled workers, but it still exists, and it is very expensive both for the state and for the individuals.

---

[3]   Recently, following Granovetter's hypothesis on weak ties (1973), Italian sociologists have studied the role of "relational nets" in individual strategies to increase professional skills (Bianco, 1996; Abbatecola, 1999).

[4]   Unioncamere , *Sistema informativo Progetto Excelsior*, 1997, 1998, 2000, 2001.

Table 6.1 *Ratio of congruent employment versus field of study.*

Field of study	Necessary for the job	Nonutilisation of a degree
Linguistics	30.6	69.3
Teaching	36.9	63.1
Socio-politics	42.3	57.7
Humanities	45.8	54.2
Economics and Statistics	61.6	38.4
Total	**67.0**	**33.0**
Psychology	68.9	31.1
Geobiologics	72.2	27.8
Law	72.7	27.3
Architecture	79.1	20.9
Agriculture	75.8	24.2
Engineering	86.5	13.5
Chemistry and Pharmacy	92.1	7.9
Medicine	98.3	1.7

Source: ISTAT, *Indagine sul destino lavorativo dei laureati*, Roma 2000.

6.3 Integration and quality as elements of flexibility

The first relevant change in defining VET in Italy, although later than in other European countries, has been the passage from VET as the first stage of qualification to VET as lifelong learning, "a persisting educational process, which is not limited to an initial period aiming to attain a job: VET is rather a process which follows workers during their professional life, to cope with jobs that are changing very often, both in time and in their characteristics. Then a form of education that requires frequent passages from work to education, re-entering with new know-how and incentives to work. VET is becoming more and more a form of learning on the job, (perhaps, by oneself or at a distance), which occurs while one's activities continue in a normal manner" (Osbat, 1985, pp. 9-10).

This is theory, however; in practice, the idea of VET has spread throughout educational policies only in recent years, guiding the reforms in progress aimed at integrating school, vocational centres (Centro Formazione Professionale (CFP)) and training. Qualification could not be realised separately by different actors: they have to plan common curricula based on common criteria. Local authorities have the responsibility of defending specific socio-economic needs, the State must enhance the equality of educational opportunities, and then protect workers' mobility, and the CFPs have to face requests both from industry and from students, in every phase of their lives. The integration between actors increases flexibility and transferability, but it needs a global improvement of the educational system: the logic of the system is to think about VET not only as a cooperative process (even if this is a good starting point), but as "goods" or "services" planned and realised with common - or at least consonant - criteria and objectives.

The theoretical approach below integration is the *high-trust model of production,* requiring greater worker participation and better basic education, based on values such as citizenship and competitive individualism (Hickox & Moore, 1993, p. 109). Society does not care for academic learning involving a limited *pool of talents* in a low qualified mass (Ashton, 1992), but it needs an education that enables flexible abilities and competencies to grow or advance in a great number of people, self-adapting in any set of circumstances. Well-qualified workers are able to cope with changing and complex responsibilities – this is of course a form of mobility – but only if they have a strong general education, closely connected to vocational and lifelong education.

At the moment, in the Italian educational system, there are elements producing more rigidity than flexibility. The provision of qualification is fragmented and its fundamental logic is not always to react to market demand; the educational service (which is not homogeneous throughout the country) varies in dimension and quality, and it is possible to find both very innovative and very obsolete courses. As a consequence, equity is not easy to guarantee, either for students and workers, or for companies. The image of vocational education is still poor: if general education and also technical education are seen as a device to increase employability, a commodity or an investment[5], vocational education is not yet seen as a "multilevel link" between work and education, where competencies could be created, maintained and developed.

Perhaps, it might be useful to have a larger presence or influence of the so-called "umbrella organisations" - assembling centres that share elements of quality (for instance, a common VET model). Umbrella organisations not only exert a lobbying role, but they could work as franchising organisations, defining the objectives common to all systems, performing cross-functions (i.e. teachers' education, assessment, audit, monitoring of changes in demand, advising, and so on). Each CFP has to define its specific mission, according to the common strategy, improving in this way the flexibility of the system as a whole. Italian centres are currently moving to transform into real "service centres", offering their diversified users not standardised "courses" but "packages", which could be personalised as far as to develop individual career guidance to "accompany" individuals to work[6]. Packages require highly qualified professionals, attention to the market, integration into the local economic system, to control the risk of rough mobility.

Nevertheless, there is a condition that is not easy to obtain to integrate different agencies, a national system of skills certification[7]: a process of inter and intra-institutional mobility could be realised only if it is possible to recognise

---

[5]   See human capital theories, from Becker (1964) onwards, even if the direct role of education in the process of creating wealth is not easy to demonstrate (Sanders, 1992).

[6]   One successful experience has been the "Janus II" project, realised by an umbrella organisation grouping a number of vocational centres in Emilia as a form of "second chance" for dropouts, in connection with the European Youthstart program. 178 young people were enrolled in 4 centres: after the initial guidance period, only 17 left, and no one left during the personalised program to get a job. The percentage of dropping out was 9.5%, versus 25%–30% of the corresponding traditional vocational courses (Sarchielli, Zappalà, 1998; Vanetti, 2000).

[7]   Isfol (a national agency which runs research and qualification programs for VET) is trying to define and maintain an updated program of educational standards and transferable educational units to create a credits system (Isfol, 1997).

interchangeable credits. Skills certification does not come from the formal educational path (what we in Italy call the legal value of the title), but from what people can actually do. These abilities and competencies can be used as an additional value in the labour market, and they determine the place the person occupies. Since this place and its characteristics are changing with increasing rapidity, the quality of work is not related to the place occupied, but to the cognitive capital accumulated throughout life, and spent in a discontinuous life (and work) career, where workplace training stresses attitudes and the opportunity for self development. Effective knowledge demands an increasing mass of information, and becomes more and more a sum of formal and informal learning. A more useful concept might be "expert knowledge", which defines not just the level to which a person has been educated, but also the degree to which he or she is able (or has become able *via* workplace training and lifelong learning) to put a wide range of skills, knowledge, competencies and other attributes to productive use. "Human capital thus constitutes an intangible asset with the capacity to enhance or support productivity, innovation and employability: It may be augmented, or may decline or become redundant. It is formed through different influences and sources, including organised learning activity in the form of education and training. Knowledge, skills, competences and other attributes combine in different ways according to the individual and the context of use" (CERI, 1998, p. 9).

Reyneri (1999) emphasises two main consequences of this process of redefining professional areas starting from competencies, not from actual job characteristics:

- the mobility of professions increases, because they do not depend on the organisation, but on their internal structure, and the professional communities to which people belong because of their competencies are the most important socialising agency to establish the professional self;
- from the economic point of view, there is a passage from internal markets to occupational markets, where mechanisms generating competencies have an essential weight, especially if these competencies are consistent with the needs of the demand.

6.4 Individual attitudes and motivation towards longer schooling

Structural determinants are fundamental in the labour market, but you cannot ignore the fact that there is a *supply-side autonomy,* connected to subjective factors, i.e. behavioural strategies, job satisfaction (that is an "emotional positive mood resulting from the positive assessment of one's own work experience", Locke, 1986), the idea one has of one's future, of one's attitudes and possibilities, and so on. With regard to these elements, the appraisal of the investment in education could also vary, particularly from the point of view of employability. For all the importance of subjective factors in the affluent society, where the survival threshold has been largely exceeded, social and economic research tends to examine only the macro level, seldom considering the supply side, even if a "causality spiral" existed (Doise, Palmonari, 1988) between the individual characteristics of the supply and the labour market structure. Every person plays an active role, behaving in a different way, for instance, depending on whether he or she thinks that finding a job is a difficult or an easy game to play.

It is difficult to say if it is the students or their families who first make the decision to invest in education: probably there is in the family group a mix of motivations[8]. In most cases, higher schooling is a value-adding facility for workers, but in Western societies, people tend to overvalue the role of education as a mobility device. Moreover, educational policies represent education as a "functional equivalent" of work (Lodigiani, 2000), an element of social cohesion, a right of citizenship loosely related to technicalities. For these reasons, positive attitudes towards educational investment last, even if the demand for qualified manpower decreases or is low, and for a long time democratisation has been considered more important than quality.

The growth in the level of mass education - not only for small privileged groups - has been quite important, because the technological gap between "starters" and "latecomers" holds back both social and economic development, and so there is social pressure for higher and more dynamic schooling. In Italy, the demand has grown strongly and continuously, but only in general education schools, not in vocational or on-the-job education. The rate of participation in secondary education grew in ten years from 69.3% in 1987/88 to 82.4% in 1997/98. Rates of transition from secondary to tertiary education were stable for ten years, about 67%/68%, but the rates of enrolment of first-year students on the cohort grew in ten years from 39 to 46.5 freshmen for each hundred young people of the same age. The success rate of the university is very low: only 38.5% of students graduate, versus 81% in the United Kingdom, 72% in Germany, and 55% in France in 1999[9].

In postmodern, or postindustrial societies, work has become an increasingly complex social object, and its meanings are pluralised. The idea of the instrumental value of work still remains, because through work it is possible to obtain the resources necessary to live; at the same time, in Western civilisation work is a central value (Ribolzi, 1991), and it plays a strongly symbolic role both for individual life and for the system of morals. Lorence and Mortimer (1985) called *work involvement* the subjective importance ascribed to work as a human activity, related to general opinions on its central position in life. These opinions are very stable: they come mainly from social stratification and are very little influenced by the actual situation of the labour market. The authors call *job involvement* the way a person identifies himself with his job. Work involvement comes from the system of values, whereas job involvement comes from the characteristics of the activity carried out.

Other authors (Warr et al. 1981) define synthetically *employment commitment* as the importance ascribed to work, both as a human activity and a component of individual identity. In their opinion, these meanings and beliefs as a whole are firmly established and not permeable to negative experiences. This stability creates positive expectations about the economic consequences of schooling, considered "the almost self-evident vehicle in promoting national economic growth, individual development, and a more equitable distribution of income".

Psychological surveys and studies also show that a "tendency towards mobility"

---

[8]   Social research shows that people tend to consider only direct educational costs, not the costs paid through public expenditure: so middle-class students tend to stay in school much longer than would logically be expected.

[9]   In Italian universities, access to most courses is free: for this reason, dropout rates are very high in free-access courses (for instance, law 70.7%, political sciences 78.2%, humanities 60.9%) and lower in courses with limited access (medicine 17.8%, dental medicine 12.9%).

as a personality trait does not exist: this tendency - if it is one - is connected to satisfaction or to a positive assessment of one's personal job, to job initial socialisation and to school experiences. It seems that the main effect produced by personal experiences is the idea that the possibility of finding a job might depend on personal efforts (*internal control*) or on circumstances that they cannot influence or determine (*external control*). The problem is that people normally try to select information to elaborate theories that provide the possibility of elaborating a system of explanation that requires few changes, and that is more consistent with the existing information that people have, ignoring "discouraging" information[10].

As for school, we have to remember that learning patterns determine to a large extent attitudes towards both work and work mobility. Going from education to work (or simply from a learning environment to a different one) is normally a problem, but this difficulty is smaller, or appears to be so, if practical knowledge and experience are very important in the curriculum, and learning *alternance* (job experience included in school time) is highly valued (Ribolzi, 1998). Students can "negotiate between two different cognitive worlds" (Benne, 1976), attaining a fundamental skill in transferring competencies to different tasks or sectors of activity. If VET is seen as strictly connected to a specific workplace, individuals become rigid; if it is connected to generic competencies (Nijhof, 1998), it increases cooperation and flexibility. Policy-makers must indeed remember that flexibility is not only the balance between the supply and demand of labour, applied to the labour market, but is also a question of individual needs and requirements.

6.5 Labour market demands and educational supply

From an organisational point of view, to motivate young people it is important to accentuate personal perspectives, but institutional conditions are an important matter when viewing VET. Technological changes, modifying production processes and work organisation have globally transformed the methods and content of vocational education and training, but the nature and the distinctive marks of the local labour markets define the competencies required for skilled workers. Knowledge of the companies' educational needs is fundamental information in educational planning. The variables of technological and organisational development create a need for qualified workers (as to level and specialisation)[11]. If educational policies establish effective links where education and work meet (job centres...), a direct relationship between the growth of educational expenditure and the growth of national income could easily be created.

The lack of empirical techniques capable of relating technological change and educational policies to economic growth has limited the use of the so-called manpower forecasting theory. To a very great degree, the difficulties of forecasting systems originated in the seventies, when the demographic trends in developed

---

[10] In higher education, for instance, we can find "investing students", who have a professional project and see university studies as an instrument to control their future, and "consumer students" whose attitude is less instrumental: they drop out more often.

[11] It is important to note that product-based technological learning activities, to which the term "learning" in "learning economy" normally refers while central to generating high-skill, "knowledge-intensive" employment, are never going to account for the majority of employment in any given economy.

countries turned dramatically upside down, and the coming of the new technologies overthrew both education and work. And, what is more, manpower forecasting looked at VET as a means of achieving economic aims, while equity and freedom were the social expectations from education.

At the present time, the need for a better link between school and the labour market has acquired growing weight. The information system is moving in two directions: on the one hand, techniques to analyse educational outputs and skills demand have improved and have been used to guide human resources planning. Educational qualifications have to match the demand for skilled workers, but they should also anticipate the further needs of scientific and technological skills. On the other hand, educational paths have become more flexible, since growing mobility creates a demand (both social and economic) which could be satisfied at best by the use of credits.

Four main methods are normally used to forecast the features of work demand, elaborating short or middle-term forecastings:

> *The combined estimation methods* based on coefficients referred to manpower and output, which are largely used by the OECD, which link work demand by occupational category to productivity and production growth in the different economic sectors. The correspondences between manpower input and goods and services output, or professional certifications, are determined by means of fixed coefficients (Psacharopoulos, 1983). This method is rigid, because the emerging production models, based on polyvalence and the possibility of replacing different skills, make it difficult to identify school qualifications with a fixed profession. Moreover, this method implies the existence of a standard occupational classification, which is very difficult to organise (Scarnera, 1999; 2000).
>
> *Cross-national comparison-based methods*, which formulate forecasts comparing occupational structures and educational levels and types in countries at different phases of development. In this model, the relationship between inputs and outputs is very rigid, and ignores "cultural" factors. As Zymelman (1980) says, a development trend that happened in Japan should not necessarily be repeated in Italy or in Latin America.
>
> *Demographic forecasting-based methods*, which work only where rigid standards exist, for instance, in schools. These methods are greatly influenced by the variability both of the coefficients and of the demographic forecastings.
>
> *Survey-based methods*, which integrate administrative type sources with widespread surveys carried out on representative business samples. Even if this method requires expensive and sophisticated methodological techniques, it gives the possibility of investigating, by direct surveying, not only the number but also the characteristics of the various occupational profiles (academic qualifications, experience and age requested, area/role in the companies, main areas of knowledge and skills requested).

In Italy there have been a number of sectoral studies, and three main general and systematic investigation projects, carried out by the Italian Statistical Central Institute (ISTAT), only for school-leavers from secondary school or higher education, by the OBNF[12], and by the Progetto Excelsior, implemented by the Italian Union of Chambers of Commerce, in association with the Ministry of Employment and the European Union, since 1997.

1. The Italian Statistical Central Institute (ISTAT) carries out systematic surveys of the transition to work of school-leavers from secondary schools or higher education. These survey results allow structural and cyclic effects in the supply and demand of skilled workers to be recognised, building up economic and noneconomic indicators to describe the correspondences between job and task characteristics, and the level or type of education. Even if there are temporal limits[13], and a large subjective component (i.e. about the utility or importance of the academic knowledge areas involved in the job), these data could be used for a number of purposes, with an effort of interpretation. For instance, thinking about transferability and flexibility, in Lombardy there is a small percentage of highly skilled, unemployed young people. It is not clear whether they cannot find a job, or they prefer to wait for a particular job. Obviously, these two conditions do not overlap, and they introduce the distinction between a *"stopgap" job* and a *"permanent" job*. This distinction is not irrelevant, because policy-makers might evaluate in a more suitable way the resources to be invested in education, if they know the attitudes of the highly skilled young people towards mobility, and the employability of their qualifications in different sectors of activity or in different geographical areas[14]. The youth labour supply is characterised by a *redefinition of entrance modalities:* the increasing age for permanent job, the creation of an "archipelago" of intermediate conditions between education and work, the existence of a multiplicity of possible stopgap jobs, seen not only as a means of survival, but also as an opportunity to choose and measure one's capabilities. The number of irregular or "anomalous" conditions multiplies before a permanent job; for this reason, official statistics, which can describe, measure and in some way forecast macro (but not micro) phenomena become useless, though their importance is increasing.

2. The OBNF study aims to specify the educational needs of industries in terms of so called "archetypes", logical schemes describing technical and practical skills connected to specific occupational tasks, and their consequences in terms of planning, control, training on the job and so on. In this study, flexibility, mobility and transferability are not relevant, because the "archetypes" are classed crossing only structural variables, i.e. their actual existence in the companies, the forecasting of development and availability in local labour markets. From this point of view, each sector or region has *critical needs* (high diffusion, high development, low availability) where it is important to *continue* to invest in education, *emerging needs* (low diffusion, high development, low availability) where it is important to *start* to invest in education, and *declining needs* (high or low diffusion, low development, high or low availability) where it is less important to invest in education, or it is better to invest in retraining and lifelong education to promote mobility.

---

[12] The OBNF (Organismo Bilaterale Nazionale per la Formazione) is a board constituted by the Unions and the employers organisation (Confindustria) within the limits of the so-called "pact for work" (20 January 1993).

[13] The research looks at the occupational situation three years after graduation, and it is normally published after two years, so that, for instance, the last one, issued in 2000, is about graduates from 1995. Of course, in the meanwhile the labour market has changed a lot.

[14] In this study there are also data broken down by gender, which do not exist in the other surveys: for this reason, their utility cannot be compared.

3. The Excelsior Project carries out surveys in order to forecast labour market trends up to two years in advance. The last and fourth survey (issued in July 2001) only analyses one year in advance: a sample of more than 90,000 companies with up to 250 employees were interviewed through a CATI system; all the companies that have more than 251 employees were interviewed by qualified interviewers. The four levels of education (degree, high school diploma, technical or vocational qualification, compulsory education) were divided into 58 groups, and combined with the needs of further education. For the first time, the questionnaire had a specific section about Continuing Vocational Training Survey (CVTS) in the year 2000: these data are brand new, and provide the opportunity to point out aspects of flexibility, mobility and transferability. I will discuss some of them to emphasise the consequences, in terms of flexibility, transferability and mobility.

6.6 Consequences of the Excelsior Project

General trends: The data coming from the Excelsior Project suggest that the role of industries as producers of lifelong learning in the VET system is relevant and is based mainly on private funds. In the year 2000, only 13% of the costs were paid out of public funds, both national and European. The percentage of Italian industries organising some kind of educational provision for their workers is close to the European average, i.e. about 12% (Table 6.2). The percentage of public funds varies from a minimum of 8.4% in small industries of 1-9 employees to a maximum of 18.5% in industries of 50-249 employees.

Table 6.2 *Permanent education run by companies for their employees: number of workers and trainees qualified by the company in the manufacturing and services sectors, costs (million lire) from public funds, 2000.*

	Employees	Trainees	Total costs	Public funds
Manufacturing	5,163,851	509,982	1,085,789	158,783
Services	4,640,378	533,901	1,272,346	147,969
Total	9,804,229	1,043,883	2,358,135	306,752

According to the entries planned in 2001, this trend will probably continue, because 39.4% of new workers are expected to need further qualification – even supposing we could negatively evaluate the fact that about 40% of them are required to have only compulsory education, without any qualification, and the majority (73.9%) will need no further qualification during work. The qualification opportunities offered are influenced by geographical area and company dimensions. There are fewer opportunities in SME but more in larger companies, 87.8% of which are offering qualification to 25% of the workers. Managers have more opportunities than blue-collar or white-collar workers, while only 30.7% of the trainees are women (Table 6.3).

Table 6.3 Qualification opportunities offered by region, by number of employees and by professional group, 2000 (percentages)

Percentage of companies offering qualification by region				
North-West	North-East	Centre	South & Islands	Total
12.6	13.2	11.5	9.4	11.9

Percentage of companies offering qualification by number of employees				
1-9	10-49	50-249	250 and above	Total
10.3	18.3	34.9	87.8	11.9

Trainees by professional group				
Blue-collar	White-collar	Managers	Total	Women
9.2	12.9	20.1	10.6	30.7

Source: Sistema Formativo Excelsior, 2001.

In VET offered by companies, the opportunities are not distributed equally, nor do they compensate for unequal starting points – on the contrary, they tend to favour people starting from the highest levels. If initial education and industrial training are seen as complements in VET, industrial training will only increase existing differences in human capital, implying the risk of some workers "missing the boat". Every industry has certain paths of entry that are starting points for the more demanding jobs offered to more experienced people who want to acquire additional education. In establishing and maintaining an employment relationship, genuine "know-how" will be emphasised rather than formal qualifications, and people will be able to acquire additional real and recognised competencies through learning at work. Production of the skills needed for work can be crystallised by thinking about what education would mean in different sectors of the economy. The increase in human capital can no longer be identified with the enhancement of formal education and training, whose main function is to instill general skills and facilitate lifelong learning.

We could also determine a *qualification rate* for each productive activity, i.e. the ratio between employees and trainees, indicating how many opportunities a worker has to take part in VET. The average value is 10.6%, and this means that only one in ten workers will probably have some kind of training or education by his company: this value varies from 9.2% for manual workers, to 12.9% for white-collar workers, up to 20.1% for managers. It is very interesting to note that, although both in secondary and higher education the percentage of women is higher than that of men in permanent education, in which companies decide freely who is to be involved, employed women are 34.4%, but women in VET only 30.7%.

The level of school qualification of the workers involved in VET is unknown, but we do know the amount of demand for the manpower forecasting as a whole by level of school education, and we also know if experience or further qualification is needed (Table 6.4): so, it is likely that additional qualification will be offered mainly to people in need of additional qualification.

Table 6.4 *Manpower forecasting by level of education and main educational needs, 2001.*

	Total	Additional qualification	Experience and additional qualification	Experience without qualification
Higher education	7.3	67.7	65.5	72.1
Diploma	32.0	49.4	44.2	54.7
Qualification	20.8	39.7	32.3	46.9
Compulsory	39.9	26.1	21.9	29.6
Total [15]	100.0	39.4	35.5	43.1

Source: Sistema formativo Excelsior, 2001.

Vocational education is required by 20.8%, and 39.7% of them need additional education. Diploma is the most required level, 32.0% of temporary employees, half of them needing additional qualifications, and, finally, higher education is required only for 7.3%, and 67.7% of them need more education. These data strengthen the fact that *the need for permanent education grows in relation to the school level,* which is the fundamental asset for lifelong learning. In this permanent process, the value of experience and of learning on the job is higher than the value of education. For each level, the demand for experience *without* additional education is systematically higher than the demand for experience *with* additional education - up to 14 points for higher education. In most cases, the need for additional qualification in companies is both great and growing, and is greater for newcomers than for employees.

   Vocational education and training have to be unlinked from the formal school system, reorganising working life in terms of the production of practical know-how and work-based training. The idea of matching the educational system and working life one-to-one could well be abolished; however, planning and implementing educational policies requires the setting up and operating of a permanent information system which runs without interruption, is fully aware of productive sectors and typologies, and which analyses the situation in both territorial and dimensional terms. Education aims at creating the new skills required for the promotion of both old and new industries. New industries are, however, by definition, new and inexperienced, so it is not easy to predict the skills. In these circumstances, there is an increasing trend towards setting up organisational processes for production systems which aim both to simplify structures and general functions and to research new ways of training, managing and using human resources. The educational system has to know how to predict accurately and well in advance the professional requirements demanded by companies, in order to organise guidance and training for those (old or young) who are to be employed.

6.7 The state of debate in Italy

The current economic situation in many European countries, including Italy, appears to be dominated by some particularly significant phenomena: the ever-increasing *use*

---

[15] The number of demanded places was 716,000.

of technological innovations, resulting in the rapid obsolescence of technical skills; the irreversible process of *economic globalisation*, which leads to a high level of transferability of production factors such as technology, capital and labour; the new and dynamic *complexity of production systems* and markets which is generating a process of dis-integration of traditional production activities. This has had a significant impact on the skills required by workers, and on their personal ability to evolve and adapt to changes in processes, technology and organisational conditions, requiring *flexibility* and *mobility*.

Vis-à-vis such changes, there has been a noticeable increase in the importance of the policy-making required to steer and preside over these changes, possibly trying to anticipate regulations and measures affecting the flexibility of the labour market and a tighter integration of the educational and production systems, enhancing *transferability*. One of the consequences of these changes is a need to rethink the matching of the demand and supply of different forms of education[16], using them to influence work policies, to reduce and control social conflict, to facilitate both people's employability and mobility and the companies' enrolment of skilled workers, in a shorter time and at lower costs, even if the transition to work is never automatic, but implies discontinuity.

To overcome this discontinuity in Western societies, institutional and cultural conditions demand a *systemic approach to VET:* no one single actor could be responsible by itself for the development of VET. Every kind of education, particularly vocational, originates and develops through the existence of *knowledge networks,* made by schools, centres, and communities of practice working together in a perspective of task division[17]. A common trend is the shift from formal to informal education: for instance, communities of practice have an increasing role as a gateway to the labour market, to maintain the competence of workers, to support local networks, and probably to facilitate the adaptation to change. A *system action* is made of components connected by internal ties (in this case educational agencies), operating as a functional unit in a fixed background or frame. A *system management* of VET needs a balance between differentiation and specialisation, in a complex, organic model, where "structures and roles act as open systems: their operational autonomy is limited by a network of informal and economical exchanges, where the game rules are created or influenced by the actors" (Cnos – Ifap, 1993).

In this system and in its background, flexibility and mobility are improved by a dynamic connected to the idea that education is not only a social problem, but exists as a personal responsibility in determining educational paths. School centrality has become too "heavy" in the face of the demand for lifelong education, and has been substituted by a network of related agencies, offering coherent qualification possibilities ("a spider's web of educational opportunities", Giovannini 1987). On the demand side, even in Italy, some buffer organisations are collecting the educational demands of particular groups, lobbying to obtain useful opportunities. However, if social actors interact in a correct way, decision-makers cannot emphasise a particular point of view reducing the complexity (the so-called *fast*

---

[16] Of course, employability is not the only aim of education, the other ones being personal development, citizenship, quality and equity.

[17] A study in the arts and crafts sector underlines the existence of competencies that are only passed on in the communities of practice: in this case, time would not need to be wasted on achievements at school, if the person could prove in other ways that he or she commended the necessary skills.

thinking). They have to consider both individual and collective needs, individual and collective aims, profiting by the results of educational research and practices.

With the structure of the educational provision being based on credits or modules, and no longer on linear sequences, transferability grows. The risks are knowledge fragmentation, individual isolation, autonomy radicalisation, where the "responsibility for one's life project" leads to a reduction in the responsibility of both school and work. To avoid these risks - which mainly damage the weakest part of the population - educational policies will have to integrate concepts that are so far opposite (education and work, general and vocational education, initial and lifelong education...) and to enhance basic education, which is a condition for transferability and mobility, even if the influence of education on one's life chances is not fully known, and swings between an excess of expectations and absolute usefulness. More specifically, in a postFordist society, vocational education and training has to be seen as the crossroads of three identities (Vergani, 2000, p. 79):

- VET is *an individual right*, in particular to profit from lifelong learning opportunities, both for one's professional and personal life. Moreover, VET could be used to maintain high worker employability, to guarantee the quality of their performance, and to enhance the correspondence between educational credits and changes in organisational and production systems;
- VET is *a strategy to support companies and productive organisations* in general, because it is a way to shape individual skills that correspond to the profiles demanded, and a tool to enhance efficiency, innovation and competitiveness;
- VET is an instrument that public institutions (local and national) can use to *sustain development and local or sectoral qualifications*, and to help people to be placed or replaced in the labour market. In this above meaning, VET could be seen as a tool for active labour policy, because it facilitates the matching of demand and supply, reducing *mismatching,* and is a factor for labour market regulation, if it is connected to the characteristics of the demand, reducing the inadequacy of training systems.

Mobility increases equity, the economists say, and Esping-Andersen (1999, p.183) states that "for any given individual, skills are the single best source of escaping from underprivilege", demonstrating that the risk of unemployment is shared by more people in a mobile workforce, and everyone has prospects of improving their conditions. At the moment, the Italian educational reforms are trying to create a balance between industry, which is asking for more specific skills, and school, which is promoting its general role of socialisation and self-realisation. It is probably too early to say whether a solution exists to these contrasting expectations. In the short term, a more specific vocational education could increase employability, but in the middle term only a more general education could protect workers from a conjunctural crisis, by helping them to retrain, increase or modify their skills. To ensure mobility, education and its relationship to working life has to be rethought: education alone cannot eliminate underprivilege, because it is tied to families and to the labour maket: if there are no jobs, education is simply "the storage of unneeded labour"(Kivinen & Peltomäki, 1999, p. 121).

Note

Luca Queirolo Palmas, University of Genova, has helpfully cooperated with me both in elaborating and revising this chapter.

References

Abbatecola, E. (1999). *Le reti di relazione nella riproduzione delle disuguaglianze e differenze di genere: il ruolo delle reti di relazione* [Relational networks role in reproducing class and gender inequalities]. In G. Cella (Ed.), *Disuguaglianze e differenze* [Inequalities and differences] (pp.239-26). Milano: Guerini e associati.

Ambrosini, M. (Ed.). (2000). *Un futuro da formare* [A future to educate]. Brescia: La Scuola.

Ashton, D.N. (1992). The restructuring of the labour market and youth training. In Ph. Brown & H. Lauder (Eds.), *Education for economic survival. From fordism to postfordism?* (pp.180-202). London: Routledge.

Beeby, C.E. (1966). *The quality of education in developing countries.* Cambridge, Ma: Harvard University Press.

Benne, K.D. (1976). Educational field experience as the negotiation of different cognitive worlds. In W.G. Bennis (Ed.), *The planning of change* (pp. 164-171). New York: Rinehart & Winston.

Bianco, M.L. (1996). *Classi e reti sociali. Risorse e strategie degli attori nella riproduzione delle disuguaglianze* [Classes and social networks. Individual strategies and resources in reproducing inequalities]. Bologna: Il Mulino.

Boudon, R. (1973). *L'inégalité des chances.* Paris: Colin.

Callini, D. (1993). *Cambiamento organizzativo e formazione.* Milano: Franco Angeli.

CERI - OECD (1996). *Employment and growth in the knowledge based economy.* Paris: OECD Documents.

CERI (1998). *Human capital investment.* Paris: OECD.

Dahrendorf, R. (1995). *Report on wealth creation and social cohesion in a free society.* London: Commission on wealth creation and social cohesion.

Doise, W., & Palmonari, A. (Eds.) (1986). *L'Etude des représentations sociales.* Neuchatel: Delachaux et Niestlé.

Esping Andersen, G. (1999). *Social foundations of postindustrial economies.* Oxford: Oxford University Press.

Gallino, L. (1998). *Se tre milioni vi sembran pochi* [If you think three millions are too few]. Torino: Einaudi.

Giovannini, G. (1987). I molti tempi, attori e luoghi della formazione: un'analisi del policentrismo a partire dall'offerta [Plurality of educational supply in education]. *Studi di Sociologia,* (25), (nr. 1), 3-17.

Granovetter, M. (1973). The strenght of weak ties. *American Journal of Sociology,* (78), 1360-1380.

Hickox, M., & Moore, R. (1992). Education and postfordism: a new correspondence? In Ph. Brown, H. Lauder (Eds.), *Education for economic survival. From fordism to postfordism?* (pp. 95-116). London: Routledge.

ISFOL, (2000). *Rapporto Isfol 2000.* Milano: Franco Angeli.

Kivinen, O. & Peltomäki, M. (1999). Apprenticeship training. In O. Kivinen, H. Silvennoinen & P. Puusteli (Eds.), *Work based learning. Prospects and challenges.* Turku: Ministry of Education, Painosalama Oy.

Lodigiani, R. (2000). Investire ancora nella formazione professionale? [Investing again in vocational education?]. In M. Ambrosini (Ed.), *Un futuro da formare* [A future to educate] (pp.25-46). Brescia: La Scola.

Machlup, F. (1984). *Knowledge: its creation, distribution and economic significance.* Princeton: Princeton University Press.

Nijhof, W.J. (1998). Qualifying for the future. In W.J. Nijhof & J.N. Streumer (Eds.), *Key qualifications in work and education* (pp. 19-35). Dordrecht: Kluwer Academic Publishers.

Osbat, L. (Ed.). (1985). *Tendenze innovative nella formazione continua in Italia e paesi della comunità europea* [Innovative trends in long life learning in Italy and in the U.E. countries]. Milano: Franco Angeli.

Psacharopoulos, G. (1973). *Returns to education: an international comparison*. San Francisco: Jossey-Bass.

Regini, M. (Ed.). (1996). *La formazione delle risorse umane. Una sfida per le regioni "motore d'Europa "* [Human resources qualification. A challenge for "European motors" regions]. Bologna: Il Mulino.

Reyneri, E. (1999). I nuovi modi di lavorare [New forms of work]. *Impesa e Stato*, (50).

Ribolzi, L. (1991). Valori e mondo professionale [Values and professions]. In L. Santelli Beccegato (Ed.), *Bisogno di valori* [Need for values] (pp. 155-171). Brescia: La Scuola.

Ribolzi, L. (1998). Qualificazione delle risorse umane e apprendimento in alternanza [Human resources qualification and alternance education]. In E. Besozzi (Ed.), *Navigare tra formazione e lavoro* [Between education and work] (pp.65-74). Bologna: Carocci.

Rifkin, J. (1994). The end of work: the decline of the global labor force and the dawn of the post-market era. New York: The Putnam Publishing Group.

Sanders, J.M. (1992). Short and long term macroeconomics returns to higher education, *Sociology of education*, (65), 21-36.

Sarchielli, G., & Zappala, S. (1998). *Construire la seconda opportunità* [Building the second chance]. Milano: Franco Angeli.

Scarnera, A. (Ed.). (1999). *Progetto interarea di classificazione delle professioni, Rapporto del primo e del secondo anno di attività* [Classification of professions. First and second year report]. Roma: ISTAT (mimeo).

Vanetti, R. (2000). Janus II. *Progetto regionale per l'inserimento sociale e lavorativo dei giovani. Azione di valutazione* [Regional program for youth job and social life entering. Assessment action]. Bologna: AECA (mimeo).

Vergani, A. (2000). I nuovi contenuti della formazione professionale [New contents in vocational education]. In M. Ambrosini (Ed.), *Un futuro da formare* [A future to educate] (pp.65-79). Brescia: La Scola.

Warr, P.B. (Ed.) (1981). *Experience of work: a compendium and review of 249 measures and their use*. New York: Academic Press.

CHAPTER 7

Developments in vocational education in Ireland

DAVID TUOHY

THE GENERAL THEME OF THIS BOOK explores the concept of flexibility, in vocational education. This chapter explores the vocational system in Ireland as a case study. Vocational education and training (VET) has been a feature of post-compulsory education and initial VET has struggled to find a distinctive place in a traditionally academic and general education at post-primary level. This case study illustrates the attempts to introduce a more flexible curriculum and the way the system had adapted to these initiatives.

The chapter is divided into three main parts. The first explores the context of vocational education in the years immediately after the founding of the State, and the changing context that led to Ireland joining the Common Market (now the EU) in 1974. The second part describes a period of expansion, where an attempt was made to integrate initial VET into a general education, and a major expansion took place at third-level and in the non-formal sector. The third part examines the emergence of an emphasis on vocational education in three recent curricular initiatives in compulsory education. It shows how these initiatives have been "colonised" by the general academic curriculum and points to the difficulty of establishing a strong vocational track in a country without either the industrial support or the historical context of such a provision.

7.1 The early years (1922-74)

In the early years of post-Independence Ireland, secondary schools were mainly private institutions run by church groups but open to government inspection. They provided an academic education that relied heavily on the classics and had little flexibility. Students took two examinations - the Intermediate (age 15) and Leaving (age 17) Certificate examinations. This gave them entry into the civil service, teaching or to university and the professions. The general skills learned were suitable to a large number of clerical type jobs, and in a largely agrarian society, this was the principal means of social mobility (Lee, 1989). However, despite expressions of social concern and a commitment to equality of opportunity in education, access to education beyond the primary stage outside urban areas was available only to about 8% of the age group (Ó Buachalla, 1988).

In 1930, the Vocational Education Bill established statutory local Vocational Education Committees (VEC) to provide continuation, apprentice and technical education. The VECs showed a great deal of flexibility in responding to local needs, and organised a wide variety of courses in the different trade areas, frequently linked to apprenticeship schemes. The courses tended to be very specific, without transferable skills. The courses suited local employment needs and also provided a limited general education – a two-year course leading to the Group (age 14)

103

W. J. Nijhof et al. (eds.), Shaping Flexibility in Vocational Education and Training, 103-112.
© 2002 Kluwer Academic Publishers. Printed in the Netherlands.

Certificate. The establishment of a mainstream continuance track involved an assurance to church groups that the vocational schools would not be allowed to impinge on the field covered by the denominationally run secondary schools. This meant that vocational schools were not allowed teach those subjects nor prepare for those examinations that gave access to university and white collar employment – a restriction that remained in place until the mid 1960s (Whyte, 1971; Ó Buachalla, 1988). The curriculum for this mainstream vocational track remained very general, with no great differentiation of vocational skills. The Group Certificate consisted of core subjects Mathematics, English and Irish language, augmented by practical subjects such as Woodwork and Metalwork for boys and Home Economics and Secretarial Skills for girls. In practice, what distinguished the two tracks was the academic ability of the students, rather than a chosen career path. In general, the private secondary schools "creamed off" the more academically able, and the rest went to the vocational schools. The general philosophy was that students with low academic ability were better suited to practical subjects. Clearly, in this scenario, vocational education held a lower status than an academic one, and inevitably, the division often reflected social class differences.

As well as a different governance structure and emphasis in the curriculum, there were different career pathways for teachers in the dual system. Teachers in vocational and secondary schools belonged to different teacher unions. In vocational schools, teachers of the "practical" subjects had specialised qualification pathways. Those who taught "academic" subjects were not required to complete a Higher Diploma in Education, as were their secondary colleagues, although in practice, many did. The two systems were quite distinct and there was very little mobility or transfer between them.

In the later 1960s, Ireland embarked on a major investment policy in post-primary education. Fees were abolished and a transport scheme organised. This enticed large numbers of young people to stay in school. New syllabi were developed to support a change in economic policies designed to move Ireland from an agrarian to an industrial economy. The emphasis was mainly on science and business studies. The new curriculum was conceived as a flexible, comprehensive curriculum. It insisted on a core set of subjects – Irish, English and mathematics, and then offered a range of "elective" subjects, including vocational subjects, to suit the talents within the student cohort. The underlying philosophy was the promotion of a general education, and students were encouraged to take a balanced selection of subjects from languages, humanities, science, business and practical groups. The new system aimed at a unified curriculum rather than promoting a separate vocational curriculum.

The country lacked the infrastructure to support an industrial expansion that might have attracted students to a more focused vocational education at second level. The response to the new curricular initiatives in fact underlined the lack of status of vocational education. The expansion in the secondary sector far outweighed the expansion in the vocational sector, as parents and students aspired to a more academic orientation, and what would have been seen as a more flexible, and financially rewarding, career track. Although some secondary schools began to offer the traditional vocational subjects, the uptake of these subjects was still centred in the vocational schools and the new Comprehensive and Community schools. The fact that all subjects were now included in the Intermediate and Leaving Certificate programmes gave the impression of a developing flexibility in the curriculum. However, the basic subject structure (organised as two or three year courses) and the examination system remained the same, and this had the effect of limiting that flexibility. The subject choices of students still reflected social class and gender differences in provision and uptake (Breen, 1986; Lynch, 1999).

School management practices also militated against the emergence of a strong vocational track. At junior level, many of the secondary schools used the general subjects of the Group Certificate examinations (after 2 years) as a trial run for the more prestigious Intermediate Certificate the following year. This utilitarian approach to preparing students for the academic process further downgraded the status of the practical subjects, and illustrated the tendency of the academic programme to "colonise" the vocational programme for its own benefit. This eventually led to the abolition of both the Group and Intermediate Certificates in favour of a single Junior Certificate.

At senior level, Leaving Certificate students sat terminal examinations at the end of two-year programmes in seven subjects. The hope was that students might be able to tailor their subject profile to suit their interests and talents. Although they now had a greater menu of subjects to choose from, organisational constraints meant that individual choices were curtailed. First, there was the issue of the core curriculum that lowered the number of options available. Secondly, the traditional structure of a two year course, which sought to balance depth and breadth within one syllabus, had major constraints on school schedules, lowering the options given to students. Thirdly, some of the practical subjects were not recognised in assessing students' merits for progress to third level courses. Consequently, students tended to choose the more academic subjects, as these were seen as increasing options for entry to third level, and this remains true today.

From a human capital perspective, policy initiatives aimed at a comprehensive curriculum. A wider range of skills was produced in the population through the different subjects on offer. However, the structure of the curriculum meant that the individual student still graduated with six or seven different subject areas. There was a greater possibility for variation in the subject profile, although in practice, the different practical subjects were now being spread more thinly among a small proportion of the student body. This meant that it was the system that became more comprehensive rather than the individual student becoming more comprehensively educated. The dominant philosophy was that of a general education. Subjects studied were not seen as reflecting a chosen career pathway, but as creating capacity for later choices. In this culture, it was extremely difficult for a distinct vocational philosophy to gain a foothold.

7.2 The period of expansion (1974-90)

Ireland's membership of the European Community gave rise to major support from the European Social Fund. Through the Department of Education, money was made available for specific training programmes at post-primary level. One focus of the investment was the development of alternative curricula for young people who experienced little success in school and who "dropped out", often with no qualifications. This formed part of the social policy related to disadvantage, as these students typically came from deprived backgrounds. The alternative programmes often incorporated work experience and had a greater emphasis on traditional 'vocational' skills. These included Vocational Preparation and Training (VPT1) programmes, which were offered to students at the end of Junior Certificate and aimed to facilitate a transfer to the world of work at age 16. VPT2 programmes also developed as Post-Leaving Certificate programmes dealing with an older age group. These programmes existed mainly in the Vocational sector, which showed a high level of flexibility and adaptability in responding to student needs in a local context.

Formal post-primary education remained a unified system. There was some evidence of the re-emergence of a distinct vocational track within the system, but the main focus of vocational education was at the end of cycles within the system. Thus, VPT1 and VPT2 programmes assumed the end of a general education and looked to the transition to the world of work. For others who had left the education system, training programmes were put in place to develop more flexibility in the workforce, and these had a strong vocational dimension. In mainstream education, the main focus for a developing vocational track was at third level. Regional Technical Colleges and Institutes of Technology were established with special emphasis on developing business and technician skills to serve the needs of the developing economy. The expansion in this sector was rapid, with the number of full-time students increasing fourfold in the past twenty years (Table 7.1). All awards were validated through the newly established National Council for Vocational Awards (NCVA), allowing for a high level of transferability and mobility among students and in their progress from Certificate through Diploma courses, and in some cases to Degree level.

Table 7.1 *Distribution of Full-time Students between Universities and Institutes of Technology in selected years.*

	1975	1980	1985	1990	1995	1997
Universities + Teacher training	26992	30671	34620	40269	55875	59651
Institutes of Technology	n.a.	10910	18953	27819	38160	41000

Table 7.2 shows the distribution of students in the Institutes of Technology by the type of courses they take. The table shows a rapid growth in Business courses, which include the use of Information Technology applications, and in more recent years, a greater concentration on Science courses, which includes training in the Health and Food sciences. This growth reflects the needs of an economy based on the service industry rather than on manufacturing.

Table 7.2 *Distribution of Full-time Students in Institutes of Technology by the Courses Taken.*

	1980	1985	1990	1995	1997
Business	2709	5302	9171	12204	12906
Engineering	4126	5424	7952	10212	10408
Science	1771	3165	4868	8361	9274
Other	2304	3202	5280	7353	8412

In the 1980s Ireland experienced a major growth in population, with over 50% of the population under the age of 21 at one stage. This put a major strain on educational resources, particularly in trying to cope with the aspiration of many students leaving post-primary schools to progress to third level. Many failed to obtain places and again the VEC schools responded by offering Post-Leaving Certificate (PLC) courses that in many cases had externally validated accreditation (e.g. City and Guilds). Some VEC schools were so successful in offering these courses that they eventually dealt only with senior students on such courses, and no longer offered a general education to junior pupils. Currently, these colleges offer a wide range of PLC courses, although the status of the courses is a matter of some debate, existing as they do in a limbo between post-primary and third level. Most of these courses are one or two year courses, offered on a modular basis, thus giving a high level of flexibility in their delivery. At present, about 70% of the school leaving cohort proceed to either further or higher education. Of these, about 30% enrol on Post-Leaving Certificate courses in institutes of further education; another 30% on certificate or diploma courses in technological colleges, and 40% on degree courses in universities or technological colleges.

The period of economic growth and expansion saw the emergence of a vocational trend in education in Ireland. This was concentrated at post second-level, and in the main depended on the general education received at second-level, rather than capitalising on the vocational content of some subjects at second-level. These developments reflect the strong culture of general education in second-level schools, and the dominance of a more academic approach to general education. Perhaps it also reflects a pragmatic response to a changing economy, where young people were not prepared to commit themselves too early to a career path, delaying their options until they had to make choices at third level.

7.3 Present developments

The early experience of the expansion of the education system was mixed. It soon became clear that the traditional academic curriculum had to be adapted to suit the expanded cohort of students, especially those who were failing within the system. As a result of a focus on the quality of the experience of these students, pilot projects in new curricular initiatives were undertaken by the City of Dublin VEC, Shannon Curriculum Unit and Tipperary North VEC (Coolahan, 1981). These new programmes incorporated a strong vocational aspect. In recent years, the success of these programmes has been recognised in the establishment of three new programmes in the senior cycle of second-level education – the Transition Year, the Leaving Certificate Vocational and the Applied Leaving Certificate. An analysis of these programmes, particularly the latter two, demonstrates the difficulty of establishing a strong vocational strand in the present culture of Irish second level schools.

Currently, the second level system offers a unified general education for all to age 15, when students complete the Junior Certificate. Some flexibility is offered in a range of elective subjects, and the level at which each subject can be taken (Higher, Ordinary or Foundation). After that, students have a number of pathways. Most schools now offer a Transition Year, an optional year that focuses on personal development. Students also have a choice of three different Leaving Certificate programmes – the traditional (academic) Leaving Certificate, the Vocational Leaving Certificate and the Leaving Certificate Applied. Currently, the syllabi for various subjects (modern European languages, Irish, Accounting and mathematics) are being revised to give them a greater vocational orientation. We shall look at some issues related to the theme of the chapter in three of these programmes.

7.3.1 The transition year

The transition year was introduced to provide students with opportunities for personal development and for exploring new learning areas and strategies. It is inter-disciplinary and student-centred in design, and aims to help students take responsibility for their own learning as a prelude to the Leaving Certificate. Teachers have flexibility in designing short courses tailored to the specific needs of students. Although not strictly seen as a vocational programme, most schools offer some form of reflective work experience in simulated or placement conditions. This helps students learn skills and evaluate life in practical situations. Insofar as there is a vocational concept underpinning the Transition Year, it deals more with the process element of work (interpersonal skills, self-esteem and confidence) rather than developing specific work skills. These process skills are seen as being easily transferred to different work situations, and again reflects the dominance of the general education philosophy in post-primary education in Ireland.

7.3.2 The Leaving Certificate Vocational Programme (LCVP)

In choosing elective courses for their Leaving Certificate, the traditional vocational subjects have been associated with weaker students. Table 7.3 compares the popularity of traditional "vocational" subjects within two student cohorts – those who took seven higher level papers in their Leaving Certificate examination, and those with no higher level papers. These groups can be taken to represent the academically able and the academically weak respectively. The comparison reveals that there is a preference for the more vocational subjects among the academically weaker group. It seems that students have internalised expectations of the subjects in which they can succeed, as these students have low failure rates in these subjects. These subjects have less dependence on linguistic ability and the gap between the language of the home and the language of the classroom is less likely to lead to failure. It is the core subjects of English, Irish and Mathematics that produce the highest failure levels (Tuohy & Doyle, 1994).

Table 7.3 *A comparison of the % of students from each of two cohorts – those who take 7 or more papers at Higher Level and those who take no paper at Higher Level – as to the uptake of vocational subjects.*

Higher Level Papers Taken	Business Organisation	Home Ec. (Social & Scientific)	Technical Drawing	Engineering	Building Construction
7 or more	15	11	9	2	1
None	51	38	18	15	12

In 1989, the Leaving Certificate Vocational Programme (LCVP) was introduced. Because of its vocational emphasis, this programme attracts funding from the European Social Fund, making it attractive to schools. In this mode, students sit the regular subjects of the Leaving Certificate Programme as the normal part of the school programme, but with an emphasis on vocational subjects and a recognised course in a modern European language. LCVP students also take three mandatory link modules, which are meant to replace one of the subject choices in the traditional programme. These three link modules are titled: enterprise education, preparation for work and work experience. The emphasis is on active learning, cross-curricular activity and links with the local environment. The link modules are taught as short courses, and have an element of continuous assessment in how they are graded. In recent years, performance in these modules has counted in a "points" system for entry to some third level courses.

In 1997, 2300 students who sat the Leaving Certificate were assessed in the LCV link modules. 1688 (73%) applied for some third level course and over 95% of these were offered a place in a third level institution. 854 (51%) students eventually accepted a place, 385 on a degree programme and 469 on a certificate or diploma course in an Institute of Technology. These figures also reflect the national profile of students leaving school (Tuohy, 1998).

Of LCV students who applied for third level courses, 1109 (67%) had attended a voluntary school, which traditionally provided the academic programme, and the others attended vocational (15%), comprehensive (2%) or community schools (11%), with 5% not identifying their school type. A study of this cohort indicated that they had a very similar profile of subject uptake as the general student body. There was no specialised vocational orientation, although a slightly higher proportion of LCV students took Home Economics, Business Studies and Biology than in the general body.

Table 7.4 *Success Rates of Students who took the Link Modules in the 1997 Leaving Certificate.*

	Distinction	Merit	Pass	Fail
All LCV students (n=2300)	607	1201	398	94
LCV applicants for 3rd Level (n=1688)	562	927	167	3

Four grades are awarded for the Link Modules – Distinction, Merit, Pass or Fail. Table 7.4 shows that the students who applied for third level places were representative of a high achieving cohort among the LCV cohort. Most of this group of students were able to include the merit points available for Distinction or Merit grades on the Link Modules among the six scores that counted in obtaining places on third level courses. Thus, the Link Modules acted as an insurance subject for a large number of students who were seeking a place on an academic course at third level, rather than providing a distinct academic track.

Table 7.5 *The percentage of two cohorts of students applying for third level places, who took the indicated number of subjects in the Leaving Certificate Examination of 1997.*

Subjects Taken	Total Cohort	LCV students
6	14	1
7	72	10
8	10	86
9	<1	3

An examination of the Leaving Certificate examination results of those who applied for third level courses revealed that 86% of the applicants who had LCV link modules sat for seven other subjects at their Leaving Certificate. However, in the general population of students, 86% have seven or less subjects (Table 7.5). This means that, for many students, the link modules were regarded as an "extra subject", rather than a course of studies replacing one of the regular choices. It seems that many secondary schools use the LCV programme as a means of increasing the options open to their students by giving them an extra subject, rather than focusing on the particularly vocational aspect of the programme. It is not immediately clear how schools were so flexible to find time for the link modules in their schedules, and what aspects of the general programme were sacrificed to accommodate them.

These LCV students also aspired to similar types of third level courses at both university and technological colleges, and in the same proportions, as their non-LCV peers. They also had similar success rates in obtaining places, including their first course option. It appears that many of the students who took the LCV pathway in the senior cycle of post-primary school remained very flexible in their career orientation, and used the link modules in a utilitarian way to enhance these options, rather than seeing the LCV as a way of acquiring a particular set of vocational skills that would be carried into third level. Further research needs to be done on the destinations of the other students who followed a vocational pathway at Leaving Certificate and did not apply for third-level places.

7.3.3 The Leaving Certificate Applied (LCA)

The Leaving Certificate Applied was introduced in 1995. It was intended to meet the needs of those students who would not normally progress to the traditional Leaving Certificate. It is designed as a two-year modular programme structured around three main elements:

- General education (minimum 30%) – arts, social, language leisure and recreation.
- Vocational Preparation (minimum 25%) – guidance, work experience, English and communication, enterprise education.
- Vocational education (minimum 30%) – information technology, mathematical applications and two specialist areas of vocational occupation.

Assessment is through a combination of continuous assessment, cross modular projects and examinations. Students who opt for this pathway may not qualify directly for third level places, but may progress to further study at PLC level. It is the intention of the government that the LCA awards will be fully integrated into the new certification system of educational and training qualifications.

Table 7.6 *Percentage Destination of Three Cohorts of Leaving Certificate Applied Students on Completion of their Programme.*

	1997	1998	1999
Employment	39	38	36
Apprenticeship/Trade courses	17	31	28
PLC courses	32	22	23
Seeking work	6	4	4
Unknown	6	5	8

The LCA has received very positive evaluations, particularly from the students who take the course (Trant, 1999). In particular, the students seem to benefit from the module approach with its continuous assessment component, particularly the attempts to develop their own projects. Teachers too have enjoyed the cross-curricular projects, and the flexible approach to module design and active learning methodologies. In the delivery of the LCA, particular attention has been paid to developing a level of esteem among employers for the vocational skills learnt on the programme. To a large extent, this has been successful, although there has been a sense that perhaps this programme might lead young people into a non-productive blind alley, because of the lack of recognition of many modules for entry into further education. However, linking the LCA with other certification programmes has ensured that there are some pathways open to students into further education, and these pathways are being used by students (Table 7.6). A quarter of the cohort proceed to PLC courses, with the option of going on to third level, particularly in the Institutes of Technology. Approximately two thirds of the LCA cohort go straight into employment, apprenticeships or trade-linked courses. Thus, the LCA makes a more direct connection with the world of work than any of the other programmes. However, the underlying philosophy maintains a flexible and general approach to the skills developed, hoping that students may be able to transfer these skills to a variety of different opportunities in later life.

7.4 Summary

The development of Irish education at post-primary level has focused mainly on the development of a general curriculum for compulsory education. Vocational preparation has been seen mainly as "capacity building" through general skills, rather than manpower development through specific skills. Job related skills have been associated with post-compulsory schooling, or as second-chance education.

In the initial stages of the development of the Irish system, there was a distinct vocational track, although this could be thought of more as a non-academic general education rather than a work-related training. Since the mid 1960s, an attempt has been made to integrate vocational elements into a general curriculum for all students, although in recent years, distinct vocational programmes have emerged in the post-primary system. This has led to a greater degree of flexibility and creativity in curriculum design, especially in the area of linking schools with the world of work. Historically, however, the academic culture is very strong in schooling in Ireland. The attempt to develop a more flexible and integrated approach has also shown the tendency to "colonise" the vocational approach and adapt it to support the aims of an academic programme. Work experience and vocational preparation tend to be seen more as part of the process of personal career decision-making rather than training for a particular type of work resulting from a career choice. The policy of retaining a high level of general education in all programmes, and integrating a vocational element into that experience, aims to develop skills and perspectives that are transferable to a number of different vocational areas. Where specific skills have been taught, vocational education has been associated with low-achieving students often in the lower socio-economic groups, and hence has suffered from a lack of esteem. As Ireland has not had a strong industrial infra-structure, the place of these skills in the economy have not been widely appreciated. In more recent years, the focus on a specific vocational development has centred on Post-Leaving Certificate courses and third-level institutions, particularly in support of a highly successful service sector.

References

Breen, R. (1986). *Subject Availability and Student Performance in the Senior Cycle of Irish Post-Primary Schools*. Dublin: Economic and Social Research Institute.

Coolahan, J. (1981). *Irish Education: history and structure*. Dublin: Institute of Public Administration.

Lee, J.J. (1989). *Ireland 1912-1985. Politics and Society*. Cambridge University Press.

Lynch, K. (1999). *Equality in Education*. Dublin: Gill and MacMillan.

Ó Buachalla, S. (1988). *Education Policy in Twentieth Century Ireland*. Dublin: Wolfhound Press.

Trant, A. (Ed.) (1999). *Reconciling Liberal and Vocational Education*. Dublin: Curriculum Development Unit.

Tuohy, D. (1998). *Demand for Third Level Places. Interests, Fields of Study and the Effect of the Points System on the Application Process for 1997*. Commission on the Points System. Research Paper No. 1. Dublin: Government Publications.

Tuohy, D., & Doyle, E. (1994). New Directions in Irish Secondary Education. *Studies, 83*, (332), 436-446.

Whyte, J.H. (1971). *Church and State in Modern Ireland 1923-1970*. Dublin.

CHAPTER 8

From a unified to a flexible vocational system: the Hungarian transition case

LÁSZLÓ ZACHÁR

8.1 Introduction

THE AIM OF THIS CHAPTER is to demonstrate the process of changing the vocational system in Hungary before and after the political change of regime. The main focus is on the theme of flexibility; how the VET system functioned before the nineties, and how it has adopted a new structure and content, as a consequence of the economic changes.

The chapter has three parts. The first explores the main characteristics of the VET system before the political change of regime in the frame of the former socialism. The second part describes the transformation of the VET system, and from this I stress the various developments which have provided answers to the different challenges, e.g. the institutional, structural, and content reforms of VET. The third part summarises directions that can solve the present problems.

8.2 The main characteristics of political-economic transformation before the 1990s and after

Hungary has a long-established record of gradual economic reform, resulting in rapid economic growth, combined with increasing macroeconomic stability. The gradual process of democratisation and economic liberalisation, initiated as early as the 1960s, has led to a higher degree of consensus about the directions of reform than that observed in other Central European countries. In the late 1980s, a Communist Party-led government initiated the political reforms, including free and democratic parliamentary elections, which it had tried so long to avoid. Economic reforms were accompanied by a gradual opening up of the economy to western markets. The increasing liberalisation of academic research, education, and culture led to the development of Hungarian civil organisations and, in some cases, the establishment of new political parties. Changes in economic and social policy were also supported by a gradual decentralisation of public administration - first to the local level, and more recently, by the setting up of a new regional administrative infrastructure (OECD, 1999).

The transitional reforms were better prepared and more advanced, as a result of a number of economic and institutional reforms. Their main impact was: the achievement of some degree of decentralisation; the beginning of a reduction in the role of the State; the emergence of a private sector; agriculture becoming quite prosperous and competitive; the economy becoming more open than others to the outside world and being managed by a young generation of technocrats.

W. J. Nijhof et al. (eds.), Shaping Flexibility in Vocational Education and Training, 113-126.

Openness to the outside world, and a relatively high degree of freedom of opinion had contributed to Hungary maintaining its high level of research in fields such as economics and sociology, which, in turn, had an impact on the transformation of public opinion.

The above-mentioned conditions may have contributed to the very rapid pace of privatisation in the 1990s, and the fact that the role of foreign investment in Hungary during that decade was considerably greater than in other Central European countries. A number of multinational firms are now operating in Hungary in very modern plants.

Besides the favourable changes, unfavourable ones have occurred too, similar to those in other Central European countries. Gross Domestic Product (GDP), for example, dropped by almost a fifth during the first three years; the level of per capita income decreased significantly, while the budget deficit worsened to a considerable extent. In 1995, a stabilisation programme was adopted, designed to restore the macroeconomic balance and to accelerate the pace of reform and privatisation. Among the changes in the economy, restructuring the labour market is of major importance, above all, the quantitative and qualitative (vocational) composition of the workforce. The key problem is whether the labour market is able to 'cope' with these economic challenges, in terms of flexibility.

8.3 The change in the demand for education and training

In the experimental transitional models in the countries of Central Eastern Europe, the economic change is a determinative process, especially its structure, speed, and social influence.

One of the main changes is that a considerable rearrangement has taken place among the branches of the national economy. These trends had started long before 1989, but during the period of transition, they accelerated. The change in the employment structure is the result of two factors: on the one hand, the liquidation, slimming down, or consolidation of state-owned companies, and, on the other, the establishment of new companies. As a consequence of all this – as seen in Table 8.1 – the structure of employment in the Hungarian economy has been completely restructured.

Table 8.1 *Changes in the distribution of employment by sectors in %.*

Branch	1985*	1990	1995	1999
Industry and construction industry	40	36.1	32.6	34
Agriculture and forestry	25	17.5	8	7.1
Services	35	46.4	59.4	58.9
Total	100	100	100	100

Note: * = estimated data.
Source: Processes shaping labour market supply and demand. Labour Research Institute, Budapest.

At present, the evolved structure of employment in Hungary is approaching that of developed countries: agriculture 7%, industry 34%, services 59%.[1]

It is necessary, however, to make a comment on this positive change. The most significant – and emotionally most distressing – problem is that, during these changes, employment decreased. Mass unemployment rose dramatically. Unemployment, which increased with stormy rapidity at the beginning of the 90s, was a completely new phenomenon in the Hungarian economy. During the period of social, economic, and employment restructuring in 1989-1992, Hungary lost 1,174,000 jobs, which reduced full employment by 22.3% (Szép, 2000).

It is obvious that the demands in such a developing economy change rapidly, but that this cannot be followed as quickly by the school system.

One important feature for judging the flexibility of the vocational training system is the adaptation of the composition of schooling by sector to the changes in the economy and employment.

From the data in Tables 8.2 and 8.3, it can be concluded that vocational technical schools and vocational secondary schools are able to follow these new demands only slowly. There are, however, differences between these two school types.

Table 8.2 *Changes in the composition of apprentices by economic sector in %.*

Branch	1985/86	1990/91	1995/96	1999/2000
Industry and construction industry	69.5	69	67	52.4
Agriculture and forestry	8.5	8.9	7.8	9.3
Services	22	22.1	24.3	38.4
Total	100	100	100	100

Source: Labour process - Labour Research Institute, Budapest.

Table 8.3 *Changes in the composition of secondary vocational school pupils by economic sector in %.*

Branch	1985/86	1990/91	1995/96	1999/2000
Industry and construction industry	42.6	49.2	47.9	44.7
Agriculture and forestry	8.1	4.3	4.1	3
Services	49.3	46.5	48	52.4
Total	100	100	100	100

Source: Labour process - Labour Research Institute, Budapest.

The tables show that the direction of change is the same as the sectoral change in the economy: the rate of pupils has decreased in the industry/construction industry sector and increased in the service sector.

---

[1] Until 1995, the cause of the transformation, however, was not a real change, because it came from decreased employment in agriculture and industry. There was no increase in the service sector - that was thus a "mathematical" change only. Since 1995, employment has increased in absolute numbers in all sectors, the service sector being the strongest. The present situation thus shows a more real "picture".

The data in the tables reveal two main features: the more radical changes occurred in vocational technical schools, where industry is at present also within the dominant sector. Secondly, the change in the rate of secondary vocational pupils has been more gradual – except in the agricultural sector. The reason for this is that, on the one hand, a significant part of secondary qualifications has always fallen under the service sector (financial, economic, and health services), while in the field of elementary qualifications, new service trades (e.g. computer operator) have developed only in the past decade. On the other hand, the role of the secondary school is not only to provide professional training, but also to prepare pupils for higher education. Interest has therefore been greater for the professions at this educational level than at the apprentice level.

The other important question is: What qualification levels are required by the developing market economy? These numerical characteristics are shown in Table 8.4.

Table 8.4 *Employed and unemployed persons by highest educational attainment in %.*

Highest educational attainment	1993		1996		1999	
	Employed	Unemployed	Employed	Unemployed	Employed	Unemployed
< 8 grades	2.1	5.8	1.2	4.9	0.8	3.1
= 8 grades	25.2	35.8	21.4	32.9	17.6	31.2
Vocational schools	27.7	33.7	30.5	36.6	32	38.7
Secondary schools	30.1	21.3	30.7	21.5	33.1	23.8
Higher ed. institutions	14.9	3.4	16.2	4.1	16.5	3.2
Total	100	100	100	100	100	100

Source: National Central Statistic Office, Time Series. Labour Force Survey.

From the data in the table, an increasing role for higher qualification can be seen in both employment and unemployment.

The data relating to employment show that the rate of higher qualified employees has increased in the past decade, but the rate of lower qualified people has decreased. The borderline is the minimum of primary (elementary) schooling. (It can be seen, for example, that the rate for those who did not complete primary education was 0.8 % in 1999 - they scarcely feature among the employed.) At the same time, the rate of higher qualified employees has increased in all categories (vocational and secondary school and higher education institutions) and in all time series (1993, 1996, 1999).

The qualification data of the unemployed show that the rate has increased in the vocational school category, and it has on average the same value in the higher categories (secondary school and higher education institutions). If a comparison is made between the rates in the employed and unemployed categories, it can be seen that the rates of the vocational schools are greater in the unemployed categories. This comparison shows a 'protection' against unemployment as a consequence of the higher qualification.

In the past decade, the number of qualified employees has increased. One of the reasons for this positive process is the higher education of young people. The second reason is the higher qualification of former employees who have returned after unemployment with a new qualification.

The transformation of the Hungarian economy proves to be playing a positive role in higher education and qualification in employment, especially in the prevention of unemployment. On the basis of data, one part of the Hungarian labour force is recorded as complying with the higher requirements of the economy. This trend towards a higher qualification of employees can be seen as a durable one.

8.4 The change in the institutional structure

The developing market economy undermined the school system formed in the period of formal socialism. Figure 8.1 illustrates the institutional structure of education and vocational training that operated before the transitional period in Hungary. From this figure, it can be seen that after grade 8 of primary school, the system basically had three types of institutions: a 4-grade grammar school, a 4-grade vocational secondary school, and a 3-grade (or 2-grade) vocational training (apprentice) school. Two of the three provided a certificate (GCSE), the apprentice school did not.

The old system had a lot of problems. Firstly, those who had only primary school education, without a semi-skilled qualification, or skilled worker qualification without secondary education (GCSE) became more susceptible to unemployment, as can be seen in Table 8.4. The second problem was the lack of continuous schooling, because the apprenticeship schools did not provide the required knowledge base for higher education. From this, another problem arose: the apprenticeship schools (vocational training schools) became unpopular (see Table 8.5). One further problem was the lack of practical placement (workshops) and the deepening gap between the content of training and the needs of employers. Table 8.5. shows the rate of pupils within secondary educational institutions by school type.

Table 8.5 *Changes in the rate of pupils within secondary educational institutions in %.*

Academic year	Grammar school	Secondary vocational school	Apprentice school	Secondary schools Total
1985/86	24.9	30.6	44.5	100
1990/91	23.9	32.6	43.5	100
1995/96	26.6	39.4	34	100
1999/2000	28.8	47.9	23.3	100

Source: Vocational Training in Hungary 2000. E.M., Budapest.

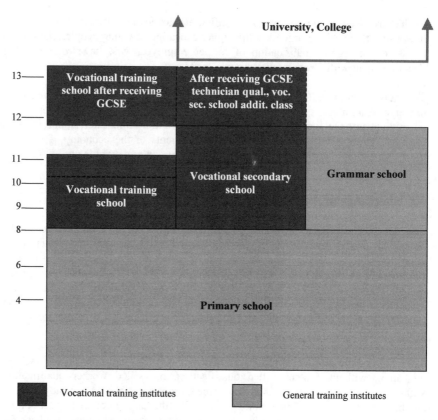

Figure 8.1 Institutional structure of education and vocational training before the transitional period in Hungary.

This reveals a continuous decrease in the pupil rate at apprentice schools: it has fallen to almost half during the past 15 years. This process has been a positive factor, because, in parallel, the rate of those pupils educated at higher level schools (grammar and secondary vocational schools) has increased. Despite this, the decrease in the number of apprentices represents a danger too, because, at the same time, there has been a continuous lack of skilled workers on the labour market in many sectors and regions.

As a result of the above-mentioned problems at the beginning of the 90s, experts were united in their opinion that the structure of VET institutions should be reformed in a way which would provide better opportunities for employment for young people and adults. A separate institutional structure is needed for the labour-market type training of adults too. The aims of the development were:

- To lengthen the duration of basic or general education;
- To increase the number of those attaining completely valuable secondary education (grammar school and vocational secondary school) (ending with a final exam, GCSE);
- To strengthen career orientation and guidance activities in schools and the career correction support of adults;

- To postpone the age when someone enters the workforce, by lengthening compulsory education or providing an opportunity for changing a career for the first time in school;
- To organise the institutional structure of vocational training outside the formal school system; so-called employment-aimed training should be assisted to a greater extent among the unemployed and those threatened by unemployment, as well as continuous training of employees (within the company);
- Finally, to elaborate and adopt a flexible vocational training system, which can create the legally guaranteed hierarchy and content for vocational qualifications, both within the school system and outside it, as well as its coordination with the professions.

In order to achieve the above policy aims and tasks, several new laws (see "references") and provisions were passed between 1991 and 1996; the main characteristics of these and their impact are summarised in the following sections.

8.5 The characteristics of the reform process

8.5.1 Changes within the school system

The 1993 Public Education Act modified both the structure of the primary and secondary school system and its main functions – including the institutional system of vocational training (see Figure 8.2).
- Maintaining the eight-grade primary school, the period of basic education was extended to the 9th and 10th grades of the secondary level of education. Completing these grades, pupils can take an examination of basic education, which is the basis for the pathways among the institutions, and the condition of entrance to ISCED 3.3 level training, the International Standard Classification of Education proposed by OECD. This classification shows the different levels of training. The 3.3 level means the accomplishment of 10th grade in any type of schools, plus the national basic examination as the entrance level to training;
- Changes in vocational education, aimed at extending the duration of education and training. The number of grades in vocational school training was increased from three to four, while at 9th and 10th grade – besides academic subjects – career orientation and vocational preparation are provided; concrete vocational training is provided at the 11th and 12th grades;
- Similarly, the vocational secondary schools only provide orientation and preparation and some basic training for a certain group of professions during the 9th–12th grades. Strict vocational training begins at the 13th and 14th grades;
- The Act raised the period of compulsory education – compulsory school attendance – from 16 to 18 years, and made it possible for students to flexibly adapt to the changed conditions, and to obtain their second vocational qualification, also with state support, tuition fee-free.

The measures described above changed the institutional structure of the vocational school system to a more differentiated and established system of pathways. The competencies of the young people became more convertible, and they were able to correct their career on the labour market.

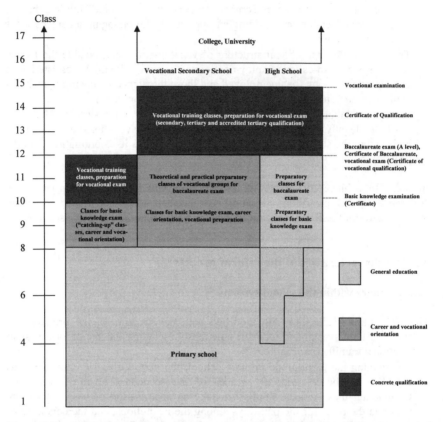

Figure 8.2 Institutional structure of education and vocational training after the transitory period in Hungary. Hungarian education and training system 2000.

8.5.2 The establishment of the "non-school type" training system

Besides school type education and training, other training systems were established (non-curricular-based, non-semester, mainly competency-based) to meet more effectively the needs of the economy and the labour market.

A four-pillar institutional structure of non-school type vocational training has been developed in Hungary since 1993. The elements of this structure are:

- A network of ten, governmentally-financed (from the central budget), regional Labour Force Development and Training centres in the seven regions and in the capital, established between 1992 and 1996, with the support of the World Bank;
- Private training provider enterprises (private ventures, small and medium-sized companies, foundations, and non-profit organisations), which are specialised in labour market/adult training. The registered number of these was 800 in 1997, and 1,500 in 2001;
- Vocational schools (financed by local authorities) which also provide non-school type training; they number 200;

- Companies (medium and large-sized), which provide continuing training on a regular basis for their own employees; their estimated number is 2,000.

The quality of training has been strengthened by official registration, which has been compulsory since 1997 for those who provide non-school type vocational training. The registration contains the programme (curriculum), the required staff, and the technical facilities of the training.

Access to training was strengthened by the 1993 Vocational Training Act, which widened the right to access to vocational training, defined the notion of vocational training and the main rules of vocational training outside the school system. According to this, training is also accepted as vocational training if it aims at the rehabilitation of the sick, the development of foreign language skills (if connected to vocational attainment), or complementary training (e.g. refresher training, job seeking, etc.). These programmes can be supported outside the school system by local labour funds.

This complex notion permitted the diversification of the training support system of the unemployed, of those threatened by unemployment, and of pre-employed young people (school-leavers), accepted by the Employment Act of 1991. It is important to mention that in Hungary the unemployed and those threatened by unemployment can obtain training offers and support from the labour centre by right of citizenship, but the person himself may also initiate a concrete training programme. Employers may also initiate retraining for their own workers, within the compass of so-called preventive training, if they are not able to employ them without training. (In this case, however, the provision of law ordains the liability of further employment for the employer.) The support may include the total costs of training, and also substitute support for wages, meals and travelling expenses.

The facilities for continuing training – the training support of employers and employees – were helped by a provisional act, passed in 1996. This act allowed the company to spend a third of its contributions from the supporting fund for training the company's own workers. The company's contribution is 0.5% of gross wages.

8.5.3 Main characteristics of non-school type vocational training

The above mentioned four-pillar non-school type training system – developed between 1993-95 – serves mainly for the training and retraining of the employable age groups. This training system is usually aligned directly to labour market demands – from employers or employees. The distribution of the trainees in a non-school type of training by the institutions (Table 8.6) illustrates that labour market training is organised mainly by profit organisations (in 1999, 60%), which can adapt flexibly to changes in demand.

It is important that the participation of non-profit organisations also increased. They trained about 1% of trainees in 1995, and by 1999 this rate had increased to 8%. (Note: the absolute number of trainees increased from 99,000 to 133,000)

Table 8.6 *Distribution of participants of the non-school type training by the economic type of provider in %.*

Provider	1995	1996	1997	1998	1999
Privat firms (profit)	52.8	52.5	55.2	55.4	60
Institutions under the central budget	21.6	24.5	21.5	22.1	18.8
Institutions coming under local authorities	12.8	10	12.3	11.2	9.3
Non profit organisations with legal entity	0.8	4.5	8.3	8.5	8.8
Other	12	8.5	2.7	2.8	3.1
Total	100	100	100	100	100

Source: Data of the non-school type vocational training. Publications of the Ministry of Education.

From the rates, it can be seen that the main providers are private firms. In 1999, they trained approx. 80,000 trainees, while central or local budget-financed institutions together trained almost 40,000. At the same time, the main topics of training focused on five professional areas between 1997-99 (see Table 8.7).

Table 8.7 *Distribution of participants of non-school type training by topic of training in %.*

Topic (qualification area)	1997	1998	1999
Economics and management	27.7	22.6	23.1
Personal services, catering, tourism	18.2	20.1	23
Computing and computer handling	17	19.3	18.4
Industrial (craft and mass production)	15	15.6	13.5
Health care	7	5.4	4
Other	15.1	17	18
Total	100	100	100

Source: Data of non-school type vocational training. Publications of the Ministry of Education.

It should be mentioned for the description of the qualification level of the workforce that 75%-85% of the trainees participated in such courses, which provided state-guaranteed qualifications during the period 1995-99.

8.6 Changes in the qualification structure

The structure of qualifications is a decisive factor of the VET system, as it determines the possibility of achievements, shows the consequences of the interdependence of qualifications and their compatibility. The new structure of vocational qualifications was defined on the basis of the Vocational Training Act and related provisions of law passed in 1993. This contains the registered vocational qualification accepted by the state, and was published in 1993 in the National Training List (OKJ). The main characteristic of the system is that professional and examination requirements are unified – independently of the provider. The minister responsible for certain qualifications is obliged to prepare and maintain these requirements, involving the representatives of the main stakeholders (tripartite system). The minister also edits the central curriculum of a certain qualification for school type training. Both in school type and non-school type training, the examination for qualification is identical.

Flexibility of access to training is optimised by the possibility of attaining a qualification in non-school type training too. Career orientation is facilitated by the OKJ, as the database contains the description of temporary jobs, and shows the proportion of theoretical and practical training time.

Since 1998, school-type accredited high level vocational qualifications have also been listed. These qualifications are based on GCSE and can be accredited during later higher education. The list can be modified annually, in accordance with the suggestion of the National Vocational Training Council (OSzT) by the Minister of Education.

Besides the appropriate institutional structure, some further key conditions for an appropriate flexibility of VET are:
- An increase in the transparency of qualifications on the basis of the similarity of training content;
- Development of a suitable choice of modular (vocational) training programmes;
- Dissemination of competence-based teaching methods;
- The introduction of special programmes for disadvantaged groups;
- Educational staff development.

The elaboration and realisation of all five groups of tasks has meant continuous developing work in the past ten years with many problems to solve. In the next section, we will go into these.

In the interests of increasing transparency, the reform of the number and structure of qualifications in the National Training List is now happening in a way that will guarantee greater flexibility, with its trade-group structure for renewing former qualifications. On the other hand, there will be so called part-trades built into the content of the basic trades – in accordance with the modular principle. The catalogue of the reduced number of qualifications granted by the state has been completed; the total number of qualifications has been reduced by approximately 30%.

The development of competence-based training methods – based on the analysis of jobs and scope of activities – has a short history of about ten years in Hungary. The development has been realised in ten regional Labour Force Development and Training Centres. The programme and curriculum-developing process is based on direct demands from the employers, and had a beneficial effect on renewing training methods. Considering so-called experimental knowledge and the acceptance of the necessity of knowledge assessment in advance, the latter will be introduced as a compulsory service – to suit the adult student.

In the interests of the effectiveness of vocational training programmes – including increasing transfer and taking prior learning into account – modular programme developments have started, which will also influence the school system, by strengthening flexible pathways, for example, widening curriculum development, modularisation, and the credit transfer system (Raffe, 1994).

The training programmes for people with reduced working abilities are financed with a higher norm by the employment centre. The continuous help for this latter stratum will be supported more vigorously by the planned Adult Training Act in the future, giving a guarantee of a state norm for labour force training. In this field, the regional Labour Force Development and Training Centres were very effective. The reason for this is not only that these institutions are supported by the state, so that the training of handicapped groups can be implemented within 'market-free' conditions, but also that the experts at these institutions first selected up-to-date methods.

The flexibility of the training staff is a basic condition for the flexibility of vocational training, and their adaptation to economic, technological and cultural developments. A system for compulsory further training was therefore initiated in Hungary in 1997, based on employer support, accredited programmes and the intensive cooperation of the higher education institutions. Meanwhile, in initial teacher training, at many universities and colleges, the topic of "the world of work" has become a part of the training: at the Technical University of Budapest: technical teacher training, at the Pécs University of Sciences: human manager training, and at the Szent István University: career guidance training. These new modules provide appropriate knowledge for students fulfilling their tasks in the development of career orientation, guidance, and correction, the modern characteristics of employees, and job seeking.

8.7 New directions and tasks of development

In the above-mentioned transformational processes, many contradictions and real problems can be seen. For example, higher qualified people with better education/training and employment positions versus lower qualified people who have reduced opportunities to find appropriate positions on the labour market and to raise a sufficient income. Many other factors too play a role in creating these problems, e.g. unsuitable social circumstances, lack of motivation, life as an unemployed person, etc. To solve the education and training problems, Hungarian experts have worked out an integrated and complex development programme for vocational and adult training, the main outlines of which are shown below:

- Motivation of adult training activities, expanding the area of the supported training into the field of general education (e.g. literacy, refresher training, preparing for vocational training, civic knowledge and competence development, etc.) and foreign language training;
- Strengthening of the equity of social groups, and the promotion of normative financial support for the training of unskilled and disadvantaged adults is needed; this support could be expanded later on for the second and further qualification. For those who cannot gain normative support, including higher education students, tax allowances must be provided;
- Promotion and strengthening of the quality of training and the further development of the existing compulsory registration of the training provider

institutions is needed, extending the registration to the institutions of the new directions (general/language training) and promoting supervision. In addition a voluntary accreditation system of institutions and programmes must be established. The state motivates the accreditation, as the trainee having the support may participate just in accredited training;

- Promotion of the development of VET contents. On the one hand, the Act would order the assessment of prior learning and the provision of different modules; on the other, it would declare the legality and equity of modular, open, and distance learning programmes;

- Last but not least, ensuring financial facilities is a key issue, which will need a unique new frame. It should control the normative state of finance – from the national budget, the training support of the unemployed – from the Labour Market Fund, and the tax allowance for those who have none of the other forms of support listed here.

These developments mean a guarantee for the promotion of the flexibility of non-school type vocational training, as they motivate the adaptation of the institutions to changing demands, ensure different resources for covering the training costs, and create interest in the development of quality assurance. In our opinion, the reformed school type education and the development of non-school type training will be able to meet the needs of the future. This will require the system to be frequently analysed, evaluated and modified.

8.8 Summary

The Hungarian vocational education and training system should meet the demands of the market economy. As demonstrated, the key issue is adaptation to the changing demands of the economy and society. As a result of this, the Hungarian VET system became more flexible step by step. The main characteristics of this are:

- Different pathways relevant to the trainee's abilities, and institutional infrastructure which can provide initial, refresher and continuing training relevant to the needs of the labour market, and a differential resource system to finance it;

- A multilevel qualification system providing multiple choices, ensuring state-guaranteed qualifications, and accepting local programmes too;

- The development of modern, effective and applicable training methods and adoption system;

- A system of assessment of prior learning.

The Adult Training Act, which was passed by Parliament at the end of 2001, provided a framework to realise the above-mentioned aims and development directions.

The continuous development work of the past ten years has resulted in a learner-centred and knowledge-based society, which is continuously evolving. The different governments - which changed after each election every four years - have contributed to these results. They have continued, fundamentally unchanged, the institutional reform of education and training and carried it out. The fact that the team of experts working in the field of directing education and vocational training has remained stable since the period of transition has played an important role in this. At the same time, it is the weaknesses that drive us to strengthen the flexibility of the VET system, as Hungary has no other fundamental reserve than the quality of its human resources.

References

OECD, (1999). *Towards Lifelong Learning in Hungary.* ISBN 92-64-17023-5
Raffe, D. (1994). The new flexibility in vocational education. In W.J. Nijhof & J.N.Streumer (Eds.), *Flexibility in training and vocational education* (pp. 13-33). Utrecht: Lemma.
Szép, Zs. (2000). *A munkaerő piac és a szakképzés kongruenciája* [The congruence of labour market and vocational training]. Budapest: Foundation "Together for the workplaces of the future".
1991. évi IV. törvény a foglalkoztatásról és a munkanélküliek ellátásáról, Budapest 1991. (Employment and assistance of unemployed people Act No. IV/1991, Budapest 1991).
1993. évi LXXIII. Törvény a közoktatásról, Budapest 1993. (Public Education Act No. LXXIII/1993, Budapest 1993).
1993. évi LXXVI. Törvény a szakképzésről, Budapest 1993. (Vocational Training Act No. LXXVI/1993, Budapest 1993).
2001. évi LI. Törvény a szakképzési hozzájárulásról, Budapest 2001. (Vocational Training Contribution Act No. LI/2001, Budapest 1996).
2001. évi CI. .Törvény a felnőttképzésről, Budapest,2001. (Adult Training Act, No.CI./2001, Budapest 2001).

CHAPTER 9

Design and effects of a flexible VET system:
a case study in Dutch agricultural education

JOS GEERLIGS AND WIM J. NIJHOF

9.1 Introduction

THE EFFECTS OF A NEW AND UNIQUE QUALIFICATION SYSTEM in the Dutch vocational system in agriculture is the main subject of this chapter. In setting up a new VET system between 1988 and 1992, policy-makers aimed at flexibility and equity as the major performance indicators of VET schools. Internal flexibility of pathways in combination with a competence-based approach was perceived as the optimal solution at the time. This chapter does not focus on learning processes, learning context or content, but on the curricular conditions to improve the flexibility and transferability of pathways at the macro and meso-level. The focus in this chapter is thus on efficiency and effectiveness indicators. This chapter is divided into four sections - the description of flexibility instruments and design characteristics; standards for measuring performance indicators; the actual measurement of flexibility in the qualification system; the analysis of the outcomes, and the evaluation.

9.2 Designing flexibility

In 1990, a new design for Agricultural VET was developed. There was an urgent need for connecting school to work to stop students dropping out, to raise their motivation, and to prove that learning at work might be as effective as formal learning in school. These initiatives were to have far-reaching consequences for the design of curricula, for pedagogy, for learning processes, and for the outcomes (Geerligs, 1999). New conditions were formulated for apprenticeship settings, in terms of quality, coaching and the guiding of students.

The design of the new system was primarily competence-based and performance-driven - a major trend at the beginning of the nineties. At the same time, the systems design became more responsive and flexible, in terms of horizontal and vertical opportunities (Nijhof, Kieft & Van Woerkom, 2001). Two pathways were designed: a full-time school-oriented pathway, and a dual track. Students could move either way between these pathways. Even free space for school teams (20% of curriculum time) to plan the content of the curriculum as specifically as possible was a sign of the flexibility approach related to the growing relative autonomy of schools. Upstreaming and downstreaming facilities for students were also optimised, by using the common core principle in educational profiles and units in different pathways (Geerligs, 1999; Lazonder, 1998).

The transforming process required new professional roles and competencies of teachers. The teacher of traditional subjects might not have been used to this

127

W. J. Nijhof et al. (eds.), Shaping Flexibility in Vocational Education and Training, 127-148.
© 2002 *Kluwer Academic Publishers. Printed in the Netherlands.*

approach. (Kieft & Nijhof, 2000). Modularisation might also enhance flexibility of educational objectives. At the macro-level, the curriculum formats were standardised and made more flexible (Nijhof & Streumer, 1994; Raffe, 1994). The fact that the QS (Qualification System) linked the content of education with part-time and full-time training, with short pathways at four qualification levels might improve the opportunities to select the optimal route. With respect to school organisation, the modularisation of programs might increase the flexibility of the school and learning. Modularisation was also expected to promote the flexibility of pathways at meso-level, by applying the principle of commonality, i.e. using the same modules in different educational profiles. The principle of commonality was to reduce duplication when students changed programs, lower the number of unqualified early leavers, and increase the flexibility of the school organisation. Problems between structure and flexibility were seen at all levels of the system: for instance, those related to the decontextualisation of the learning processes, integration of work and learning, modularisation of the curriculum, and commonality as a means of transfer and efficiency. A QS was therefore to contain as little guidance on structure as possible.

The thesis was that the new QS would create optimal conditions at the systems level for improved internal flexibility, enabling more students to qualify in a shorter time. The new QS also assigned complete occupational divisions to Institutes of Agricultural Education (IAE), and four qualification levels to IAE's, with a reference to European qualification formats, such as ISCED and SEDOC. These levels were: Q-Level 1: Start qualification (Entrant); Q-Level 2: Basic; Q-Level 3: Professional; Q-Level 4: Expert. This meant that the management and teachers at IAE's were able to allocate a student to a higher or lower-level group to match his abilities and motivation to standards. This might increase the flexibility of pathways and enable more students to leave school with a diploma. It might also decrease the length of stay at school, through greater efficiency of the learning process. The allocation of time, together with linking requirements for goals with students' characteristics, would ensure that the curriculum was more easily understood. It was expected that more students would attain a diploma in a shorter time. The use of a new taxonomy of qualifications for justifying and designing units and attainment targets could have both short-term and long-term effects on flexibility (Van de Lagemaat, 1986; Olbrich & Pfeiffer, 1980). For instance, the management of IAE's could apply the *principle of commonality* to issue a lower-level diploma to an early school-leaver, based on the political principle that no one would leave the system without an entrant or start qualification. Commonality would also increase opportunities for management to link the school and work-based programs. Consistency of the program would increase student motivation and enhance the efficiency of the learning process. Integration of subjects into units would make programs more flexible. The long-term effect might be that students would develop higher levels of cognition and transfer, and enter other occupations as well.

A second facility was that IAE's might *exempt a student* from a unit after an appropriate assessment. This facility might prevent undesirable repetition. Schools would apply it once they had a procedure for assessment, and it would then improve the efficiency of the process. An undesirable side effect was that management and students searched for exemptions.

Attainment targets with decontextualised action structures would increase the opportunities for teachers to utilise multiform practical experiences, and enable modification to meet regional and individual demand (Van de Lagemaat, 1986). Once established, it would support an individualised provision. Decontextualisation might enable general principles to be discovered and transferred. This flexibility could have a major impact on students' motivation and their cognitive skills, and might make schools more efficient (Nijhof, 2001; Soden, 1993).

9.3 Other initiatives that influenced internal flexibility

Other relevant initiatives around 1990 were the merging of schools, lump-sum funding, the normalisation and dualisation of pathways, an open legal status for teachers, and a quality-control system for the schools. Merging schools increased their size and, thereby, broadened the provision. Their larger capacity might in the long run increase their flexibility; in the short term, the advantages of scale might be thwarted by the policies of the old locations. The lump-sum funding might strengthen the advantages of scale and greater freedom, and so improve the internal efficiency of IAE's in the long term. Normalisation of pathways was an aim of the schools and might make the provision easier to understand, which, in turn, was to improve the efficiency of the IAE's. Dualisation increased the work-based component of all courses in the educational route. As a result, all students would need to stay at school longer. The effect in the short term was that more students would leave school without a diploma. Once the work-based component could be utilised in the courses, students' motivation might increase and more students attain a diploma.

The introduction of *a quality-control system* for schools tended to encourage self-reflection on all the possible changes mentioned above, since it took into account what was considered important to the new occupational divisions, the lump-sum funding, and the open legal status (Hoeben, 1993; 1997). These were all general prerequisites for the successful implementation of the new QS, and could have a considerable impact on all points of flexibility.

Swinkels-Kuijlaars & Van Wijlick (1995) concluded that the new design principles had been accepted, but that schools felt overloaded and abandoned, with problems of many kinds (Ros, Swinkels-Kuijlaars, Theunissen, Visser, Jongmans & Geijsel, 1996). The majority of teachers shared the opinion that this new qualification system (QS) facilitated the upstreaming and downstreaming of students without any loss of time. Lazonder (1998, p. 76) drew two further conclusions. Firstly, flexibility, as designed and developed in the QS, had actually been implemented in the schools. Secondly, the number of students that utilised flexibility was, however, low. Horizontal streaming - from the educational to the training route, or vice versa - did not exceed one percent per school year, while vertical streaming was only relevant as upstream within schools (4.5%). A further observation was that the utilisation of this facility was very poor. Babeliowsky (1995), De Bruijn (1992) and Raffe (1994) also observed that students did not appear to utilise the possibilities of upstreaming and downstreaming.

9.4 The desired measurements

So far, we have seen that the new QS shapes conditions and prerequisites at the macro and micro-level for the internal flexibility of the learning system, enabling more students to qualify in a shorter time. To test this hypothesis, the required and possible measurements are described below.

Increase in internal upstreaming and downstreaming
The changes in conditions for using pathways, levels and courses in students' careers before and after the implementation of the QS need to be measured. It is expected that students will utilise more pathways.

Qualified (early) school-leaving
The proportion of registered students that left school with a diploma after the implementation of the QS should be higher. The division of qualified school-leavers that qualified at the Q level of first registry or another Q level, in particular at lower levels, needs to be measured to obtain indications about the effects of upstreaming and downstreaming. An increase in qualified 'early school-leaving' is expected.

Shortening of pathways
The time students need to attain a diploma should be measured as a ratio of the normal course length before and after the implementation of the QS. The QS is expected to shorten the length of stay. The time students spend per block should be calculated, to compare the efficiency of the new pathways. It is expected that students will utilise school-time more effectively. The higher performance of the system through the accreditation of prior learning should be measured. Exemptions may pervert data about the improved outcome of schools.

9.4.1 How the flexibility of IAE's is measured

IAE's supply data each year about students under a code number to the Ministry of Agriculture (MA). The data and attainments of students have been monitored in a central electronic database, the MA register, since 1986. Cohorts in the period before the QS was implemented and before the pathways of SSAVE (Senior Secondary Agricultural Vocational Education) were normalised, are from 1987 to 1989. These three cohorts will be called Old (1987-1989). In 1990, the pathways of the educational routes were normalised and dualised, which is why students in the 1990 and 1991 cohorts experienced the dualised structure. These two cohorts will be called Dual (1990-91). Dualisation and the New QS were implemented together in 1990 in three so-called experimental 'gardens'. In 1992, the new QS became compulsory for all schools.

9.4.2 Indicators to test increased flexibility

Two indicators may measure the overall effect of flexibility: the success rate and the cost-benefit ratio. The success rate is the number of students leaving school with a diploma, expressed as a fraction of the number of students who entered that course in the first year. With a high success rate, more students obtain a diploma. The cost-benefit ratio is the number of school years students take per course year to attain a diploma. 'Are these two indicators valid criteria for the effect of the QS?' This question will be analysed below.

The success rate and the cost-benefit ratio for Dutch VET were monitored by the Central Statistical Office (CBS, 1990). Cohort data have been collected since 1975 and results were published until the school year 1988. The success rate of SSAVE has been stable during the past fifteen years and shows that between 33% and 75% of registered students gain diplomas (CBS, 1990). The success rate and cost-benefit ratio of SSAVE are relatively good, in comparison with Dutch Vocational Education in general. This favourable score is possibly due to the extra SSAVE-B pathway. Streaming is one of the areas in which education can improve (Scheerens & Bosker, 1997). From a flexibility point of view, students in SSAVE have a good chance of obtaining a diploma in a short time. As this example shows, the indicators allow a generalised conclusion on flexibility. The QS has strengthened the definition of outcome and differentiation, which is why effectiveness and efficiency were expected to improve after the implementation of the new QS. However, the two CBS indicators are interrelated, and that is a problem.

The cost-benefit ratio as defined (Kooy, 1984) is a function of the success rate. A high cost-benefit ratio may mean that everyone gains a diploma, even if some students must repeat a year; it may also mean that many students leave school without a diploma. That is why the cost-benefit ratio indicator has to be replaced by two other indicators: the relative length of stay of qualified school-leavers (LS-Q), and the relative length of stay of early school-leavers (LS-E). The relative length of stay is the ratio of registered school years to normal course years. This indicator can be calculated independently for each cluster of students in a sample. Three indicators remain, and these are clear and straightforward.

9.5 Reflections on a forerunner of dualisation: The SSAVE-B-project (1975-1985)

In this section, reflection will be given to an innovation that was introduced between 1975 and 1985. At that time the so-called SSAVE-B project was set up to enlarge and utilise work-based experiences. The SSAVE-B pathway was a specific provision to educate the 'practice-oriented successors on farms'. Much was done to improve this pathway. This project could be seen as a forerunner of modern versions of competence-based education, which has a long tradition, also in the USA (Saylor, Alexander & Lewis, 1981). The 2-year SSAVE-B had a work-based program of 12 weeks in two years, and the 3-year SSAVE-B had a work-based program of 54 weeks over three years (Table 9.1). The expansion of the work-based program was called dualisation. The pathways of the two alternatives had a similar school-based program.

Table 9.1 *The pathway structure of the 2- and 3-year SSAVE-B courses.*

	Course Time	School-based Program	Work-based Program
SSAVE-B	84 weeks over 2 years	72 weeks	12 weeks
Dualised SSAVE-B	126 weeks over 3 years	72 weeks	54 weeks

From 1975 onwards, the Minister of Agriculture encouraged the agricultural schools to change the 2-year SSAVE-B route into a 3-year dualised route. The aim was to motivate students with a linked school and work-based program, and to improve the integration of subject matter. At the end of 1984, the SSAVE-B pathway was dualised for about 40% of the schools and 50% of the students (APS, 1984).

The calculation of the success rate and the length of stay (of qualified and early school-leavers - LS-Q and LS-E) in 1987 and 1988 shows the effects of the 2-year SSAVE-B and the 3-year SSAVE-B pathway.

The students registered in the 2-year and the 3-year pathway who attained a diploma at level 3 were counted. The 3-year pathway scored a low success rate in comparison with the conventional 2-year pathway. In the 3-year pathway thus more students left school without a diploma than in the 2-year pathway (Table 9.2).

Table 9.2 *SSAVE-B outcome of the 2- and 3-year SSAVE-B entrants (87-89).*

	n		Score		
1987 – 1989	2-year pathway	3-year pathway	2-year pathway	3-year pathway	Difference
Success rate	3,293	4,040	73.5%	63.2%	10.3%*
LS-Q	2,423	2,552	1.13	1.12	0,01
LS-E	870	1,488	0.82	0.67	0,15*

* = $\alpha < 0.001$

This effect may be comparable with the low internal effectiveness of Dutch apprenticeship schemes (in 1988-1990 the average success rate for the 27 main branches was 54%). The length of stay of qualified school-leavers (LS-Q) in the 2 and 3-year pathway was the same (Table 9.2). Similar proportions of students repeated course years in the two pathways. The relative length of stay of the early school-leavers (LS-E) between the 2 and 3-year pathway differed significantly. Based on the costs of a full course of US $ 4,600[1], the total cost of early school-leaving is calculated in Table 9.3.

A comparison of total costs and losses showed that the costs of early school-leaving took up 20% and 26% respectively of the total costs of the 2 and 3-year pathways. The calculation of the financial loss, however, is not complete. The loss of motivation and costs of the student were not estimated or included. The value of a possible difference in outcome of the two pathways has not been estimated either. Nevertheless, the data about the isolated effect are straightforward, relevant and significant. The dualised pathway was expected to motivate students, rather than

---

[1]   Comparison of prices for 1998 (MA, costing unit of the Department of Science and Knowledge Dissemination).

discourage them. That is why the effect of dualisation was unexpected and disappointing. The 10-year SSAVE-B experiment did not improve effectiveness or efficiency, and the poor outcome was not reported, or even recognised. The effect is still relevant since all SSAVE pathways were dualised in 1990.

The second hypothesis to test the effects of changes in SSAVE in the early 1990s is the following. Dualisation improves students' results by shortening the length of stay and producing more qualified school-leavers. This hypothesis is likely to be rejected.

Table 9.3 *The loss in US $ of early school leaving in 2- and 3-year SSAVE-B.*

1987 - 1989	2-year pathway	3-year pathway	Difference
LS-E	0.82	0.67	
Years/early School leaver	0.82*2 = 1.64	0.67*3 = 2.01	
Costs/early School leaver	1.64*4,600 = $ 7.544	2.01*(2/3*4,600) = $ 6.164	$ 1,380
Total costs (1987 – 1989)	870*7.544 = $ 6.563.280	1488*6.164 = $ 9.172.032	

9.5.1 Data and algorithms

Utilising the MA registry data requires a comparison of the normal number of course years for a course with the actual number of school years. This comparison is the basis for calculating the indicators. A course takes 2, 3 or 4 course years in SSAVE. The number of school years differs between graduates, because of the variance in success in subsequent years. Between one school year and the next, a student is promoted to the next year (a), repeats the course (b), or leaves school with (c) or without (d) a diploma (Kooy, 1984, p. 20). The learning career of a student can be monitored with this algorithm. Figure 9.1 shows an example of progression from the first course-year.first school year (t.t) to the second course-year.second school year (t+1.t+1).

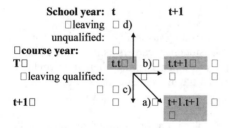

Figure 9.1 Scheme for student up and down streaming in 1st year (Kooy, 1984).

The completion of a four-year course may take six school years, since students are not allowed to repeat more than two course years. Data collected over a period of six years provides detailed information about the school careers of students of a certain cohort. The scheme as presented can be filled with absolute data (the actual number of students) or with relative data (the fraction <1 and >0). The sum of the relative data in the squares of a completed scheme gives the average total length of stay.

The application of the success rate and relative length of stay, from data in the register of the Ministry of Agriculture, is not possible without adaptations. Adaptations of conventions are needed to interpret dualised pathways in the traditional system. The algorithm is designed for a standard year-group system. The courses in SSAVE did not have the same number of course years in every school until normalisation in August 1990. Since the introduction of QS, IAE's have turned from a timetabled and year-group system and introduced, sooner or later, a unit-group system. This means that the production structure in the schools has been in transition. The degree of transition differs between schools. As a result, the registry of data depicts a degree of transition too (Table 9.4). For example, a student with 78 blocks at the beginning of the 5th school year on a full time 4-year Manager course is counted as having passed to the 4th course year because he has > 3*25 blocks.

Table 9.4 *The 'passes' in the QS, based on credits attained.*

Full qualification	Credits in full qualification / course years (Review DC '94)	Credits / course year 'new passes'
Operator	20/2	10
Supervisor	45/3	15
Manager	100/4	25

A student can be counted as a graduate when a diploma in the IAE is attained, or when the specific diploma of the course of entry is attained in the first course year. The MA register data counts any diploma attained at any IAE. When a student attains more than one diploma, the highest-level diploma counts. When his diplomas are of the same level, the first diploma counts. The logic of these choices is ruled by efficiency.

9.5.2 Algorithms of the indicators

The algorithm will be discussed for each measurement.

Increase in internal upstreaming and downstreaming
Analysis of student upstreaming and downstreaming, as in Figure 9.1, indicates the change of pathways, levels and courses in students' careers before and after the implementation of the QS. The frequency of students taking alternative routes to attain a diploma was expected to increase after the implementation of the QS.

Qualified (early) school-leaving
The ratio of registered students leaving school with a diploma before and after the implementation of the QS is calculated. Given -
N = number of students in the first year of a course (t.t in Figure 9.1)

$$R = \frac{S}{N}$$

S = number of students that qualify from the course (Σ c in Figure 9.1)

R = success rate (is the % qualified) (Kooy, 1984, p. 23) -

Qualified school-leavers that qualify in the course for which they first enrol or another course, in particular at a lower level, are identified and separated. These categories are divisions of N. The ratio of registered students leaving school with a diploma is also measured before and after the dualisation of the educational route. In 1990, all schools started with dualised pathways. A few 'experimental garden' IAE's started in 1990 with the QS. The majority of the IEA's, however, started with the QS in 1992. This difference in take-up is used to separate the dualisation effect. The higher performance of the system due to the improved effectiveness of courses and also the certification of early school-leavers (with a lower grade diploma) and by exemptions is measured in the database.

Shortening of stay in pathways

The time students need to attain a diploma is calculated. Given -

J_s = total number of actual school years of all qualified school-leavers

(Σ -.t+n (n=0, n=∞) for qualified school-leavers in Figure 9.1);

C = the normal number of course years;

E_s = relative length of stay of qualified school-leavers (LS-Q).

$$E_s = \frac{J_s}{S * C}$$

E_s is compared before and after the implementation of the QS, and the dualisation effect can be separated as described above. In addition, the performance of early school-leavers is calculated. Given -

J_{n-s} = total number of school years of all early school-leavers;

E_{n-s} = relative length of stay of early school-leavers (LS-E) -

$$E_{N-S} = \frac{J_{N-S}}{(N - S) * C}$$

The MA register can also be used without application of the algorithms above. This has been done, for example, for comparing the average time students at levels 1, 2 and 3 spend per block. This provides a test of the actual credits students attained per year. The number of exemptions given to students has also been taken from the MA register without application of the algorithms.

9.6 Desired standards of flexibility of schools

The initiatives in SSAVE with an expected short-term impact on the flexibility of the IAE's have been described in section 9.2. Indicators were designed to measure the degree to which more students attain a diploma in a shorter time. The assumption is that positive scores are signs of flexibility. How are these scores to be weighed precisely?

The problem is that no hard standards are available to weigh the scores. SSAVE scored well in comparison with other Dutch VET, thus the best standard is an improvement on one's own performances in the past. As a consequence, the scores of SSAVE from before 1990 are compared with those of SSAVE from 1990 onwards.

9.6.1 Measuring flexibility

Collecting data is routine for IAE's and the Ministry of Agriculture. The Ministry supplied the data to calculate upstreaming and downstreaming, success rate and length of stay. The developed algorithms were run. The next section discusses the objects, standards and procedures of the measurements. Three comparisons of data were made. First, the increased internal upstreaming and downstreaming was analysed, followed by qualified (early) school-leaving and, finally, the shortening of stay in pathways.

9.6.2 Upstreaming and downstreaming

The hypothesis is that the QS will intensify upstreaming and downstreaming. In the MA register, it was observed that vertical streaming in S-SSAVE (Q-level 2) was rare; 4 students (< 0,25%) of the 1987-1989 cohorts (n = 1869), streamed up to SSAVE-B. This changed after the implementation of the QS. In the 1992 cohort (n = 760), 137 level-2 students (19,4%) streamed up: about 100 times more.

The learning paths of the 762 students were analysed with the help of the student streaming scheme (Figure 9.2). A rich pattern of upstreaming and downstreaming was observed. The majority of the students (623) stayed in the level-2 pathway, a minority (139; 22.3%) streamed up. Some level-2 students (39) changed in the second year to the level-3 (Supervisor) pathway, others (94) in the third year.

Of the stayers (77.7%), 46 % attained a diploma, and of the streamers (22.3%), 12%. The altricials and the nidifugous were equally successful (> 50%). In Figure 9.2, the students of the Operator cohort of 1992 utilised 19 routes in different combinations and length of stay. The utilisation of routes (averages of 3, 2, or 1 cohort) is summarised in Table 9.5.

1st year	2nd year	3rd year	4th year	5th year	n	Sub totals
Operator					219	
	Operator				352	
		Operator			50	
			Operator		2	623
			Supervisor	Manager	1	
		Supervisor			43	
			Supervisor		39	
				Operator	1	
				Supervisor	9	
				Manager	1	94
		Manager	Manager		1	
				Manager	1	2
	Supervisor				4	
		Supervisor			25	
			Supervisor		6	
			Manager		1	
				Manager	3	39
	Manager	Manager	Manager		3	
				Manager	1	4
Total					762	762

Figure 9.2 The routes of the 1992 cohort in the Operator pathway.

Table 9.5 *Utilised routes by first entries in SSAVE.*

Cohorts (n=) All IAE's	Old (87-89) n = 3	Dual (90-91) n = 2	QS (92) n = 1
Level 2	5.7	12.0	19.0
Level 3	24.0	28.5	30.0
Level 4	25.0	25.5	27.0

Before the dualisation initiative, on average 5.7 pathways were utilised by the 1987-1989 cohorts. For early school-leavers, one, two or three school years are counted as three different routes. The average in the dualisation period (1990-1991) was 12 routes for Operators. The analysis shows an increase in the number of routes used. At level 2 (S-SSAVE), the 1987-1989 cohorts only used the S-SSAVE pathway with different lengths of stay. The QS changed this. Many more routes are used at level 2 and 3. The observation is a relevant increase in internal upstreaming and downstreaming. These observations do not match the conclusions of Lazonder (1998) that vertical streaming does not exceed 4.5%. A different basis for analysis may explain the different conclusion. It is likely that differences can be explained by differences in the datasets. The MA register is based on records supplied by schools, with reference to unique student numbers - no student can be forgotten, no one can be counted twice. Lazonder used an inquiry[2] addressed to the school management. It is likely that unless teachers and managers consult the registry system of the school for the inquiry, they will underestimate vertical streaming in the school. The QS

---

[2] The inquiry was held in March 1997 about the school year 1995-1996.

138 Jos Geerligs and Wim Nijhof

enhances upstreaming and downstreaming. The question is, however, whether the increased streaming opportunities have improved the effectiveness of IAE's.

9.6.3 Qualified (early) school-leaving

On the basis of the design principles of flexibility as portrayed in section 9.2, the thesis is that the QS will enhance qualified school-leaving. The development of the success rate between 1987 and 1993 has been analysed from the MA register. The results are given at qualification levels 2, 3 and 4 for all IAE's and for the three experimental 'all gardens' (Table 9.6).

Before the implementation of the changes in SSAVE, the average success rate for all IAE's was 72.23 %. SSAVE-A, at level 4, had a high score (77.72 %). The success rate was low at Q-level 2, and gradually increased at levels 3 and 4. A possible explanation for the different scores is that SSAVE-A was the pathway with the best status and was attractive to teachers. In addition to that, students with insufficient ability or motivation were placed in the SSAVE-B pathway, and after 1983 also in the S-SSAVE pathway.

The 1987-1989 cohorts of the 'all gardens' showed a pattern similar to other schools. The 'all gardens' scored better than SSAVE on average (with the exception of the lower S-SSAVE pathway, with a score of 36.42% of students attaining a diploma). Better schools may pick up improvements faster (Van Gennip, 1991). Before 1990, the success rate at the higher levels in SSAVE was better than at Q-level 2 ($\alpha < 0.001$); in 'all gardens' the difference exceeds a factor 2.

Table 9.6 *Success rate development in SSAVE between 1987 and 1993 in %.*

Innovations Levels	old (87-89)	dual (90-91)	QS (92)	Difference dual-old	Difference QS (92)- old	Difference QS (92)- dual
All IAE's	72.23	64.79	70.41	-7.4 **	-1.8	+5.6**
Q-level 2	55.27	43.84	53.86	-11.5 **	-1.4	+10.0**
Q-level 3	70.11	64.19	69.80	-5.9 **	-0.3	+5.6**
Q-level 4	77.72	72.38	75.38	-5.3 **	-2.3	+3.0*
All gardens	75.63	68.56	75.24	-7.1 **	-0.4)	+6.78*
Q-level 2	36.42	38.97	52.34	+2.6	+15.9*	+13.4
Q-level 3	74.42	66.48	70.47	-7.9 *	-4.0	+4.0
Q-level 4	80.85	77.10	81.46	-3.7	+0.6	+4.2

* $\alpha < 0.05$

**$\alpha < 0.001$

The first change for all schools was the dualisation of pathways. The success rate of the 1990 and 1991 cohorts dropped significantly by 7.4 percentage points. This is a severe decline in student performance.

The effects are difficult to explain. The school and work-based components and pedagogy hardly changed because of the dualisation initiative, and one would have expected no change in the success rate. However, at Q-level 2 the change in the success rate was large and significant in all IAE's (- 11.5 %). The drop in the success rate after the dualisation initiative was almost the same for all IAE's and for the experimental 'all gardens'. The implementation of dualisation had a direct, significant and negative effect on the success rate of students. The second hypothesis was not confirmed: dualisation does not improve students' results.

The second change in SSAVE came when the QS became compulsory for all IAE's in 1992. Data for the 1992 cohort showed a *significant recovery* of the average success rate of students from all IAE's. The difference between the old 1987-1989 cohort and the QS 1992 cohort, however, is not significant. The explanation of the improvement is not easy. It might be attributed to the implementation of the QS. It is not very likely that the cause of recovery is dualisation. It would be in contrast with the observation in the 1987-1989 cohorts of the 2 and 3-year SSAVE-B course (Table 9.6), where 15 years after dualisation there is still a large difference in success rates. The recovery is more likely to be due to the new QS.

Lower levels appear to be more subject to unqualified school-leaving than does level 4. An analysis of early and nonqualified school-leavers in the first year of entry shows the effects of dualisation and of QS, and it eliminates the effect of course duration. That is why a comparison was made of the early, nonqualified (ENQ) school-leavers in the year of enrolment.

Table 9.7 shows that early, nonqualified school-leavers in the first year of entry at Q-level 2 are the most vulnerable (over 20% ENQ school-leaving) and particularly the most vulnerable to change (the largest increase in ENQ school-leaving due to dualisation, 5.4%). This vulnerability is also visible at level 3, but is far less pronounced. The change in ENQ school-leaving is significant at level 4. This was possibly due to the fact that in a level-4 course it became slightly more difficult to attain 100 credits at a relatively high pace in 1992. Dualisation makes the pathways longer and may force a no-go decision at an earlier stage; this should result in a shorter length of stay.

Table 9.7 % ENQ school-leaver in year of registry between 1987 and 1993.

Levels	Innovations	Old (87-89)	Dual (90-91)	QS (92)	Dual-old	QS-old	QS-dual
All IAE's							
Q-level 2		21.6	26.9	28.0	+5.4*	+6.4*	+1.0
Q-level 3		16.2	17.2	15.3	+1.0	-0.9	-2.0
Q-level 4		9.8	11.6	12.2	+1.8*	+2.4*	0.6

* $\alpha < 0.05$

9.6.3.1 Qualified early school-leavers

Further analysis should reveal whether 12.5% ENQ school-leaving in the first year is acceptable in an overall picture. This analysis can also help to test the hypothesis about the increase in internal flexibility due to the QS; particularly the effect of increased upstreaming and downstreaming on qualified school-leaving.

Table 9.8 gives a breakdown of the success rate. The first column approaches the success rate from an entry-level starting point. The qualification level is given for each entry. When more diplomas have been attained, only the highest diploma level is counted.

Table 9.8 *Composition of the success rate between 1987 and 1993 in %.*

Innovations Levels	Old (87-89)					Dual (90-91)			Difference dual - old for regular	QS (92)				Difference QS - old for regular
Diploma level: Entry level:	Tot. %	2	3	4	Tot. %	2	3	4		Tot %	2	3	4	
All IAE's	72	4	31	37	65	6	27	32		70	7	29	34	
Q-level 2	55	**55**	0	0	44	**41**	3	0	-14.1**	54	**43**	10	1	-12.6**
Q-level 3	70	0	**68**	2	64	0	**58**	6	-10.3**	70	4	**60**	6	-7.6**
Q-level 4	78	0	7	**71**	72	0	10	**62**	-9.0**	75	0	14	**61**	-9.7**
Garden c	72	1	33	38	79	7	37	35		80	9	33	38	
Q-level 2	24	**24**	0	0	62	**52**	10	0	27.9*	70	**61**	9	0	36.4*
Q-level 3	72	0	**68**	4	81	2	**70**	9	1.7	76	8	**68**	0	0.1
Q-level 4	77	0	3	**74**	81	0	17	**64**	-10.2	85	0	18	**67**	-7.7

* $\alpha < 0.05$
** $\alpha < 0.001$

The negative effect of dualisation in all IAE's on the success rate of diplomas attained at the level of entry is significant. The QS hardly compensates for the losses; the negative and significant effect on the success rate persists for diplomas attained at the level of first entry. This means that the compensating effect of the QS observed in Table 9.8 is mainly due to diplomas attained after streaming - thus an effect of commonality. 'Garden c' shows a remarkably better effect, probably due to the QS, at level 2 and 3 for diplomas attained at the level of first entry. The diplomas attained at the level of first entry do not differ much between the *1987-1989 cohorts of all IAE's* and *the 1992 cohort of 'garden c'*. Most of the extra in 'garden c' results from upstreaming and downstreaming, particularly at level 4.

A focus on the upstreaming and downstreaming effects of dualisation and QS initiatives yields the following. For the 1987-1989 cohorts, entry level 2 qualifies only at level 2; level 3 has 3% qualifying above their entry level and none below; level 4 has 10% qualifying below entry level. This situation hardly changed after dualisation in 1990-1991. After the QS initiative, however, the upstreaming and downstreaming yielded significantly more qualifications. In the 1992 cohort the upstream from Q-level 2 to Q-level 3 was considerable; 10 out of 54 is around 18.5% of the level-2 entrants that attained a level-3 diploma. It is likely that students were placed more easily in the level-2 stream than before. This would explain the increase in numbers of students and also the upstream. The 20% upstream, however, represents smaller numbers of students than needed to explain the improved success rate (for example, in 'garden c'). Therefore, it is likely that the QS improved the entire pedagogic climate of the level-2 pathway. The QS increased upstreaming of level-2 entries and enhanced significantly qualification at higher levels (support for the first hypothesis). This effect was probably due to the commonality of full qualifications.

In the 1992 cohort, the significant numbers streamed down from level 3 to level 2; 4 % out of 70% of qualifiers at level 2, and even in the 'garden c' 8% out of 76%. This is a clear result of commonality. The number of level-3 entries that attained a level-4 qualification, increased significantly from 2 to 6 percentage points; the successful upstreaming and downstreaming was about 10%.

In the 1992 cohort, the downstream at level 4 had also grown to a significant 14% out of 75% of qualifiers at level 3, and in 'garden c' as many as 18% out of 85%. This again was a clear result of commonality.

These observations put the recovery from the dualisation initiative into perspective. Since the dualisation initiative, the number of students at level 4 failing to qualify in the pathway of entry, has grown substantially. In the 1987-1989 cohorts, 71% of the level-4 entries attained a diploma at that level. After dualisation in 1990 and 1991, this dropped to 62%. After the QS initiative in 1992, the success rate was 61%. For 'all IAE's' these changes are significant. With regard to the attainment of a qualification in the pathway of entry, the decrease due to dualisation was > 10%. This is in line with the observations in the 2 and 3- year SSAVE-B project. The conclusion is that the new QS has improved the flexibility of SSAVE and restored the success rate. The negative effect of the dualisation initiative is offset by the diplomas attained at levels other than the level of first entry. A further conclusion was that of the 1987-1989 1993 cohorts, 50% of the NQ school-leavers left school in the first year. Thus, the ratio of NQ school-leaving between the first year and the following years did not change due to dualisation and QS implementation.

In comparison, De Bruijn (1997, p. 298) concluded that in VET in general the flexible curriculum structure had a negative influence on the success rate. In contrast, the observation in this study was that the introduction of the QS had a positive impact on the success rate. This effect was probably due to the kind of integration of this pathway in the system. It was likely that in the general vocational education system the isolated position of dualisation and the way it was utilised by schools had greater negative effects than De Bruijn had observed.

9.6.3.2 Shortening of stay in pathways

Another aspect of testing the hypotheses on QS and dualisation is their effect on the length of stay, which was supposed to be shortened by the initiatives. The central question in this section is 'Are students attaining their diplomas in a shorter time?'

The development of the length of stay was analysed separately for qualified and nonqualified school-leavers between 1987 and 1993. The length of stay is the ratio between school years and normal course years. In Table 9.9, it can be seen that of the 1987-1989 cohorts, the nonqualified school-leavers at level 2 had a length of stay of 0.83, and the qualified school-leavers 1.07. This means that on average a nonqualified school-leaver stays at school for 2 * 0.83 = 1.66 years before leaving without a diploma. The qualified school-leaver in the 1987-1989 cohorts stayed on average 2 * 1.06 = 2.12 years.

The comparison of the 1987-1989 cohorts with the 1990-1991 cohorts shows that the dualisation measure, which led to an absolute increase in the length of stay, significantly shortened the relative length of stay. The 1990-1991 cohorts in the 'gardens' also showed a significant decrease in the length of stay - this decrease was about a factor 3 greater than in 'all IAE's' (all IAE's totalled: -0.03/-0.01 and all gardens totalled: -0.08/-0.03). Shortening the length of stay by nonqualified school-leavers was about a factor 3 greater and more significant than that of qualified school-leavers.

In the 1992 cohort, except for level 2, a significant, continued and gradual decrease in the length of stay was observed in all schools, and in the three 'gardens'. This change due to the QS was about 3 times greater than the change due to dualisation. These observations support the assumption that the decrease in the length of stay was mainly attributable to the implementation of the QS.

Table 9.9 *The length of stay in pathways in SSAVE between 1987 and 1993.*

	Old (87-89) diploma: n/y	Dual (90-91) diploma: n/y	Difference dual-old	QS (92) Diploma: n/y	Difference QS (92)-old	Difference QS (92)-dual
All IAE's	0.69/1.09	0.67/1.08	-0.03*/-0.01*	0.61/1.04	-0.09**/-0.06**	-0.06**/-0.05**
Q-level 2	0.83/1.07	0.83/1.10	-0.01/-0.04*	0.74/1.09	-0.10**/-0.03	-0.09**/-0.01
Q-level 3	0.69/1.13	0.65/1.11	-0.04*/-0.02*	0.64/1.08	-0.05*/-0.05**	-0.01/-0.03**
Q-level 4	0.64/1.07	0.57/1.06	-0.07**/-0.01	0.52/1.00	-0.12**/-0.08*	-0.06**/-0.07**
All gardens	0.69/1.09	0.62/1.06	-0.08**/-0.03**	0.52/1.01	-0.17**/-0.08**	-0.09*/-0.06**
Q-level 2	0.84/1.03	0.79/1.04	-0.04/0.01	0.81/1.12	-0.02/0.09*	0.02/0.07*
Q-level 3	0.69/1.11	0.65/1.08	-0.04/-0.03	0.49/1.06	-0.20**/-0.05*	-0.16*/-0.03
Q-level 4	0.65/1.08	0.46/1.05	-0.18**/-0.03*	0.40/0.97	-0.25**/-0.11**	-0.06/-0.08**
Garden c	0.63/1.07	0.45/1.04	-0.18**/-0.03	0.48/0.95	-0.15*/-0.11**	0.03/-0.09**
Q-level 2	0.84/1.00	0.72/1.03	-0.12/0.03	0.71/1.07	-0.12/0.07	-0.00/0.05
Q-level 3	0.57/1.10	0.39/1.05	-0.18*/-0.05	0.44/1.05	-0.13/-0.05	0.05/0.06
Q-level 4	0.63/1.03	0.37/1.03	-0.26**/0.00	0.42/0.88	-0.21*/-0.15**	0.05/-0.14**

* $\alpha < 0.05$
** $\alpha < 0.001$

The experimental gardens showed a significantly stronger progression in the decrease in the length of stay in their third year of QS than did all IAE's in their first year. The approval of the hypothesis that QS, and to a minor extent dualisation, shortens the length of stay in schools applies to qualified and to early school-leavers.

9.6.3.3 The relevance of the change in the success rate and length of stay

Before a further analysis is made of the change in the length of stay, first an explanation of the relevance of the measured changes will be given. This is why the set of available data from the tables presented was used to calculate a very tangible entity: the cost of the diploma for one set of entrants. For the comparison, the number, success rate and length of stay of all students need to be taken into account. The data for the example with level-4 students is collated in Table 9.10. The cost of one school year is US $ 4,600, and on that basis the total costs for one diploma is calculated. The total cost of qualified students is the product of registered students, success rate, course years, length of stay (yes) and US $ 4,600. The total cost of nonqualified students is the product of registered students, 1 - success rate, course years, length of stay (no) and US $ 4,600. The cost of qualified plus nonqualified students devised by the product of registered students and success rate provides the cost per qualified entry.

Table 9.10 *The costs of qualified Q-level-4 entries in the educational route.*

All IAE's	Old (87-89)	Dual (90-91)	QS (92)
Students that registered at Q-level 4	8.588	4.367	2.762
Success rate (all qualifications)	77.7%	72.4%	75.3%
Length of stay (no/yes qualified)	0.64/1.07	0.57/1.06	0.52/1.00
Total cost qualified students	$ 131.4*10^6	$ 61.6*10^6	$ 38.3*10^6
Total cost non-qualified students	$ 22.5*10^6	$ 12.7*10^6	$ 6.5*10^6
Total cost of the cohort at Q-level 4	$ 153.9*10^6	$ 74.3*10^6	$ 44.8*10^6
Cost per qualified 'Q-level 4 entry'	$ 23,060	$ 23,510	$ 21,520

Both the success rate and the length of stay determine the costs. At the systems level, the dualisation initiative (1990 - 1991) increased the costs to qualify a level-4 entry by ($ 23,060 - $ 23,510 =) $ 450. The costs of the declining success rate (77.7% - 72.4%) of 5.3 percentage points were compensated by a decrease in the length of stay (0.64/1.07 - 0.57/1.06 =) 0.07/0.01 points. The cost of a diploma at level 4 did not change much between 1987 and 1993 - an actual decrease of 2 %.

The product of success rate and length of stay provided an overall effect of these initiatives, and allowed the conclusion that the QS enhances success rate and shortens the length of stay. The combination of these effects results in significant improvements in the efficiency of the system.

The second conclusion is that dualisation decreases the success rate severely and shortens the length of stay slightly. The combination of these effects leaves the efficiency of the system unchanged. The changes are relevant - the three 'gardens' show that a cost reduction at the systems level of between 10% and 20% is a realistic target.

9.6.3.4 Possible explanations for the changes in length of stay

The development of the length of stay was analysed by means of data at the level of units and blocks. The source document was the MA register. The normal number of credits that a student should attain per school year is given in Table 9.11. For each level of the educational route, the total of units attained and the total of students registered at each level is taken (LNV, 1998). The division of the two provides the actual credits attained per student per school year.

Table 9.11 *Credits attained per student per school year in educational route.*

School years:	92-93	93-94	94-95	95-96	96-97
Operator (Q-level 2)	10.7	11.9	11.9	12.1	12.4
Supervisor (Q-level 3)	15.3	15.1	15.3	15.9	16.5
Manager (Q-level 4)	22.8	23.5	24.2	26.2	25.3

The data in the table is about credits in school years. From the table it can be seen that at levels 2 and 3 (and at level 4 from 1995-1996 onwards) the credits attained per student were increasing. This means, theoretically, that all students could have attained a diploma with an average length of stay < 1. Neither of the two is true - the success rate was not 100% and the length of stay at the system level was > 1. This means that students left school with certificates, but without a diploma. The data in Table 9.11 suggest that there was hardly any waste in the IAE. That means that all the waste measured (diploma costs, calculated at an annual cost of US $ 4,600, higher than $ 9,200, $ 13,800 and $ 18,400 for level 2, 3 and 4 respectively) is 'a qualification at the certificate level' (and not at the diploma level).

Many school-leavers with certificates do not lack ability, but leave school for different reasons. One traditional reason may be that the leaver changed his/her mind; he/she may go to another school or to employment for reasons that the system is familiar. Another reason is that the school-leaver is acting as a customer and a selective shopper. This possibility is not characteristic, but is a phenomenon observed in the IAE's.

Although the traditional teacher may not be happy with this development, it is certainly a sign of flexibility and of service to the client. The positive interpretation of the observed development would mean that the effect of the QS initiative is underestimated by considering success rate and length of stay measured only at diploma level. The full effect of the QS initiative can also be measured at the level of certificates or credits.

9.6.4 Effects of exemptions on the length of stay

The assumption was that students in the educational route would have a surplus of competence greater than the required basic units. As a consequence, schools should be keen to apply exemptions. The hunt for exemptions, however, could decrease the attainment levels and debase the system – not if the student is being given credit for previous attainment. Exemptions have been included in the count of units attained and certificates awarded, which is why they are counted separately.

The 325 level-2 students of the 1992 cohort attained 2,795 blocks in the school year 1992-1993, of which 22 blocks by exemptions: this is 0.8%. The analysis of the way IAE's assigned exemptions to students allows some relevant conclusions. The pattern of the assignment of exemptions in the 1992 and 1992[3] cohorts was regular (with the exception of a 12.9% peak for a small number of level-2 students in the 1992 cohort in the school year 1995-1996). Exemption was rare at level 2, and between 2% and 4% at levels 3 and 4. It is not visible from Table 9.12 that the experimental 'gardens a and b' assigned exemptions mainly at level 4, and that 'garden c' did not assign exemptions at all. 'Garden' c transformed units into weekly periods of subject matter.

---

[3] The pattern in the 1991 and 1992 cohorts is not representative of the cohorts of other years, and differences between schools are considerable. 'Garden b', for example, granted 15.7% exemptions of the total of certificates attained at level 4 in the first school year of the 1996 cohort.

Table 9.12 *The assignment of exemptions in the 1992 and 1993 cohorts.*

School year	Cohort 92				Cohort 93			
	Student	Blocks	Exemp-tions	%	Student	Blocks	Exemp-tions	%
92-93:								
Q-level 2	325	2,795	22	0.8				
Q-level 3	1,334	17,346	675	4.0				
Q-level 4	2,088	44,502	1,527	3.4				
93-94:								
Q-level 2	389	6,032	27	0.4	488	4,061	35	0.9
Q-level 3	1,346	19,835	365	1.8	1,348	17,587	494	2.8
Q-level 4	2,048	49,730	1,663	3.3	2,333	46,807	1,363	2.9
94-95:								
Q-level 2	52	637	12	1.8	569	8,839	39	0.4
Q-level 3	1,372	24,880	550	2.2	1,232	17,771	483	2.7
Q-level 4	1,686	39,631	711	1.8	1,960	47,757	1,844	3.9
95-96:								
Q-level 2	6	62	8	12.9	67	896	2	0.2
Q-level 3	239	3,399	9	0.3	1,321	24,696	103	0.4
Q-level 4	1,781	55,774	814	1.5	1,835	45,427	830	1.8
96-97:								
Q-level 2	2	22	0	-	7	96	2	2.1
Q-level 3	3	419	5	1.2	195	2,838	79	2.8
Q-level 4	264	6,715	247	3.7	1,528	44,236	841	1.9

These observations mean that exemptions, because of their infrequency, are not the cause of measured differences between the data from all IAE's, from all 'gardens' and from individual 'gardens'. Exemptions, however, were granted, and that means that the system was flexible in this respect. The length of stay of qualified and nonqualified school-leavers needs to be analysed separately. The observation is that the two indicators have dynamics of their own. The dualisation initiative of 1990 shortened the length of stay slightly and significantly. The QS initiative had a strong and significantly positive effect on the 1992 cohort. To the effect of QS on the success rate and the length of stay can be added the cost of a diploma per qualifying entrant. In 'all IAE's', 'all gardens' and individual 'gardens', all the diplomas had become less expensive.

9.7 Conclusions and discussion

This study focuses on internal flexibility as one of the key instruments to promote highly qualified and skilled workers for the future. The design of new pathways based upon competence and work-related conditions, conditions of time, and curricular conditions, like the principle of commonality and the use of exemptions based on prior learning, have shown that the concept was attractive to teachers but difficult to implement. Three formats of innovations have been compared in this study. The 'old' innovation of work-related education, dualisation, and the new qualification system. Dualisation was expected to improve students' motivation and be a prerequisite for the linkage of a school and work-based program for the learning of transferability. The analysis casts doubt on the assumed positive influence of dualisation on students' motivation. It seems that long courses detract more from motivation than work-based programs can add. The contribution of the work-based program to the learning of transferability is assumed to demand much development time of schools. The consequence is that no results are expected now. As a result, the short-term outcome of dualisation is negative.

The generalised conclusions from the data are the following. The year 1990 had a major impact. Indicators that were fairly constant at the time changed significantly. This change was due to the normalisation and dualisation of the pathways - the effect was observed in schools with and without the new QS. The negative effect of normalisation and dualisation on success rate and length of stay was almost as dramatic as that measured between the second and third-year pathways of SSAVE-B between 1987 and 1989. The experimental 'gardens' recovered more quickly than the other schools from the 1990 calamity. In 1992, the recovery of the success rate in the experimental 'gardens' was almost complete.

A significant shortening of the length of stay in 'all IAE's' and the experimental 'gardens' was observed after dualisation and implementation of the QS. The QS effect was about three times stronger than the dualisation effect. The dualisation effect may have been caused by an earlier no-go decision, due to the increased course length. The QS effect was probably due to increased upstreaming and downstreaming and utilisation of the commonality principle.

An increase in internal upstreaming and downstreaming was observed. The QS increased the ratio of students that leave school with a diploma. This effect is strongest for level 2. Qualification in pathways other than the first entry pathway increased. A negative effect was that of level-4 entries, fewer students attaining a level-4 diploma. The negative dualisation effect on the success rate was strong, but not lasting, as a result of the QS.

Students spent less than the normal time on blocks. The time allocation to courses was efficient. This means in the context of the new QS that, in addition to the measured success rate at diploma level, substantial numbers of certificates were issued to students leaving the IAE without a diploma. Flexibility in certification might be an important means to qualifying for the labour market and to avoiding unemployment.

IAE's granted exemptions to students at levels 3 and 4. For the 1992 and 1993 cohorts, exemptions covered 2%-4% of the total number of certificates attained. This is reasonable; it should be slightly more for level 4.

IAE's became more effective and efficient for all target groups. Progression increased. Undesirable repetition decreased because of the high level at which certificates were issued. Thus the flexibility of the organisation improved.

It is obvious that these conclusions do not cover all possible aspects of flexibility (Nijhof, Kieft & Van Woerkom, 2001). The focus here was on internal flexibility in terms of effectiveness and efficiency as defined by indicators. School-to-work transitions, transferability, the mastery of cognitive and metacognitive skills, was not the subject of this study. The utilisation of educational and training pathways, dualisation, the principle of commonality of full qualifications, modularisation of units, decontextualised attainment targets, and the integration of subject matter together all contributed to success rates, length of stay, and cost benefits. While the results are inconsistent for different qualification levels and are limited to the population of agricultural students and institutions, further in-depth studies are needed to find out what the optimal conditions for internal and external flexibility should be.

References

Babeliowsky, M. (1995). Schoolloopbanen en studierendement in het voortgezet onderwijs. *International Journal of educational Development, 17 (3)*, pp. 323-334.

Bruijn, E. de (1992). *Modularization in Dutch vocational education and training*. Amsterdam: Stichting Centrum voor Onderwijsonderzoek, Universiteit van Amsterdam.

Bruijn, E. de (1997). Het experimentele en het reguliere: Twintig jaar voltijds kort middelbaar beroepsonderwijs. *Thesis*. Amsterdam: SCO-Kohnstamm Instituut.

CBS, Centraal Bureau voor de Statistiek (1990). *Indicatoren voor door- en uitstroom in het AVO en MBO*. Den Haag: SDU.

Geerligs, J. (1999). *Design of Responsive Vocational Education and Training*. Delft: Eburon (Thesis University of Twente, Enschede).

Gennip, J. van (1991). *Veranderingscapaciteiten van basisscholen*. Nijmegen: ITS.

Hoeben, W.Th.J.G. (1993). Evaluatie van onderwijsbeleid. In Nijhof, W.J., Franssen, H.A.M., Hoeben, W.Th.J.G. & Wolbert, R.G.M. (Eds.), *Handboek Curriculum. Modellen, Theorieën Technologieën* (pp. 165-191). Amsterdam: Swets & Zeitlinger.

Hoeben, W. Th. J.G. (1997). Kwaliteitszorg in het beroepsonderwijs. In Nijhof. W.J. (Ed.) *Ontwikkelingen in het beroepsonderwijs en de Volwasseneneducatie. Onderwijskundig Lexicon.* (pp. 103-128). Alphen aan den Rijn: Samsom H.D. Tjeenk Willink.

Kieft, M., & W.J. Nijhof (2000). *HRD Profielen 2000. Een onderzoek naar rollen, competenties en outputs van bedrijfsopleiders*. Enschede: Twente University Press.

Kooy, H.J. (1984). Indicatoren van de doorstroming in het onderwijs. *Statistisch magazine, 1984, nr. 2*: 19-27.

Lagemaat, D. van de (1986). *Onderwijzen in Ondernemen. Thesis*. Culemborg: Educaboek.

Lazonder, A.W. (1998). *Aspecten van de flexibiliteit van de kwalificatiestructuur*. Wageningen: Leerstoelgroep Agrarische Onderwijskunde LU.

LNV, Minister van Landbouw, Natuurbeheer en Visserij (1998). *Statistische Informatie Agrarisch Onderwijs 1997*. Den Haag: LNV.

Nijhof, W.J., & J.N. Streumer (1994). Flexibility in vocational education and training: an introduction. In Nijhof, W.J. & Streumer, J.N. (Eds.), *Flexibility in training and vocational education* (pp. 1-13). Utrecht: Lemma.

Nijhof, W.J. (Ed.) (2001). *Levenslang beroepsbekwaam*. Den Haag: Elsevier.

Nijhof, W.J., Kieft, M., & Woerkom, M. van (2000). *Reviewing flexibility: A systems approach to VET*. Luxembourg: Office for Official Publications of the European Communities. ISBN 92-894-1482-0

Olbrich, G., & Pfeiffer, V. (1980). Lernzielstufen: Darstellung und Anwendung eines Hierarchisierungssystems für Lernziele in der beruflichen Bildung. *Berichte zur Beruflich en Bildung 25*. Berlin: Bundesinstitut für Berufsbildung.

Raffe, D. (1994). The new flexibility in vocational education. In Nijhof, W.J. & Streumer, J.N (Eds.), *Flexibility in training and vocational education* (pp. 13-33). Utrecht: Lemma.

Ros, A.A., Swinkels-Kuijlaars, H.P.C. Theunissen, J.J.C.M. Visser, J.J.C.M. Jongmans C.T., & Geijsel, F. (1996). *Over vernieuwingen gesproken. Onderzoek naar het innovatief vermogen en de invoering van de basisvorming en de kwalificatiestructuur op de AOC's*. Wageningen: Vakgroep Agrarische Onderwijskunde, LU.

Saylor, J.G., Alexander, W.M., & Lewis, A.J. (1981). *Curriculum planning for better teaching and learning*. New York: Holt, Rinehart and Winston.

Scheerens, J., & Bosker, R.J. (1997). *The foundations of educational effectiveness.* Oxford: Pergamon.

Soden, R. (1993). *Teaching thinking skills in vocational education.* Sheffield: Employment Department.

Swinkels-Kuijlaars, H.P.C., & Wijlick, W.G.A.M. van (1995). *Verkenning discrepantie landelijk VLO-beleid en de feitelijke uitvoering door AOC's.* Den Bosch: Kompact-groep KPC.

CHAPTER 10

Valuing learning outcomes acquired in non-formal settings

GERALD A. STRAKA

10.1 Introduction

THE CONCLUSIONS OF THE EUROPEAN COUNCIL held in Lisbon in March 2000 initiated the orientation of education policy towards lifelong learning, which "is no longer just one aspect of education and training; it must become the guiding principle for provision and participations across the full continuum of learning contexts" (MLL, 2000, p. 3). This vision is regarded as the common umbrella under which all kinds of teaching and learning should be united, and it demands a fundamentally new approach to education and training (MLL, 2000).

In order to take action on lifelong learning, six key messages have been formulated: (1) new basic skills for all, (2) more investment in human resources, (3) innovation in teaching and learning, (4) valuing learning, (5) rethinking guidance and counselling, and (6) bringing learning closer to home. Focusing on message (4), the objective is to "improve significantly the ways in which *learning* participation and *outcomes* are understood and appreciated, particularly non-formal and informal learning" (MLL, 2000, p. 15 [italics added]). Far more has to be done in this area for the benefit of much wider segments of the population and the labour market. Target segments include "non-traditional learners" as well as those who have not been active in the labour force because of unemployment, family duties or illness. Regardless of the type of learner, innovative forms of certifying non-formal learning are important; absolutely essential is the development of high-quality systems for the Accreditation of Prior and Experiential Learning (APEL). To realise these aims, the Commission of the European Communities will establish, by the end of 2003 and based on the systematic exchange of experience, an inventory of methodologies, systems and standards for the identification, assessment and recognition of non-formal and informal learning (MLL, 2001, p. 17).

In this short review, the term "learning" is used in different ways: e.g. lifelong learning as a vision, a common umbrella uniting all forms of teaching and learning; innovation in learning; valuing learning; bringing learning closer to home; non-formal and informal learning; innovative forms of certifying non-formal and informal learning; assessing and recognition of non-formal and informal learning. This tenor is also found in a recent CEDEFOP publication entitled "Making Learning Visible: Identification, Assessment and Recognition of Non-formal Learning in Europe" (Bjornavold, 2000). In this CEDEFOP publication and in some passages of the Commission's papers a similar phraseology can be identified – sufficient reason to analyse some of these terms. Therefore, a concept of learning from the individual's perspective is developed and compared with the CEDEFOP definitions of learning: formal, non-formal and informal learning. The assessment triangle, with the three corners cognition, observation and interpretation, is introduced as a model providing a framework for analysing recently introduced

149

W. J. Nijhof et al. (eds.), Shaping Flexibility in Vocational Education and Training, 149-165.
© 2002 Kluwer Academic Publishers. Printed in the Netherlands.

forms of certifying learning outcomes: the German "continuous IT training", the Norwegian "Realkompetanse project", and the Finnish "Recreational Activity Study Book". The results are related to flexibility, mobility, transferability and fairness ... with surprising results.

10.2 What is "learning"?

Particularly since the publication of Senge's (1990) "The Fifth Discipline", learning has become a key word in practice and theory around the globe. In the meantime, not only are organisations, regions and various entities engaged in learning, new forms of learning are assumed to be necessary for the individual too. A close look at these formulations reveals that learning is used as a metaphor simply to characterise the changes in internal and external relations of institutions (Straka, 1998). From the individual's perspective, there is also strong support for the thesis that mankind has not changed learning over the past millennia (Schott, 2001). Some types of learning may have become more important in the "information age" or "knowledge society", so "new forms of learning" are more adequately labelled "new types of teaching, training or coaching". It seems that the Commission was aware of this problem: "lifelong learning is the common umbrella under which all kinds of teaching *and* learning should be united" (MLL, 2000, p. 4). However, it is questionable whether such a broad notion of lifelong learning is informative. Being informative means that phenomena that do not fit within the concept are to be ruled out (Albert, 1968). If everything is subsumable, the concept is not informative and is thus useless for political programming and supervision. Therefore, learning will be modelled from the original perspective of the individual.

In the course of a lifetime, an individual interacts with the socio-culturally shaped physical and social environment. The individual enters this process with *internal conditions*, e.g. abilities, skills, knowledge and motives. From the individual's perspective, the environment includes supervisors, colleagues, technical equipment, etc., which are subsumed within the concept of external or *environmental conditions*. It is the individual's behaviour that maintains the interaction with these environmental conditions, made possible by internal conditions (Gagné, 1973). Examples of such activities are *viewing* a picture, *comprehending* a statement, *handling* a piece of work. With words such as "viewing", "comprehending" and "handling", we are describing – albeit vaguely – *behaviour*. In this context behaviour is directed at "something" (a picture, a statement or a piece of work). From a cognitive perspective, this something means *information* generated by the individual's (cognitive) behaviour based on the internal conditions and/or perceived signs or symbols from the environment (Straka & Macke, 2002).

When asked why an individual realises, maintains, discontinues or avoids a particular behaviour, or what reasons are behind the behaviour (conscious or unconscious), then we are dealing with the motivational part of the individual-environment relation. *Motivation* relates behaviour to something (e.g. content) that aligns it – turning it towards or away – with a certain intensity. There is yet another dimension to the interaction. It is the *emotion* embracing the subjective experience from an affective and non-rational angle (which can be pleasant or unpleasant). Emotion is connected with impressions such as joy or anger, or with physical processes such as sweating or shuddering, and is often accompanied by expressional behaviour such as facial expressions or gestures (Pekrun & Schiefele, 1996; Boekaerts, 1999).

All four dimensions (behaviour, information, motivation, emotion) presuppose one another. They do not exist separately but come into being only through mutual action, i.e. they generate one another. However, this does not mean that one or other of the dimensions cannot be at the forefront during certain phases of an event (Becker, Oldenbürger & Piehl, 1987). For example, although reading a text considered highly important and interesting, a person when very irritated retains nothing. After a while the irritation subsides and the individual reads the text attentively, compares what has been read with what is already known, sees here and there additions to previous knowledge, and is pleased at having learnt something new. This is not surprising for we know that a person easily understands and retains things of interest.

The individual's interaction with socio-culturally shaped physical and/or social environmental conditions, or the relationship between subject and society, results in consequences relating to the environment and/or the individual (cf. Figure 10.1).

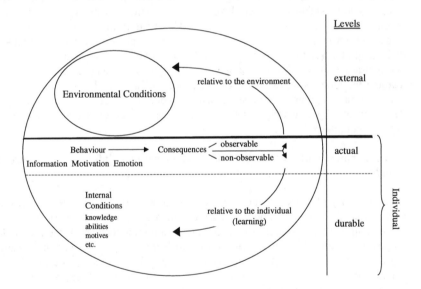

Figure 10.1 Learning.

Environment-relative consequences arise, for example, from handling a piece of work or giving potential information. Individual-relative consequences exist in the fact that a person's knowledge and abilities have permanently changed, and therefore learning has taken place. Accordingly, *learning* has taken place if, and only if the *individual-relative* consequences of the interaction between behaviour, information, motivation and emotion lead to a permanent change in the internal conditions of the acting individual (Straka & Schaefer, 2002).

CEDEFOP's concepts of learning will be analysed on the basis of this conceptualisation of learning. Referring to Lave, they define learning as "a cumulative process where individuals gradually internalise more and more complex and abstract entities (concepts, categories, and patterns of behaviour or models)" (Bjornavold & Tissot 2000, p. 204).

"Internalising" is part of the actual learning process and the "internalised entities" are equivalent to the internal conditions. The attributes "complex and abstract" describe the properties of internalised entities and, with "more and more", indicate a never-ending path of development. However, there are conceptions of development where distinct plateaus of mental development are postulated, remaining constant for some time. A well-known example is Piaget's conception of intellectual development, where the ability for formal operating represents the highest stage of development. However, Oerter (1980) reports that certain people never attain the ability of formal operation during their life span. Another example is the validated concept of learning hierarchies, according to which certain types of skills are cumulatively acquired but not inevitably internalised as more and complex and abstract entities (Gagné, 1962; Eigler & Straka, 1978). Furthermore, the learning process itself remains a black box in which entities with some features are internalised. To summarise, Bjornavold and Tissot's definition of learning describes, using such terms as "entities like concepts", some types of internal conditions and their potential relations. Besides this "cumulative" but unspecific process of internalisation, this definition of learning is result- or development-oriented, not learning-oriented. However, learning as a process is individual and autonomous, and with a certain regularity idiosyncratically "coloured" by the personal history and development of the learner. These activities can be described and systematised beyond "cumulative"[1].

10.2.1 Formal, non-formal and informal learning – informative differentiations?

In the glossary of the CEDEFOP study, formal, non-formal and informal learning are defined and commented on by the authors themselves (cf. Figure 10.2).

Learning is an individual process producing a durable change in the individual's internal conditions. No one is able to learn for someone else; the action of learning always has to be realised by the individual, even if that individual is a member of a community of practice. The signals of the other members of the community are consciously or unconsciously selected and interpreted – and to a large extent internalised – by the learner on the basis of internal idiosyncratic conditions (Straka & Macke, 2002). As a consequence, *learning and its results are always non-formal.* Where might these differentiations of formality come from?

---

[1] In another part, where learning is much broader but similarly defined structurally, it is added that the word *"learning"* designates both the learning process and its outcome (Bjornavold & Tissot 2000, p. 201). Indeed, a process becomes the function of learning if there is an individual intent to realise durable change in the internal condition (= outcome) or if this change took place even without an aim. However, if no outcome has occurred, no learning but "only" action took place. Learning is indissolubly linked with an internal outcome, but the internal structure and its change is a matter of psychic developmental theories.

FORMAL LEARNING	NON-FORMAL LEARNING	INFORMAL LEARNING
Formal learning is "learning that occurs within an organised and structured context (formal education, in-company training etc.), and that is designated as learning".	Non-formal learning "is learning embedded in planned activities that are not explicitly designated as learning, but which contain an important learning element".	Informal learning results "from daily life activities related to work, family, or leisure".
Comment: "Formal learning may lead to a formal recognition" (Bjornavold & Tissot, 2000, p. 204).	*Comments*: "As opposed to formal learning, non-formal learning encompasses (a) what is sometimes described as *semi-structured learning*, that is learning embedded in environments containing a learning component (i.e. quality management); and (b) accidental learning resulting from daily life situations (including at the workplace) and defined below as *informal learning*" (Bjornavold & Tissot, 2000, p. 204).	*Comments*: "Informal learning is part of *non-formal learning* (see def. above). It is often referred to as *experiential learning* and can to a certain degree be understood as *accidental learning*" (Bjornavold & Tissot, 2000, p. 205).

Figure 10.2 Formal, non-formal and informal learning.

One source is to be found in earlier didactic textbooks starting with the introduction of learning in "natural" and "educational" settings. Natural settings are the family, the neighbourhood, nature, etc., whereas educational settings are those arranged to initiate and support learning (cf. Huber, 1972; Stöcker, 1975). Theories of organisations that differentiate between the formal and informal organisational structures in companies are another source (cf. Pfeiffer, 1976). Both strands may have contributed to characterising environments according to different degrees of formality. Similar considerations seem to have been the origin of CEDEFOP's definition of "formal learning", expressed as "learning that occurs within an organised and structured context (...)". However, the wording of this definition is tautological: "Learning (...) designated as learning", i.e. learning is learning! The same tautology is to be found in the definition of non-formal learning: "learning (...) not explicitly designated as learning".

One aim of concepts is to classify phenomena clearly in order to be informative (Albert, 1968). This claim will be analysed in respect to these three definitions. Formal learning "occurs within an organized and structured context"; non-formal learning "is embedded in planned activities (...) which contain an important learning element"; informal learning results "from daily life activities related to work, family, or leisure". The criteria for "formal learning" are the properties of the context or the environment, for "non-formal learning" the embedding in planned activities of the learner or of others, which remains unclear. "Informal learning" results from activities related to selected contexts such as work. Comparing these passages, it can be concluded that the criteria for formality are different in these definitions ("environment", "activities", "activities and environment"). Can we conclude that the context for formal learning is organised and structured? for informal learning unorganised and unstructured? and for non-formal learning somewhere in between?

Is the difference between non-formal and informal learning the existence of an important or unimportant learning element? What are the criteria for importance?

These inconsistencies might have been the reason for the authors' comments after each definition. Non-formal learning earns the lengthiest comments. Part (a) specifies the environment containing a learning component. But why is this specification not part of the definition and why is the addition "quality management" not an example? Part (b) even increases the inconsistency of the definitions by introducing the unspecified term "accidental learning" as a characteristic of non-formal learning and by the additional explicit reference to informal learning. However, the comment postulates that "informal learning is part of non-formal learning". To differentiate between these two learning types, the undefined attributes of experiential and accidental learning are introduced. Questions like the following may be raised: Does "accidental learning" take place only in non-formal and informal contexts, and not in formal contexts? Does no "experiential learning" take place in formal settings, whatever the criteria for formality might be?

An answer will be given by combining environmental conditions with learning types. The environmental conditions are grouped around the poles "formal" and "non-formal"; the learning types are differentiated into explicit, accidental/incidental and implicit. The criterion for formality is the degree of educational or non-educational structuring (Straka & Macke, 2002). This combination demonstrates (cf. Figure 10.3) that the learning types are not exclusively related to one of the educational or other arranged settings (cf. Straka, 1997, 2000, 2001). For example, a school peer group as an informal setting needs a formal educational structure to be established, but the learning types occurring within this setting tend to be more implicit or accidental than explicit, and are not always in accordance with the goals of the "formal" or educationally structured environment. Another example is the dual system in Germany. The vocational school is an educational environment in which approximately one and a half days a week are spent. But what type of environment is the workplace where the other three and a half days a week are spent? If authenticity is taken seriously, this time should be used to act and learn in places or on tasks that are arranged to realise company goals – in this case, company not educational purposes are of primary importance – and not in educationally structured apprentice workshops established far away from the production line. Following this logic means that time spent on the shop floor within the framework of the dual system in Germany is learning under non-educational or non-formal environmental conditions, where explicit but also accidental or even implicit learning may take place as part of "experiential learning". Taken from this angle, validation of "non-formal learning" has been carried out millions of times in Germany since the dual system was introduced[2].

---

[2] It should be noted that the Memorandum on Lifelong Learning differentiates "three basic categories of *purposeful learning activity*": formal learning (in education and training institutions, leading to recognised qualifications), non-formal learning (alongside mainstream systems, typically without formal certificates, and followed by further concretisations), and informal learning (a natural accompaniment to everyday life) – but with the addition *not necessarily intentional*, the same problem arises.

| Environmental conditions | Formal | Non-formal |
Learning types	(public) school and training systems	workplace, family, peers etc.
Explicit	xx	x
Accidental/incidental	x	x
Implicit	x	xx

Figure 10.3 Environmental conditions and learning types.

Given the difficulty of separating informal, non-formal and formal conditions of learning, we agree with Eraut (2000), who advocates the use of formal and non-formal[3] environmental conditions or settings. The reason is that informal learning is often treated as a residual category to describe any type of learning which does not take place within, or follow from, a formally organised learning program or event. "However, for those who believe that the majority of human learning does not occur in formal contexts, the utility of such a catch-all label is not very great" (Eraut, 2000, p. 12). Therefore we recommend differentiation only in respect to formal and non-formal environmental conditions (Eraut, 2000), of which the "formality" can be characterised as follows:
- a prescribed framework for learning (e.g. school syllabus, training regulations for companies);
- an organised event or package;
- the presence of a designated teacher or trainer;
- the external specification of the outcomes;
- the award of a designated qualification, credit or certificate;
- accreditation or recognition of the qualification, credit or certificate, affiliated with the right of access to further education, etc. (e.g. the "Abitur" guarantees access to higher education; the successful termination of primary VET in crafts is a prerequisite for becoming a foreman/forewoman in Germany).

Although these conditions may have an impact on learning types, they are not constitutive for learning itself. Formal and non-formal environmental conditions represent the two poles; between these many differentiations are possible, being more closely related to the one or the other. Examples would include:
- a woman with certified organisational skills acquired at home while raising children;
- a certified painting workshop in an adult education institution;
- a Microsoft certificate acquired under specific educational conditions;
- an "IT agent" certificate from dual primary VET education in Germany;
- a "bank clerk" certificate in Germany;
- an NVQ certificate at level 3 "Providing financial services (banks and building societies)" in the UK;
- a "bilan de compétence" in France or a PhD degree from a department of a regular university.

---

[3] If there is a preference for the mysterious term "informal", it might be used instead of the term "non-formal".

These examples are based on assessments made by individuals who have learned in environmental settings of varying formality.

10.3 Valuing what and how

Assessment as reasoning evidence can be modelled with the use of an assessment triangle. The corners represent the three key elements underlying any assessment. Referring to the model of a person's interaction and learning with the culturally shaped environment, *cognition* represents a model of the person's internal conditions and mental actions in a domain. A set of beliefs about the kinds of *observation/performance* that will provide evidence of a person's cognition, and an *interpretation* process for making sense of the evidence are the two other corners (NRC, 2001).

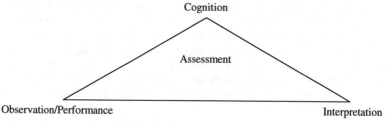

Figure 10.4 The assessment triangle (NRC, 2001, p. 39).

The cognition corner refers to a theory or set of beliefs about how people represent knowledge and develop cognitive competence in a domain. An expert in control may have acquired extensive, well-structured and deeply understood knowledge in this field. This affects not only what such a person takes notice of, but also how he or she organises, represents and interprets information in the environment – which in turn affects the abilities to remember, reason and solve problems (NRC, 2001, p. 31).

The observation corner represents a description or set of specifications for assessment tasks to elicit illuminating actions from people. Examples include descriptions of:

- what a person says or does in a meeting;
- what a person says or does with specific kinds of support[4];
- written or oral responses;
- the choice of an alternative in a multiple choice item;
- demonstrations;
- documentation of projects realised in the workplace;
- on-demand tasks or work samples;
- portfolios.

The interpretation corner encompasses all methods and tools used to reason from fallible observations. It expresses how the observations derived from a set of indicators (i.e. tasks, work samples or behaviours) give evidence about the knowledge, skills or general internal conditions being assessed. The "how" varies

---

[4]   Compare levels A to D of the Norwegian Realkompetanse project later in this text.

dependent on recent probabilistic measurement models such as the Rasch model used by TIMSS and PISA, the one-dimensional model to the classical measurement conception where the observations/performance scores and estimated errors are the indicators for the non-observable internal conditions or processes.

The three corners of the assessment triangle are interrelated. For the relations between cognition and observation, the personal constructs, or a theory or model of how people develop cognition and competence, provide clues to the types of situation that will elicit evidence about these internal conditions or processes. Connections between cognition and interpretation can be based on defined internal conditions and processes, or on a conception of how people develop competence, and can provide recommendations about the types of interpretation method appropriate for transforming data about personal performance into assessed results. A link between observation and interpretation (i.e. knowing the possibilities and limitations of various interpretation models) helps in designing a set of observations that is at once effective and efficient for the task at hand (NRC, 2001, p. 44 seq).

10.4 Assessments for learning outcomes in non-formal settings

In recent times, and probably also initiated by *Making Learning Visible* (Bjornavold, 2000), some types of assessing learning outcomes beyond formal schooling have been introduced. As examples of this trend, the conceptions of German continuous IT training, the Realkompetanse project and the Finnish Recreational Activity Study Book are briefly reviewed.

10.4.1 New methods of assessing vocational competencies in Germany

Based on the recognised IT occupations of the German dual system, a new continuous IT training system began in May 2002[5]. The system consists of within-company career paths at three levels. The lowest level covers 28 special profiles, including software developer, network administrator, IT key accounter and elogistic developer. The second level addresses operative functions, differentiating between IT engineer, IT manager, IT consultant and IT commercial. The third level addresses strategic functions and is divided into IT systems engineer and IT business engineer. The European Credit Point Transfer System (ECTS) treats certificates gained at these levels as equivalent to the BA or MA certificates of the higher education system. The basis for these certificates is "work process-oriented continuous training" during which the employee works on actual problems encountered in company projects in order to combine work and learning. The project work has to be documented, discussed with the company coach and checked against "reference projects" (Grunwald, 2002, p. 179).

The certification will be run with a private certification body in order to satisfy the general criteria for institutions certifying personnel in accordance with the German Industry Norm (DIN EN 45013).

---

[5]	(http://www.bmbf.de/pub/it-weiterbildung_mit_system.pdf, http://www.apo-it.de and http://www.kib-net.de).

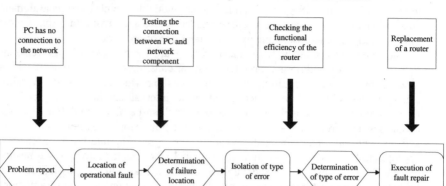

A simple practice project: Fault management of a network administrator

Part of the reference project: Abstraction of the practice project

Figure 10.5 From the practice to a reference project (an example for a network administrator).

10.4.2 The Realkompetanse project

The Realkompetanse project of the Norwegian Ministry of Education and Research started in August 1999 and will formally come to an end in July 2002. Its aim "is to establish a system that gives adults the right to document their non-formal and informal learning *without having to undergo traditional forms of testing*" (VOX, 2002, p. 9 [italics added]). Realkompetanse includes "all formal, non-formal and informal learning (…) *Formal learning* is normally acquired through organised programmes delivered via schools and other providers and is recognised by means of qualifications or parts of qualifications. *Non-formal learning* is acquired through organised programmes, but is not typically recognised by means of qualifications, nor does it lead to certification. *Informal learning* is acquired outside of organised programmes and is picked up through daily activities relating to work, family or leisure" (VOX, 2002, p. 11).

The validation process in general combines dialogue-supported performance assessment and portfolio assessment, possibly in conjunction with tests (VOX, 2002). It covers documentation methods in work life and in the civil society/third sector, validation in respect to upper secondary education, and validation for admission to higher education.

The documentation of non-formal and informal learning in the workplace consists of two parts: a curriculum vitae and a skills certificate. The curriculum vitae is similar to that put forward by the European Commission and the Forum on Transparency of Qualifications and contains personal data, work experience (employer, position, period, areas of responsibility), education, valid licences and publicly approved certificates, courses (title, period, year of completion, important content), other skills and voluntary work (type of activity, skills, and closer description of responsibilities), and additional information. The skills certificate or the competence card from the workplace describes what the employee is able to do as part of the job. The categories are personal data, main areas of work responsibility (with a closer description of responsibilities), specifications of professional skills needed to carry out main responsibilities, personal capability, social and personal skills, management skills, and additional information. These specifications are graded at four levels, from level A (carries out elementary tasks under supervision) up to level D (has very good insight into subject area of profession, may be in charge of development at own workplace). The certificate is signed by the employee and on behalf of the business/company.

10.4.3 The Finnish Recreational Activity Study Book

The Recreational Activity Study Book of the Finnish Youth Academy was designed as a tool to make learning visible in settings outside the formal system. The target group is all young people over 13 years of age. By March 2002 there were more than 55,000 owners of the study book in Finland, and over 250 formal educational institutions value the entries in the book. This conception of valuing learning results in non-formal settings is supported by the Finnish Ministry of Education and Culture and the Finnish Forest Industries Federation. The major youth and sports NGOs behind the development include the Center for Youth Work of the Evangelical Lutheran Church of Finland, the Nature League, the Guides and Scouts of Finland, the Finnish Red Cross and the Swedish Study Centre in Finland.

The concept of the Recreational Activity Study Book distinguishes nine settings or types of learning activity: regular participation in hobby activities, positions of trust and responsibility within citizens' organisations, activities as a leader or coach, participation in a project, courses, international activities, workshop activities (apprenticeship), competitions and other activities. Adults responsible for the records are instructed to focus on the learning and development of the young people, i.e. not only on what has been done but also on how it has been done and how it is to be documented. The book records the organisation responsible for the activity, a description of the activity, the young person's own evaluation of learning, the date(s) and duration of the activity, performance (success and development), the signature of the adult responsible and contact information, and the stamp of the responsible organisation.

The Recreational Activity Study Book links messages to the young people, the employers and the formal educational institutions. This book serves the young as a curriculum vitae on non-formal learning, which can be useful when applying for further education or a job. It provides the employers with information about the job-seeker's activity and goal-orientation and shows that young people learn valuable skills outside the formal education system. It enables the formal educational institutions to get to know something about the applicant's experience relevant to the particular field of education and shows that the youth and sports NGOs offer a good learning environment that can be used to complement or support formal education (Savisaari, 2002).

10.5 Summarising evaluation with the assessment triangle

The specifications of recently introduced forms of assessing learning outcomes acquired in non-formal settings in Germany, Norway and Finland will be analysed against the background of the assessment triangle. In the German case, documented authentic projects will be related to "reference projects" that describe the processes on a general level. Such a concept is structurally equivalent to the differentiation into classes or patterns of behaviour and realised singular behaviour (Holland & Skinner, 1961). As a consequence, there is the danger of moving further towards the specification of the observation/performance corner by disregarding the interpretation and particularly the cognition corners. Also missing is a concept of competence development in company settings. Even if there is an idea of developing from a novice to an expert in a certain domain, theoretical considerations are necessary and have to be tested. Otherwise the same problem might come up as in programmed instruction: successfully mastering short "frames" (learning step) is only one of the conditions to become an expert – and these frames are actually replaced by projects or complete tasks.

In the Norwegian and Finnish cases, valuing learning outcomes in non-formal settings is also closer to the observation corner than to the cognition corner. Interpretation seems to be largely based on the personal, and even idiosyncratically coloured theories of competence and competence development of assessors who, in many cases, are not trained for this task. The implicit vision behind all three concepts seems to be a notion of cumulative development of whatever path and structure – also found in the Bjornavold & Tissot definitions already discussed.

The analysis results are in accordance with the actual theoretical and practical considerations in formal vocational education. They indicate a trend away from mastering subject matter concepts and structures, and general cognitive, key and meta competencies, to performance competencies based on skills necessary to master tasks or task demands in a specific domain. The reason for this development lies in the findings and observations that people have difficulty in applying what was learned in school to real life situations, because the knowledge learned remains inert to a large degree (cf. Resnick, 1987). General competencies alone have virtually no practical utility. The more general a rule or strategy, the smaller is its contribution to the solution of a concrete problem. The cognitive sciences have convincingly demonstrated that content-specific skills and knowledge play a crucial role in solving unfamiliar tasks (Bransford et al., 2000). Generally, key competencies cannot adequately compensate for the lack of content-specific knowledge (Weinert, 1998).

In an analysis of nine concepts of competence and competencies, Weinert (1999, p. 26) concludes that they "should be understood primarily as the mental conditions necessary for cognitive, social and vocational achievement". He recommends a functional approach. Which cognitive competencies do we need to master tasks and task demands (Weinert, 1999, p. 27)? As neither a comprehensive theory of human abilities nor a sociological classification of environmental demands exists, the starting point is prototypical, typical and specific characterisations of classes of performance demands, performance, criteria and indicators of competencies. Some of these ideas seem to be the implicit guiding principle of the continuous IT training regulations in Germany. Perhaps the PISA definition of competence and the interpretations might give some hint as to which way to go. "PISA assesses the ability to complete tasks relating to real life, depending on a broad understanding of key concepts, rather than assessing the possession of specific knowledge [in three literacy domains: reading, science and mathematics]. (...) The domains covered by PISA are defined in terms of: the *content* or *structure* of knowledge that students need to acquire in each domain (e.g. familiarity with scientific concepts or various text types); the *processes* that need to be performed (e.g. retrieving written information from a text); and the *context* in which knowledge and skills are applied (e.g. making decisions in relation to one's personal life, or understanding)" (OECD, 2001, p. 19). This definition completely matches the learning model of this chapter: the structure of knowledge corresponds to the internal conditions, the processes to the internal and observable behaviour, and the context to the environmental conditions[6].

10.6 Consequences for flexibility, mobility, transferability and fairness

Specifying tasks or task demands to be mastered in companies or NGOs contributes to an increase in the flexibility of a formal VET system – not seldom criticised for its stability or immobility before the background of megadynamic changes in technology, global economy or cultures. Behind such general trends, however, very particular settings are the reality, which may contribute to unintended side effects of such types of assessment, as Eraut points out: "In order to serve as a basis for the design of valid performance-based assessment, [the NVQs] had to be tied to particular working practices. But as national qualifications, they were expected to be transferable so that a qualification obtained in workplace A was equally valid for workplace B. How then could a national set of standards be reconciled at a detailed level with the diversity of working practices found in a liberal market economy?" (Eraut, forthcoming). This view indicates that some problems might arise concerning transferability and mobility.

Mobility – considered as moving from one region, country, state, company to another – is easier if the certificates for competence are transparent. In this context such questions may come up as: Are the descriptions of the certified competences valid, especially if they are written by a person untrained in filling out competence cards from the workplace? Is there no need for formulations valid for more than one workplace? The "reference project" against which the realised singular project in a specific company is checked (cf. IT-Weiterbildung, 2002) seems to offer a solution. The competence card in Norway comparable to the curriculum vitae of the EC, a type of standardised work reference (Arbeitszeugnis), indicates aspects to be taken in account. Study results seem to support this trend in assessment. They revealed that, when hiring people who have not long finished primary vocational education, the work reference is regarded as much more important than the grades in the final examination of the German dual system (Schmidt, 2000). However, the significance of work references is a problem, ranging from unclear (especially if assessment is not made by experts in that particular field) to a validity of $r = 0.26$, which is higher than the significance of an analysis of the application documents (Schuler, 2000), although both are still low.

Validity is a core problem concerning all these methods used beyond the standardised measurement of competencies. Even if the records describe graded personal mastery of tasks or task demands, these statements represent explicit or

---

[6] A similar competence and assessment concept underlies some recognised training occupations in Germany, e.g. the insurance clerk (Breuer, 2001; Berufsbildungswerk der deutschen Versicherungswirtschaft, 1998), the mechatronician (Breuer & Müller, 2001) and the IT occupations (Breuer & Müller, 2000).

implicit non-visible skills and knowledge (cf. European Curriculum Vitae, Norwegian competence card and the Finnish Recreational Activity Study Book). Personal traits are internal conditions with the status of invisible constructs. According to the Standards for Educational and Psychological Testing of the American Educational Research Association (AERA), the American Psychological Association (APA) and the National Council on Educational Measurement in Education, six aspects should be considered: the content, substantial, structural, generalisability, external and consequential aspects (AERA, APA and NCME, 1999). Miller and Linn (2000) conclude and recommend in their validation of performance assessment that there is a limit to generalisability if the number of tasks is small and generalisations across different forms of assessment might not be comparable.

The European Forum on Transparency of Vocational Qualifications has attempted to make the certificates of different VET systems transparent, and the key message to certify acquired competencies in non-formal settings is the right way to increase mobility in the European Community. However, the Forum should not cease meticulous comparisons of formulations on a linguistic level. Instead, via observations and testing, it should try to make the knowledge and skills "visible" too, with indicators valid in regard to such measurement standards and requirements as those of the companies, labour market and NGOs. If validity is not guaranteed, the certificates of competence are nice to have but of no market value.

Transferability is seen as an individual competence, and the underlying mechanism is transfer (Nijhof, Kieft & van Woerkom, 2001). The concept of transfer stems from the classical behavioural learning theory track. In this concept, transfer is the intervening variable representing the phenomenon that someone who has learned something in workplace A is able to apply it in workplace B – which, as Eraut (forthcoming) points out, differs from A. The actually discussed, recommended and excellently recorded methods of valuing learning in formal and non-formal settings seem to pay tribute to this tradition without noticing it. If the stream of vaguely defined competences is brushed aside, the competences to be documented are to a large degree descriptions of observed behaviour, records of cognition on the basis of introspection, methods that involve quite a lot of biases and errors, or products (e.g. portfolios) created in more or less precisely defined environmental settings. However, behaviour, self-reports and products are not the transfer itself. In order to infer intersubjectively reproducible from these indicators that transfer is a process driven by cognitive actions via interpretation, theoretical considerations are needed. For example, transfer may be realised consciously (explicitly) and/or unconsciously (automatically, implicitly), with actions subsumed to problem-solving strategies, application, routinised patterns or even the limbic system. The basis for this process and these actions are the person's knowledge, skills and corresponding meta-knowledge, interests and emotional dispositions in a certain domain, i.e. all characteristics of an expert (cf. Bransford, 2000). A conceptualisation of expertise in a specific domain is needed, and, if linked with a developmental purpose, also a vision of human resource development on the basis of representative tasks or task demands to be mastered and performed (cf. Rauner, 1999).

Valuing the level of individual expertise transferable to similar venues of work and other activities brings a lot of benefits to the mobile person concerned, such as entering or re-entering the workforce, changing workplaces, earnings. These aspects, positive for the individual, may not be so for companies. Experts will be kept in the company; certificates may increase the demand for higher wages. These are among the reasons why valuing and certifying competences acquired in the workplace is not a hot topic in Germany, especially in the tariff-bound wage systems with regulations for upgrading.

Valuing competencies acquired in non-formal settings may offer chances to segments of "non-traditional learners" and various social groupings, such as those re-entering the workforce, people from regions of the European Community with no established VET system, employees working without any certificate of their competences, or young people engaged by NGOs who might somehow try to enter the workforce. However, despite case and qualitative studies, there is not enough known about the quality of what is learned in non-formal settings. Does learning during the process of work, or at home or in NGOs contribute to transferable knowledge and skills not tied to the specific environmental settings? Do these new (for politicians) venues for learning contribute to higher-order, domain-appropriate thinking skills and deep understanding? Baker, O'Neill and Linn (1993) state in their article "Policy and validity prospects for performance-based assessment" that expectations regarding these assessments are extremely high. "There is a danger that potentially positive aspects of performance-based assessment will be lost when the unrealistic high expectations are not realized. (...) A better research base is needed to evaluate the degree to which newly developed assessments fulfil expectations" (Baker, O'Neill & Linn, 1993, p. 1216).

In this context some paradoxes can be identified. It is stated that schools and their certificates have a marginal prognostic value for mastering life outside the formal settings ("university of life") (cf. Resnick, 1987). However, competencies acquired "out of school" are evaluated using the standards of the formal system. To make the argumentation even more paradoxical, because work, the family and the NGOs are such wonderful learning arenas, the learning outcomes have to be valued in order to become eligible for the formal schooling.

There is still another threat to this policy. Research shows that job-related continuous learning in non-formal settings is an important aspect for the employed aged 19 to 64 in Germany. In the year 2000 two out of three employed said they practised this type of self-education. However, people who failed to complete dual education, blue-collar workers, immigrants and working women were under-represented (Kuwan & Thebis, 2001). Findings confirming that some people do not attain the formal operating ability during their life span provide another example (Oerter, 1980). As a consequence, valuing learning outcomes acquired in non-formal settings might support the Matthäus principle – giving more to those who already have – if no support grounded in learning theory is added.

References

AERA, APA & NCME (1999). *Standards for Educational and Psychological Testing.* Washington, DC: American Educational Research Association.

Albert, H. (1968). Modell-Platonismus. In E. Topitsch (Ed.), *Logik der Sozialwissenschaften.* Köln: Kiepenheuer & Witsch, S. 407 seq.

Baker, E.L., O'Neill, H.F. & Linn, R.L. (1993). Policy and Validity Prospects for Performance-Based Assessment. *American Psychologist* (1210-1218), 48.

Becker, D., Oldenbürger, H.-A. & Piehl, J. (1987). Motivation und Emotion. In G. Luer (Ed.),

Allgemeine experimentelle Psychologie. Stuttgart: Fischer. pp. 431-470.

Berufsbildungswerk der deutschen Versicherungswirtschaft (1998). Bedingungswerk 1 der SÜDSTERN-Versicherung. *Abschlussprüfung im Ausbildungsberuf Versicherungskaufmann / Versicherungskauffrau*. Karlsruhe: Verlag Versicherungswirtschaft.

Bjornavold, J. (2000). *Making Learning Visible*. Thessaloniki: CEDEFOP.

Bjornavold, J. & Tissot, P. (2000). Glossary. In J. Bjornavold, *Making Learning Visible*. Thessaloniki: CEDEFOP. pp. 199-221.

Boekaerts, M. (1999). Self-regulated learning: Where we are today. *International Journal of Educational Research* 31 (445-458).

Bransford J.D. et al. (2000). *How people learn*. Washington, DC: National Academy Press.

Breuer, K.U. (2001). Authentic Assessment in Vocational Examinations: Approaches within the German Dual System. In L.F.M. Nieuwenhuis & W.J. Nijhof (Eds.), *The Dynamics of VET and HRD Systems*. Enschede: Twente University Press. pp. 141-152.

Breuer, K.U. & Müller, K. (2000). *Umsetzungshilfen für die neue Prüfungsstruktur der IT-Berufe*. Bonn: BMBF.

Breuer, K.U. & Müller, K. (2001). *Mechatroniker/Mechatronikerin*. Umsetzungshilfen für die Abschlussprüfung. Gestaltungshilfen für die Zwischenprüfung. Bonn: BMBF and VDMA.

CV (n.d.). *Curriculum Vitae*. A co-operation between trade and industry and the educational system in Nordland. Edited by the Project Manager Mrs. Pettersen (ingerlise@kongsvegen.vgs.no).

Eigler, G. & Straka, G.A. (1978). *Mastery Learning, Lernerfolg für jeden?* München: Urban & Schwarzenberg.

Eraut, M. (2000). Non-formal learning, implicit learning and tacit knowledge in professional work. In F. Coffield (Ed.), *The necessity of informal learning*. Bristol/UK: Policy Press.

Eraut, M. (forthcoming). *NVQs in England: Description and Analysis of an Alternative Qualification System*. Paper presented at the BMBF Expert Meeting 6 and 7 June 2002, Bonn.

Gagné, R.M. (1962). The Acquisition of Knowledge. *Psychological Review*, 69, 355-365.

Gagné, R.M. (1973). *The Conditions of Learning*. New York: Holt, Rinehart and Winston.

Grunwald, S. (2002). Zertifizierung arbeitsprozessorientierter Weiterbildung. In M. Rohs (Ed.), *Arbeitsprozessintegriertes Lernen*. Münster: Waxmann. pp. 165-179.

Holland, J.G. & Skinner, B.F. (1961). *The analysis of behavior*. New York: McGraw Hill.

Huber, F. (1972). *Allgemeine Unterrichtslehre*, Bad Heilbrunn: Klinkhart.

IT-Weiterbildung (2002). *IT-Weiterbildung mit System. Neue Perspektiven für Fachkräfte und Unternehmen*. Bonn: BMBF.

Kuwan, H. & Thebis, F. (2001). *Berichtssystem Weiterbildung VIII*. Bonn: Bundesministerium für Bildung und Forschung (BMBF).

Miller, M.D. & Linn, R.L. (2000). Validation of Performance-Based Assessment. *Applied Psychological Measurement* (367-378), 24, 4.

MLL (2000). *A Memorandum on Lifelong Learning*. Commission Staff Working Paper. Brussels: Commission of the European Communities.

MLLR (2001). *Making a European Area of Lifelong Learning a Reality*. Communication from the Commission. Brussels: Commission of the European Communities.

Nijhof, W.J., Kieft, M. & van Woerkom, M. (Eds.) (2001). *Reviewing flexibility. A systems approach to VET*. Luxembourg: Office for Official Publications of the European Communities.

NRC (2001). National Research Council. *Knowing What Students Know: The Science and Design of Educational Assessments*. Committee on the Foundations of Assessment. J. Pelligrino, N. Chudowsky & R. Glaser (Eds.). Washington, DC: National Academy Press.

OECD (2001). *Knowledge and Skills for Life*. First Results from PISA 2000. Paris: OECD Publications.

Oerter, R. (1980). *Moderne Entwicklungspsychologie*. Donauwörth: Auer.

Pekrun, R. & Schiefele, U. (1996). Emotions- und motivationspsychologische Bedingungen der Lernleistung. In F.E. Weinert (Ed.), *Psychologie des Lernens und der Instruktion*. Göttingen: Hogrefe. pp. 153-180.

Pfeiffer, D.K. (1976). *Organisationssoziologie*. Stuttgart: Kohlhammer.

Rauner, F. (1999). Entwicklungslogisch strukturierte berufliche Curricula: Vom Neuling zur reflektierten Meisterschaft. *Zeitschrift für Berufs- und Wirtschaftspädagogik* (424-446).

Resnick, L.B. (1987). Learning in School and Out. *Educational Researcher* (13-20), 12.

Savisaari, L. (2002). *Youth Academy & Recreational Activity Study Book System*. Helsinki: Nuorten Akatemia. www.nuortenakatemia.fi

Schmidt, J.U. (2000). Auf dem Weg zu einer neuen Ordnung im Prüfungswesen? *Berufsbildung* (3-7), 65.

Schott, F. (2001). Lebenslanges Lernen in der Wissensgesellschaft als Herausforderung an die Erwachsenenbildung? Anmerkungen und Vorschläge aus psychologischer Sicht. In I. Ambos & E. Nuissl (Hrsg.), *Forschung zur Erwachsenenbildung*. Dokumentation des Forschungsworkshops in Hofgeismar im Januar 2001 auf CD-Rom. Bielefeld: Bertelsmann.

Schuler, H. (2000). *Psychologische Personalauswahl*. Göttingen: Angewandte Psychologie.

Senge, P.M. (1990). *The Fifth Discipline*. New York: Doubleday Current.

Stöcker, K. (1975). *Neuzeitliche Unterrichtsgestaltung*. München: Ehrenwirth.

Straka, G.A. (Ed.) (1997). *European Views of Self-Directed Learning*. Münster: Waxmann.

Straka, G.A. (1998). *Auf dem Weg zu einer mehrdimensionalen Theorie selbstgesteuerten Lernens*. Forschungs- und Praxisberichte Band 1. Homepage: www.los-research.de. Bremen: Universität.

Straka, G.A. (Ed.) (2000). *Conceptions of Self-Directed Learning*. Münster: Waxmann.

Straka, G.A. (2001). Action-Taking Orientation of Vocational Education and Training in Germany – a Dynamic Concept or Rhetoric? In L.F.M. Nieuwenhuis & W.J. Nijhof (Eds.), *The Dynamics of VET and HRD Systems*. Enschede: Twente University Press. pp. 89-99.

Straka, G.A. & Macke, G. (2002). *Lern-Lehr-Theoretische Didaktik*. Münster: Waxmann.

Straka, G.A. & Schaefer, C. (2002). *Validating a More-Dimensional Conception of Self-Directed Learning*. Paper presented at the International Research Conference of the AHRD, Feb 27 – March 3, 2002, Honolulu, Hawaii, USA.

VOX (2002). *The Realkompetanse Project*. Validation of non-formal and informal learning in Norway. Oslo/N: VOX.

Weinert, F.E. (1998). Vermittlung von Schlüsselqualifikationen. In S. Matalik & D. Schade (Eds.), *Entwicklungen in Aus- und Weiterbildung – Anforderungen, Ziele, Konzepte*. Baden Baden: Nomos. pp. 23-43.

Weinert, F.E. (1999). *Concepts of Competence*. München: Max Planck Institut. www.statistik. admin.ch/stat_ch/ber15/deseco/weinert_report.pdf

CHAPTER 11

Resources for flexibility: critical comments

FERNANDO MARHUENDA

11.1 Introduction

WHAT I INTEND TO DO IN THIS REVIEW CHAPTER IS THE FOLLOWING: first, to point to what I consider to be the central questions related to flexibility from a pedagogical and curricular perspective, thus outlining those areas in which 'educational tools and resources' may be found. Second, I will comment on each of the previous six chapters in this section, using the questions I have given as the guidelines for my own reading of those chapters. Third and last, I will try to extract overall conclusions from the chapters, according to the said agenda, and attempt to give some hints on study work and research to continue this line.

The six chapters which describe and analyse educational tools and resources for flexibility in VET systems across several countries in Europe are very different in scope. Some of them provide foundations and data about recent reforms in national systems, in which flexibility is a central element, like the cases of Scotland, Hungary, and Ireland. One focuses on the evaluation of a flexible system in the agricultural sector; another takes assessment mechanisms as the core of the chapter. There is one more chapter, which, taking as its starting point recent developments in the Italian system, provides general and critical reflections on VET that may well apply to many other countries, not just Italy. Furthermore, the elements which the respective authors have chosen in order to assess flexibility are different. Yet, there are several issues which may be found in most of the chapters, and these are the ones I will try to highlight here, in an attempt to develop an overarching frame with which to provide some reflections on resources used at different institutional levels by different agents in different cultural, historical, and economic contexts, in order to achieve and broaden flexibility in VET systems.

11.2 Educational tools and resources for flexibility

I approach flexibility from a curricular perspective: I will take the elements which shape both the curriculum and the curriculum tradition underlying them, in order to find which are the elements that foster flexibility, what is its meaning and scope, and what are its implications for the organisation of teaching itself.

The components of curriculum are well known: aims or objectives, content, methodological strategies, and assessment of learning. There are certain elements surrounding these, like the role of the teacher and the students, all available curricular materials, the arrangements regarding time and space allocated to the different subjects or content packages, and the organisational framework in which the curriculum is embodied.

W. J. Nijhof et al. (eds.), Shaping Flexibility in Vocational Education and Training, 167-180.

There are different perspectives in the field of curriculum studies, and my own is a deliberative one (Marhuenda, 2000a). However, because of the very nature of VET, at the crossroads between education, economy, and the labour market, I will also assume a critical approach. I do this in the belief that vocational education and training may not be seen as a simple extension of the labour market, in which everything - the content of VET - and everyone - the beneficiary - is a 'commodity' (Marhuenda, 2000b). If VET is an educational offer, and a part of educational policies, the needs of individuals - not only of the markets - have to be taken into account. These needs are related to their development as professionals, thus connected to their vocational and personal identities, not only to their competencies and qualifications.

The issues which one must consider from this educational perspective are the following:

a) Whatever teaching practices may result from the flexibilisation of education, what are their expected impact upon learning processes? Teaching is, after all, a practice for the sake of learning, even if it is not a causal relation (Fenster-macher, 1989);

b) The flexibilisation of VET systems has to take into account its impact upon the formation of vocational identities: the contribution of VET to personal development as workers and citizens is of particular importance for certain groups. The role of work experience here is also of relevance (Marhuenda, Cros and Giménez, 2001), flexibility is a feature of such schemes whenever there is an individualised training plan which adjusts an occupational profile to the nature of the placement and the needs of the trainee;

c) The accreditation of qualifications and knowledge is clearly an issue in current VET, yet, very often, the assessment procedures behind it are not properly addressed. Assessment, like teaching, is closely related to the learning processes which individuals develop; and the kind of assessment facilitates different ways for the appropriation of knowledge;

d) The aim of flexibility is to improve VET systems: this means increasing the quality of VET, the quality of education and training policies, but mainly practices, and, by extension, improving the quality of work, including here as well the nature of teachers' work. Pedagogies for flexibility have to be compatible with pedagogies for education - thus, pedagogies for the development of people's capacities;

e) Pedagogy is effected, it 'happens', in the classroom, through the interaction of teacher, student, and content, and it is in that relational process that the educational value of flexibility has also to be activated and assessed: delivery issues, methodologies, and classroom processes, are the elements with which to find out what the educational aspect of flexibility is, as Nijhof (2001) pointed out;

f) A flexible VET system does not always guarantee the achievement of flexibility in the workforce. There is no such isomorphism. And, furthermore, the flexibility of the workforce - particularly of young workers - is not always a desirable effect, in so far as it hinders, rather than fosters, human development;

g) The measure and efficacy of VET flexibilisation could also be related to flexible policies in the labour market. This is also related to the flexibilisation of organisational forms in the educational system, particularly providing greater autonomy to vocational schools with regard to their own educational projects.

Examples of how this has worked - though not in vocational schools - are shown in both Apple and Beane (1998) and in Darling-Hammond (2000). Yet, flexibility as a policy principle is often used for opposed tendencies, as shown by Apple (2001): current policies reject, rather than devolve, power and autonomy to schools in the name of flexibility. One issue of particular interest here is that of the flexibilisation of only part of the system (VET), while the other levels remain untouched and, therefore, highly regulated by the administrators of the school system;

h) Flexibility in the curriculum has been one of the axes of certain curriculum traditions. Nevertheless, today we are experiencing the expansion of 'national curricula', together with a trend towards the standardisation of qualifications;

i) The content of education is the main element of the curriculum: *what content is of most worth* has long been considered the key curricular question. What are the effects of vocationalising education? The content of VET is changing, but it cannot be reduced to a series of skills and competencies, as some would have us believe. There is a permanent content of VET behind each programme. Work itself, its nature and characteristics, could well be considered as the cross-curricular axis behind each vocational scheme. Without this in mind, it is rigidity, not flexibility, that is being achieved.

11.3 Dealing with the flexibility issue: assessing the contributions

In this section, I will look at the analyses and explanations given by the authors of the chapters in this section. I will focus on the elements upon which they rely as academics in order to assess flexibility, trying to avoid reassessing the judgements they have made about the reforms and experiences on which they have commented. This has been their contribution, and mine does not consist of comparing the different programmes or policies within or among the countries portrayed in the section. This would also be a difficult task, because of the different nature of the data provided and the contextual information, which is also very varied. I will, therefore, try to point to the key areas they touch on and raise some questions on how flexibility is understood in different countries, by different academics, and what the consequences are of trying to make it a driver for reform.

11.3.1 Institutional responses to a flexible unified system

The chapter written by Howieson, Raffe and Tinklin gives us enough background and data on the reform. Both the discussion it portrays and the wider implications defined at the end of the chapter highlight the main issues. They show how important are some of the issues we are using to interpret flexibility and the relations between some of them.

The element which serves as the conducting line for the chapter on reforms in Scotland is that of the relations between the system and the schools in the system, with regard to who holds the autonomy and the extent of flexibility. This is shown through a series of questions, which are either indicated by the data or highlighted in the discussions.

What we have in this case is a single framework, which runs with common rules but different curricula (different content, length and level) as well as different institutions, different age groups, and different levels of study. This single framework allows for great flexibility at the ground level. Yet, many questions arise about the value of such flexibility: how will it work in a system with significant imbalances between public and private institutions? This is an issue of particular importance if we consider that the educational system is being marketised and commodified, thus subject to a competitive and changing economic area, and, hence a subsequent labour market. From this perspective, the very meaning of apparently nonconflictive issues has to be considered twice: the definition of the mission of the colleges, the trends towards homogenisation through assessment practices, the role of decentralisation of the system and its relation to regionalisation. Since they are at the same time both relevant in terms of the labour market and dangerous, given the current economic practices, which tend to delocalise production and services.

Changes in the educational system are, therefore, accompanied by changes in school organisation. They are, however, not always consistent in their aims, but are sometimes contradictory, and show a struggle to survive in the system and to readdress it towards aims which are educational, and thus subject to political and social discussion. What this all shows, in the end, are the following key issues:

a) How flexible are institutions to introduce reforms, thus making use of flexibility to counteract its effects, when these are not perceived as adequate or desirable?

b) Does flexibility increase the autonomy of particular institutions, and what sort of autonomy is this? Is there any chance of applying flexibility to resources, material, or staff availability?

c) What does this mean in the context of competition among institutions?

d) In summary, can a flexible system be used differentially and produce effects which are not only different but also contradictory? Is this due to the way that individual schools manage such flexibility, or to the side-effects of a policy of flexibilisation, which is applied in an unequal context? Or is it rather a matter of the model of flexibility which each school represents?

If different coexisting forms of flexibility are not compatible, the purpose of flexibility will most probably not achieved. If so, we might ask ourselves whether the aims which flexibility is attempting to pursue can be achieved through other means, checking flexibility against other policies which might be effective in different ways.

These questions are not mere speculations when we look at other areas which the authors' text also highlights. It is worth noting that there is not much in their chapter about teaching practices, though there is a lot with regard to teachers' work, if not in extension, at least there are a few important concerns. There are several remarks on the impact upon teachers' work. It seems that rigidity, less autonomy, and double control are increasing. The question then is: do we require a flexible teaching body in order to introduce flexibility into the system? If the answer is 'yes', we face a double problem. First, whether the flexibilisation of education as a labour market will contribute to satisfying educational standards, or will transform postsecondary education into a jungle of training provision, in which the educational institutions will work as trademarks that may be franchised by others or fall into subcontracting practices that will make a divide in the educational offer: one of elite and the other lacking clear coherence. The second problem is: what are the conditions required from the student body in order to benefit from such an educational offer? And, of course, how will those requirements be achieved? Will compulsory education be good enough for such a purpose? Do we then need rigid compulsory education in order to guarantee flexible postcompulsory education or VET?

The former is obviously related to the issue of the individualisation of education and flexibility at different levels. From this point of view, we should compare the choices offered by the system with the opportunities chosen by the students, not only from a statistical point of view, but also by looking in detail at the nature of the options and choices. We would then be in a position to answer the question of whether there is freedom to choose, and whether this guarantees equal opportunities. Here, another issue emerges: who should be prioritised by flexibility policies and practices? Who is being empowered by them? Who is benefiting from them? And this should be done both internally - to the educational system - and externally - who in society is favouring and supporting flexibility in the VET system? And is it only in the VET system? Are there any opportunities to defend a flexible system for the non-professionalising pathways of education? The authors make some hints on this when, analysing the data presented in Table 5.6, they refer to the "reduced ability to respond to the needs of many adult learners" (Chapter 5, this volume).

All of the above is realised through various curriculum and assessment mechanisms. The coexistence of different pedagogies and assessment regimes is not problematic - on the contrary, it helps sustain the individualisation of learning, in as far as the status and progression of those forms are also kept at equal levels. This goes beyond the transparency of qualifications and standards; it has to do with comprehensiveness, inclusion, and prestige. There is the reasonable fear that, due to the emphasis put on accreditation and the assessment practices addressing this, the flexibility of the system is guaranteed by restricting flexibility in pedagogies. The attention that assessment has received may risk the chance of having differential ways of delivering: more assessment needs more planning and it involves a powerful drive for teaching.

On top of this, there are also doubts about the flexibility of the curriculum: its modularisation, as well as its time-driven design, skip flexibility both on the part of the user and on the part of the content. Or is there no relation between flexibility and openness of the curriculum? Here, we may also introduce a new element: what is the hidden curriculum of a flexible VET system (Garrick, 1998), and what might its effects be? Does modularisation contribute to enhancing or hindering, by fragmenting, core skills? Can core skills be effectively achieved through modularisation?

Furthermore, maybe we have to reach the conclusion that a flexible curriculum introduces rigidity into assessment, which, in its turn, restricts flexibility in teaching, as may be seen from the discussions in Chapter 5. And yet, we are not clear about the extent of such flexibility; after all, are different levels of achievement possible within each of the five levels offered by 'Higher Still'?

11.3.2 Demand and supply of qualifications: systems' change towards flexibility

Luisa Ribolzi contributes to this section with a chapter using data on reforms in Italy to illustrate broad concerns about the contribution of VET to social progress, with a strong link to individual progress, under the form of the subjective dimension of learning. It not only explains the system, but also tries to understand how individuals use it and approach VET in order to face the labour market.

Thus, the text starts by expressing the convenience of relating flexibility and mobility to education and the educational system, rather than reducing it to employability and a feature of the workforce and the labour market in which they move. It does so in the attempt to "take seriously the hypothesis that learning is the main characteristic of social and economic development", and to check what impact such a hypothesis has on educational policies: do they take it as seriously as they say they do?

Ribolzi analyses deregulation practices in the labour market, showing that they have led to its segmentation - thus making it harder to achieve any mobility other than geographical - and identifying the groups that are experiencing flexible forms of occupation, namely the 'traditionally weak' ones. It would be a good exercise to see how the VET system is reflecting or addressing these trends - the segmentation, fragmentation, and flexibilisation of those at risk - and whether its impact is reinforcing or counteracting what is happening in the labour market.

Ribolzi explains that flexibilisation is finding its place within the VET system, through the integration of different actors in the definition of vocational curricula, while some of these actors are benefiting from the growing interest in continuing vocational education, with work experience and open distance learning as its 'star' features. Together with this, she identifies traces of commodification of the provision of training; rigidities of the system which imply educational problems; a need for the standardisation of factors other than the curriculum, in order to make packages 'marketable'. She also gives hints on the role of general education as the basis for flexibility and adaptability, which support equity in education, while at the same time questioning the benefit of the liberalisation of the training provision and the interest of companies and continuing education in issues such as equity, citizenship, democratisation, and social cohesion. It is with regard to these that she introduces reflections on work in postindustrial societies, with its effect on individual involvement in work.

This contribution is significant if we consider that there are good reasons in her chapter to make of work *per se* a content for vocational education programmes, beyond the technicalities of each profession or job which the programme addresses, and considering elements of ethics and identities. This is the case too for her comments on socialisation practices at work and in school, thus recovering the weight and importance of the hidden curriculum, in order to foster personal development, to increase the opportunities for vertical mobility, and to face labour market demands and changes from a proactive point of view. As she very clearly states, "flexibility is also a question of individual needs and requirements".

Ribolzi's contribution on labour market demands and education supply is an intelligent and flexible overview of vocational education, taking into account the different types of needs of the different actors and people involved and facing flexibility in a broader manner than is usually done on the part of the labour market. She claims the need to take into account sectoral differentiation and to consider the different roles that might be expected from initial and vocational education. This is of great help in establishing an internal differentiation of generic statements which do not contribute to better adjusting work and education - in both ways - and thus relocating vocational education, respecting its relative role in relation to the preparation of workers and citizens, and clarifying the responsibilities of the individuals and those of the system - both the educational and the productive.

11.3.3 Developments in vocational education in Ireland

Tuohy's contribution consists of the history of the VET system in Ireland since the proclamation of the Republic at the beginning of the 20th century. The main issues which are covered in the chapter with relation to my proposed guidelines are the following:

Curriculum and assessment are very clearly devised as two different control systems over education. Several statements are made on recent reforms related to the "development of a general curriculum for compulsory education". What is not so clear is whether it is in such a development that flexibility lies. These are the developments of the Leaving Certificate in its different forms, in which flexibility is laid basically upon assessment and content: the structure of the curriculum is to be modular. Yet, Table 7.3 and comments around it (Tuohy, this volume) show failure at the core contents of curriculum, which introduces serious questions on the 'principle of commonality'; neither is it clear where flexibility is needed. It seems that the real problem before the latest reforms was "the development of alternative curricula for young people who experienced little success in school and who 'dropped out', often with no qualifications. This formed part of the social policy related to disadvantage". That was also - and still is - a problem throughout Europe. In fact, had that problem not been there, there would have been fewer attempts to reform postcompulsory curricula, and these would not have been as vigorous. This is also confirmed by the fact that many of the new reforms have left some room for previous system structures to which those students who are academically oriented still go, and which seem not to be so much in need of flexible structures. The issue, then, is to what extent such reforms have succeeded in solving that problem, or whether the problem remains unsolved, while it is other students who are benefiting from the reforms. Tuohy also mentions something about this, when explaining the differences between full-time and part-time students: part-time students would apparently benefit more from a flexible system, though data are provided on full-time students. This is of particular relevance in the case of VET, since part-time students are usually those who work, and for whom VET has a different meaning.

Some reference is also made, though veiled, to the old Deweyan ideals, which might apparently suit flexibility policies nowadays: "(...) the strong culture of general education in second-level schools, and the dominance of a more academic approach to general education. Perhaps it also reflects a pragmatic response to a changing economy, where young people were not prepared to commit themselves too early to a career path, delaying their options until they had to make choices at third level." Is this not flexible enough? Do students need greater choice? What are the conditions upon which they can make effective that choice? Does it have to consist of a choice of content, a choice of level, or both? Why not leave choice to delivery, why not let them choose the teacher? Is there any choice of the assessment procedures - if not of the assessment system? Is it vocational orientation which will contribute to making those conditions effective? Does flexibility depend upon the guidance that the students receive?

There are but few other forms of flexibility: the transition year seems to have it embedded. Yet, flexibility runs the risk of fragmenting knowledge, which would not be good for the 'academically weak' groups. The dualisation of pathways seems to happen: the preference for 'more vocational subjects' among the 'weak' is accompanied by a failure at the core subjects. How is this to be judged in terms of access to knowledge? Furthermore, is this contributing to the use of labelling practices in both the school system and the labour market? And what can we say of the apparently 'subverted' use of the certification - LCV - described towards the end of the chapter?

Maybe, if failure is the problem, the solution lies not only in changing the content, modifying its levels, and organising it differently, but also in the very pedagogical relation which occurs in school and is relatively independent of the content. If the forms of delivery remain untouched, whatever changes are made to content will not reach the students, or will by reducing and simplifying the content itself, rather than reinforcing those young people who are 'academically weaker' or 'at risk'. Of course, this pedagogical relation is firmly linked to the assessment practices, and to these we turn in the next section.

11.3.4 From a unified to a flexible vocational system: the Hungarian transition case

The chapter prepared by Zachár has a different scope to the previous ones. Here, we find a report on the context in which current reforms take place, most of them under the name of flexibilisation, surrendering the former VET system to the needs of the new order. The chapter is full of hope about current changes: one example is the confidence in OKJ, which has not proved very useful in other countries. This might be expected when reforms have just started - as opposed to those countries in which current reforms are addressed to counter the effects of previous recent reforms. There appears to be a certain internationalisation, even Europeanisation, of the rationale behind Hungarian reforms, something that is not so easy to identify in Western European countries. Such reforms also seem coherent in the scenario of a country undergoing deep transformations in both the economy and the political regimes; and, furthermore, VET seems to be playing a role in the strategy of consolidation of the new situation and of the modernisation of the country. This is the reason why VET is closely and undoubtedly linked to the restructuring and stabilisation of the labour market and the economic situation. Nevertheless, such a link seems more appropriate for the case of continuing education than for initial vocational education. What is the effect on pedagogies going to be if such training is attempting so hard to adapt to employers' demands, like "enforcing a system for compulsory further training"?

Furthermore, when reading the chapter, the question arises whether changes in the VET system are being addressed with regard to its structure or to the content of vocational education itself. Is the system generating new qualifications? Are these qualifications useful for the new companies or for those already existing? What schemes for work experience are possible within these new qualifications? More questions are raised when considering the rapid pace of change in the Hungarian VET system within a decade: how have these changes affected teachers' qualifications and jobs?

Some of these questions come from comparing data provided in the tables in Zachár's chapter. The decrease in the numbers of those employed in agriculture has been accompanied by a stabilisation in the composition of apprentices, while there has been a considerable drop in the case of secondary vocational schools, yet it remains a relatively strong sector in the economy of the country. Table 8.5 (Zachár, this volume) provides some hints about the behaviour of secondary vocational schools and apprentice schools during these years, yet it does not show how differently they react to each of the sectors of the economy. It seems that the apprentice system was able to adapt to rapid changes in different domains, while the vocational education system, more modern and recent, is not able to respond adequately, or at least seems to be slow, and maybe even reluctant to change. Might this then be a lesson for other countries, and should this reinforce the ability of a rather old system - apprenticeship - to face the challenges of modern economies?

In this sense, the reforms portrayed in the chapter seem reasonable and have clear aims, like improving basic education, increasing the number of people with qualifications, increasing the number and quality of career orientation services, and delaying the age for entering the labour market. It seems, though, that many of these reforms are reinforcing the role of general education, rather than that of vocational education. This is consistent with the attempt to organise 'employment-aimed training', thus to establish a system of continuing training.

What is most surprising, nevertheless, is the aim to "adopt a flexible vocational training system" precisely in order to guarantee a "legal hierarchy and content for vocational qualifications both within the school system and outside it". Flexibilisation here is used as a means to regulate the system, to introduce coordination into it, and to establish mechanisms of comparability and control. In this sense, we wonder whether the effectiveness of the VET system depends upon flexibility, or are there other elements in or around the system which contribute to its adequacy and success, where flexibility plays only a secondary role. In the system, which up to now has been relatively deregulated, and which entailed great flexibility, there might have been other elements within it which contributed to its success in adapting to the changes, without a strong emphasis on flexibility measures.

This may well be connected to the commodification of vocational education, as shown by the data on the different training centres which have taken the initiative in providing updated skills and qualifications: 10 regional development centres, 200 vocational schools, for 1,500 private training providers and approximately 2,000 companies. The differences in numbers make it understandable that a regulatory framework will be welcomed, even more so if we consider the conditions and preparation of the training staff in charge of leading such reforms that are expected to further modernise the country, as can be presumed from the data shown in Tables 8.6 and 8.7 (Zachár, this volume).

On the part of the students, the tendency among young students to gain two different vocational qualifications is remarkable. What sort of professional identities might be fostered through such a strategy: is it a mosaic or polyhedral identity, where reluctance to change is suppressed? Where are the anchors for such identities? Or is the profession no longer a key element in the processes that young people go through to reach maturity?

It also seems that the educational - VET - system of the country might have acted as the pilot-area for expanding ideas and reforms, with the support of funding institutions like the World Bank. And, indeed, it seems that the effort devoted to the reform of VET is much greater than that at other levels of the system. Interestingly enough, though, there seems to be a broad national consensus on the need for such reforms, which has allowed for a succession of them throughout the nineties, despite the political changes in government. Furthermore, Hungary seems to be one of the countries in which VET is kept under the control of the Ministry of Education, as oppossed to what is happening in other European countries, where it has been transferred to the Department of Employment or even the Department of Finance, for its expected role as an 'active measure' against unemployment.

11.3.5 Design and effects of a flexible VET system: a case study in Dutch agricultural education

The chapter written by Geerligs and Nijhof provides good reflections on flexibility, based upon the reform of VET in a sector with strong peculiarities among VET itself. The chapter is outstanding at providing measurements for flexibility and at using them to define the desired standards of flexibility of schools. It would be very interesting to try to apply such measures - upstreaming and downstreaming, qualified school leaving, and shortening of pathways - in order to evaluate reforms introducing flexibility into VET systems in other sectors in the Netherlands and in other countries. The final part of the discussion, at the end of the chapter, is also good at pointing out other dimensions of schooling that may be affected by flexibility policies.

The main achievement of the chapter, however, is to draw on the effectiveness and the efficiency of flexibility, relying upon typologies and levels of flexibility described by the authors elsewhere (Nijhof & Streumer, 1994). Thus, what are the benefits and the freedom introduced by flexibility for both teachers and students - for the latter, not only of choice, but also of moving across different pathways?

To start with, it seems that flexibility increases the proletarisation of teachers. This is a trend which is also shown by data in Chapter 5 but, most significantly, by literature on the teaching profession, see also Chapter 13 of this volume. This is happening as there are increasing controls upon both the input - the curricular prescriptions and the core curriculum - and the output - accreditation procedures - of the educational system. Here, traditions from continental Europe - in prescribing curricula - and of Anglo-Saxon countries - focused on examination bodies, rather than on the delimitation of curricula - have merged to increase the pressure upon teachers, who have to comply nowadays with requirements on both sides, with their corresponding paperwork and their limitation on teachers' work to address everyday issues in their classrooms that have to do with their teaching, rather than with their 'planning' or 'keeping records of achievement'.

How can we then talk about the autonomy of school and the teachers in it if, at the same time, we have pressures to design a core curriculum which has to be developed and delivered through materials in a similar way?

Will this be meaningful? What is then the worth of a curriculum? Whose needs are addressed by it: those of the individual, of society, democracy, VET, or the labour market? These are old Deweyan questions which different curriculum traditions have addressed differently. The value of the curriculum is, of course, linked to its format and structure, and to its code. And flexibility is being introduced in VET at the time of the 'invisible code', as Lundgren (1992) puts it. According to his views, this helps to perpetuate such a code.

Yet, all of these are aspects surrounding the real aim or principle towards which flexibility should be addressed: "that no one should leave the system without an entry or start qualification". If that is the issue, basically the possession of an accreditation, it is therefore not strange that both management and students search for exemptions with regard to their own curriculum pathways. This is probably undesirable, as the authors state, basically because learning is left to the margins: what counts is not the learning processes, but the knowledge one is able to certify. Here, we come to the question of whether anything is better than nothing, despite 'anything' not being a degree. Maybe such accreditations have a labelling effect, which is undesirable, since it prevents the young person from getting a job.

We can also see how the pace and speed of reforms affect its impact. This requires further investigation, for which there is no room in the chapter: is there a 'national' bias towards flexibility? How can we measure flexibility - and its desired effects - where the system has not been reformed? How does flexibility operate at other levels, and has it got any substitute addressed to the same aims but which have been achieved - or attempted - through different strategies? How can we evaluate not only the results of flexibility - its effects - but also the pedagogies and the organisation of school work in those programmes which have been reformed? Furthermore, are there any undesired effects, like the 'dualisation of pathways', which are achieved through the flexibilisation of the system?

11.3.6 Valuing learning outcomes acquired in non-formal settings

The chapter written by Straka is different to all the previous ones in its focus: it deals with assessment systems in various countries, with regard to flexibilisation in the recognition of vocational qualifications. In doing so, its perspective is different to the most usual ones that describe qualification structures and systems. Straka's point of view is on examination - assessment practices - and the subsequent learning which is fostered by the ways in which those exams are arranged and prepared.
The focus on assessment also has an impact on how work interaction is reviewed, when it comes to learning on the job in nonformal learning sites. That space, which has been the domain of teachers and students, is where a great deal of flexibility and decentralisation is currently happening. Yet, those are forms of flexibility and autonomy that are not the preferred ones to the school system.

Straka relates flexibility in curriculum, teaching, and assessment to the learning processes of students and to the learning outcomes of such processes. Thus, we may require flexibility in the way the content is delivered, as well as in the ways it is acquired - apprehended - by students. And, due to the fact that learning processes are often addressed to the examination techniques to which students will be submitted, the types and parts of the exams are a central element for the development of certain learning processes and outcomes, both in the short and in the long term. Straka uses examples from Germany, Norway, and Finland. All of them have in common the wish to be able to accredit and give merit to learning which has taken place without the provision of institutional teaching, not only traditional teaching, but also any form of open or distance learning. This current meritocratic emphasis is consistent with the rapidly expanding, yet confusing - as Straka shows - notion of learning, which has been used too often as a keyword in policy documents, with no clear meaning, or an undefined one.

The main critique that Straka draws on these trends is that most of these initiatives are in different ways a rebirth of the behavioural notion of learning, which may not be so appropriate, either for the current economic and productive system - the knowledge economy - or for those who have not succeeded in formal education, and for whom the recognition of learning in nonformal situations might be an opportunity. Embedded in that behavioural definition is the neglect of the interpretative and cognitive aspects of knowledge, including nonacademic knowledge, and the narrow focus on that knowledge which may be observed and written down in certain forms. This is perceived in the ways in which assessment reforms in those countries are considering issues like novelty or dexterity in the mastery of competencies; the level of detail to which such competencies have to be written; how they handle the emphasis on recognition across borders, while, at the same time, there is an insistence on writing 'national' catalogues of competencies; the fragmentation of skills, rather than the integration of knowledge. Such control over learning might be better assessed if we thought of turning such assessment criteria into curriculum guidelines: would we be able to teach all those competencies? Is it possible to identify so clearly so many contents of the hidden curriculum of vocational education, of learning a profession, and of becoming a citizen?

There are serious questions, therefore, as to whether such attempts to assess learning out of formal settings, which resemble so much the Tyler rationale, will be better able to meet the needs of a qualified workforce. An even more worrying doubt is whether these practices and policies will make any contribution to fostering citizenship, both at the individual and the societal level. At the individual level, with the danger of greater exclusion of those already at risk, with the growing distance in terms of merits accredited. At the societal level, with the commodification of leisure and voluntary work, in terms of acknowledging credit to something which is done supposedly under voluntary conditions, therefore, in a free manner. This consideration of competencies as a property, which should at least be signalised, is consistent with the view of the curriculum - both the training curriculum and the *curriculum vitae* - as an accumulation of knowledge. The paradoxes and conflicts that these raise are clearly addressed in Straka's chapter.

11.4 Conclusions and perspectives on further research

I started this chapter by making clear my perspective with regard to how I was approaching the different chapters under review. I have used those features to read the chapters and raise the issues which those guidelines might help to highlight. I will now briefly comment on what has been the result of such an exercise. I will finish by giving some hints for further research.

The clearest conclusion is that teaching practices have hardly been studied in the chapters. Yet, as I have tried to show in these pages, there is plenty of room there for making flexibility effective in VET , thus comprising the possibility of having an impact upon learning, which is what should count in the end.

There is also the need to develop further studies on how flexibility reaches the content of curriculum - and not just its structure: the knowledge that is selected to be taught in different VET qualifications and the ways in which it is portrayed. This is of particular importance at a time in which flexibility policies are related to the modularisation of the curriculum, and to the fragmentation and deconstruction of knowledge into skills and competencies.

Some of these issues look completely different from the point of view of equal opportunities: the right to education is the right to learn (Connell, 1997; Darling-Hammond, 2001) and the right to be able to hold the accreditations, rather than to merely sit down and 'receive lectures'. The expectations that young people have are important here, and they are, at the same time, connected to related pedagogical elements, such as motivation. These pedagogical issues are not always compatible with system measures, like the homogenisation, comparability, and transferability of qualifications. Many of these, developed under the rationale of 'quality systems', are basically neoliberal attempts which are in the same strand as the capitalisation of knowledge and the marketisation of education, particularly VET. Yet, improving flexibility, in so far as it contributes to the transferability of pathways, is also an aspect which contributes to keeping education - and VET - as a public service from which all have the right to benefit. Whether or not important learning contents are achieved through this, and whether there is an appropriate age to introduce flexibility - and below which that right to education must be solved through other means - is something to evaluate.

More research is also needed into the extent to which different curriculum traditions are helpful to vocational education and to its flexibilisation. Such traditions have a say in areas such as the design and development of curricula, the role of teachers, the allocation and use of teaching aids and curriculum materials and textbooks, as well as in assessment practices. Otherwise, it seems that the only way to handle curriculum in VET is that of the Tyler rationale, which has proved to be one of strong rigidity in compulsory primary and secondary education.

The remaining questions in this chapter have to do with the kind of research - rather than its focus or content - that might contribute to improving what we already know about flexibility in VET:

a) That analyses on reforms happening in a region or a country are undertaken by scholars of other regions or countries. This would contribute to advance comparative work in avoiding a certain 'defensive' approach, in which all reforms seem to improve the previous schemes or systems. It is the educational features of the system which have to be looked after, rather than its national features;

b) To develop conceptual and analytical frameworks which can be applied to the study of each of the different circumstances, in order to develop an evaluation of reforms and programmes. To develop models and theories, and to use those already existing. Otherwise, the risk of commenting on what is being described is too hard to avoid, in the absence of such frameworks - in this section of the book, we have found examples of such frameworks in the development of matrixes and measures for undertaking such analyses. The lack of theory in most of these areas is a problem both for - and of - research;

c) To consider in depth why flexibility is an option basically in postcompulsory education, while it is not fostered in primary, compulsory - or even secondary - education, where the trend towards reinforcing core curricula seems to be growing. What are the problems then in the transition from primary to postcompulsory education? These are troubling questions if we think of flexibility as an opportunity - a way out - for dropouts; or is it more an option for those who have succeeded in school? We are tempted to think so if it is mainly the students who have succeeded who are in a position to benefit from the features embedded in it. If so, does flexibility solve problems, or does it introduce new ones? Is the flexibilisation of the system then a closing of options for some students?

d) To develop research teams with researchers from different study areas: economists, psychologists, educators, sociologists, etc. The subject of vocational

education and training and the relations between education and work require it to
be so.

References

Apple, M.W. (2001). *Educating the right way*. New York: Peter Lang.
Apple, M.W., & Beane, J. (1998). *Escuelas democráticas*. Madrid: Morata. [*Democratic schools*, 1995, Alexandria: ASCD].
Connell, R.W. (1997). *Escuelas y justicia social*. Madrid: Morata. [*Schools and social justice*, 1993, Philadelphia: Temple University Press].
Darling-Hammond, L. (2001). *El derecho de aprender*. Barcelona: Paidós. [*The right to learn*, 1997, San Francisco: Jossey-Bass].
Fenstermacher, G. (1989). "Tres aspectos de la filosofía de la investigación sobre la enseñanza", in Witrock, M. (ed.) *La investigación de la enseñanza (I)* Barcelona: Paidós, pp. 150-179. [Three aspects of philosophy on research on teaching, in *Handbook of research on teaching*, 1986, New York: MacMillan].
Garrick, J. (1998). *Informal learning in the workplace*. London: Routledge.
Lundgren, U.P. (1992). *Teoría del curriculum y escolarización*. Madrid: Morata. [*Between education and schooling: outlines of a diachronic curriculum theory*], 1991, Victoria: Deakin.
Marhuenda, F. (2000a). *Didáctica general*. Madrid: De la Torre.
Marhuenda, F. (2000b). *Trabajo y educación*. Madrid: CCS.
Marhuenda, F., Cros, M.J. & Giménez, E. (2001). *Aprender de las prácticas: didáctica de la formación en centros de trabajo*. Valencia: Universitat de València.
Nijhof, W.J., & Streumer, J.N. (Eds.) (1994). *Flexibility in training and vocational education*. Utrecht: Lemma.
Nijhof, W.J., Kieft, M., & Woerkom, M. van (2001). *Reviewing flexibility. A systems approach to VET*. Luxembourg: Office for Official Publications of the European Communities.

SECTION IV

PROFESSIONAL CONDITIONS

CHAPTER 12

Professionalism as a path for the reform of VET systems

LORENZ LASSNIGG

12.1 Introduction

THE ROLES AND RESPONSIBILITIES AS WELL AS the qualifications and competencies of teachers and trainers have been well represented on the agenda for the reform and improvement of education. There have been serious disputes about these issues, as the teachers and their interest organisations have been especially blamed for problems in public education by the proponents of the market-oriented public choice theory, which has gained influence in broad chapters of the policy community at national and supranational levels. More recently, new proposals for the improved "professionalism" of teachers have been made, which might be seen as attempts to reverse the rather defensive position of these groups. When we look at vocational education and training (VET), however, we can see that the questions grouped around professionalism are much more complex. What we may term "VET professionals" turns out to be a kind of hybrid category in recent research, including not only teachers and trainers but also several other professional roles and positions.

Thus, "professionalism" is a multifaceted issue when we apply that term to VET. First, we have to take into account the ambiguities and dynamics at the conceptual level. Second, there is at least a dual meaning of this term in VET, concerning the roles of the teacher and trainer on the one hand and the professional mastering of the respective occupational content to be taught on the other. The teaching and training functions are consequently seen as a key factor in the development of a well-functioning and responsive VET system. There is a need to bring more systematic reasoning into the question of what "professionalism" might mean in VET.

12.2 The concept of professionalism

The concept of professionalism is used in an open and dynamic way, to explore certain facets and potentials of that phenomenon in the area of VET systems. On a more theoretical level, the concept is complex in itself, and has been in flux since its "classical" period in the 1960s. Initially, high-status occupations with considerable power were described as professions, with the following characteristics usually being attributed to them (cf. Torres, 1991; Alisch, Baumert & Beck, 1990):

- specific expertise or knowledge base, which tends to be closely related to a specific scientific discipline;
- a system of regulation and control, within which the processing of a specific occupational area is reserved specifically for this profession by the state, and which is subject to auto-control;

W. J. Nijhof et al. (eds.), Shaping Flexibility in Vocational Education and Training, 183-205.
© 2002 Kluwer Academic Publishers. Printed in the Netherlands.

- a specific code of ethics, which provides the basis for auto-control, and in conjunction with this, a special system of values;
- a type of self-organisation, which also regulates access to the profession, and special training as well as certain practical requirements.

It is easy to see that professional groups of educators fulfil very few of these criteria - "VET professionals" usually even less so than other categories of teachers and trainers. The consequence of this was that teachers were classed as a *semi-profession* (Etzioni, 1969; cf. also the early twist in the meaning of the term into "bureaucratic professions" by Leggatt, 1970, p. 160; see also Hodkinson & Issitt, 1995, p.8).

Since then, attention in the theoretical discourse has shifted to focus more closely on the process of creating and developing professions, definitions were made more flexible, and the dissociation from other forms of occupations is seen in a less absolute, more fluid way (Abbott, 1988). It is particular discussions about the definition and control of a certain occupational field, and the institutionalisation of a specific knowledge base, as a basis for the legitimisation of occupational autonomy, (DiMaggio & Powell, 1991). More recently, in line with the development of neoliberalism, the relationship of professionalism and managerialism has come up as an important question of analysis (cf. Exworthy & Halford, 1999). Nittel (2000) has made a distinction between three aspects of the "professional complex", with distinct theoretical references: *professionalism*, meaning competent performance of an occupational field, and referring to an action-theory perspective of work performance; *professionalisation*, meaning the collective processes of establishing a degree of visibility and power for an occupational group; and *profession*, meaning a certain established category of occupations, referring to macro-level theories of society concerning the functional differentiation and overall structures of the division of labour. These meanings do not necessarily combine to give a holistic, theoretical and empirical view, thus the former categories may be used for professional fields other than professions.

However, the reasoning in this contribution concentrates on the questions of how the status of a *profession* may be achieved in VET, which developments in this direction can be observed, and how professionalism in this meaning may affect VET reform and development. Professional work was originally seen in contrast to work in bureaucratic hierarchies, and consequently the spread and predominance of Taylorism and the Fordist model in the sixties and seventies led to an image of de-professionalisation, with some people even talking of the "proletarisation" of professions. Professional forms of work, however, proved more able to survive than had been predicted by this research, with the new production concepts and the post-Fordist paradigm in particular stressing re-qualification and re-professionalisation. Nowadays, it is the relationship between professional work and bureaucratic hierarchies which is being studied. "The dominance of bureaucratic hierarchies is over", writes Lynne Zucker (1991, p. 160) in her study of the interplay between "bureaucratic authority" and "expert authority". Different forms of complementarity and interplay, which can be studied in more detail in the system of vocational training and coordination between training and employment, have taken over from the dichotomy between hierarchy and profession and their mutual exclusiveness.

A link between professionalism and innovation research is provided by the study of the content of professional work (cf. Eraut, 1994) in relation to the development of learning organisations and the learning processes in the interplay between tacit knowledge and codified knowledge. Professional work stands out particularly due to the great importance of its implicit components, which implies particular conditions and also difficulties in shaping formal training for learning these qualifications. The pedagogical and learning-oriented concepts of communities of practice, which are highlighted in some other chapters of this volume, are another approach to bring this aspect to the fore. The current analysis, however, concentrates more on the institutional and policy-oriented aspects of this topic.

Clearly, there are differing views about what innovation means, where it comes from, and how it is brought about. Concerning our issue of professionalism in VET, the main question related to innovation is what role the VET system, and consequently VET professionals, might play in the process of knowledge production in their respective areas. In conceptual terms, we have here the well-known distinction between the linear and the systemic models of innovation, which are related to the different forms of knowledge, informal and formal, tacit and codified, practical and theoretical, etc. (cf. OECD, 2000).

Against the background of these concepts, the structure of VET systems and the distinctive roles and positions of VET professionals and their division of labour can be seen as a complement to the distribution of knowledge and the organisation of the process of knowledge production. The horizontally fragmented and vertically layered VET systems, combined with a segmented division of labour among VET professionals, reflect the linear model of innovation, with its segmented allocation of the different stages of knowledge production to different institutions. Professionalisation against this background is related to the more inclusive and interactive structure of knowledge production in the systemic model of innovation.

The starting point for the analysis of the main categories of "VET professionals" is a comparative review of research in the field of the vocational training system (VET) on the one hand, and in the newly emerging field of human resource development (HRD) on the other.

Contrasting vocational education and training (VET) and Human Resource Development (HRD) can be productive for the purpose of understanding jobs, roles, tasks, and positions, since we can draw on a more developed analysis of roles and positions in the HRD field, as compared to the VET field. Research into professionalism in HRD is conceived of as a kind of model or counterfactual for VET professionalism, as it starts from a holistic perspective of roles to be performed in that field, bringing together the various functions involved, which are normally much more segmented and scattered in the VET field. The relation of education and training-related functions and managerial functions especially is solved in a gradual manner in the HRD concept, as compared to the tendency to create a deep split between them in VET, where the managerial functions are in fact allocated more or less to the political level.

The analysis follows four steps:
1. the patterns of professionals working in HRD are reviewed concerning their roles, positions, and tasks in different national systems;
2. the categories of professionals in VET systems are analysed;
3. an exemplary analysis is presented of the pattern of the division of labour, and the respective conflicts and linkages among these categories of professionals in a national system;
4. an overview is given of research into these patterns in other systems.

12.3 HRD practitioners: their roles, positions and tasks in Europe and the USA

12.3.1 Roles

In contrast to the dominant role of teachers and trainers in vocational training, the classification of HRD practitioners covers a much broader spectrum of roles. This field may also be studied as an example of how a certain occupational group has been developed towards professionalism. The activities leading up to the creation of the *American Association for Training and Development* (ASTD) were an important step towards the professionalisation of the HRD field, with systematic investigations and developments of the roles and functions of HRD practitioners having been undertaken since the eighties. In the nineties, this approach was put to good use on a broader European scale, particularly through the activities of the University of Twente.

The classification of HRD roles in the USA (McLagan & Suhadolnik, 1989, p. 20) is important in this context, the professional *roles* being a basic conceptual element in establishing the professional field.

Table 12.1 *Roles of HRD practitioners.*

1.	Marketer
2.	Needs Analyst
3.	Researcher
4.	HRD Materials Developer
5.	Organisation Change Agent
6.	Instructor/Facilitator
7.	Programme Designer
8.	HRD Manager
9.	Administrator
10.	Individual Career Development Advisor
11.	Evaluator

Source: McLagan and Suhadolnik, 1989, p. 20.

Various studies considered the usability of this classification in the analysis of European HRD practitioners (cf. de Rijk et al., 1994; Valkeavaara, 1996, 1998; Odenthal & Nijhof, 1996). Similarities and differences emerged with the US structure[1], which, in turn, can be seen to be in motion (McLagan, 1996)[1]. The European surveys, which are possibly distorted by sampling errors and the small sample size, tend to coincide on a high dominance of four roles, with the Instructor/Facilitator as a leading role being ticked by 85%-95% of respondents. The following three roles, which may be termed the main roles were ticked by 50% of respondents in Germany, and they were also frequently mentioned - although in different configurations - for the other European countries looked at. The remaining

---

[1]   The 1989 role structure has been revised for a new study of HRD roles in the USA. New roles are Organisation Design Consultant and Performance Consultant, the original specialised roles of Evaluator and Needs Analyst have been absorbed into the more complex new roles, (cf. also Odenthal & Nijhof, 1996, pp. 88-89). A European project also analysed developments in large companies in the direction outlined by the ASTD. An overall shift from the more "practical" roles in training towards the more "strategic" roles linking HRD to corporate needs can be observed (Tjepkema, Horst, Mulder & Scheerens, 2000, 85-86).

roles from the ASTD classification were much less frequently ticked by participants (e.g. in Germany, by a maximum of one-third of respondents), and can be seen as more highly specialised roles in Europe:

Table 12.2 *Distribution of HRD roles in European studies.*

Leading role	Main roles	Specialised roles
Instructor/Facilitator	Programme Designer	HRD Materials Developer
	Organisation Change Agent	Marketer
	Needs Analyst	Individual Career Development Advisor
		Evaluator
		HRD Manager
		Researcher
		Administrator

Source: Classification Lassnigg, based on results by Odenthal and Nijhof, 1996.

There are different degrees of emphasis on the specialised roles from one European country to another: in Ireland and England, the roles of HRD Manager and Administrator were regularly ticked, whereas in Germany, HRD Materials Developer, Marketer and Individual Career Development Advisor and Evaluator are the most frequently encountered specialised roles; in Italy, Individual Career Development Advisor and Evaluator were mentioned comparatively rarely; in England, Researcher and HRD Materials Developer play a comparatively more important role.

12.3.2 Positions, roles and tasks

Another perspective to analyse the occupational field of HRD practitioners are the *positions* in terms of the job titles performed in the enterprise sector. The most important positions comprising the different roles are summarized in Table 12.3.

Table 12.3 *Positions of HRD practitioners.*

Trainer	Personnel or Executive Manager
Advisor	HRD Coordinator, Counsellor
Training or HRD Manager	Researcher
Director or Head	

Source: Odenthal and Nijhof, 1996.

More detailed analysis of the most important roles and tasks performed within the different positions reveals a large degree of overlapping between the job titles in terms of roles (see Figures 12.1 and 12.2 based on Odenthal & Nijhof's survey 1996, and de Rijk & Nijhof, 1997).

Closer consideration of the empirical distribution of roles amongst German HRD practitioners produces the following picture (see Figure 12.1). There are four overlapping types of job titles, each of which has to carry out similar tasks: Trainers

(41%), HRD Managers, Counsellor-Coordinators (20%), Advisors, Director-Heads (26%), and Personnel or Executive Managers (4%). All these headings have the *instruction/facilitation* and *programme design* roles in common, carried out by more than two-thirds of practitioners. These can be seen as a core function. Trainers also act as *organisation change agents*, whilst HRD Managers and Counsellor-Coordinators, in addition to their core functions, also perform *needs analysis*. Advisors and Director-Heads perform *all the roles mentioned* (the small group of Personnel or Executive Managers also perform the role of *HRD Manager*, which would appear to be redundant).

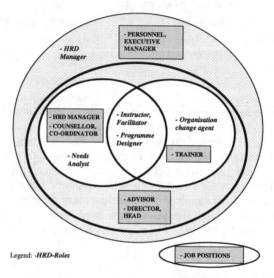

Legend: *-HRD-Roles*   *- JOB POSITIONS*

Job positions are represented by circles, and are comprising all roles falling within the circle; areas of intersecting circles show common roles of inter-secting job positions.

Figure 12.1 HRD roles and self-reported job positions of German HRD personnel. (Odenthal and Nijhof, 1996; Table 4.23 Design of figure by the author.)

A study from the beginning of the 1990s (Arnold & Müller, 1992) gave a similar picture. An important distinction was drawn between full-time personnel within companies on the one hand and part-time personnel and external trainers, who have become the main force for further education in companies, on the other. The profile of full-time personnel, especially that of the trainers, is even more complex than observed in the HRD studies. As an example, the full-time trainers also perform needs analysis, whereas this role tends to be performed by HRD Managers or Counsellors, according to the quantitative studies. Arnold & Müller (1992; see also Nittel 2000, 180-181) point to an ongoing process of enriching the educational personnel towards the performance of management functions and of supporting organisational and cultural change in the enterprises.

The most important tasks performed by European practitioners in the course of their work were also surveyed (see Figure 12.2). Here, once again, there is a lot of overlapping between tasks. Six out of ten categories of tasks are regularly mentioned in more than two headings of job positions, including two tasks in four headings (design and develop HRD interventions; deliver HRD interventions), and two tasks in three headings (consultancy/advise and manage/develop the department). Only four of the ten categories of tasks were more regularly ticked specifically for certain headings (recruitment, management development, research, report/publish).

In conclusion, two task areas or roles provide the focus of activity for European HRD practitioners: training/facilitation and organisational change agent. On average, for the four European countries, a quarter of respondents indicated these roles as being the most important; in Germany, the most important role focused more heavily on Instructor/Facilitator (41%) than on change agent (13%). Despite the high proportion of direct teaching activity or learning support, the activities of HRD personnel are quite closely tied in with the organisational development processes. For example, there are no major differences between internal and external HRD practitioners as regards their professional activities. A recent study of HRD professionals in large learning-oriented organisations across Europe confirms the predominant role of training activities by HRD personnel, whereas in some organisations, HRD professionals operate as change agents, starting and supporting the change process towards a learning organisation" (Tjepkema et al. 2000, p. 9). The authors suppose that their "outcomes might indicate that HRD practices to some extent fall behind HRD visions"(ibid., VII). Even in the learning-oriented organisations studied, one of the main inhibiting factors for the innovation of HRD towards these visions was a lack of clarity about HRD's role (besides the well-known lack of time for learning, and for performing HRD tasks on the part of managers, and a lack of motivation on the part of managers, or employees; ibid., VII, 43-45).

12.4 Categories of professionals in VET

The division of labour between different professional profiles in the area of formalised vocational training, as compared with these occupational roles and headings in the HRD field, can be analysed on the basis of some empirical studies of the different categories of teachers and trainers in particular. The comparative CEDEFOP study of *Teachers and Trainers in Vocational Training* (CEDEFOP, 1995a, p. 15; 1995b p. 12; CEDEFOP, 1997) initially distinguishes between three basic types of VET professionals:
- technical and vocational teachers;
- full-time trainers; and
- part-time trainers and temporary trainers.

Distinct *functions*, which are attached to the five basic stages of the training process, are put forward as an additional basis for developing particular professional profiles. "In those countries where training is more developed and has a longer tradition, it is possible to establish a second means of classification based on the function fulfilled by the teacher or by the trainer (...) there are five basic stages in the training process, around which new occupational profiles are emerging: mainly needs analysis and design, organisation of the training, the design and drawing up of the didactic material, the training itself, and evaluation. Around these functions, new areas of expertise are becoming apparent. They are related to education and training

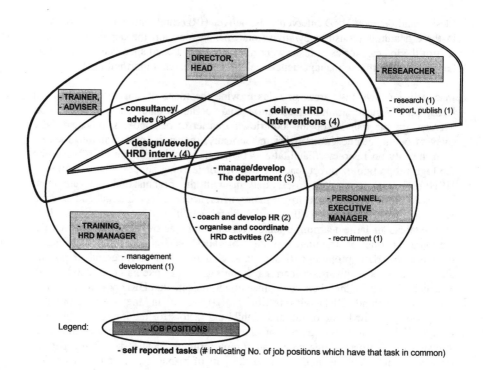

Legend:

- JOB POSITIONS

- **self reported tasks** (# indicating No. of job positions which have that task in common)

Job positions are represented by circles or segments, and are comprising all tasks falling within the circle or segment; areas of intersecting circles or segments show common tasks of intersecting job positions. *Source*: de Rijk and Nijhof, 1997, 8, Tab. 3 (Design of figure by the author).

Figure 12.2 Self-reported tasks and job positions of European HRD personnel.
management and the organisation and planning of teaching" (CEDEFOP, 1995b, pp. 12-13)[2]. A somewhat modified classification of six different functions in the vocational training field, which is more closely related to professional categories in vocational training systems, is provided in CEDEFOP (1997).

Table 12.4 *Functions and professional categories in VET.*

Tutoring (tutor, coach, guide, master);	Development (developer, designer);
Teaching (teacher, trainer, instructor);	Management (training manager, principal, director);
Counselling (counsellor, consultant);	Policy-making

Source: Quotation from CEDEFOP, 1997, p. 15.

---

[2] This functional analysis, based on the training cycle, also underlies the British approach to skill development from the time of the Industrial Training Boards until the developments in the Training and Development Lead Body (CEDEFOP, 1995a, pp. 157-158, p. 171).

A comparison of the two types of classification - that in the HRD field on the one hand, and that in the VET systems on the other - reveals one fundamental difference: in the HRD field we are dealing with complex profiles, which are often directly related to management and guidance functions, whilst in the VET field there is a segmentary division, which is typical of Taylorism and Fordism. Teaching and support functions tend to be quite distinct from the other functions, such as analysis, planning, development, design, evaluation, etc. The more organisational tasks are usually carried out outside the actual training organisations within the administrative superstructure, often even outside the education sector in the area of the political and corporative organisations of interest groups. This pattern corresponds to the model of bureaucratic organisation.

Studies of teachers and trainers in vocational training in the countries of the European Union produce a basic pattern, in which the areas of vocational training schools as well as apprenticeship and other forms of vocational training - the latter being more deeply rooted in the employment system (e.g. labour market training) - overlap with the HRD field. In the school sector, there is a great deal of regulation, supervision, and information, but much less in the other areas. Thus, for example, it was not even possible in the CEDEFOP studies to simply find comparative figures for the different categories of trainers and tutors. Some important findings from the comparative CEDEFOP "cartographic" studies were:

- The *division of VET professionals according to the three basic types* of teachers, full-time trainers, and part-time /temporary trainers was clearly found in most of the different countries (there is little information about tutors, a category which seems to merge with that of trainers).

- The *teacher category is closely related to the structure of the respective vocational training systems.* In many countries, these systems are highly regulated, differentiated, or fragmented, and this structure is reflected in the structure of teachers and their training system (particularly obvious in France, for example). If the vocational training sector is less regulated, there is a greater diversity as well as a less pronounced structuring in the educator area (e.g. in England, where at the same time the clearest linkages of VET and HRD are to be found).

- Usually *educators tend to be bound very specifically to a subject*, which can be general, occupational, or technical. There are often various more or less hierarchical levels of educators, sometimes linked with types of schools at different levels. Moreover, in the area of vocational training subjects, there are more theoretical (higher value) and more practical (lower value) categories of educators with different training pathways. Training of staff for the general subjects usually takes place at the higher education level, whilst this is less often the case for staff for vocational training subjects. Educators for practical subjects often have vocational training at the middle level (skilled worker). Thus, a rather rigid structure of VET professionals exists in various countries.

- In most countries, *educators for professional subjects*, most of whom have had to go through the relevant training at the higher education level, are required to have several years' *practical experience in industry*. (England is an exception, for example, where there is no regulated professional training for this staff, as is Italy). In many countries, there are ongoing discussions as to whether the emphasis in teacher training for professional subjects should be placed more on the pedagogical or on the practical-occupational side. This type of discussion is taking place in Germany, for example, and also in Switzerland for the staff in full-time or part-time vocational training schools (cf. Bader & Hensge, 1996; Ruetzel, 1996; Straumann, 1996).

- Whilst there is a good level of information in the teacher field, *the information base for trainers is very poor in all countries.*[2] A distinction is often drawn between trainers within companies on the one hand, and trainers in extra-school institutions for vocational training, which usually fall within the scope of responsibility of labour market policy, or labour market authorities, on the other. Occupational training programmes for disadvantaged young people are carried out in this area in project form, but the institutions are intended for both young people and adults. Specific rules on qualifications usually apply to these trainers, but it is rare to come across any specific training requirements. (In Italy, for example, there are exhaustive job descriptions within the framework of collective contractual regulations.)

- A further category of trainers who are covered by regulations are the *in-house company trainers in apprenticeship systems*. In this field once again, a large proportion of trainers do this as a sideline without being trained, and trainers are expected to lean more heavily towards the practical side, with pedagogical requirements taking a back-seat role. In Germany, for example, a large percentage of employees - one in six, according to estimates - are involved in training, but most of them minimally so and as a sideline. (Around half of all trainers only for a few hours, and less than 10% devote more than half their working hours to training; cf. Neubert 1996; a similar situation is to be found in Austria; cf. Lassnigg & Steiner 1997.)

- The *structures for training and further training of trainers tend to be vague and complex*, and are often rooted in the market economy sector. Although efforts are being made in the training establishments linked to labour market policy to take as much account as possible of economic requirements, there are, all the same, considerable differences between the training establishments and the in-house training processes. Ellström (1999) describes these differences between a "factory culture" and a "learning culture" and the tensions related thereto using a comparison between training on the labour market and the Swedish "employer-sponsored training".

- One important characteristic of teachers and trainers in the vocational training sphere is that *they belong to two professional categories*: on the one hand, their own area of expertise, and on the other, their role as educators. Usually the lion's share of their training has been with reference to their field of expertise, with training for teaching activities amounting to very little[3].

---

[2] In some reports, it is clearly pointed out that the education system "does not officially recognise the trainer function" (e.g. Finland in CEDEFOP, 1998). The category of trainers provides in fact a direct relationship to the HRD field, and the studies indirectly point to a prevailing tendency to neglect that field.

[3] This corresponds to a certain extent to the paradigm of teachers in higher education as conceived in Humboldt's principle of "Education through Science": "anyone who has a scientific grasp of his subject can also teach it" (orig. German; Thonhauser, 1995, p.115; cf. also Stinchcombe, 1990).

12.4.1 Old and new professionals in Austria as an example for the division of labour

Some basic patterns in this field can be sketched out using a stylised picture of the different types of VET professionals in the Austrian VET system (Lassnigg & Stöger, 1999; Lassnigg, 1999a).[4] By comparing different areas from the whole scope of VET and HRD, a kind of overall and inclusive professional structure is generated, within which we can draw a distinction between "old" and "new" professionals. The "VET professionals" in the formal vocational training system can be broken down into four categories of "old professionals":

- teachers, trainers, tutors;
- administrators, principals, managers;
- politicians, lobbyists;
- researchers.

There are three important areas of VET and HRD which lie outside the traditional formal VET system, and can be seen as the basis for the emerging categories of "new professionals":

- adult education (including further training, labour market and publicly supported in-service training);
- HRD in the company sector and on the market for consultancy;
- a new area of intermediate organisations (centres for innovation), which have no direct training function as such but play an important role in providing incentives, triggering innovation, and playing a coordinating role.

These areas are clearly gaining importance, and the professional categories of people working within them cannot be subsumed within the traditional categories of VET professionals. Moreover, they are normally not even subsumed within that field of professional competence.

The most important characteristics and aspects of the division of labour among VET professionals can be indicated by a stylised comparison of the HRD roles on the one hand, and the categories of "old" and "new" professionals in the Austrian example on the other (cf. Figure 12.3).

Firstly, the distinction of the four categories of "old professionals" broadens the traditional focus, which tended to concentrate on educators (teachers, trainers, tutors) alone, as the wider organisational professional categories are included. In so doing, it becomes clear that professional demands in the area of VET also cover a broader scope of functions and categories than would appear when viewed from the point of view of professionalising the teaching profession.

Secondly, the cross-classification of VET professionals and HRD roles shows that, in spite of their different field of application (economic organisations) and different aim (implementation of company strategies), the latter can still reveal important aspects of professionalisation in the education sector. What emerges in particular in the formal education system is the segmentary distribution of the various roles in different contexts (administration, politics), and it becomes clear that there is a potential overlapping with the development of learning organisations. Firstly, training organisations can themselves be conceived of as learning

---

[4] This section owes very much to the work in the project "New forms of education of professionals for vocational education and training (EUROPROF)", which was carried out in the Leonardo da Vinci programme (European Commission ID 3366).

organisations, and secondly, training also plays an important role in the development of learning organisations in the business sector.

The distinction between the contexts of the formal education sector on the one hand, and the HRD field, adult education, and the intermediary organisations on the other sheds light on the different configurations of "old" and "new" professional profiles. Roles are matched in a segmented manner to the various vocational categories amongst the "old" professionals, with teachers teaching, administrators administrating and developing, politicians taking decisions, researchers carrying out research, etc. Conversely, the "new" professionals have more complex role profiles.

There are also some similarities concerning the pattern of roles between certain categories of "old" professionals and certain areas in the "new" context - between teachers-trainers-tutors and adult education, between administrators/managers and professionals in the HRD field (with the difference that the latter are more active in the direct teaching-learning processes), and between politicians-lobbyists and the professionals working in intermediary organisations.

This stylised pattern, which needs to be analysed in greater depth by further research, warrants a few additional comments. Administrators-managers have a complex role profile and concentrate a very important strategic function in their field. This corresponds to the bureaucratic model, but it should be stressed that this category of "de facto" VET professionals is not usually taken as such. With the exception of more recent attempts at the professional preparation of school heads, there is next to no training for these categories. Legal training continues to play an important role in administration, and to some extent, this is a case of promotion positions for teachers, which are still often filled according to political criteria. The organisational context of the "new" professionals is less bureaucratic and demands more complex profiles, which are necessitated by the fact of working in a more flexible environment. Linking learning functions with organisational activity in development and planning raises the question as to how useful similar combinations might be amongst the "old" professionals.

As opposed to the conceptual integration of an overall professional structure in VET and HRD, the categories of VET professionals described live and work in different "worlds", are not particularly coordinated, and sometimes even work against each other. There are certain lines of conflict among them, and there exist certain linkages too, each influenced by and influencing the functioning of the VET system.

	"OLD" PROFESSIONALS VET System[a]				"NEW" PROFESSIONALS. Other Frameworks[b]		
	Teachers Trainers Tutors	Administrators Principals Managers[c]	Politicians Lobbyists	Researchers	Adult Educ.	HRD	Inter-Med.
Common roles							
- Instructor/ Facilitator	xxxxx	x			XXX	XXX	
- Programme Designer	xx	xxxxx	xx	x	XX	XXX	X
- Org. Change Agent		xxxxx	xx	(x)		XXX	XXX
- Needs Analyst		xxxxx	xxxxx	xx	X	XXX	XXX
Specialised roles							
- Materials Developer	(x)	xx			X	X	
- Marketer		(x)	xxxxx		X	X	XXX
- Indiv. Career Devel. Advisor	x				X		
- Evaluator (Inspector)		xxxxx	xxx	xx	X	X	XXX
- HRD Manager		xx				X	
- Researcher				xxxxx		X	
- Administrator	x	xxxxx			X	X	

Notes: [a] The counselling function is mainly performed outside the VET system within the labour market organisations; within VET the teachers perform these activities. [b] Personnel in HRD, further education (F-E), intermediary institutions (INT). [c] The functions of development are performed mainly in this category.

Figure 12.3 Stylised pattern of roles and professional categories in Austrian VET.

12.4.2 Toward a generalised picture of the division of labour

The experience and results of research into the division of labour between the different categories of VET professionals were processed in the EUROPROF project, and reveal some similar basic patterns and tensions (cf. Attwell, 1997a; Brown, 1997; Heidegger, 1997; Heikkinen, 1997a). Attwell (1997a, p. 261) describes a simultaneous process of convergence and divergence for both sides - VET and HRD - which has the following characteristics:

- extending the role of VET professionals, mainly through increased activity in the field of further education (developing new programmes for new groups of learners);
- greater involvement in processes of organisation learning (linking learning with labour processes);
- increased concern for training and further training of the unemployed (counselling, development and organisation of new programmes);
- new roles in the management of learning processes, as a result of decentralisation processes in vocational training;
- increased emphasis on context-related learning and learning in the workplace leads to a shift of activities from traditional teaching in the classroom to

activities involving the shaping of learning processes in practice (mentoring, coaching, simulation, support, etc.).

A few examples of specific developments could serve to illustrate this general trend. Studies in France have revealed that role extension is occurring not only in schools, but also in the area of further training (de Bligniere, 1997).

Reforms in vocational training in Spain since the early nineties have meant in particular that new players have been more involved in the administrative and political fields (social partners, regional administrations, labour administration, etc.), and have done away with the monopoly of the vocational training school system, which was seen as increasingly inefficient (Cellorio, 1997). Similar trends towards greater involvement of external "VET professionals" from amongst the social partners and the regions can be seen in many countries, including Denmark, the Netherlands, Finland, and the United Kingdom, accompanied by relatively pronounced professionalisation (Nielsen, 1996; Santema, 1997; Heikkinen, 1997a, b; Shackleton, Clarke, Lange & Walsh, 1995).

One important question concerns the position and duties of teachers in the vocational training schools, as well as trainers in companies. Teachers are often seen as a central category, which should act as the "spearhead of change and progress in teaching and learning processes" (Attwell, 1997a, p. 258; Papadopoulos, 1994). It is generally felt that an extension and adaptation of their role and function would be desirable, but there are considerable contradictions attached. On this point, the studies in the EUROPROF project refer to different experiences in various countries. Vocational training policy in Finland tried to extend the teachers' activity profile, but this did not prove entirely successful. Anja Heikinnen (1996). At the opposite end of the scale, a study in the Netherlands shows that teachers are very much involved in non-teaching duties, and see this in positive terms (Stoel & Streumer, 1996). At the same time, however, it also says that most teachers teach traditionally (ibid., p. 16).

These differences possibly reflect the different positions and role definitions which teachers have in the respective vocational training systems; they may, however, to some extent, also reflect the sense of some teachers of their professional identity being grounded in their teaching responsibility (cf. Halford & Leonard, 1999, pp. 111-112). For example, the developments in Finland are seen within a marked situation of tension between the traditionally strong and central role of teachers and the technocratic top-down reform politics of the eighties and early nineties (Heikkinen, 1997b, pp. 216-218). The growing significance of informal and work-based learning means increasing importance of and increasing demands for in-house trainers. At the same time, they are usually in a weak position, usually work part-time as trainers, and have little or no professionalisation in their training function - although there is more marked professionalisation in their "own" profession. This even applies to Germany, where this role is the most highly professionalised. This relation of tension seems to be very pronounced across the board within this group, and is sometimes seen as the path towards the "pedagogisation" of labour processes: "... instead of creating a separate group of VET professionals, pedagogical knowledge should increasingly be a component of everybody's 'professionalism', especially those working in jobs involving planning, management and development" (Heikkinen, 1997a, p. 125; CEDEFOP 1996).

A summary of the general shortcomings in the VET professionals' training system levels the following criticism (Heidegger, 1997, pp. 18- 19):

- there is no integration of VET and HRD;
- there is no connection between vocational training and reducing unemployment;
- there is insufficient interaction between the different categories of "VET professionals";
- the opportunities and contributions for shaping the professional position are not valued;
- pedagogical skills are usually kept separate from occupational subject areas;
- occupational competence (know how) and knowledge (know what, know why) are usually kept separate;
- prospects in planning and management are often fundamentally different from the points of view of vocational training practitioners;
- theory and practical application are kept separate, with both sides being incorporated in different positions/persons;
- the development of cooperative learning environments is not taken into account.

Thus, the basic structures and problems of the division of labour amongst VET professionals are mirrored and reflected in their training. Correspondingly, in studies into the opportunities for the professionalisation of the vocational training field quite strong suspicions and tensions between some groups came to the fore (Heikkinen, 1997a, p. 130).

12.5 Pathways towards professionalism

12.5.1 Policy strategies and professionalism

Some major trends in influential recent proposals for policy strategies at the supranational level concern improvement in the internal coordination of the various subsectors of the education and training systems, and changes in the patterns of the allocation of roles and functions among the main actors in the policy process, namely the state, with its varying subsections and agencies at regional and local levels, the providers of education and training, and the various groups of what are preferably called "clients" (students, parents, and economic and societal actors). Somewhat paradoxically, this does not mean a strengthening of the position of the professionals working in these establishments. Especially with the position of teachers, implicitly or explictly, the opposite is frequently the case. Their position as a strong interest group in hierarchical public systems should be weakened by that strategy. Management functions become more important internally, and exposure to external influences should be strengthened through various channels.

Reforms in vocational training have often attributed a passive role to educators. In the technocratic tradition of the sixties and seventies, an attempt was made to change their work through the development and organisation of new teaching plans, curricula, or other rules governing work organisation.[5] The dominant proposals of today, which are quite strongly influenced by the public choice paradigm, also aim

---

[5]   The most extreme version of this strategy is "...to make the learning process 'teacher proof'..." (Haddad, Carnoy, Rinaldi & Regel, 1990, p.57) through the central control of curricula and the communication media.

at indirectly changing the behaviour of educators by strengthening external influences, for example, through quasi-market structures. Teachers have been - and still are - at the centre of contemporary attempts to reform education in several countries. They are clearly seen as a major force for development, but in their established mode as a strongly unionised interest group within public service, they have been seen as the main obstacle to reform. Thus, the weakening of that position can easily be shown to be a core element of the neoliberal policy proposals. The study by Whitty, Power and Halpin (1998, pp. 12-14) of ongoing market-oriented reforms, which has drawn on a lot of relevant literature, produces the following stylised picture, in terms of the consequences of reform for the various "stakeholders" in the system:[6]

- school heads are becoming a central figure, their role becoming more that of "corporate director", "business executive", or "entrepreneur"; in contrast to the discourse about "new managerialism" with flat hierarchies, it is noted that "...the gap between the manager and the managed grows" (p. 12);
- for teachers, there is the "greatest divide between school management texts and empirically informed research": instead of autonomy and professionalism, work is becoming more intense, collective agreements are being undermined, and organisational power is being challenged;
- for pupils and classwork, it is noted that the reforms have not raised standards, and that traditional aspects of teaching have been strengthened ("increasing fragmentation and unitisation of the curriculum", "marginalisation of non-assessed fields", "more rigid compartmentalisation of students", "a new 'hidden curriculum' of marketisation") (p. 13);
- for the political steering and administration of schools, a "highly delimited" involvement of external "stakeholders" was noted, with an unequally strong representation of people with "professional business-related expertise" when compared with "lay members without that expertise", and trends towards the "commodification of parents"(p. 13).

In the following, some attempts are reviewed which have outlined ideas or approaches for dealing with professionalisation.

12.5.2 Strengthening teacher professionalism

As we have seen in the analysis of VET professionals, teachers are the most established group among them. An approach could thus be the direct opposite of the neoliberal one, to establish teachers as a real profession in the traditional sense, and to include other related categories (trainers, facilitators, instructors, evaluators, developers, etc.) in that profession. This strategy has been proposed by Hargreaves and Evans (1997). Attempts in this direction are the strategies in the paradigm of action research, which combine the approach of *the reflective practitioner* with a strong emphasis on the self-evaluation of the education and training establishments

---

[6] It may well be that the results are a bit overstated, but they nevertheless square with de Moura Castro and Cabral de Andrade's (1997) assessments about the internal logic of the bureaucratic interpretation of education and training systems, as well as with the expectations which can be deduced from the institutionalist analysis of educational institutions. Sinclair, Ironside & Seifert (1996) present similar results for the USA and Great Britain; for vocational training policy in Greece, the high priority attached to reducing costs with no regard for quality is flagged (Patiniotis & Stavroulakis, 1997).

as a preferred development strategy. Teachers as researchers of their own practice and experience are more strongly involved in the process of knowledge production, which, in turn, is focused on the borderline between informal and formalised knowledge, or between tacit and codified knowledge. However, this strong focus on teachers does not give enough attention to the complex structure of VET systems, and the various groups and categories of professionals in this field.

The VET Professional as an educator

Another variant of a "strong" professionalism strategy stems from the study of VET professionals in Finland (Heikkinen, 1997a, b; see Chapter 13 by Anja Heikkinen in this volume). It picks up on the existing division of labour between the various categories of VET professionals, the distribution of status between them, their different prospects and duties, as well as the conflicts between them. The question is whether there are enough points in common to warrant an all-embracing professionalisation process. An essential aspect therein is the historically central position of teachers as protagonists of vocational training, in contrast with the educational conception of vocational training. These two conceptions are related to the tensions between vocational professionalism and *professionalism as an educator*. The professionalism of educators is seen as a guarantee of the *educational* conception of vocational training; "...it created a common background for the conception of vocational education - a paradigm of vocational education - among teachers, administrators, players in industry, students and parents" (ibid., p. 215). Educators are simultaneously seen as a link between the different "worlds", and they possess considerable powers of definition for vocational training in their respective fields.

The potential of the in-house HRD field in companies is felt to be undeveloped, the trainer function to be marginal and ignored, staff development of little status, low priority, and not very up to date from the point of view of method (Heikkinen, 1997a, p. 123-126). A personnel developer is quoted in summary form, "business is always business: the economist always beats the training manager in the enterprise, in hierarchy and decision-making...training is no king in working life yet - it is quite the reverse" (ibid., p. 124), (Keep, 2000).[7]

Maintaining the different categories of VET professionals and improving their cooperation on the basis of a mutual understanding of their respective roles is suggested as a strategy for professionalisation, since "...the underlying rationale is that the core of VET professionalism is occupational expertise, practical knowledge and a living connection to industry and occupational life" (Heikkinen, 1997a, p. 129). "New planning and coordinating mechanisms should be developed which would not destroy the educational core in vocational education" (Heikkinen, 1997b, p. 218). An important element in professional development is "professional autonomy for self-definition" (Heikkinen, 1997a, p. 132). In the field of company activities there is a call for the widest possible diffusion of pedagogical knowledge, and further training in administration, planning, research, politics, and the representation of interests is seen as an important task.

---

[7]   This view is to some extent reinforced by the European HRD study cited above, which sees much work left to be done to upgrade the HRD functions in the enterprise sector, even in large learning-oriented organisations (Tjepkema, 2000, 91-95).

The VET professional as a "connective specialist"
Michael Young and David Guile (1997) have developed a professionalisation strategy for the United Kingdom, predominantly against the background of informally organised vocational training. This strategy is aimed at developing the profile of a "professional of the future", building on the traditional elements of professionalism, and tacking on additional elements. This produces a profile of the VET professional as a "connective specialist" (ibid., p. 210).

Table 12.5 *Traditional and new elements of VET professionalism.*

Traditional elements	New elements
Technical competence;	Research and innovation capacity;
Underpinning knowledge;	Customer/client awareness;
Practical experience;	Flexibility (polycontextual, boundary-crossing skills);
Ethic of responsibility.	Telematic-based learning.

Source: Young and Guile, 1997.

This profile certainly represents a further development of VET professionalism in the United Kingdom, in which expansion of the NVQ-concept, which has been criticised for being too narrow, comes to the fore. "The current pattern in the UK mirrors closely that of the provision of VET itself...(i.e. it is uneven and fragmented); furthermore, there are signs that it could become trapped in the competence dogma of NVQs" (Young & Guile, 1997, p. 206).[8] Organisational roles are, however, not part and parcel of this profile. On the question concerning the mechanisms for implementing this profile, reference is made to the building of an infrastructure for vocational training as a political task, within which tasks are allotted to the providers of educational activity, the companies and social partners, as well as the political institutions (Young & Guile, 1997, p. 210- 211).

EUROPROF cornerstones for VET professional training
A further strategy was proposed within the framework of the EUROPROF project, in the shape of a general framework for the development of a European "community of practice". Whilst initially the project was aimed at integrating the numerous different roles within a broad professional profile (Attwell, 1997b, p. 6), the study of structures in the different European countries highlighted the high degree of fragmentation of different categories of VET professionals, but also a trend towards convergence. Since direct, formal integration and cooperation do not appear to be a realistic option, a general framework of "cornerstones" for the training of VET professionals is being suggested as a step towards professionalisation, which will provide a basis for reform in the individual countries and systems, and also a basis for the development of a European Network of players in research and practice. The following aspects have been put forward as the cornerstones of this framework for

---

[8]   In the United Kingdom, attempts at professionalisation link up with the HRD field, because on-the-job learning processes traditionally play a major role in vocational training (cf. also CEDEFOP, 1995a).

the development and further development of training for "VET professionals" (Attwell, 1997a, p. 263-264):

- training programmes at university level, including career guidance and mechanisms for continuing professional development in practice;
- training in participation in shaping production processes (anthropocentric production);
- training in social innovation and entrepreneurial skills;
- linking pedagogical training with vocational training, taking work process knowledge into account;
- training in functions of vocational training planning;
- multidisciplinarity, particularly linking VET and HRD;
- opportunities and points of departure for mobility in Europe;
- training in the implementation of research activities;
- cooperation with organisations in the world of work, and the social partners;
- efforts towards learner-centred training programmes, and cooperation between different organisations, both national and international;
- efforts towards situated learning and rich, context-oriented learning environments.

12.6 Conclusions and perspectives

The following tentative conclusions and perspectives can be drawn when the analysis of VET professionals is related to reform of VET systems, the division of labour, and potential professionalisation in this field.

a) The development of training organisations in the direction of learning organisations is certainly not feasible with the traditional structure of the segmentary division of labour. Neither does this structure appear to be particularly well suited to the strengthening of links between the informal learning processes in companies and the formal ones in the formal training organisations. If the analysis of the roles and positions for HRD personnel is taken as an example, there is a great variety of starting points for professionalisation processes in the overall field of "VET professionals". It seems highly unlikely that a generally "correct" path or a "correct" general profile of VET professionals exists. We can conclude, anyway, that the traditional strategy of professionalisation - which would mean professionalisation of the teaching profession (as, for example, more recently proposed in Hargreaves & Evans 1997) by the development of the specialised knowledge base for their reserved occupational area, and the strengthening of their autonomy in terms of self-organisation, guided by a special code of ethics - does not turn out to be feasible for VET professionals. This is because it would reinforce the emphasis on teaching, and, in turn, strengthen the split from their other roles and functions, especially planning, development, decision-making, etc.

b) To develop a field of professionalisation which combines or amalgamates VET and HRD professionals, and in any case takes up the trainers as a crucial professional category, seems to be an important element of a professionalisation strategy in VET. The softer recommendations for the improvement of the NVQs in the U.K. given by Hodkinson & Issitt (1995), which conceive of teaching as a kind of reflective practice, and work out some important dimensions of professional practice, give useful hints for its development. On the other hand, some visions in HRD, which are focused on the spread and integration of learning into corporate strategies, and which propose the development of stronger linkages between internal and external activities and infrastructures, may be taken as another important element of a professionalisation strategy. This is common in the proposals discussed above.

c) Turning to ideas for constructing occupational realities through the institutionalisation of vocational training, control of the appropriate knowledge base is a strategic element, which must also be taken into account in the development of professional profiles. For VET professionals, the particular problem arises as regards linking the pedagogical or HRD knowledge base to the contextual knowledge base in the occupational field within which the activity takes place. The type of linkage of these elements, as well as their weighting, differs very greatly from one approach and strategy to another.

d) Concerning the relationship of professionalism and education and training reform, we may finally point to a kind of paradox. Although VET professionals seem to be a crucial force for the further development of VET systems, they are linked so tightly to the existing structures that professionalisation will hardly work as an instrument for reform. And this, in turn, reduces the likelihood of reform. Furthermore, involvement in the construction of the symbolic institutions of qualification and occupational structures seems to be a crucial issue for the development of VET as well as for professionalisation. This runs against a "technical-naturalistic" view of qualification demands (cf. Lassnigg, 1999, 2001), which puts its main pressure on the analysis of and passive adaptation to these demands. Involvement in the development of meso-level policy strategies, linking the VET side and the employment side at the level of organisations, seems to be a core activity for promoting professionalism. To overcome the above-mentioned paradox, these activities may be based on the categories of new professionals situated in HRD, or in innovation centres and the like. Professionalism is thus clearly one path for reform, although one which is not easy to follow.

Note

Thanks especially to Phil Hodkinson for his encouraging comments, to Anja Heikkinen for her inspiring questions and editorial recommendations.

References

Abbott, A. (1988). *The system of professions: an essay on the division of expert labour.* Chicago: University of Chicago Press.

Alisch, L.-M., Baumert, J., & Beck, K. (Eds.). (1990). Professionswissen und Professionalisierung. *Braunschweiger Studien zur Erziehungs- und Sozialarbeitswissenschaft, Band 28*; in collaboration with *Zeitschrift für Empirische Pädagogik.* Braunschweig: Sonderband.

Arnold, R., & Müller, H.-J. (1992). Berufsrollen betrieblicher Weiterbildner. *Berufsbildung in Wissenschaft und Praxis*, H.5., 36-41.

Attwell, G. (1997a). New roles for vocational education and training teachers and trainers in Europe: a new framework for their education. *Journal of European Industrial Training 21* (6-7), 257-265.

Attwell, G. (1997b). Towards a community of practice for vocational education and training professionals. In A. Brown (Ed.), *Promoting vocational education and training: European perspectives*. Hämeenlinna: Tamperen yliopisto/LeonardoDaVinci-EUROPROF.

Bader R., & Hensge K. (1996). Aus- und Weiterbildung von Lehrern und Ausbildern. In P. Diepold (Ed.), *Berufliche Aus- und Weiterbildung* (pp. 181-187). Beiträge zur Arbeitsmarkt- und Berufsforschung (BeitrAB) 195. Nürnberg: IAB.

Brown, A., (Ed.) (1997). *Promoting vocational education and training: European perspectives*. Hämeenlinna: Tamperen yliopisto/LeonardoDaVinci-EUROPROF.

CEDEFOP (1995a). *Teachers and trainers in vocational training. Vol I*. Luxembourg: EUR-OP.

CEDEFOP (1995b). *Teachers and trainers in vocational training. Vol II*. Luxembourg EUR-OP.

CEDEFOP (1996). *The role of the company in generating skills: the learning effects on work organisation. Reports on The Netherlands, the United Kingdom*. Luxembourg: EUR-OP.

CEDEFOP (1997). *Teachers and trainers in vocational education and training. Vol III*. Luxembourg: EUR-OP.

CEDEFOP (1998). *Teachers and trainers in vocational education and training. Vol IV*. Luxembourg: EUR-OP.

Cellorio, X.M. (1997). The Spanish VET system at the turn of the century: modernization and reform. *Journal of European Industrial Training 21* (6-7), 220-228

de Bligniere, A. (1997). The professionalisation of VET in France. Paper presented to 10 Year Anniversary Symposium ITB (Institut für Technik und Bildung) Bremen, 19-20 February.

de Rijk R.N., Nijhof, W.J., & Mulder, M. (1994). *The HRD profession in the 90s: table report of a survey on the HRD profession in four European countries*. Enschede: Universiteit Twente. (unpublished manuscript)

Diepold, P. (Ed.). (1996). *Berufliche Aus- und Weiterbildung*. Beiträge zur Arbeitsmarkt- und Berufsforschung (BeitrAB) 195. Nürnberg: IAB.

DiMaggio, P.J., & Powell, W.W. (1991). The iron cage revisited: institutional isomorphism and collective rationality in organisational fields. In W.W. Powell & P.J. DiMaggio (Eds.), *The new institutionalism in organisational analysis* (pp. 63-82). Chicago: UCP.

Ellström, P.-E. (1999). The role of labour market programmes in skill formation: the case of Sweden. In W.J. Nijhof & J. Brandsma (Eds.), *Bridging the skills gap between work and education* (pp. 55-68). Dordrecht: Kluwer.

Eraut, M. (1994). *Developing professional Knowledge and Competence*. London: Falmer.

Etzioni, A. (Ed.). (1969). *The semi-professions and their organization: teachers, nurses, social workers*. New York: Free Press.

Exworthy, M., & Halford, S. (Eds.). (1999). *Professionals and the new managerialism in the public sector*. Buckingham: Open University Press.

Haddad, W.D., Carnoy, M., Rinaldi, R., & Regel, O. (1990). Education and Development: Evidence for New Priorities. *World Bank Discussion Paper No 95*. Washington, D.C.: World Bank.

Halford, S., & Leonard, P. (1999). New identities ? Professionalism, managerialism and the construction of self. In M. Exworthy & S. Halford (Eds.), *Professionals and the new managerialism in the public sector*. Buckingham: Open University Press.

Hargreaves, A., & Evans, R. (Eds.) (1997). *Beyond educational reform. Bringing teachers back in*. Buckingham: Open University Press.

Heidegger, G. (1997). Key considerations in the education of vocational education and training professionals. In A. Brown (Ed.), *Promoting vocational education and training: European perspectives* (pp. 13-24). Hämeenlinna: Tamperen yliopisto/LeonardoDaVinci-EUROPROF.

Heikkinen, A. (1996). Vocational Education as a "life project"? Reflections from the case of Finland. EUROPROF Research paper. University of Tampere.

Heikkinen, A. (1997a). A comparative view on European VET professionalism - Finnish perspectives. In A. Brown (Ed.), *Promoting vocational education and training: European perspectives* (pp. 123-132). Hämeenlinna: Tamperen yliopisto/LeonardoDaVinci-EURO-PROF.

Heikkinen, A. (1997b). Vocational education as a 'life project'? Reflections from the case of Finland. *Journal of European Industrial Training 21* (6-7), 213-219

Hodkinson, P., & Issitt M. (1995). The challenge of competence for the caring professions: an overview. In P. Hodkinson & M. Issitt (Eds.), *The challenge of competence. Professionalism through vocational education and training* (pp. 1-12). London: Cassel.

Keep, E. (2000). Learning Organisations, Lifelong Learning and the Mystery of the Vanishing Employers. *Paper at the ESRC Centre on Skills, Knowledge & Organisational Performance*, University of Warwick (http://www.openuniversity.edu/lifelong-learning/papers/index.html).

Lassnigg, L. (1999). Bildung - Beruf - Beschäftigung. Koordination, Innovationsdynamik und „Systemgrenzen". In C. Honegger, S. Hradil, & F. Traxler (Eds.), *Grenzenlose Gesellschaft* (pp. 484-501). Opladen: Leske+Budrich.

Lassnigg, L. (1999a). "Old" and "New" professionals in Austrian Vocational Education. *Sociological Series* No. 40. Institute for Advanced Studies, Vienna.

Lassnigg, L. (2001). Steering, Networking, and Profiles of Professionals in Vocational Education and Training (VET). In P. Descy & M. Tessaring (Eds.), *Training in Europe*. Second report on vocational training research in Europe 2000: background report, Vol.1, 11-70.(download German version: http://www.equi.at/en_fs_projekte.htm > qualification).

Lassnigg L., & Steiner P. (1997). *Die betrieblichen Kosten der Lehrlingsausbildung*. Materialien zur Wirtschaft und Gesellschaft Nr. 67. Vienna: AK.

Lassnigg, L., & Stöger, E. (1999). Professionals for vocational education and training in Austria. *Report for the EUROPROF Project*. Institute for Advanced Studies. Vienna.

Leggatt, T. (1970). Teaching as a profession. In J.A. Jackson, (Ed.), *professions and professionalization* (pp. 155-177). Cambridge: Cambridge University Press.

McLagan, P.A. (1996). Great ideas revised: creating the future of HRD. *Training and Development* (January), 60-65.

McLagan, P.A., & Suhadolnik, D. (1989). *Models for HRD practice: the research report*. Alexandria VA: ASTD.

Neubert, R. (1996). Arbeitssituation, berufliches Selbstverständnis und Qualifikation ausbildender Fachkräfte. In P. Diepold (Ed.), *Berufliche Aus- und Weiterbildung* (pp. 201-206). Beiträge zur Arbeitsmarkt- und Berufsforschung (BeitrAB) 195. Nürnberg: IAB.

Nielsen, S.P. (1996). The dynamics of change in Denmark: The role of the social partners. *EUROPROF Research paper*. Copenhagen: DEL.

Nijhof, W.J., & Rijk R.N. de (1997). Roles, competencies and outputs of HRD practitioners. *Journal of European Industrial Training 21* (6-7) pp. 247-256.

Nittel, D. (2000). *Von der Mission zur Profession? Stand und Perspektiven der Verberuflichung in der Erwachsenenbildung*. Bielefeld: Bertelsmann – DIE.

Odenthal, L., & Nijhof W.J. (1996). *HRD Roles in Germany. Studies in Human Resource Development*. Enschede: Twente University Press.

OECD (2000). *Knowledge management in the learning society*. Paris: OECD.

Ofner, F., & Wimmer, P. (1998). Alternative approaches to financing lifelong learning. Country report Austria. *Research report* commissioned by the Federal Ministry for Education and Cultural Affairs. Vienna.

Papadopoulos, G.S. (1994). Linkages: a new vision for vocational and technical education. In OECD (Ed.), *Vocational education and training for youth* (pp. 169-179). Paris: OECD.

Patiniotis, N., & Stavroulakis, D. (1997). The development of vocational education policy in Greece: a critical approach. *Journal of European Industrial Training 21* (6-7), 192-202.

Rützel, J. (1996). Professionalisierung von Berufspädagoginnen und Berufspädagogen für eine gewandelte Praxis. In P. Diepold (Ed.), *Berufliche Aus- und Weiterbildung* (pp. 219-222). Beiträge zur Arbeitsmarkt- und Berufsforschung (BeitrAB) 195. Nürnberg: IAB.

Santema, M. (1997). Regional development and the tasks of vocational education and training professionals. *Journal of European Industrial Training 21* (6-7), 229-237.

Sinclair, J., Ironside, M., & Seifert, R. (1996). Classroom struggle? Market oriented education reforms and their impact on the teacher labour process. *Work, Employment and Society* 10 (5), 641-661.

Shackleton, J.R., Clarke, L., Lange, T., & Walsh, S. (1995). *Training for Employment in Western Europe and the United States.* Aldershot: Elgar.

Stoel, W.G.R., & Streumer, J.N. (1996). *The changing role of teachers in secondary vocational education.* EUROPROF Research paper. Enschede: University of Twente.

Straumann, M. (1996). Berufsbildung und Berufspraxis als Grundlage für die Aus- und Weiterbildung der Lehrkräfte an gewerblich-industriellen Berufsschulen in der Schweiz. In P. Diepold (Ed.), *Berufliche Aus- und Weiterbildung* (pp. 223-233). Beiträge zur Arbeitsmarkt- und Berufsforschung (BeitrAB) 195. Nürnberg: IAB.

Tippelt, R. (1997). Initiativen der UNESCO: Ausgewählte aktuelle Konzepte zur Bildungsplanung und zur Kooperation von beruflicher und allgemeiner Bildung. In K. Schaak & R. Tippelt (Eds.), *Strategien der internationalen Berufsbildung. Ausgewählte Aspekte* (pp. 123-147). Beiträge zur Bildungsplanung und Bildungsökonomie 6. Frankfurt/Main: Lang.

Tjepkema, S., Horst, H.M., Mulder, M., & Scheerens, J. (2000). *Future challenges for HRD professionals in Europe.* Final report, TSER-project ERB-SOE2-CT-2026. Enschede.

Torres, D.L. (1991). What, if anything, is professionalism? Institutions and the problem of change. In P.A. Tolbert & S.R. Barley (Eds.), *Organisations and professions. Research in the Sociology of organizations. A research annual* (pp. 43-68). Vol. 8. Greenwich Conn.: Jai.

Valkeavaara, T. (1996). HRD roles in Finland - preliminary results. In E.F. Holton (Ed.), *Academy of Human Resource Development. Conference Proceedings.* Minneapolis.

Valkeavaara, T. (1998). Human resource development roles and competencies in five European countries. *International Journal of Training and Development* 2 (3), 171-189.

Whitty, G., Power, S., & Halpin, D. (1998). *Devolution and Choice in Education. The School, the State and the Market.* Buckingham: Open University Press.

Young M., & Guile D. (1997). New possibilities for the professionalization of UK VET professionals. *Journal of European Industrial Training 21* (6-7), 203-212.

Zucker, L.G. (1991). Markets for bureaucratic authority and control: information quality in professions and services. In P.A. Tolbert & S.R. Barley (Eds.), *Organisations and professions. Research in the Sociology of organizations. A research annual* (pp. 157-190). Vol. 8. Greenwich Conn.: Jai.

CHAPTER 13

Transforming VET policies and professionalism:
a view from Finland

ANJA HEIKKINEN

13.1 Introduction

IN MOST WESTERN COUNTRIES THE TENDENCIES to remove national boundaries from the globalising financial markets, and to subcontract and accelerate production and distribution led to the incorporation of flexibility, mobility and transferability into the central objectives of education, employment and labour market policies during the 1990s (Atkinson & Meager, 1986; Poon, 1988; Sayer & Walker, 1992; Finegold & Soskice, 1990; European Commission, 1996; Vartia & Ylä-Anttila, 1996). Since education is commonly considered in relation to nation states, national industries and labour markets, it is natural that "transnational" or comparative discussions on flexibility, transferability and mobility tend to take a system theoretical (and functionalist) point of view. The basic categories are (national) VET systems and employment systems, challenged by global mega trends in economy and society, globalisation, turbulent change and informationalisation (Longworth & Davies, 1996; Nijhof, Kieft & van Woerkom, 1999; Castells, 2000). Most visions present learning and knowledge as the driving force of economies, societies, organisations and individuals. Discourses on economy and education increasingly merge. The catchwords flexibility, mobility and transferability pertain to learning psychological and economic meanings.

In the current discourse, transferability and mobility as individual behaviour and qualities are subsumed into flexibility. Educationally they refer to the outcome of learning as the life-long learning and employable worker, economically to the flexible use of human beings as a workforce. "Flexibility, enacted organisationally by the network enterprise, requires networkers, and flextimers, as well as a wide array of working arrangements, including self-employment and reciprocal subcontracting. The variable geometry of these working arrangements leads to the coordinated decentralisation of work and to the individualisation of labour." (Castells, 2000, p. 372)

The main imperative of flexibility is to stimulate VET work to respond and enable the visions to become reality. VET professionals, as part of the institutions of the VET system, should manage, steer or coordinate the provision of VET to the employment system and organise flexible learning arrangements for the acquisition of mobile and transferable behavioural patterns and qualifications (cf. Lassnigg, 2000). It is questionable, however, whether VET professionals can meet these expectations. Firstly, VET and employment hardly constitute systems with a shared meaning in almost any European country. Furthermore, different VET actors have been crucial in defining VET and VET professionalism, not just the technicians of the system. The third problem is whether we can speak of VET professionalism at all or consider it to have a similar meaning in different countries.

W. J. Nijhof et al. (eds.), Shaping Flexibility in Vocational Education and Training, 207-225.
© 2002 Kluwer Academic Publishers. Printed in the Netherlands.

The attempt to make VET professionals transnationally responsible according to universal or abstract criteria is not new. The most traditional programme originates from *management theories* such as scientific management, psychotechnics, motivation and organisational psychology, and work/industrial psychology, which have been developing in the USA since around 1910 (Drucker, 1942; Jacques, 1996; Glimell, 1997; Szell, 1992; Michelsen, 1999; Kettunen, 1994, 2001). Along with the transition to the organisation of scale, the "manager" was manufactured together with the "employee". The management of employees (later called staff or personnel and human resources (HR) management) was conceived as an extension to and compensation for education in homes, schools and other communities. Increasingly, specific expertise, legitimised by university degrees, was developed for getting the right man into the right place, for "engineering the souls" of workers by encouraging and motivating them to work for the company. The HR expertise was needed in organising the human (resource) system alongside the mechanical system of production, and in the social division and integration of work. The ideas of early Human Resource Development (HRD) have been influential in developing VET pedagogy in Europe since the 1920s and 1930s.

Elaborate attempts to define universal VET expertise have focused on *curriculum design and didactic processes* – in which specific occupational or industrial expertise is of more secondary importance. A sophisticated model of curriculum design, facilitating learning processes relevant to employment (employability and trainability), is presented by Nijhof (1998; cf. Achtenhagen, 1998). The model stresses the competence of the professional in defining the successive phases of input, process and output of a successful learning process, where the characteristics or intentions of students (learners) and teachers, as well as the skills and competence requirements of the labour market, are externally given. The models, building on constructivist and social learning theories, stress the (culturally) decontextualised nature of professional competence in designing authentic, empowering or situated learning environments or architecture (Lave & Wenger, 1991; Wenger, 1999; Evans & Hoffman, 2000). The legacy of previous approaches, enriched by the liberal adult education tradition, is visible in the university study programmes of VET professionals. In typical textbooks, the professional is described as follows:

- he/she has changing roles as a teacher/trainer, a member of the VET teacher/trainer community, a manager of learning environments and a supporter of learning processes; the VET professional is a reflective and self-conscious didactical and managerial expert (Armitage et al, 1999; Wenger, 1999);
- he/she is a facilitator of self-directed learning, a co-learner and an expert on methods of critical (self-)reflection, emancipation and empowerment; his/her expertise is based on critical self-learning and reflection (Mezirow, 1990; Brookfield, 1995);
- he/she is a researcher, coordinator and consultant, promoting programmes and processes for developing work and organisation; he/she is an expert on theories and methods of learning and research, on assessment and evaluation, and on communicating results (Engeström, 1998; Toulmin & Gustavssen, 1996).

Comparisons of VET teachers or HRD officers as professionals have typically focused on their roles and job profiles in organisations and have only marginally studied them according to the criteria of professionalisation theories (e.g. Odenthal & Nijhof, 1996; Valkeavaara, 1998; Brown, 1997; Lassnigg, 1997). From countries with a distinctive VET tradition emerges a further type of universal professionalisation of VET work (Sloane et al, 1998; Heidegger, 1997; Lassnigg, 2000). Analyses of the professionalisation of VET from German-speaking countries may serve as an example for others. For instance, Sloane et al (1998) analyse the degree of professionalisation of VET work by asking the following questions (cf. Pätzold, 1992; Zabeck, 1992, Brechmacher & Gerds, 1997): In which issues and how developed are educators as experts? In which issues and how widely are educators acting autonomously? And in which issues and how widely do educators have a collective orientation? They identify three ideal-typical groups with the potential for professionalisation, but do not discuss their interrelations. The expertise of VET teachers is based on pedagogy. They are autonomous in their pedagogical work, but subsumed into the bureaucratic curriculum regulations; their collective orientation is towards the VET institute and other teachers. The trainers are experts in occupational work processes, have autonomy in shaping occupational identities, but are restricted by regulations governing examinations and certificates and by the demands of productivity. They are orientated towards the work site community, with its occupational positions and hierarchies. The expertise of HRD officers has a fragmented (disciplinary, experiential) basis. They have autonomy in shaping learning environments but are restricted by customer and market demands, and their market-led and competing positions hinder the development of any collective orientation.

The classification is close to the ideal-typical categorisation of VET work on the basis of its functions. However, it ignores the functions of promoting production-consumption systems and providing knowledge and understanding for developing VET (Heikkinen, 1997a). Furthermore, in comparisons, the professionalisation approach raises fundamental problems because VET functions, excluding those of teachers, have been carried out mainly along with other occupational tasks. Nor does this approach pay any attention to the tension between professional and organisational identities (cf. Harney, 1998; Müller-Jentsch, 1999).

The earlier reflections on VET work build the basis for analysing the potential of VET professionals as promoters of flexibility, transferability and mobility; however, their cultural and ideological opaqueness should be deconstructed. If the historicity of the functions and divisions of VET work is not recognised, the dominant discourses and policies of change may be taken for granted and determined. The meanings given by the VET professionals themselves should be recognised. Transnational analysis should mean not only comparing systems but also collaborative reflections on the historical and cultural constitution of different meanings and practices of VET. How was VET constituted as a form of education? What were the functions and divisions of VET work and the ways of becoming a "VET professional"? How were VET and VET work negotiated and who were involved?

The maturation of an educationally responsive cross-cultural profession depends on whether the historically formed negotiations about the functions and division of VET work can be transformed into new combinations of transnational, national and subnational processes. In the following sections, concerns are raised about the recent pressure in Europe (or the EU), based on certain definitions of flexibility, transferability and mobility, and about promoting the manufacture of new transnational or hybrid VET experts. Exploiting the old VET professionalism, they might constitute new VET functions such as (a) European "busnocracy", i.e.

responsibility for the efficiency of a transnational educational service cluster towards the leading productive clusters; (b) management of didactic processes; and (c) engineering of uncertainties in learning organisations in Europe. The context of discussion is Finland, but the challenge is more general. Could a historicised and positioned approach to VET professionalism enable an alternative understanding of flexibility, transferability and mobility as educational responsibility to the citizens of Europe and the world?

13.2 The contested heritage of the "old VET professionalism"

If the interpretation of the emergence of national (mass) education systems is extended to VET, it can be argued that political and occupational citizenship – participation in the nation state and having an occupational position in the national industry – have become increasingly integrated (Boli, 1989; Heikkinen et al, 1999). However, recent VET cultural projects have been dominated by economic aims at societal and individual levels – project Europe, as a part of the project of globalisation, is challenging the established systems, forms and agency of education. The Finnish view of shared transformation and challenges may differ from other national perspectives. This is not a story of professionalisation because the word does not exist in the Finnish language; occupation refers to "means of livelihood", independence and self-sustainability, while service or office refers rather to the external mission in work. Nor did the occupationalisation of VET work follow the typical theories of professionalisation. This section argues that the transformation of VET forms, functions and agency took the following course: among administrators, away from promoting industry and towards evaluating educational services; among VET teachers, away from promoting occupation and towards managing didactic processes.

13.2.1 VET as a form of education – the legacy from vocational teachers and civil servants

VET teachers (previously including ambulatory advisers and counsellors in agriculture, home industries and home economics, and administrators in branch ministries) have been the most influential actors in the formation of Finnish VET. The category of *administrators* as VET professionals emerged after Finland's separation from Swedish governance at the beginning of the 19th century, and is linked to the establishment of branch ministries with the explicit aim of promoting national industries (Heikkinen et al, 1999). The boards and staff dedicated to VET in branch ministries were involved in Finland's competitive political, economic and cultural projects, which reached their peak through the political consensus of World War II. The importance that VET as a form of education had achieved is well illustrated in the statement by its major proponent Aarno Niini, head of the Department of VET at the Ministry of Trade and Industry from the 1940s to the 1960s:

> "When stating new guidelines for vocational education, we have to, on the one hand, define the general aim of education, and, on the other hand, specify the aims and functions of different forms of schools and education. The prevailing aim of Finnish education must be the formation of personality, which is willing and capable to consciously build the Finnish culture. In our definitions, we have to stress capability

as much as will. Thus, in the similar way that we ... consider societal and economic activities to belong into the cultural life, because cultivation of the spirit is highly dependent on them, we also include ... the provision of occupational cultivation into educational activities ... In the area of general education, we can expect that every citizen acquires some basic knowledge, adopts and manages certain common, shared habits and customs. In vocational education, on the contrary, educational activities should be divided into various parallel and sequential institutional forms, which correspond to the multiplicity of occupational life-forms themselves."

The school-based VET guided by teachers was "obviously more recommendable, both because of its efficiency and functionality as education and because of promoting the spiritual development of the learners," (Council of VET, Minutes, 1945).

The emergence of *vocational teacherhood* started by separating vocational education from general education, which was interpreted as either education for citizenship or encyclopaedic education. In the middle of the 19th century, this was primarily carried out by excluding general subjects from the curriculum, but later by developing pedagogical missions for different branches of VET (VET paradigms), separate from purely moral and intellectual education. Further, there was a separation from work-based training and instruction in skills. Teachers and state-controlled schools were preferred to skilled craftsmen and private provision. The idea of the teacher as a proponent of distinctive vocational education expanded. The first teachers of vocational education were administrators and leaders from different industries. A third, formal condition for creating vocational teacherhood in all occupational branches was the development and expansion of full-time schools and teachers. Since the turn of the 20th century, specific teacher categories based on education in relation to occupational order and hierarchies in working life have emerged in each industrial branch. In most branches, teachers specialise in practical work, vocational theory or general subjects. A shared conception of vocational teacherhood was strengthened when teachers, starting to collaborate in the 1980s, established their own unions. A condition was VET teacher training, which started in the late 19th century, gradually spreading to different branches and to different teacher categories. Since the 1960s-70s, the negotiating networks have become increasingly important when VET is used for the occupationalisation of any work. Finally, Finnish VET has been strongly influenced by educational challenges during crucial periods of social and political change (Heikkinen, 1997b).

Until recent years, administrators and teachers shared the concept of *VET as a form of education*. VET aimed at enabling the learner to survive (cope) in working life; to internalise proper attitudes to, and norms of work; to understand and adopt the typical methods and behaviour (techniques and habitus) of the occupation or industry; to participate in the work process (in organisations) and in the wider society; and to survive (cope) in private life during his/her individual life-course (Heikkinen et al, 1996, 1999).

"Would it be too much to hope that education is realised mainly by empathic living together (AH: with the students)? There surely is a lot of personal development beside all (AH: training) ... I would say that from a good teacher, these (educational) matters also come out just alongside everything else he/she does." (Retired civil servant, Office of Technical Education)

"Well, mainly it was teaching, but sometimes you had to do with education ... We used to have such special parties ... and one night they had it in a pub ... I left at ten o'clock and the boys could stay, but I told them: 'Remember that lessons start at eight o'clock tomorrow.' They knew it belongs to the training of engineers that you are never late from work; and everyone was there eight o'clock – so that may be what you call education." (Retired male teacher, technical college)

Vocational teacherhood has been heterogeneous in terms of career, recruitment and status (Heikkinen et al, 1997; Goodson & Hargreaves, 1996; Hargreaves, 1994). General teachers, either proponents of encyclopaedic knowledge or educators for citizenship, have been rather subsumed under authorities from universities, administration and teacher training in defining their practice and identity. Both primary school and gymnasium teachers have usually made a career for life within educational institutions, but VET teachers have come into teaching after occupational experience and often hesitated before making their choice. Despite branch-specific differences, the distinctiveness of VET teacherhood has been based on being:

- a master/craftsman in his/her occupational field (owner of occupational skills, techniques, habitus);
- a member of an occupational network (proponent of occupation);
- a gate-keeper to an occupation (to membership of an occupation);
- a guide to an occupation (mutual awareness of expectations and competences between students, educational institutes, work sites and employers);
- a promoter of entrepreneurship (self-initiative, independence, coping/survival in life);
- a sociology of occupation (theoretical and technological aspects of occupational competence) (Heikkinen et al, 1996; Heikkinen, 1997b).

During the post-war period, being a *proponent of the occupation* (member of occupational network) became the ideal, the core of VET teachers' identity. Besides confirming the pedagogical distinctiveness of VET, research indirectly revealed a further aspect of Finnish VET, which it seems to share with general education. It is something teachers are silent about, i.e. the tensions and conflicts in working life. When they compare themselves and teacherhood with other occupations in their sector, they may even stress such experiences. When describing their teaching, however, they barely mention any political or economic problems in working life.

In the school context, the problems were individualised. Students were simply being prepared for the hardships of real working life in order to lessen their vulnerability. Conformism to the prevailing order of work belonged to the distinctiveness of post-war VET.

The *administrators* defined their professionalism according to their role (as they perceived it) within occupational networks and industry. Even when it was no longer officially required, they felt obliged to demonstrate their competence by having had occupational education, work experience and experience as a VET teacher. However, when comparing their own expertise, older civil servants stress the superior competence of VET teachers. Similarly they stress the sharing of VET among teachers and administrators.

"In curriculum planning, of course we thought that teachers have brains. And they used to be experts in their occupation, at least as long as I worked in the office, until 1991 ... Relations were good and we maintained communication by correspondence and telephone calls and inspection visits, too – and through regional negotiations ... Of course they were also dependent on central administration, because we nominated them into their jobs ... We followed and learnt what was going on in the field ... Good heavens, I felt like they were my own children." (Retired civil servant, Office of Agricultural Education)

What distinguished VET administrators from teachers was that they saw themselves much more as *promoters of (the branch) industry* than promoters of their occupation. In developing their expertise, administrators used their personal contacts not only in their occupational network but also in their branch industry. Even though they may stress work as the final educator in gaining occupational expertise, VET administrators do believe they have a genuine role in promoting industry. The representatives of industry are conceived to have a narrow short-term superficial understanding of VET, and to lack commitment and competence – without which even industry cannot prosper in the long run.

"I had good contacts to the central organs of industry, based on my previous acquaintances and I discussed very much with them ... Representatives of working life would have good chances to influence VET, if only they want ... But their attitude seems to be that they do not have time and others have the responsibility ... I assume the people in working life think that it is the task of civil servants and they only need to worry every now and then ... In these matters they are like dogs at the bowling alley: they just run in from one door and fell a couple of skittles and then they disappear through another door." (Retired civil servant, Office for Technical Education)

Comparing the self-conception of administrators with that of VET teachers reveals a further difference: administrators believe they understand and influence VET in a wider context. Despite the changed vocabularies, it seems that the classical image of a civil servant as someone who can transcend the particular interests of societal groups and *understand the good of the totality* (the nation state) is still influential.

13.2.2 Expansion in VET, cutback in pedagogical mission

In most European countries, systems of national welfare and industries were introduced after World War II. Paradoxically, the related expansion of educational opportunities reduced the distinctiveness of VET as a form of education. In Finland, equal promotion of VET in different sectors of industry and in all regions of the country continued until the 1960s, by which time all industries had established their specific VET organs and staff in the branch ministries.

Although later than in other Nordic countries, the success in managing the rapid social change without conflicts and tensions has resulted partly from the stabilisation of the Finnish system of industrial relations since the 1960s. The principles of representativeness, consensual adjustment of interests to economic growth, and social security were adopted as components of general social and political development. The interests of leading export industries became increasingly understood as a national good, and were incorporated into workers' education in company communitarianism and into promoting productivity – claiming to meet their basic needs. During the 1960s, schoolish VET expanded and differentiated according to occupational branches and fields; it was to be arranged for all kinds of jobs and occupations, particularly at the operative level. Distinctive administration and teacher training in different branches of vocational education were established and gained weight in relation to individual institutes and teachers. The idea of distinctive vocational pedagogy became important when the number of workshop teachers increased.

The branch-industry-related development started to crack under the hegemonic policies of equal opportunity and technocratic planning. During the period 1968 to

1973, all VET administration was centralised, falling under one VET board of the Ministry of Education.

During the 1970s, modernisation politics caused the collapse of rural industries, rapid migration and urbanisation. Along with the moderating regional policy, teachers and schools were replaced by regional student selection. New pedagogical challenges emerged with the increase of unselected students from suburbanising and migrating families. The decreasing status of industrial or manual labour undermined the learning of occupational skills and increased motivational and disciplinary problems. The expanding technocratic society led to the increasing centralisation of planning, student recruitment, teaching, assessment and administrative procedures. The laws of the late 1970s provided 1.4 study places per age cohort in post-compulsory education. In the declining fields of agriculture, forestry and cheap commerce – but also in manufacturing – an over-supply of VET was created. Unionisation of teachers and the expansion of local and national administration restructured internal staff relations. Professionalisation and territorial and status battles became important for teachers' self-conception. Although signs of recession had been visible earlier, the economic boom and progressive educational programmes improved the status of vocational education. The unifying reform of vocational education was implemented during the 1980s. National curricula and teacher training were increasingly regulating teaching in institutes, and the separate provision of general subjects changed the character of vocational studies. Gradually the coordination of all forms and fields of education was merged under one board of education in 1991. Both VET administrators and teachers conceived the development as colonisation of VET by (politically motivated) general education. The major problem was the occupational relevance of curricula.

13.2.3 Evaluators of VET services and managers of didactic processes

The tendencies of the 1970s were fulfilled in the reforms of the 1990s, where VET (and VET governance) was divided between upper secondary and higher education. VET had been separated from branch industries and transformed into a unified subsystem of education, thereby losing its distinctiveness and internal diversity (Heikkinen et al, 1996, 1999). In the context of dramatic economic recession and unemployment, teachers had to face the pedagogical problems of students' heterogeneity, rootlessness and need for guidance. The regional fusions of institutes with their forced cooperation brought both pressure and options for creating a new teacher identity. The uncertainty and competition caused stress and a scramble for the academic qualifications that started to regulate their status. Teachers complained of feeling permanently incompetent. They feared that education was being sacrificed for the sake of the developmental and competitive projects of institutes and to enable teachers to improve their "competence".

The transformation of the self-conceptions of VET teachers and administrators is controversial. The "old ones" defend the ethics of obligation towards an entity (i.e. towards the nation state or national industry and towards the occupational community or network), which transcends the short-term and branch-specific, company-specific or purely individual interests. Intermingling with the emerging ethics of competition and the market, which dominate some of the "younger ones", a problematic combination may emerge. An authoritarian commitment to the competitiveness of European clusters of industry and the success of one's institute in the educational markets is linked with the promotion of individualism and competitiveness among learners.

13.3 The novelty of new VET professionalism?

13.3.1 Work site and occupational communities as educators

Education for work by the communities of livelihood themselves has been the oldest and widest form of VET in any country. However, different solutions in regulating on-the-job learning to off-the-job learning have developed in different countries and different branches of industry. Whereas Finnish work has been dominated by rural industries (until the 1950s) and also (since the 19th century) by large textile, wood processing and metal industries, craft training has remained marginal. The ideas of scientific management and improving the quality of human labour were adopted at the beginning of the 20th century, especially after independence and the construction of national industry. World War II was crucial for developing consensus between competing political and industrial projects all over Europe. In Finland, engineers were the dominant group in organising industrial relations and regulations during the war, and reconstruction and war payments till the end of the 1950s (Michelsen, 1999; Tulkki, 1996; Tuomisto, 1986). Career guidance, and industrial and work psychology were the leading principles in developing a national system for training, allocating and managing the nation's labour force. The same theories and models were widely adopted throughout most branches of industry, in VET institutes and teacher training, and in the training of managers and supervisors. While the labour movement and leftist parties did not gain the right to collective negotiations until 1940, great emphasis now had to be laid on the "human factor of production" in order to adjust the rationalisation interests of industry to the economic and political demands of workers and small farmers. Moderating tensions was based on nationalist consensus: "The compromise was rather a necessary obligation, where we ended to in order to maintain the national good (welfare), which was defined beforehand. The national good has ever since shown itself as a necessity, which narrows the perspective of political choice and will." (Kettunen, 1997, p. 172)

Even more than in other Nordic countries, on-the-job learning was a marginal aspect of negotiations between employers and employees (particularly in the private sector). As in the Netherlands and the UK (see Hytönen et al, this volume), whether separate or integrated, HRD work remained unquestionably part of management functions. Until the 1970s, learning in industry used to be, on the one hand, learning the machine and, on the other, becoming a member of the team and/or worker community. The employer (middle manager/engineer) controlled both processes in terms of recruitment and placement of workers; workers, however, often backed by the union, controlled the learning of skills and the joining of the worker community.

Occupational communities were controlling the training and division of work, which followed the traditional split between male and female living spaces. In the 1970s, participation in formal VET was considered to benefit only the employer, and on-the job training was seen as the responsibility of the bosses.

"In those days you just went into a group and ... some other worker taught you all ... It was teamwork, you just could not only do your own job and say that nothing else belongs to it, everything had to be done together ... Only men, the machinists, they never touched women's work ... when I went to work with the handkerchief machine, I would have needed some training, because it was already quite automatised, and especially about the maintenance ... The boys, the men, they had already had some tinkering with all kinds of technical things at home ... In earlier times, vocational education did not belong to our culture: if a worker was studying it had to be for something else than work ... I think the occupational communities and their borders have been so strong ... Therefore we created such kings (AH: the paper machinists) into the worker community, and the employer as much as we (workers) certainly accepted such system, which maintained the hierarchies in work." (Female worker, pulp and paper factory)

In all branches of industry, the establishment of the technocratic welfare state constituted a rupture in VET, particularly in the caring occupations, which were regulated by the state. In technical work, workers lost their local power to define division of work and processes of growth based on their informal and collective organisation.

Collective and occupational negotiations were replaced by national representative discussions about national education policy, based on corporatist economic and political interests. The centralisation of VET negotiations between the state, employers and the unions of big industry culminated in the unifying reforms of upper secondary education in the late 1970s. In care work, the creation of the welfare society and the gathering of all VET under the Ministry of Education promoted the professionalisation and unionisation of health and social work, as well as the increasing influence of nursing (health) science and social sciences as the definers of occupations and occupational growth. Still, the expansion and unification of VET created a gap between practitioners and newcomers. At school, students learnt to respect theory, not the experiential and physical aspects of work, even in health care.

"I think we used to be more with the patients; these younger people remain distant ... It may be impolite to say, but it seems to me that they are more interested in paperwork and planning. But just planning and reporting will not care the patient. The patient needs a human being near her/him." (Middle-aged head nurse in a hospital)

13.3.2 Informal learning as a response to the imperative of flexibility

Whenever the systems of production and consumption, the order of industries and the utilisation of human work have transcended the level of nation states, the psychic and social adaptation of the human factor has gained new attention. While society as a nation state has been replaced by a national innovation system, new regional and national policies and networks are emerging for controlling and managing the local and national innovation processes (Kettunen, 2001). They should develop and strengthen local experience in order to confirm the operation of global markets and industrial clusters (Lundvall & Borras, 1999; Vartia & Ylä-Anttila, 1996). "Capital circulates, power rules, and electronic communication whirls through flows of exchanges between selected, distant localities, while fragmented experience remains confined to places." (Castells, 2000, p. 370)

Learning is an excellent metaphor for the emerging order of work. The global projects of endogenous economic growth, national innovation systems and knowledge-creating companies are linked to the promotion of learning economies, organisations, and employees as enterprising selves. In globalised informationalised networking economies, any site of work is turning into a "company" or "organisation", which then becomes the main reference for employees' identification.

Informal (on-the-job) learning is very high on the agenda of economic and educational policy as a response to the turbulent changing markets. Formal and institutional VET, teachers and bureaucracy are described as obsolete and even dysfunctional as far as the successful learning of individuals and organisations is concerned (Cressey & Kelleher, 1999). At organisational level, the management of knowledge creation processes and of persuasion and motivation to change gains weight as the substitute for formal VET, which used to promote the formation of subjective occupational identities and occupational citizenship. There is less concern about the hidden curricula and facilitators of informal learning. In Finland, trainers in a few traditional craft occupations and in health care, alongside HRD officers in big private or public organisations, have been the most established professionals in on-the-job learning. However, often without formal recognition, the responsibility for support learning has belonged to the co-workers.

The VET work on work sites continues to be non-transparent and inaccessible to any wider extra-organisational societal negotiations. Workers engaged in HRD activities feel confused by the rhetoric of the positiveness of learning.

"I do not think there is much tradition (AH: of systematic personnel training) before 1980s. Then became this permanent downsizing and reduction of workforce, which means that those who stay have to be more skilled ... But now the problem is that such training cannot be effective, if we only have the amount of people who barely can run the machines, there should also be a kind of reserve for others to be able to progress ... Sometimes I feel guilty, because I am involved in changing other people's jobs, but according to the regulations I will be the last to go away and turn off the lights, although other workers are in permanent chaos." (Female worker, pulp and paper factory)

While most Finnish HRD officers are women and work in the public sector, many share the pressure and ethical dilemmas of teachers in their work (Filander, 2000). Worker interviews confirm both the internal complexity of VET as a form of education and the many functions of VET in relation to occupational growth. For example, entrance jobs, practice periods and on-the-job training are considered potential platforms for negotiation responsibilities in VET. However, the workers' expectations about organising such platforms are diffuse. They hope there will be occupational ideals, and safe and caring adults both in VET institutes and on work sites to support others in developing a sense in work and an occupational identity. Still, they consider the functions of VET work to differ.

"I think educator needs to have patience to listen and teach even during bad moments, and understand someone who is not so quick ... A highly skilled worker ... is not necessarily the best educator or trainer, who must be jovial and stand jokes. And I think in education, e.g. in vocational school, there always is something more than just training into occupation. If we started to train our skills and knowledge here, that might be rather boring and hard for the youngsters, and I would never have time to really teach them ... Nor could I change place with a teacher. He/she could never get a touch into this work, he/she could not know how the workers are. You have to know, what Seppo is like, some mornings he is little down, you have to understand your workers from the way they walk through the door and see in which mood they are. It is not just technical know-how." (Carpenter, entrepreneur)

Still, the responsibility for education and educational collaboration is delegated to schools and teachers. Even if workers criticise them for alienation from the realities of occupational work, very few would like, or indeed have the time or other resources to share their obligations. Concerns about the erosion of occupational identities are expressed in worries about eroding manual skills and personal practical theory in their occupation. The wish for collective negotiations about the aims and contents of VET and a proper division of VET work can be identified. Teachers are expected to find their feet in occupational practice, to concentrate more on the basics of occupation, to define occupational knowledge and skills in greater mutual understanding. It is not opposition to theory or schoolish learning, but a call to recognise workers' experience and knowledge and for work sites, occupational groups and educators to collaborate in developing theories and curricula. The alienation of schoolish (or official) VET is primarily ascribed to the domination of general (core/key) competences and to the over-emphasis on ICT competences.

Blaming teachers while simultaneously expecting them to assume the educational functions of work sites and the occupational community is paradoxical. Indirectly, this tells us about people's feelings of incompetence and the lack of opportunities in taking educational responsibility outside schools. Considerations about the potential of VET workers should not ignore "the importance of focusing on the demand side, that is on the jobs people get rather than simply the training they receive." (Brown & Lauder, 2001, p. 266)

13.3.3 Realities of the work site: erosion of time, space and community for occupational growth

The complaints about "peace for work" are, paradoxically, now coming from employees. Work is characterised by chaos, hecticness and loss of the psychic, cultural, social and feeling of belonging (attachment, engagement) (Heikkinen et al, 2001). The young demonstrate this, both at school and on the work site, by demanding occupationalisation and guidance in their studies and support and role models (parental care) from older workers and the working community. The oldest workers and teachers demonstrate this through nostalgic demands for bringing back the good old days, when there were identifiable communities and occupations (with which to agree or disagree) and people with whom to share the history of work, occupation and education.

> "What worries me, is the hastiness and senselessness of the working life, don't you see it in the university? In this construction business, they have to finish a big blockhouse in three months, what sense is there, why could they not slow down the speed. I can see it clearly here how crazy the rhythm has become in this life ... Maybe it is something more general what is sought in the society, certain "quality" in life or whatever quality, I think the quality of personal lives should be more important than all pompous organisations and tremendous growth and continuous increase in stock market and such." (Carpenter, entrepreneur)

Short contracts and increasing workloads have become the norm in the public sector as well. There is no longer any time or space for the occupational growth of young and casual workers.

> "Nowadays, the students are strong in theory, and an older worker tends to be quiet in order not to look stupid – or checks her knowledge somewhere. But on the other hand, she knows the practice of the house and she can think about situations from the patient's point of view. Also the physicians give feedback to old nurses, that the nurses who had the old training, are much better in nursing. Obviously it is because of the manual competence, because they have such short practice periods nowadays." (Older hospital nurse)

The middle-aged workers and teachers demonstrate their anxiety, exhaustion and ethical despair under the demands and challenges of constituting continuity, stability, reliability, community and parenthood in a world where these are being eroded. Workers in permanent and responsible positions feel that too much is being demanded of them.

In learning economies and organisations, new versions of the mixed worker – so common before the 1950s – are emerging. Whether employee or expert, the flexible worker should have a broad profile of generic competences and appropriate personality traits for permanent adaptation to change. The erosion of security, control and ownership of work reduces ethical autonomy and promotes egoism and the marketing of all human relations inside and outside work. "I characterised such a state (AH: personality system in state of flux) as flexible personalities, able to engage endlessly in the reconstruction of the self ... Nowadays, people produce forms of sociability, rather than follow models of behaviour." (Castells, 2000, p. 381)

The dominance of schoolish VET was a takeover of the embodied, experiential and collective knowledge and skills of workers by occupational and teaching experts (Jacques, 1996; Young, 1971). Even if in principle they became more accessible and open, the legitimising of divisions of work and occupational hierarchies was delegated to the schools. In contemporary economic and education policy, the development of knowledge and skills in isolation from work sites is increasingly considered too expensive and inefficient. The leading principle of permanent change as progress transforms the meanings of work and learning. The co-constitutive role of researchers is well expressed by sociologists who preach the loss of meaning of schoolish education as "an isolated island", where learning has become the prevailing form of work (e.g. Kivinen & Silvennoinen, 2000). Instead of searching for the joy of work or willingness to work, educators preach now joy of and willingness to learn.

The disappearance of education for work from the home or housing community, the prolongation of general education and the intensification and speed of working life make workers doubt whether an informal learning of occupation is possible. Occupationally oriented education, schools and teachers are more important than ever. Schools and teachers are the focus of enormous expectations, which are targeted at transferring the educational functions that used to belong to parents, homes, neighbours or housing communities to work sites, older workers, masters and entrepreneurs. Despite the celebration of work-based and organisational learning, it is questionable whether they are bringing back the control of occupational knowledge and skills to the workers as personal, embodied and collective knowledge. On the contrary, in knowledge creation and knowledge and learning management, workers are conceived as the human machinery that should be more efficiently engaged in detached and disembodied knowledge creation and learning that can be easily transferred and updated (Svensson et al, 2000; Nonaka & Takeuchi, 1995; Nonaka & Konno, 1998).

13.4 The changing landscape of VET work

Despite different historical and cultural understandings and divisions of VET work, the imperatives from a globalising economy and new ways of utilising human labour – flexibility, mobility and efficient transfer between learning and work – transcend nation-state and culture-specific responses in VET. In countries with strong and regulated systems of initial VET, concerns focus both on finding ways of "coordinating" the supply and demand of qualifications and competences at national and transnational levels, and on continuing VET (e.g. Lassnigg, this volume). In Nordic countries, a combination of school and teacher-led promotion of life-long learning and self-directed enterprising selves with developing learning organisations and national innovation is emerging. In most countries, the various actors in VET are being forced to reconsider their functions and mutual relations.

13.4.1 Identity, expertise and power

In most countries, VET work outside teaching and the civil service has until recently been only marginally recognised and collectively discussed. Increasingly, however, the new discourse on VET professionalism is focusing on its functions: the provision of skills, knowledge and habits that enable effective performance and participation in the work process, and the development of the human factor to contribute to the success of the organisation or industrial cluster. By reflecting on the experiences of Finnish administrators, teachers and workers, suggestions on the transformation of VET work can be made.

Firstly, the identity of VET teachers and administrators as co-constitutors of occupational order and national industry is eroding. Teachers are becoming managers of didactic processes instead of being promoters of their occupation; administrators are becoming evaluators of educational services, instead of being promoters of branches of industry. Their power to co-define VET and occupational work is weakening. Secondly, the emerging expertise among VET teachers and administrators is decreasingly based on occupation. The responsibility for acquiring specific knowledge and competence is increasingly delegated to work sites, and the developmental functions to consultancy and research. Thirdly, it seems the power of the new VET professionals – HR developers and trainers in the workplace, and planners, evaluators and trainers of VET professionals in university departments and institutes – is growing. They are increasingly co-defining "VET" (as HRD or life-long learning) and employability. The tendency towards the economisation of education looks more dramatic in countries that previously have consensually committed themselves to promoting national industry, occupational citizenship and the welfare society.

University departments and teacher training colleges play a crucial role in creating the new VET professionals. The following example is based on MA and doctoral programmes of adult and continuing education in my department. Reflecting on statistical data and images in literature and publicity, students suggested types of professional identities practised in different fields and based on different expertise.

VET workers may continue to exploit eclectic strategies in legitimising their work. The images and metaphors from (popular) liberal adult education are useful for the continuity and security for students, even if the aims and functions of VET seem to converge in the promotion of learning. VET professional is not a tempting metaphor for an expert who should be a proponent of the new flexi-worker, a designer of effective learning processes and a developer of scenarios, evaluations and quality con-trol in organisational knowledge creation processes (Nonaka & Takeuchi, 1995; Wenger, 1999). Alongside the portable commitment to organisation, expertise is developed that is flexible, without limits or boundaries. The identity of the future expert on flexibility is constituted as hybrid. The new expert is also an example of gender-blending: nurturing and emotional competences are combined with market and production orientation (Tomassini, 1999; cf. Silverman, 1999; Heikkinen et al, 2001).

Tabel 13.1 *MA and doctoral programmes of adult and continuing education.*

Profile/identity	Typical field of VET work	Basis of expertise
Didactic/teacher	VET institutes, academic and civic education	Didactisation, master of educational technology (ICT), diagnosing learning needs
Master	(Adult) VET institutes, work sites	Master in work process knowledge, model/example, authority
Co-wanderer	Liberal adult education, associations, self-directed learning	Co-learner, supporter, equal participant
Researcher	University, academic centres of learning, project/consulting work	Research skills management, collection and reporting of knowledge, "external" adviser
Manager	VET institutes, companies	Managing, financing and coordinating learning environments, "external" provider
Engineer of uncertainty (agent of change)	Organisations (companies)	Motivation, persuasion; social, strategic and manipulating skills
Academic secretary	Any field	Planning, managing, networking, "internal" guide, adviser

The hegemonic conceptions of universal (VET) expertise seem to follow the tradition of (masculine, Western) industrial management theories (Jacques, 1996). The expert in effective knowledge management cannot be created without abstract disembodied knowledge that is detached from the personal knower who is physically both collectively and culturally bounded (Fitzsimons, 1997; cf. Senge, 1990). In company-based learning, neither individual workers nor trainers or extra-organisational collectives have much to say, compared with the public forms of VET (Svensson et al, 2000).

Similar trends are identified elsewhere (Lassnigg, 1997, 2000; Brown, 1997; Hodkinson, 1998; Hytönen et al, this volume). A new professionalism is emerging, challenging the established forms and conceptions of VET. Educational autonomy – distance from immediate market pressure, focus on personal development – in VET work is challenged by revitalised Fordist and technocratic forms of management, by quality control and by external evaluation. Despite differences, VET institutions and practitioners face the imperatives of transnational economies, industries and political processes. Increasingly, education is being transformed into an infrastructure of transnational companies and into a service industry for maintaining the competitiveness and social cohesion of European, national and regional economic areas. Still, reflections on new VET professionals seldom reflect on the need for democratic negotiation and policy processes that would transcend the national, mainly public forms of VET. For example, Hodkinson (1998) hopes that the educational professionalisation of teachers and trainers could, despite internal complexity, occur on the basis of common theory, collaboration and career prospects. However, VET work may be too fragmented and marginal for actors to share the aims and mission to constitute a profession (cf. Brown, this volume). Lassnigg (1997, 2000) proposes a new VET professionalism as the coordination between labour markets and bureaucracy. Both suggestions capture essential aspects of the changing VET work. However, they ignore the potential of mutual interests among bureaucracy, industry and VET, especially in the welfare and public services. In Nordic countries, most bureaucrats have an occupation in the publicly and politically controlled labour market of their branch. The distinctive role of civil servants as VET professionals does not receive any attention. In the context of nation states, bureaucrats have enabled democratic negotiations about VET among competing factions. If they turn into "educational busnocracy" (cf. Fitzsimons, 1997; Marshall, 1999; Beck, 1986), serving the interests of European/global businesses instead of the interests of the people of Europe and the world, the other VET workers may not be able to mobilise themselves into anything like an educational profession.

13.4.2 Flexibility as cross-cultural, cross-functional educational collaboration

The mental and behavioural structures of actors do not change as rapidly as the reform discourse. A historicising and positioning approach would recognise the mutually constitutive nature of the psychic and the social. "When we speak about the structures of the psyche, we in fact observe the 'interim balance sheets' from a (historical social) interaction process, which guide the interactions of the future." (Siltala, 1999, p. 430) Even policy makers and employers who are committed to the rhetoric of work-based and self-directed learning, competitiveness and continuous change do not seem to believe that working life (social partners, work sites, etc.) could take the responsibility for VET. They continue to expect it from the VET institutes and teachers (Heikkinen et al, 1997). This is paradoxical compared with the hostility towards schools, teacherhood and formal learning. There is a reluctance towards replacing them with professionals covering all functions of VET. The consensual hope of negotiating the varying contents and forms of VET is still alive.

The governance and negotiations about the functions and division of VET work – historically and culturally developed in nation states – between regional and local actors and agencies are increasingly being transformed into European ones. Who is given the voice by the European "busnocracy" in discourses on flexibility, transferability and mobility and VET? While flexibility, mobility and transferability as imperatives for VET work, professional or not, are complex and controversial, a shared perspective could unfold from questioning the place of work and education in life. This would imply revisiting the relations between the economic and the educational in the context of personal, collective and planetarian reproduction of the means of livelihood.

"Cultures are real, lived experiences turned into reason, engendering reasons for action and thus embodied in material life and material goods ... we should expect that different social groups, situated in different objective conditions as to their capacity to earn a livelihood, will have distinct experiences giving different meaning to a cultural concept that at first might appear as homogeneous. Culture should not be the easy way out from economic questions: culture is the difficult way into placing economic questions in the larger framework of social reproduction." (Narotzsky, 1997, pp. 222-223)

The challenge is how to transcend the narrow foci of enterprising self and competitive organisation and create connected local, national and transnational negotiations to revitalise "the foundations of social progress, based on prosperity, security, opportunity, and participation in democratic life." (Brown & Lauder, 2001, p. 227). Educationists could collaborate in raising silenced voices and ignored views about the recognition and fair division of work as a whole, and about participation in negotiating the aims of collective reproduction of the means of livelihood.

References

Achtenhagen, F. (1998). General versus vocational education - demarcation and integration. In Nijhof, W.J. & Streumer, J.N. (Eds.), *Key qualifications in Work and Education* (pp. 133-145). Dordrecht-Boston-London: Kluwer.

Armitage, A., Bryant, R., Dunnill, R., Hammersley, M., Hayes, D., Hudson, A., & Lawes, S. (1999). *Teaching and Training in Post-compulsory Education*. Buckingham-Philadelphia: Open University Press.

Atkinson, J., & Meager, N. (1986). *New Forms of Work Organisation*. Brighton: Institute of Manpower Studies.

Beck, U. (1986). *Risikogesellschaft*. Frankfurt am Main: Suhrkamp.

Boli, J. (1989). *New Citizens for a New Society*. The Institutional Origins of Mass Schooling in Sweden. Oxford: Pergamon Press.

Brechmacher, R., & Gerds, P. (1997). Grundmodelle der Gewerbelehrerbildung im historischen Wandel. In Bremer, R. (hg.), *Schritte auf dem Weg zu einer gestaltungsorientierten Berufsbil-dung* (pp. 218-223). Bremen: Donat.

Brookfield, R. (1995). *Becoming a Critically Reflective Teacher*. San Francisco: Jossey Bass.

Brown, A. (Ed.) (1997). *Promoting vocational education and training: European perspectives*. University of Tampere.

Brown, P., & Lauder, H. (2001). *Capitalism and Social Progress*. Wiltshire: Palgrave.

Castells, M. (2000). The Information Age: Economy, Society and Culture (volume III). *End of Millennium* (2nd edition). Cornwall: Blackwell.

Council of VET. (1945). Minutes. Helsinki: Archives of National Board of Education Interviews from AMKER and EUROPROF-projects, Department of Education, University of Jyväskylä.

Cressey, P., & Kelleher, M. (1999). *Advances and paradoxes of corporate learning practices*. Presentation in FORUM workshop, held at Evora, November 1999.

Drucker, P. (1942). *The Future of Industrial Man*. New York: J. Day.

Engeström, Y. (1998). *Developmental work research* (in Finnish). Helsinki: Edita.

European Commission (1996). *White book: Teaching and Learning in Learning Society*. Luxembury.

Evans, K., & Hofmann, B. (2000). *Reconceptualising Re-enter as a challenge to vocational education and training*. Paper presented in Final Conference of Re-enter project, 27-28 November 2000, University of Flensburg.

Filander, K. (2000). *The riptide in developmental work* (in Finnish and English). University of Tampere.

Finegold, D., & Soskice, D. (1990). The Failure of Training in Britain: Analysis and Prescription. In Esland, G. (Ed.), *Education, Training and Employment (volume III): Educated Labour - the Changing Basis of Industrial Demand* (pp. 214-261). Kent: Addison-Wesley and Open University.

Fitzsimons, P. (1997). The Politics of Self-Constitution. *Journal of Philosophy of Education* 1/1997.

Glimell, M. (1997). *Den produktiva kroppen. En studie om arbetsvetenskap som ide, praktik och politik* [The productive body. Study of work science as idea, practice and politics]. Stockholm: Symposion.

Goodson, I., & Hargreaves, A. (1996). *Teachers' Professional Lives*. London: Falmer Press.

Hargreaves, A. (1994). *Changing Teachers, Changing Times*. London: Cassell.

Harney, K. (1998). *Handlungslogik der betrieblichen Weiterbildung* [The action logic of in the company-continuing education]. Stuttgart: Hirzel.

Heidegger, G. (1997). Key considerations in the education of vocational education and training professionals. In Brown, A. (Ed.), *Promoting vocational education and training: European perspectives* (pp. 13-24). University of Tampere.

Heikkinen, A. (1997a). Vocational Education as a Life-Project? *European Journal of Industry and Training, August 1997.*

Heikkinen, A. (1997b). Education or training - changes in vocational teachers conceptions of their work. *Cambridge Journal of Education, 27, 3/1997*, 405-424.

Heikkinen, A. (2000). Gender Bias in Nordic Vocational Education. *Schweitzerische Zeitschrift fur Bildungswissenschaft, 2/2000*, 357-376.

Heikkinen, A., Borgman, M., Henriksson, L., Korkiakangas, M., Kuusisto, L., Nuotio, P., & Tiilikkala, L. (2001). *There is so little time: the vanishing time, site and space for occupational growth* (in Finnish). Saarijärvi: Research Centre for Vocational Education.

Heikkinen, A., & Henriksson, L. (2000). *Paradoxes in manufacturing the life-long learning employee for organisations.* Paper presented in conference "Life-long learning - one focus, many systems", 17-19 August 2000, Ruhr-Universität Bochum. (Forthcoming in Harney, K., Rahn, S. & Heikkinen, A. (Eds.), Peter Lang Verlag).

Heikkinen, A., Korkiakangas, M., Kuusisto, L., Nuotio, P., & Tiilikkala, L. (1999). *From promotion of industry towards quality control of educational services. Vocational education in administration* (in Finnish). Tampere: University of Tampere.

Heikkinen, A., Korpinen, P., Kuusisto, L., Nuotio, P., Tiilikkala, L., & Vesala, M. (1996). *"Skills must be provided, education, too..." Finnish vocational education experienced by the teachers* (in Finnish). Tampere: University of Tampere.

Heikkinen, A., Tiilikkala, L., & Nurmi, H. (1997). *The new professionalism of vocational education?* (in Finnish). Tampere: University of Tampere.

Hodkinson, P. (1998). Technicism, Teachers and Teaching Quality in Vocational Education and Training. *Journal of Vocational Education and Training, 50, 2/1998*, 193-207.

Jacques, R. (1996). *Manufacturing the employee. Management knowledge from the 19th to the 21st century.* London-Thousand Oaks-New Delhi: SAGE.

Kettunen, P. (1994). *Protection, performance, subject* (in Finnish). Helsinki: Suomen Historiallinen Seura.

Kettunen, P. (1997). *Order of Work.* Tampere: Vastapaino.

Kettunen, P. (2001). *National work* (in Finnish). Helsinki: Yliopistopaino.

Kivinen, O. & Silvennoinen, H. (2000). Conditions and options for learning in school and work (in Finnish). *Aikuiskasvatus, 4/2000*, 306-315.

Lassnigg, L. (1997). *"Old" and "New" Professionals in Austrian Vocational Education.* Paper presented at ECER conference, September 1997, Frankfurt am Main.

Lassnigg, L. (2000). *Steering, Networking and Profiles of Professionals in Vocational Education and Training.* Manuscript for CEDEFOP. 2nd European Report on VET Research.

Lave, J. & Wenger, E. (1991). *Situated Learning. Legitimate Peripheral Participation.* Cambridge University Press.

Longworth, N. & Davies, W. K. (1996). *Life-long learning.* London: Kogan Page.

Lundvall, B.-Å. & Borras, S. (1999). *The globalising learning economy: implications for innovation policy.* Luxembourg: Office for Official Publications of European Community.

Marshall, J. (1999). The Mode of Information and Education. In Popkewitz, T. & Fendler, L. (Eds.), *Critical Theories in Education* (pp. 145-168). London & New York: Routledge.

Mezirow, J. (Ed.) (1990). *Fostering Critical Reflection in Adulthood.* California: Jossey Bass.

Michelsen, K.-E. (1999). *Fifth estate: engineers in Finnish society* (in Finnish) Vammala: Vammalan kirjapaino.

Müller-Jentsch, W. (1999). Berufsbildung - eine Arena industrieller Beziehungen. *Zeitschrift für Pädagogik. Sonderheft 40/1999*, 233-248.

Narotzky, S. (1997). *New Directions in Economic Anthropology*. London-Chicago: Pluto Press.

Nijhof, W.J. (1998).Qualifying for the future. In Nijhof, W.J. & Streumer, J.N. (Eds.), *Key qualifications in Work and Education* (pp. 19-39). Dordrecht-Boston-London: Kluwer.

Nijhof, W.J., Kieft, M., & Woerkom, M. van (1999). *Mapping the Field. Definitions and Depositions*. Umbrella study for COSTA11 project. Enschede: University of Twente.

Nonaka, I., & Konno, N. (1998). The concept of Ba. Building a Foundation for Knowledge-creation. *California Management Review, (40)*, 3/1998.

Nonaka, I., & Takeuchi, H. (1995). *The Knowledge-creating company*. Oxford: Oxford University Press.

Odenthal, L., & Nijhof, W.J. (1996). *HRD roles in Germany*. De Lier: Academisch Boekencentrum.

Pätzold, G. (1992). Zur Professionalisierung betrieblicher Ausbildungstätigkeit in Deutschland. In Stratmann, K.(Hrsg.), Historische Berufsbildung. *Zeitschrift für Berufs- und Wirtschaftspäda-gogik. Beihefte 7/1992*, 258-279.

Poon, A. (1988). *Flexible specialisation and small size*. London: SPRU.

Sayer, A., & Walker, R. (1992). *The New Social Economy. Reworking the Division of Labour*. Cambridge, MA: Blackwell.

Senge, P. (1990). *The Fifth Discipline. The Art and Practice of Learning Organization*. New York: Doubleday.

Siltala, J. (1999). Sociological and psychological self (in Finnish). In Näre, S. (Ed.), *Sociology of emotions, part II* (pp.379-465) (in Finnish). Hämeenlinna: Karisto.

Silverman, M. (1999). *Facing Postmodernity*. London: Routledge.

Sloane, P.F.E., Twardy, M., & Buschfeld, D. (1998). *Einführung in die Wirtschaftspädagogik* [Introduction to vocational pedagogy]. Paderborn-München-Wien-Zürich: Shöningh.

Svensson, L., Ellström, P.-E., & Åberg, C. (2000) *Pursuing and Exploring Workplace Learning: A Discussion Based on the Ideas Behind a Regional Research and Development Centre*. Presentation in FORUM workshop, held at Wageningen, November 2000.

Szell, G. (1992). Neue Technologien und alte Technokratiedebatte [New technologies and the old technocracy-debate]. In Ehlert, W. (hrsg.), *Sozialverträglische Technikgestaltung und/oder Technizierung von Sachzwang?* (pp. 29-52). Opladen: Westdt. Verlag.

Tomassini, M. (1999). *New Meaning of Learning Organisation and Spaces of Human Resources Development within the Globalizing Learning Economy*. Presentation in FORUM workshop, held at Evora, November 1999.

Toulmin, S., & Gustavsen, B. (1996). *Beyond theory. Changing organisations through participation*. Amsterdam-Philadelphia: John Benjamins.

Tulkki, P. (1996). *Public service or industrial work? The training of Finnish engineers as a societal phenomenon, 1802-1939* (in Finnish). Turun yliopisto: Painosalama.

Tuomisto, J. (1986). *Aims of industrial training* (in Finnish). Tampere: University of Tampere.

Valkeavaara, T. (1998). Human Resource development roles and competencies in five European countries. *International Journal of Training and Development, 2*, (3), 171-189.

Vartia, P., & Ylä-Anttila, P. (1996). *Technology policy and industrial clusters in a small open economy - the Case of Finland*. Helsinki: ETLA.

Wenger, E. (1999). *Communities of Practice. Learning, Meaning and Identity*. Cambridge: Cambridge University Press.

Young, M. (Ed.) (1971). *Knowledge and control: new directions for the sociology of education*. London: Macmillan.

Zabeck, J. (1992). *Die Berufs- und Wirtschaftspädagogik als Erziehungs- wissenschaftliche Teildisziplin* [Vocational pedagogy as a sub-discipline of education]. Hohengren: Baltmannsweiler.

CHAPTER 14

HRD as a professional career?
Perspectives from Finland, The Netherlands, and the United Kingdom

TUIJA HYTÖNEN, ROB POELL AND GEOFF CHIVERS

14.1 Introduction and definition of the problem

DURING THE PAST FEW DECADES, WORLDWIDE CHANGES in technology, the economy, demography, organisation, and working life have led to an increase in the attention paid to learning in work organisations. Such ongoing changes in the world of work have raised new challenges of flexibility, mobility, and transferability for the organisation of work and economies. They have also had an impact on the organisation of the initial and further vocational education and training (VET) of the workforce, both in traditional training institutions and within organisation-specific settings. As a result, the development of professional skills and knowledge about learning in the workplace has become much more important in organisations (e.g. Gerber & Lankshear, 2000). This field of organisational activity, which is known as human resource development (HRD), is increasingly being recognised as a crucial investment in human learning by employers in various enterprises and public sector organisations throughout Europe. Given the aims of developing vocational skills included in HRD, it can be viewed as one specific field of professional practice within VET. In this view, HRD practitioners responsible for the organising and promoting of the learning endeavours in the workplaces can be seen as one group of "VET professionals". Thus also they are actors in the definition and constitution of VET.

Many commentators have stated that organisations need to improve the professional expertise of the practitioners responsible for HRD issues, in order for lifelong learning to be incorporated into their ongoing business (e.g. Longworth & Davies, 1996; Nijhof, 1996). However, although the need to develop specialised knowledge and understanding within HRD is recognised, professional practice in this field has not gained very much acclaim as yet. HRD practitioners seem to be under constant threat of being out-sourced, depending on the overall economic success of the enterprise. Moreover, evidence of its contribution to the economic success of an organisation is hard to show, at least in a short-term perspective. Paradoxically, although HRD is seen as a key factor to promote lifelong learning in enterprises, it belongs to the margins within organisational activity. This sense of marginality seems to be shared by HRD practitioners themselves as well (Marsick & Watkins, 1990; Valkeavaara, 1999b).

The reasons for the insecure and undefined position of HRD as a field of professional practice are manifold. They are found, for instance, in its short history as a field of organisational activity, in the many definitions it is given in literature, in the lack of unified basic education in HRD, and in the modest amount of research into the nature of HRD work. Besides, HRD practitioners hold very different organisational positions. They can be found working, for instance, as internal part-

227

W. J. Nijhof et al. (eds.), Shaping Flexibility in Vocational Education and Training, 227-242.
© 2002 *Kluwer Academic Publishers. Printed in the Netherlands.*

time consultants, internal full-time practitioners, or as external short-term consultants (e.g. Nadler & Nadler, 1991). This also has an impact on how actual HRD practices are formed, as well as on how they are recognised and evaluated.

The purpose of this chapter is to describe HRD as one specific field of professional practice within vocational education and training (VET) and HRD practitioners as one specific group of "VET professionals". As the question mark in the title of this chapter shows, we intend to question the usability of the term 'profession' as far as current HRD practice in the European context is concerned. The nature of HRD work does not seem compatible with traditional definitions of a profession. We will examine HRD work through the experiences of its committed practitioners, who have entered HRD as a professional career. They are referred to in this chapter as HRD practitioners or, alternatively, as HR developers. This definition includes those who have a full-time responsibility in their organisations for a wide range of HRD activities, from training to education, from organisation development to career development, and so forth.

Specific questions to be addressed in this chapter focus on the processes of being and becoming an HRD practitioner. Firstly, what are the nature and contents of HRD as a field of practice? The following paragraphs will deal with this question by looking at HRD as an occupational activity, as a flexible field of professional practice, and as a locally constructed field of professional expertise. Secondly, in which ways can people become HR developers? And how can they develop their expertise while on the job (e.g. through problematic situations or via specific learning programs)? These two questions are dealt with in the final paragraph. Input for tentative answers is drawn from recent studies focusing on HRD practitioners in Finland, the Netherlands, and the UK. These studies provide empirical evidence from individual HRD practitioners about their experiences, their professional practice, the nature and contents of their expertise, and their personal career development within the field of HRD.

14.2 HRD as an occupational activity

The 'textbook' definition of HRD in the literature says it is a field of organisational activity aimed at maintaining and developing the human resources of an enterprise in order to promote organisational effectiveness, through training or other developmental interventions. These are directed, for instance, at the reorganisation of work tasks or the recognition and support of learning opportunities in the course of everyday work. How this definition translates into reality depends very much on the viewpoint of each particular stakeholder in the workplace. Despite its organisational aims, HRD is about working with people, that is, men and women, young and old, managers and workers, highly educated and less educated, experts and novices. Naturally, therefore, the needs, values, and beliefs of people play an important part in HRD. Table 14.1 presents an example of the different interpretations of staff training as one part of HRD found among various interest groups in Finnish working life. Different kinds of training have had an important role within HRD practice in Finland. Staff training has also been the largest and fastest growing sector of the adult education system during the past few decades. Over the past five years, more than half of the employed workforce (1995: 52% - 2000: 56%) has participated yearly in staff training in Finland (Finland Statistics).

Table 14.1 *Possible interpretations of HRD among various Finnish interest groups.*

Employers[1]	Employees[1]	Labour Unions[1]	Educational Policy and Administration
Staff training is invested in: * in order to improve performance * to increase efficiency * to compete in the markets * to have economic success	Staff training is attended to: * in order to develop one's competence * to get better and more demanding jobs * to increase salary * to strengthen job security * to promote a career	Staff training is supported: * in order to reach better agreements and contracts * to secure and strengthen the status of the professions * to increase salaries and benefits	HRD on the whole is autonomously administrated by the employers, but it can be steered through various national and European projects and funding, in order to increase national and European competitiveness (e.g., Ministry of Labour, Ministry of Education, EU-projects)
HRD Practitioners			
HRD aims to combine the various interpretations and to support communication between the different interest groups for the wellbeing of individuals and organisations			

[1] *Sources*: Finland Statistics, 1997; Rinne, Silvennoinen & Valanta, 1995.

Employers, employees, and labour unions all have their own interpretations of what is important in HRD, what the interests to invest in it are, and what the returns looked for are, either from an organisational or a personal perspective. HRD is administrated fairly autonomously by the employers. Still, public employment and education policies can have an impact, mainly indirect, on the running of developmental processes in enterprises. Employers seem to put the emphasis on organisational performance and efficiency, employees on personal development and benefits, and labour union interests are in professional security and benefits. Given the 'textbook' definition of HRD, it seems that what is left for HRD practitioners themselves is to try to bring the different interpretations together in a constructive way. This, however, hardly reflects an occupational field of their own.

While there have been various shifts in HRD practices at least since the 1920s, the current image of 'old-school' HRD emphasises the development of existing skills, knowledge, and attitudes, that is, vocational and ideological qualifications for the job. Learning experiences were provided mainly through formal training, separated from everyday work, and mostly on the terms of the organisation. 'New-school' HRD, and current VET as well, are considered to be increasingly concerned with facilitating the ability to learn and develop in the workplace, at individual, group, and organisational levels. In addition, the enhancement of informal learning in different contexts, and flexible ways of dealing with change have gained priority. Accordingly, the image of 'new school' resembles the time before the first organised, formal HRD practices and the development of a formal VET system, when the emphasis of professional development was on informal and incidental learning while working. Current key questions in both HRD and VET concern, for instance, encouraging strategic alignment of HRD, e-learning, competence management, and learning in the workplace. VET and HRD seem closely related in terms of their aims and practices. When striving for high quality performance or promoting the development of skills and knowledge, HRD is connected to both initial and further VET and its division of work. This is because HRD also has a central role in fostering occupational growth in employees through the development of task and organisation-specific professional skills and knowledge (cf. Anja Heikkinen's chapter).

Besides the increased interest and volume in organisations, HRD as a specific field of professional expertise and career has gained increasing attention from educational administration, training institutes, and academic research. HRD practitioners may be less professional in terms of traditional characterisations of a profession than most teachers in formal VET institutions. Nevertheless, HR developers and vocational teachers have things in common as well: they can be considered key people in promoting vocational development, educational innovation, and organisational change in their workplaces. Furthermore, the work of HRD practitioners and VET teachers is determined largely by the demands of organisational contexts and the challenges of flexibility, mobility, and transferability as targets of vocational development. HR developers work under a variety of formal job titles, such as training manager, (training) designer, trainer, consultant, HRD manager, and project manager. They do not share a unified basic education for their occupation. Therefore, the best way to recognise them as a group of professional practitioners may be through their commitment to HRD as a personal occupational career. Alternatively, one could emphasise their common work practices, which include the responsibility for organising and supporting other people's learning within the organisation.

14.3 HRD as a flexible field of professional practice

A literature review shows that there are many approaches that can be used simultaneously to define HRD as a field of professional practice. These approaches include, for instance, HRD as a performance and production-driven part of human resource management, as a learning and development-driven field of adult education, or as an occupational growth-driven field of VET (which is mainly continuous) for adults in various workplace contexts (Heikkinen, 1997; Barrie & Pace, 1998; Kuchinke, 1999). The numerous approaches indicate the complex and multidisciplinary nature of HRD as a field of professional practice. Judging from the traditional definitions of a profession, HRD represents an applied field of organisational activity rather than an independent professional field. Complexity and multidisciplinarity unavoidably bring contradictions and a demand for flexibility to the work of HR developers and how the core of their professional practice is acknowledged. However, it may be more fruitful to view these various approaches as complementary rather than contradictory. In addition, despite the complexity of HRD practice, there are probably some common cores transferable to all contexts. One of these common cores is that HRD practice is concerned with humans, that is, with people working in organisations (Webb, 1996, pp. 35-36).

In Finland, HR developers are usually classified according to their work tasks as a specific group of adult educators and trainers. Furthermore, they can be seen to constitute a subgroup of VET professionals (Heikkinen, 1997). To illustrate this, adult education and learning theories have contributed greatly to HRD practice and the professional development of HRD practitioners, especially in public sector organisations since the 1970s. The same tendency can also be observed in larger Finnish enterprises (Valkeavaara, 2001). A brief look at the history of HRD in Finnish organisations shows that, starting in the 1940s, HRD was considered in enterprises, and especially line management, to have a responsibility for employee learning and development. The overall expansion of adult education in working life in the 1970s brought separate staff-training departments, company-specific as well as general training centres into the training market. The latest trends, including the learning organisation, return responsibility for learning and development to management again (cf. Anja Heikkinen's chapter). At the same time, the emphasis of HRD practitioners' work has shifted from the organisation of training to the promotion of learning and development.

A similar story can be told about HRD and VET in the Netherlands (De Vries, 1988; Van der Klink, 1999), although Dutch HRD practitioners would not generally be considered a subgroup of VET professionals. A local guild system was in place in the Netherlands before the 19th century. From the 19th century onwards, vocational schools were established, gradually causing a separation of learning from everyday work. This institutional separation in VET still exists today, although the past decade has seen a marked increase in reintegration efforts. HRD practitioners started taking their positions in individual large companies after World War II, but this development did not occur on a broad scale until the 1970s. The 1980s saw central training departments on the rise, before HRD was decentralised again in the 1990s, with the introduction of ideas like the learning organisation and workplace learning. While HRD practitioners would have been regarded mainly as technical skills trainers about twenty years ago, the past decade has witnessed a tendency to think of HRD people rather as learning and development advisers. Simultaneously, the responsibility for actually dealing with learning and development issues has supposedly shifted to line management and employees themselves.

In the United Kingdom, the role and status of VET professionals have fluctuated, with much higher status being accorded during periods of national emergency than in normal times, at least until the 1980s. The low status of vocational education has been described as an aspect of the so-called 'British Disease' in regard to ever-weakening international industrial performance since at least the Great Exhibition in London in 1851. Despite the efforts of Prince Albert, who brought progressive thinking about vocational (especially technological) learning from Germany, it was not until World War I that the British began to take the matter seriously. Training initiatives introduced under wartime conditions were allowed to decline between the World Wars, so that in the 1930s, the main governmental concern reverted back to training the unemployed, and craft apprenticeship in traditional industries was left to employers and trade unions to organise. The Second World War reactivated concern about the lack of skilled workers in British industry, and the rapid training of women to carry out skilled war work or replace men in conventional jobs challenged the old 'time-served' craft apprenticeship tradition. Trainers in the military established very successful HRD programmes and did much to raise the general profile of VET in the postwar years. Industrial Training Boards were set up, which did much to encourage training in industrial and commercial sectors with little previous tradition of formalised in-company training. Full-time training managers appeared on the scene in industry and the public sector.

The mid-1980s saw much angst in the UK about the lack of competitiveness of UK companies relative to their equivalents in Germany, Japan and the USA (for example, in the car industry and computing). Government-sponsored reports claimed that much of this was due to the lack of training and development of the UK workforce. The past 15 years have seen a whole host of governmental initiatives from National Vocational Qualifications and the Investors in People Standard, to the 'New Deal' programme for the long-term unemployed (leading to NVQs). Larger organisations have introduced well-structured and well-resourced HRD departments, with an increasing emphasis on flexibly-delivered learning to employees. HRD staff are becoming professionalised through achieving qualifications from universities and/or professional bodies, and vocational lifelong learning is becoming embedded in larger organisations. Smaller work organisations rely on public sector VET providers, or contracting from the ranks of self-employed HRD professionals and small training consultancies, which have proliferated in recent years. Concepts of the line manager as trainer, and worker-controlled learning challenge the role of the HRD professional in larger and smaller organisations alike.

In general, HR developers can partake in various 'tribes' of adult educators based on their actual goals, concerns, and perspectives on learning (Darkenwald & Merriam, 1982, in Edwards, 1997, pp. 166-167). HRD practitioners can be characterised as progressives coaching individual growth, as guerrillas creating a new and better order, or as organisational maintainers promoting the effectiveness of the enterprise. Perhaps the characterisation currently most used for HR developers is the change agent, who works in the interests of organisations, industry, and the economy. At the same time, however, HRD practitioners can be described as activists. They can even be agents striving to satisfy the needs and broaden the opportunities of individuals with little power in organisations (see also Heikkinen, 1997). In earlier times, HRD practice was mainly rooted in maintaining organisational effectiveness according to management interests. It is typical of contemporary working life that HR developers are being challenged to build their professional practice on all those tribes simultaneously. This strongly suggests that flexibility is another common core in HRD practice.

14.3.1 Role changes of HR developers

During the past decade, a number of empirical studies were conducted to examine the changing roles of HRD practitioners in work organisations. For example, the 1990s saw a series of surveys being conducted to compare the nature of the HRD profession across several European countries (e.g. De Rijk, Mulder, & Nijhof, 1994; Odenthal & Nijhof, 1996; Van Ginkel, Mulder, & Nijhof, 1997; Valkeavaara, 1997). These surveys concerned self-evaluations by HRD practitioners of the actual work roles, outputs, and professional competence considered important and beneficial to their everyday work practice. The survey questionnaires adopted the descriptive model for the work of HRD practitioners established by the American Society for Training and Development (McLagan & Bedrick, 1983; McLagan, 1989; McLagan 1996). A comparison of the results from five of the participating countries (Valkeavaara, 1998a) suggested that the roles of organisational change agent, instructor, HRD manager, and programme designer appeared to best define the current activities of HRD practitioners (see also Lassnigg, this volume).

Typical HRD roles in the Netherlands were distributed quite evenly across the role alternatives presented in the survey questionnaire. The change aspect of HRD practice was highlighted, particularly in Finland and the United Kingdom. The emphasis on the role of change agent in Finland was unsurprising, given the drastic changes in working life during the survey. These forced organisations and HRD practitioners, particularly in the public sector, to reconsider their activities. The central role of change agency can also reflect recent trends in HRD and organisational rhetoric (e.g. the ideal of a learning organisation). The comparison of country-specific results indicated a diversity of roles across European HRD practitioners. It provides further evidence of the diversity (including cultural diversity) in HRD as a professional field. The work of HR developers at present cannot be described in one explicit role, although some aspects tend to get more emphasis than others.

Analysis of the Finnish survey results yielded more evidence of organisational change issues constituting one common core of HRD practice. Table 14.2 describes four dimensions in the professional practice of 164 Finnish HRD practitioners, in terms of their individual work roles and outputs (Valkeavaara, 1998b). *Change agents* (n=51) are HRD practitioners who see themselves performing mainly as supporters of organisational change and development. *Designers* (n=37) are practitioners who characterise their performance mainly as organising specific HRD interventions. *Managers* (n=50) are practitioners who spend most of their working time managing, marketing, consulting, and administrating the HRD function. *Trainers* (n=26) are HR developers whose performance relates mainly to training delivery, needs assessment, materials development, instruction, research, or career development.

Table 14.2 *HRD work in Finland, in terms of roles and outputs (n=164, adopted from Valkeavaara, 1998b).*

Change agents (n=51)	Designers (n=37)	Managers (n=50)	Trainers (n=26)
* Resolve conflicts for an organisation or groups * Changes in group norms, values, culture * Planning organisational change * Implementing change strategies * Sales and business leads * Data analysis and interpretation	* Promotional and informational HRD material * Marketing HRD products, services, and programmes	* Resource acquisition and allocation for HRD * Strategy of HRD department * HRD budgets and financial management * Programme and intervention designs	* Facilitating structured learning events * Facilitating group discussions * Feedback to learners
* Client awareness of relationships within and around the organisation * Recommendations to management regarding HRD systems * Concepts and theories/models of development/change * Designs for change			

As Table 14.2 shows, four rather open-ended core dimensions of performance can be identified as constituting HRD work. The outputs in the lower cell represent the most typical performance outputs of all HR developers, regardless of their perceived role. This general part of HRD work seems to be oriented towards change, negotiation, and seeking support for the HRD function. Furthermore, the outputs refer to more implicit information services and symbol analysis, rather than to concrete and measurable products. Consequently, HRD can also be characterised as pragmatic, a professional activity which takes place in the informal processes of an organisation. It is constantly being actualised in processes dealing with the management of tacit and informal knowledge in organisations.

14.3.2 New HRD roles?

Although the roles of HRD practitioners are shown and believed to be changing towards promoting organisational change and learning in enterprises, the empirical evidence to that effect is certainly less than conclusive. "The HRD literature is somewhat normative and rhetorical in exhorting line managers to take responsibility for training and development. The reality is that this is the exception rather than the norm." (Horwitz, 1999, in Sambrook & Stewart, 2001).

For example, Sambrook and Stewart (2001) reported on an investigation of 28 European learning-oriented organisations in seven countries. They pointed to a gap between normative theories and actual practices: "As structures and cultures change, so do HRD practices and roles. Instead of trainers, HRD practitioners now become consultants, who also have to manage the link between their activities and company strategy. An important element in this changing role is the shift from training to facilitating learning. As this new role for HRD becomes clearer in theory, many uncertainties remain for HRD professionals, especially on the question of how to translate this into practice." Many of their findings, however, do not paint a very innovative picture of current HRD activity. In 23 of the 28 cases, HRD tasks at hand could be labelled as traditional, with providing and coordinating training among the most important ones. Although HRD practitioners use many strategies to realise their envisioned role, those related to training are still very significant. Moreover, quite contrary to the dominant rhetoric, "among the least important strategies are instruments and initiatives to increase employee responsibility for learning. These outcomes might indicate that HRD strategies and practices do, to some extent, fall behind HRD visions."

Poell and Chivers (1999) conducted a qualitative study in the United Kingdom, interviewing 19 HRD practitioners who mainly worked within large corporations or were self-employed. Within the UK context, the system of national vocational qualifications (NVQs) and government programs such as *Investors in People* reflected an influential tendency towards standardised HRD programs, which is rather at odds with the dominant learning rhetoric. Supporting personal development remained an important field of activity for HR developers, along with organisational consultancy and, unsurprisingly, training delivery. Although managers and employees were increasingly expected to take on responsibility for learning, HRD practitioners encountered resistance to these changes in practice. Managers often tended to resent being made responsible for training issues that had formerly been dealt with by trainers. Some trainers themselves resisted taking on a more facilitative consultant-like role. In about half the cases, HR developers experienced a lack of recognition for training issues in organisations.

These results from the UK context are in accordance with a qualitative study of 20 Finnish HRD practitioners, who worked mainly in HRD management positions within public-sector organisations and private enterprises (Valkeavaara, 1999a).

This study suggested, for instance, that the ideals of the learning organisation, such as open communication, collaboration, and management involvement, constitute the primary source of problems for these HR developers in their everyday work practice. Furthermore, taking on the role of change agent caused HR developers notable unease and uncertainty. As much as HRD practitioners sensed the expectations and possibilities to act as challenger or change agent, they also perceived the resistance to this activity as problematic to their professional practice. The question to what extent HR developers can really be involved in shaping organisational change is certainly valid. Are they constrained in actual practice to propagating changes put forward by management? What is the cost involved to their position as professional experts in HRD issues?

14.4 HRD as an inclusive and locally constructed field of professional expertise

The core characterisation of expertise in any professional field includes an understanding of the processes behind the activity. It also entails a profound notion of how problems and the complexity of work are addressed. Finally, experts understand all the materials used, and they engage in continuous development (Bereiter & Scardamalia, 1993). Consequently, professional expertise is tightly bound to professional practice. It consists of specific knowledge and skills needed in practice. In addition, it comprises applying, developing, and transforming this knowledge and these skills.

According to Bereiter and Scardamalia (1993, p. 6), professional expertise is easiest to identify and reward when it differs dramatically from what ordinary people can do, for instance, problem-solving in well-defined fields of physics or medicine. Identifying the content of expertise in HRD, however, turns out to be rather difficult. For instance, organisational recruitment policies for HRD practitioners seem to imply that anyone with school experience can somehow train and enhance human development. This is probably the situation in enterprises where responsibility for HRD has been given to line managers. These are usually experts in their respective fields, but rarely do they have any formal knowledge, practical experience or real interest in making learning and development issues their main field of work. They get the job because it is considered a good way of integrating HRD into strategic management. Typical consequences of this policy are a high number of HRD interventions, combined with a discussion about the ineffectiveness of HRD.

Comparing HRD practitioners with VET teachers in schools and institutes brings up questions about the specific knowledge and skills making up their professional expertise. Studies of HRD practitioners suggest that making specific discipline-based definitions of knowledge and skills is problematic. A comparison of HRD in five European countries revealed, for instance, that the common core of professional expertise seems to consist of skills and knowledge in three areas: interaction and information processes, organisational operations, and learning processes. Altogether, sixteen different competencies were found to be part of the country-specific top five, being valued most often as very important by HRD practitioners. For instance, one country-specific finding was that relationship-building skills turned out as important competencies among British and Dutch respondents, while the Finns deemed understanding adult learning as very important (Valkeavaara, 1998a).

A further analysis of the Finnish data suggested four competency dimensions to expert knowledge and skills in HRD: analytical, managerial, coaching, and developmental (Valkeavaara, 1998b). Especially important were the analytical dimension (intellectual and thinking skills, communication skills, and acquiring information) and the coaching dimension (observing and identifying situations, giving feedback, and coaching groups and individuals). This suggests that HRD expertise includes making training and development theories and techniques available to people in the organisation. Furthermore, a qualitative study of twenty Finnish HR developers revealed communication skills to be an important aspect of professional expertise in HRD (Valkeavaara, 1999a). The study suggested that communication skills constitute practical knowledge for HRD practitioners, integral to their whole practice. For instance, HR developers made conscious attempts to enhance dialogue in organisational settings. In some problematic situations (e.g. contradictions between management and employees), they tried to find room for different perspectives, and to match the different points of views between groups.

To summarise our current understanding, HRD in organisations comprises an extensive, practically-oriented, and applied field of professional expertise. It is based on a broad variety of underlying theories and understanding of work and organisational psychology, learning and adult education, and business and management. Formal qualifications or criteria to judge HRD expertise, however, are difficult to find. Therefore, a great deal of expertise in HRD is acknowledged through social recognition, which can be based on, for instance, various business interests. Recent studies have also shown HRD to be a highly-contextualised and locally-determined domain of professional expertise (Garrick, 1998; Valkeavaara, 1999a). HRD does not take place in a vacuum, but rather in flexible and complex business environments. Therefore, HR developers need to cross boundaries between different types of work practices, knowledge domains, and skills required. Despite certain common dimensions in HRD expertise, it is largely constructed locally, according to specific organisational requirements.

14.5 Sources of professional career development in HRD

So far, we have established that HRD work as a field of professional practice has a manifold nature and rather ill-defined contents of professional expertise among its practitioners. It can, therefore, be assumed that entering a professional HRD career is not a clear-cut early career move from school to work. It is difficult to adopt traditional definitions of a career for HR developers, which usually refer to an objectively definable, linear, and hierarchical continuum of workplaces or tasks. A qualitative analysis of the career stories of twenty experienced Finnish HR developers (Valkeavaara, 2001), for instance, revealed four different ways of pursuing a career in HRD. Firstly, some had entered their present organisation and HRD work straight after graduating from university. Secondly, some had been involved in HRD tasks from the outset of their professional careers, although they had worked for several organisations. A third group had been employed by the same organisation throughout their careers, after vocational and/or university education. These particular HR developers, however, had started out in work related to their initial education, only gradually moving into HRD work along their careers. Fourthly, some had gained work experience related to their initial education in a variety of organisations, followed by recruitment into HRD by their present employer.

Understanding the professional career development of HRD practitioners would be possible by using a subjective approach, which defines career as a continuous learning process in a professional context. Career development can be viewed as a process of self-socialisation, focusing on the proactive adaptation of individuals to changing skill and role demands in organisational contexts (e.g. Nicholson & West, 1989; Heinz, Kelle, Witzel, & Zinn, 1998). Individuals conduct different activities throughout this process, such as acquiring new skills and knowledge, through intentional further training and informal learning from everyday work experience. On the whole, the work of HR developers can be presumed to include many opportunities for learning from experience, serving as a resource for professional career development. For instance, characteristic of the work of HRD practitioners are the many ill-defined and changing situations they encounter, the continuous adaptation to various organisational contexts required, and the constant need to tackle problematic situations. The career of an HR developer can, therefore, be understood as a continuous interpretative process of active career-building, which comprises all experiences gained balancing organisational and individual requirements.

The focus on intentional acquisition of professional knowledge and skills can be found, for instance, in studies dealing with continuing professional development for HRD practitioners (Valkeavaara, 1998b; Poell & Chivers, 1999; Sambrook & Stewart, 2001). Valkeavaara (1998b) asked Finnish HRD practitioners to evaluate their personal interests in the further development of various competencies related to HRD. The results showed the greatest interest in analytical competencies (including intellectual and thinking skills, communication skills, and acquiring information), and in coaching competencies (including observing and identifying situations, giving feedback, and coaching groups and individuals). Sambrook and Stewart (2001) were also aware that changes towards more consultancy and learning-based roles require different skills and attitudes. However, their study of 28 learning-oriented organisations showed that only one company engaged in deliberately increasing the skills of HRD professionals. HRD practitioners need to be aware and take care of the internal development of the HRD function. There are risks of losing power, and even the disappearance of the HRD function. To help overcome this, HRD professionals need to clearly identify HRD's contribution to the organisation. However, there is still little evidence to indicate HRD's added value to the business. The study of 19 HRD practitioners by Poell and Chivers (1999) also asked about their own CPD, focusing on self-initiated activities undertaken in order to become a more professional consultant. In almost half of the cases, HRD professionals indicated that they worked with associates, were actively developing their consultancy skills, or marketed both themselves as consultants and the products they developed.

One example of looking at the relation between everyday work experiences of HRD practitioners and the development of a professional career in HRD is the study conducted in the Netherlands by Poell (1998). The study was aimed at comparing the strategies employed by HRD practitioners, managers, and employees in organising work-related learning projects on the shop floor. It concluded that HRD professionals were far from influential in this domain, and needed to come up with well-elaborated new strategies to professionalise their discipline. Positioning itself as a tool of management had done little to make HRD a more professional occupation. Poell argued that if HRD professionals in modern organisations were to become more influential, they would have to act more independently of the strategies preferred by management.

Another example of analysing everyday work experience as a source for professional development is the study conducted in Finland by Valkeavaara (1999a). This study regarded the development of professional expertise as a learning process, an active problem-solving process in a specific context. It looked at the nature of the problematic situations that HRD practitioners encounter in their work, at the solutions they have sought in those situations, and at the things they had learnt from those experiences. Data were gathered from twenty full-time HRD practitioners with a high level of education and long experience in HRD. The study provided a collection of stories about problematic situations, resolutions, and lessons learnt. Stories describe the processes and outcomes of HRD practitioners' learning in the workplace. These are summarised in Table 14.3.

Table 14.3 *Summary of problem stories, resolution stories, and lessons learnt by HRD practitioners in everyday work (adopted from Valkeavaara, 1999a).*

Problem stories
* Relationships and cooperation with middle and line management in the organisation * Resistance to change on different levels of the organisation * Personal experiences of HRD expertise being rejected * Working and communicating with different people * Lack of personal knowledge and skills * Practical problems in training situations

Resolution stories
* Influencing by talking and building dialogue in the organisation * Finding and experimenting with alternative practices * Critically evaluating and developing one's own knowledge and skills * Problem-solving by doing and enhancing participation

Lessons learnt
* How to deal with situations through progressive problem-solving * How to involve members of the organisation in development processes * Acquisition of a personal sense and understanding of the change process

Chivers, Poell, and Chapman (2000) looked at the relationship between continuous professional development for HRD practitioners and the handling of everyday work challenges. The study focused on a graduate programme preparing HRD practitioners for a Master's degree in Training and Development (MTD). Data for this particular study were gathered over the course of ten years, in which the course was developed and improved at the University of Sheffield (UK). Starting from the premise that HRD professionals face many challenges and need all the help they can get to work effectively, the study asked whether the MTD course was providing them with as much help as it could. Evidence was found of a close relationship between the three main strategies that alumni employ to overcome problems at work, and the main benefits they perceive from completing the MTD course. These are summarised in Table 14.4.

Table 14.4 *Alumni overcoming work problems and benefiting from the MTD (from Chivers, Poell, & Chapman, 2000).*

Main ways to overcome problems	Main MTD Benefits
* Direct interventions to influence learning climate * Negotiation with stakeholders, especially managers, and trying to get involved in new projects at an early stage * Self-development by undertaking consultancy work, marketing themselves, selling on products and services	* Self-confidence * Increased credibility and recognition * Increased status for training, making it more strategic * Gaining more knowledge, thinking more widely * Becoming more reflective, seeing the bigger picture

These various studies show that HRD practitioners can and do engage in their own continuing professional development in many ways: through self-directed learning, through company-specific training (albeit limited), and in an academic context. Self-directed learning through everyday problem-solving seems to be a more dominant model of CPD than is company-specific training in HRD expertise. The important dimensions of learning through everyday work seem to include social interaction, participatory practices, understanding change process and continuous development. Various academic programmes in HRD are becoming more popular in Finland, the Netherlands, and the UK. These currently seem to be the most important ways for HR developers to sustain their career development, with a formal qualification representing their HRD expertise.

14.6 Discussion

This chapter has aimed to present HRD as one specific field of professional practice within vocational education and training (VET). We have examined through the experiences of its practitioners to what extent the concept of a profession can describe current HRD practices in three European countries. Specifically, we looked at the work of HR developers by treating the field of HRD as an occupational activity, as a flexible professional practice, and as a locally-constructed field of professional expertise. We also paid attention to the ways in which people can become HR developers and develop their expertise on the job, providing empirical data about individual careers and professional development within the field of HRD.

The various studies presented do not provide strong evidence to support HRD being seen as a high-status profession. The picture emerging shows a broad field of professional practice with a strong confidence on practical knowledge and a need for further development. However, setting out to become a well-defined training and development profession may not be the only, or even preferred, way for HRD practitioners to support their practice and position in organisations. Perhaps the HRD community could also strengthen its expertise by evaluating more carefully the underlying assumptions and the actual outcomes of their efforts. Awareness of the different approaches to HRD will probably give a wider range of choices to practitioners (Kuchinke, 1999). Moreover, differences in practice and expertise need not be detrimental, as Edwards (1997) suggested regarding adult educators. Workers in adult education need to be able to construct themselves not as a uniform community, but as a community of differences, inclusive rather than exclusive (Edwards, 1997, p. 170). In other words, differences in HRD practices could be seen as creative and innovative resources to the field covered by HR developers. In this connection, it would be good to look across sector, industry and cultural boundaries as well. In most cases, 'organisation' is unquestionably taken to mean 'company' or 'business', even though historically HRD was first recognised in public-sector organisations.

The currently eclectic disciplinary basis for HRD expertise could also be regarded as a sign of flexibility, which may contain opportunities rather than threats in modern organisational practice. One opportunity embedded in the multidisciplinary basis is the holistic perspective on organisational activities. This can make the role of HRD more independent of the dominant management perspective, steering clear of possibly reactive management initiatives, and moving towards proactivity. Although this would currently go against mainstream HRD debates, at the same time it could improve the recognition of HRD as a field of expertise that makes a difference to organisational practice. Furthermore, it could reduce the currently rather local nature of HRD expertise to the benefit of increased flexibility, by defining its common cores independently of organisation-specific management issues.

The various studies presented seem to agree that HRD practitioners in the examined countries have their understanding of organisational processes, organisational changes, and flexibility issues as a common core. This directly reflects the current challenges in working life. Compared to other professional groups, then, HRD practitioners contribute to the development of working life mainly through their expertise in dealing with such crucial challenges in various business environments. Particularly, their expertise is fuelled by an understanding of human learning and development in different contexts. HR developers are specialised in helping other people to learn, to develop their work, and to develop themselves through their work. They supposedly know a lot better than nonspecialists how to make explicit use of their previous experience and knowledge in enhancing and supporting people's learning. It is important, however, to remember that HRD practitioners are not the only ones doing this job. For example, human resource management increasingly seems to incorporate aspects of HRD, even though studies of HR managers show that responsibility for learning issues is missing from their competence (e.g. Lawson & Limbrick, 1996). Another field of practice closely related to HRD is organisation development. But many OD interventions are conducted by external consultants, who lack the long-term perspective and profound organisation-specific knowledge of in-house HR developers.

It would not be wise for the community of HRD practitioners to ignore the potential dangers inherent in new challenges of flexibility, mobility, and transferability facing the world of organisations. With theory increasingly emphasising strategies other than training-based, and organisational practice apparently more resistant to innovative learning strategies than usually assumed, HRD as a profession is badly in danger of getting stuck in between. It seems crucial to develop new HRD work protocols and methods that can guide HR developers in supporting self-directed employee learning and in delegating responsibility for workplace development issues to managers. Only when the body of knowledge in this area reaches a degree of refinement similar to that of its traditional training domain will HRD practitioners be fully equipped to face the challenges of modern organisational life. Further developing this core competency of the HRD profession will provide a central problem and a major challenge to HR developers and researchers in the field alike.

References

Barrie, J., & Pace, W. (1998). Learning for organizational effectiveness: Philosophy of education and human resource development. *Human Resource Development Quarterly, 9*(1), 39-54.
Bereiter, C., & Scardamalia, M. (1993). *Surpassing ourselves: An inquiry into the nature and implications of expertise.* Chicago, IL: Open Court.
Chivers, G.E., Poell, R.F., & Chapman, R. (2000, January). *The development of HRD practitioners for changing roles in the European workplace of the next Millennium.* Paper presented at the first European conference on HRD research and practice across Europe 2000, held at Kingston, UK.
Darkenwald, G., & Merriam, S. (1982). *Adult education: Foundations of practice.* New York: Harper & Row.
Edwards, R. (1997). *Changing places? Flexibility, lifelong learning and a learning society.* London: Routledge.
Finland Statistics (1997). *Adult education survey 1995.* Helsinki: Tilastokeskus.
Finland Statistics. Adult Education Survey 2000. Available in <URL:http//www.stat.fi/tk/he/aku00_ennakko4.html> (21.5.2001).
Garrick, J. (1998) *Informal learning in the workplace. Unmasking human resource development.* London: Routledge.
Gerber, R., & Lankshear, C. (Eds.) (2000). *Training for a smart workforce.* London: Routledge.
Ginkel, K. van, Mulder, M., & Nijhof, W. (1997). Role profiles of HRD practitioners in the Netherlands. *International Journal of Training and Development 1*(1), 22-33.
Heikkinen, A. (1997). A comparative view on European VET-professionalism: Finnish perspectives. In A. Brown (Ed.), *Promoting vocational education and training: European perspectives* (pp. 123-137). Hämeenlinna: University of Tampere.
Heinz, Kelle, Witzel, & Zinn, (1998). Vocational training and career development in Germany: Results from a longitudinal study. *International Journal of Behavioral Development 22* (22): 77-101.
Klink, M. van der (1999). *De effectiviteit van werkplekopleidingen* [The effectiveness of workplace training]. PhD thesis. Enschede: University of Twente.
Kuchinke, P. (1999). Adult development towards what end? A philosophical analysis of the concept as reflected in the research, theory, and practice of human resource development. *Adult Education Quarterly, 49*(4), 148-163.
Longworth, N., & Davies, W. K. (1996). *Lifelong learning.* London: Kogan Page.
Marsick, V., & Watkins, K. (1990). *Informal and incidental learning in the workplace.* London: Routledge.
McLagan, P. (1989). Models for HRD practice: The Models. Washington D.C. : American Society for Training and Development.
McLagan, P. (1996). Great ideas revisited. *Training and Development Journal, 20*(1), 60-65.
McLagan, P., & Bedrick, D. (1983). Models for excellence: The results of the ASTD training and development competency study. *Training and Development Journal, 7*(6), 10-20.
Nadler, L. & Nadler, Z. (1991). Developing Human Resources (2nd printing.). San Francisco: Jossey-Bass.
Nicholson & West, (1989). Transitions, work histories and careers. In M. Arthur, D. Hall and B. Lawrence (Eds.) *Handbook of career theory.* Cambridge: University Press., pp. 181-201.

Lawson, T. & Limbrick, V. (1996). Critical competencies and developmental experiences for top HR executives. *Human Resource Management* 35 (1), 67-86.

Nijhof, W. (1996). Towards the learning society: teaching and learning in the European year of lifelong learning. *Lifelong Learning in Europe, 1*(1), 46-50.

Odenthal, L., & Nijhof, W. (1996). *HRD roles in Germany.* [Studies in Human Resource Development, 13.] De Lier: Academisch Boekencentrum.

Poell, R. F. (1998). *Organizing work-related learning projects: A network approach.* PhD thesis, University of Nijmegen.

Poell, R.F., & Chivers, G.E. (1999, September). *HRD consultant roles in different types of organisations.* Paper presented at the European Conference on Educational Research (ECER), Lahti, Finland.

Rijk, R.N. de, Mulder, M., & Nijhof, W. (1994, June). *Role profiles of HRD practitioners in four European countries.* Paper presented at the IRNEDT Conference, Milan, Italy.

Rinne, R., Silvennoinen, H., & Valanta, J. (1995). *Työelämän aikuiskoulutus* [Adult education in working life]. [Report of the Research unit for the sociology of education, 29.] Turku: University of Turku.

Sambrook, S., & Stewart, J. (2001). The changing role of human resource development practitioners in learning (oriented) organisations. In M. Kelleher, P. Cressey, & R.F. Poell, *Learning in learning organisations: European perspectives.* Luxembourg: CEDEFOP.

Valkeavaara, T. (1997). HRD practitioners analysing their work: What does it tell about their present role in working life? In P. Remes, S. Tøsse, P. Falkenkrone, & B. Bergstedt (Eds.), *Social change and adult education research: Adult education research in Nordic countries 1996* (pp. 14-40). Jyväskylä: University of Jyväskylä, Institute for Educational Research.

Valkeavaara, T. (1998a). Human resource development roles and competencies in five European countries. *International Journal of Training and Development, 2*(3), 171-189.

Valkeavaara, T. (1998b). Exploring the nature of human resource developers' expertise. *European Journal of Work and Organizational Psychology, 7*(4), 533-548.

Valkeavaara, T. (1999a). "Sailing in calm waters doesn't teach": Constructing expertise through problems in work - the case of Finnish human resource developers. *Studies in Continuing Education, 21*(2), 177-196.

Valkeavaara, T. (1999b). Ongelmien kauttako asiantuntijaksi? Henkilöstön kehittäjien kokemuksia työnsä ongelmallisista tilanteista [To become an expert through problems? HR developers' experiences of the problematic situations in their work]. In A. Eteläpelto & P. Tynjälä (Eds.), *Oppiminen ja asiantuntijuus* [Learning and expertise], (pp. 102-124). Juva: WSOY.

Valkeavaara, T. (2001). Constructing professional expertise in HRD: The career stories of human resource developers. In J. Streumer (Ed.), *Proceedings of the Second conference on HRD research and practice across Europe 2001* (pp. 337-355). Enschede: University of Twente, Faculty of Educational Science and Technology.

Vries, E.K. de (1988). *Het leven en de leer: Een studie naar de verbinding van leren en werken in de stage* [Life and learning: A study into the connection between learning and working in apprenticeships]. PhD thesis. Nijmegen: University of Nijmegen.

Webb, G. (1996). *Understanding staff development.* Buckingham: Open University Press.

CHAPTER 15

Challenges of supporting learning of newly qualified professionals in health care

ALAN BROWN

15.1 Introduction

IN THIS CHAPTER I WILL DISCUSS the challenges of how best to support the learning of health care professionals working in hospitals in the United Kingdom. In particular, I will focus upon how best to support the learning of newly qualified radiographers and physiotherapists working in National Health Service (NHS) hospitals. These groups are chosen for two reasons. First, NHS hospitals are very clear examples of organisations where the commitments to flexibility and transferability have been given particular emphasis within the broader political aim of modernising the NHS (Department of Health, 1997). Second, the focus upon the continuing development of these two professional groups provides insight into the relative role traditional 'VET professionals' (tutors and trainers) have to play in helping newly qualified practitioners achieve flexibility in the application of their skills, knowledge and understanding in work contexts. The role of such formal support for learning needs to be contextualised by a consideration of the value of support offered by more experienced colleagues, self-directed learning and learning through the experience of work itself. In particular, I will argue the role to be played by 'VET professionals' in support of the continuing learning of health care practitioners is partly dependent upon the extent to which peers and more experienced colleagues, who are not 'VET professionals', actively support less experienced colleagues. Before examining how best to support their learning we need to have some understanding of what the newly qualified have to learn before they can consider themselves, and others regard them, as experienced practitioners with acknowledged expertise in an environment characterised by flexibility, transferability and work intensification.

15.2 The challenge of learning while working for newly qualified hospital radiographers and physiotherapists

The Institute for Employment Research at the University of Warwick has completed a study into the extent, causes and implications of skill deficiencies in Health and Social Care. The following analysis draws heavily upon this study of the skill implications of changes in the patterns of work of radiographers and physiotherapists working in seven hospital departments and highlights the range of pressures impinging upon the development of these groups of staff (Brown, Green, Pitcher and Simm, 2000). The organisational changes in hospitals and the National Health Service, changes to professional training and development, changing ideas about the nature of practice and philosophies of care, changing patterns of work and

243

W. J. Nijhof et al. (eds.), Shaping Flexibility in Vocational Education and Training, 243-257.
© 2002 Kluwer Academic Publishers. Printed in the Netherlands.

demand for services, the adoption of new technologies and new techniques have created a turbulent environment for practice for health care professionals working in hospitals. Newly qualified radiographers and physiotherapists still have much to learn. In order to make a successful transition in becoming an experienced practitioner the 'novice' will need to negotiate six major learning challenges involving:

- Successful engagement with major (and changing) work activities;
- Successful interaction with others;
- Successful learning from experience;
- Alignment of professional and personal values;
- Commitment to continuing professional development;
- Coping with the demands for flexibility, transferability and work intensification in the workplace.

The context in which the work takes place, a hospital department with demanding performance targets, itself acts to reinforce some tensions between working and learning. For example, decisions about balancing the competing requirements for service delivery and how to support skill development most effectively have a number of dimensions. These include professional judgement about the most appropriate approach to care and practice; organisational issues around how to cope with the particular context in which health care is provided; caseload management; and departmental management. This means that in any particular setting there is not a single model of best practice as to how health care professionals should act. Rather hospital departments have to make contextualised decisions about how best to optimise service delivery and skill development in the settings in which their practice is grounded (Brown et al, 2000).

It is also important to remember that decisions about effective service delivery by people working as professionals are at least in part bound up, either implicitly or explicitly, with particular models of professional practice. These also tend to be holistic, and it is apparent that lists of required skills or behaviours related to the tasks to be performed can be apparently never ending, but still not get to the heart of professional practice (Benner, 1982). It can be particularly difficult to map the full complexities of performance in professional practice (McAleer and Hamill, 1997). By the same token, my six challenges could be criticised for separating out things that are by their nature inter-related. I am aware that the challenges could be reconfigured and they overlap. Still they are not being put forward for their explanatory power, rather they just serve an illustrative purpose, allowing me to unpack some of the complexities involved in thinking about learning while working as a means of professional development.

15.3 Successful engagement with major (and changing) work activities

The most obvious learning challenges facing newly qualified radiographers and physiotherapists while working in hospitals relate to the successful completion of their core professional tasks in practice. Considerable learning for newly qualified radiographers and physiotherapists comes from their engagement with work as they move towards becoming experienced practitioners in their own right. The challenge of work itself can lead to significant learning, particularly for the newly qualified. For example, the work of radiographers includes using a range and variety of equipment, solving problems arising under pressures of time and limited space, managing patients under varying circumstances and working as part of a team. The precise skill needs in radiography also depend partly on the equipment used and the service provided, for example whether the hospital provided therapeutic as well as diagnostic radiography. Technical and professional knowledge, interpersonal skills and sensitivity are required. Radiographers are at the interface between patient and clinician, and need well-developed inter-personal skills to deal with internal and external customers. The increased sensitivity to the need to recognise individual difference in patients means that skills of patient management have increasingly come to the fore, as radiographers have to deal with patients with very different levels of tolerance and anxiety under varying medical circumstances (Eraut, Alderton, Cole and Senker, 1998a). All those who come into contact with patients are now expected to explain or reassure, as appropriate.

Additionally, the work of radiographers is becoming more complex, with the technical and IT skill demands increasing and the underpinning knowledge base also expanding. The range of tasks radiographers have to perform has increased too, including the need to mark up X rays with issues for doctors to consider. Skills associated with intra-hospital team working are becoming more important and this can be a particularly sensitive issue for radiographers, as this could be seen to present a challenge to existing hierarchies, as it requires doctors and consultants to acknowledge the expertise of others. This was illustrated by Eraut, Alderton, Cole and Senker (1998b) who describe a case where the sensitivities were such that radiographers "put red dots on pictures to casualty officers where they had noticed something broken, thus contributing to diagnoses by often relatively inexperienced doctors without trespassing on their traditional territory" (p.44).

The work of hospital physiotherapists can be similarly challenging as within the major Health Trusts they may practise in a range of environments. These include outpatient services, respiratory care, orthopaedics, paediatrics, health care of the elderly, neurology, primary and community care, women's health, mental health and so on. The work of physiotherapists has both clinical and psychosocial aspects, including prevention of disease and injury, diagnosis, assessment and treatment of patients and management of rehabilitation. As with radiographers, one response to the variety of work is to use job rotation to help the newly qualified to develop the ability to apply their skills in a range of contexts. Within physiotherapy departments two-year rotations for junior staff were the norm and any additional support was normally provided in-house during this period. There is a strong tradition of learning through working within both radiography and physiotherapy with the expectation that you do not become fully experienced until several years after formal qualification.

As well as learning from job rotation the newly qualified need progressive exposure to more complex clinical cases. Such learning though often needs to be supported by a process of active reflection and review whereby it is possible to discuss and share with others ideas about the most effective ways to tackle a range of problems in practice. This exposure to a variety of cases and contexts facilitates learning through observation and listening as well as from direct experience (Eraut et al, 1998b). Indeed, where the more complex cases are initially handled by more experienced colleagues this is a classic form of learning through legitimate peripheral participation (Lave and Wenger, 1991).

Over time, as they get more experienced, practitioners will be expected to change how they work, for example in relation to how they carry out their initial diagnoses. One characteristic of effective performance of experienced physiotherapists and radiographers is that, like other professionals, they have learned to make some decisions rapidly and intuitively, while others require much more deliberation, analysis and discussion (Eraut, 2000). Newly qualified practitioners have to learn to make these distinctions and this requires a readiness for experienced practitioners to discuss their interesting cases as well as those of the novice, if the novice is to learn to model appropriate patterns of thought.

However, besides negotiating the traditional professional transition pathway between novice and expert practitioner, there are a wide range of other issues, targets and goals, associated with more flexible working, that affect individual performance in hospital radiology and physiotherapy departments (Brown et al, 2000). For example, greater emphasis is being placed upon moves towards more patient-focused care; patient self-management; empowering patients; and different models of in-patient rehabilitation (e.g. linking physiotherapy and occupational therapy). Consequently newly qualified practitioners are faced with additional considerations, such as how best to support multi-disciplinary working within hospitals or partnership working with other services. Such shifts have implications for the mix of clinical and other skills that newly qualified health professionals will need to treat patients, and require highly developed inter-personal and communication skills. Some health care organisations had adopted service strategies that actively embrace partnership working with other service providers such as Social Services departments in order to deliver a more holistic approach to service delivery. This has had significant skill implications in terms of multi-disciplinary working and understanding the perspective of others. Similarly, moves to offer more holistic care have led to the need for multi-skilling among physiotherapists and occupational therapists.

15.4 Successful interaction with others

The newly qualified health care practitioner has to learn to be able to sustain relationships with a range of people, including being able to develop and sustain therapeutic caring relationships with patients. Thus, for example, physiotherapists need the ability to engage and motivate patients to take responsibility for their own rehabilitation. The newly qualified also need to be able to work with colleagues, not least in order that they are able to learn from more experienced colleagues. That this can come through both from watching them in action and through discussions is apparent, although Eraut et al (1998b) point out that the extent of such support varies between different communities of practice, with feedback from colleagues being a particularly prominent feature of the work of diagnostic radiographers. Professionals then learn from each other, and the educative function may sometimes be explicit as when radiography staff 'educate' each other in the most effective way to use new equipment. It is also common for the newly qualified to learn from colleagues in a variety of less formal ways too.

Morrison (1992) points out that those working in the caring professions also have to deal with issues of emotional involvement, stress and work constraints. This means it is important to have mechanisms where individuals can talk these issues through with colleagues, either formally or informally (Brown et al, 2000). Taylor (1992) argues that such an approach is vital, as those working in the caring professions need to relate to each other as people, not just in terms of their professional roles. They need to be regarded as people who share the everyday common human qualities of their patients. The case studies bear this out, the more departments become over-loaded then the more important it is for colleagues to feel supported.

Newly qualified practitioners have to learn to work with and from other staff too, including other professionals. Any attempts to bring greater flexibility and transferability into health care are intimately bound up in ideas about practice as it is, how it might or should be, and relations between occupational groups (Webb, 1996). This is most evident in current attempts to offer a more holistic approach to health care, and this has implications for intra-team training, if the goal of multi-disciplinary working is to be achieved. For community physiotherapy outreach work and relations with GP practices will become more important in delivering a more decentralised and comprehensive service. The ability to communicate effectively across services and disciplines has therefore become a core competence and inter-personal skills when dealing with the public, for education and prevention as well as treatment, have become even more important for those working in this area.

It is also worth noting the necessity of not considering the learning and development of radiographers in isolation, but rather focusing upon the skill utilisation of the team as a whole if they are to deliver an efficient, high quality service. Thus radiology departments that adjusted the skills mix according to whether they were able to recruit radiologists, experienced radiographers or the newly qualified, then needed a plan for the effective utilisation of the particular skills mix they had. Intra-team skill development was particularly important in achieving this flexible response. It was even more apparent in physiotherapy that the training and development of both physiotherapists and assistants and how they worked together was a vital component in the recruitment and retention of staff.

Newly qualified health care professionals are likely to make a successful transition to becoming experienced practitioners if they are members of a number of networks. Professional networks, regional collaboration and programmes of continuing professional development are all important in the dissemination of good practice, but more informal networks also played a significant role in spreading good practice (Brown et al, 2000). At departmental level it is particularly important to ensure that newly qualified practitioners are tied into such networks. The learning of newly trained practitioners was also facilitated if:

- Regular mutual staff discussions were encouraged;
- Mentoring relationships were in place;

- Formal reviews of practice were held;
- Informal relationships led to work-related discussions at which more 'provisional' or 'riskier' comments could be made without pretending to be authoritative (such discussions were often held after work and/or in settings away from work).

It is important to acknowledge the role of informal relationships as a means of supporting learning and not to focus solely upon the successful interaction with others in formal settings. Although learning through personal networks is important for less and more experienced health professionals alike (Eraut et al, 1998b), the former also have to learn who holds different types of knowledge, how to access it and so on. One key link was often colleagues with whom the individual had trained and who were now working in different hospitals. Such contacts could be particularly important for the newly qualified who did not always initially at least wish to share some of their doubts about aspects of their own work with their new colleagues. Personal networks could also lead to access to required knowledge through chains of contacts.

15.5 Successful learning from experience

One line of argument sometimes advanced by managers was that the move to graduate entry for the professions allied to medicine had intensified the requirement for further learning while working after formal qualification. The issue was that new entrants, particularly to physiotherapy, might have insufficient experience of exercising the *practical* skills they need to do the work, resulting in the need for very intensive on-the-job training once they were qualified. In the context of a pressurised workplace environment, however, such training does not always coalesce with the 'reflective practice' approach instilled within degree-level training (Brown et al, 2000).

Skill deficiencies of recently qualified graduates may relate to their relative lack of knowledge of the particular contexts in which they are working. In particular, they may need support for learning to implement practical principles in particular contexts. This inexperience is partly due to the necessity for teachers to describe practice in generic terms, such that learners will have sets of practical principles with which to cope with the variety of possible practice settings (Brown et al, 2000). On the other hand, the shift of professional training into higher education may lead to rather less emphasis being given to 'practical knowledge' and greater emphasis on (academic) scientific knowledge. This may be partly due to teaching by academics who have a disciplinary (academic) background, rather than by professionals with practical experience. This may mean that students are not provided with authentic examples of 'knowledge use' in practice (Eraut, 1994). Whatever the reasons, the perception is that graduates lack sufficient understanding of how knowledge is used in practice, and that this makes their subsequent learning from experience even more vital.

It may be that graduates are also less proficient at some practical tasks, simply because they have had much less practice than those trained under the old system. The exposure to a range of experience over time may be particularly significant in the build-up of implicit or tacit knowledge rather than explicit knowledge. The profession as a whole is of course aware of this in the sense that they recognise that new graduates require additional training and that is one reason for widespread use of job rotation in the first two years following graduation. Experienced practitioners, however, may feel that they are increasingly stretched by other duties to give as much time to supervision and support as they would in more ideal circumstances.

Learning from their own experience is important for the newly qualified, but so is learning from the experience of others. Newly qualified practitioners need opportunities to discuss and practise thinking about complex cases handled by their more experienced colleagues. This approach to seeking to tackle complexity through interpretation and a shared search for understanding gets to the heart of "the discursive nature of professional practice" (Webb, 1996, p.111). Such an approach does not involve copying the precise way others tackle problems, but rather following the general approach of drawing on knowledge, abilities, skills and attitudes used in an integrated, holistic way (Gonczi, 1994).

The value of extended dialogue to reflective practice is now widely acknowledged, and without this departments could lose their sense of shared purpose, and just react as individual practitioners, without any impetus to improve the quality of practice. This extended dialogue underlines the social nature of learning and working and should, from an activity theory perspective, enable practice in the department (or activity system) to be transformed. By this means both internalisation (socialisation of new staff) and externalisation (developments of new reactions within the activity system) of learning would be facilitated (Engeström, 1992).

Various forms of organised learning support can be used to facilitate the learning from experience of the newly qualified. For example, rotation, clinical supervision and mentoring could all be organised more or less formally (Eraut et al, 1998b). The mentor could be just offering support on a serendipitous basis or taking great pains, as in the case of a more experienced radiographer offering support to a less experienced colleague: *"this woman goes out of her way to show her relevant things that come up when she's not there, shows her lab reports on mammograms she has done, etc, thus building up her expertise more quickly" (p.40).*

Learning could also take place as a result of cascading experience, particularly where increased multi-disciplinary work and teamworking placed greater communication demands on staff in addition to those required for dealing with patients. For example, in a radiology department, where a new MRI scanner had been recently introduced, there was a need for radiography staff to 'educate' other professionals in the potential dangers of using the equipment incorrectly and the need to adhere to protocols. This sometimes created problems if the other professional was in a superior position and the situation required assertive handling by the junior, as this could present a challenge to established organisational cultures (Brown et al, 2000).

One way learning from experience has become more formalised is through the increasing expectation that health care professionals will engage with their work in a way that makes greater use of formal evidence than in the past. The call for evidence-based practice to be used as a basis upon which to make clinical judgements requires greater attention to be given to an understanding of the nature of research and what constitutes clinical evidence (including issues of validity, reliability and generalisability) (Gray, 1997; Greenhalgh, 1997; Sackett, Richardson, Rosenberg & Haynes, 1997). In this area of learning through evidence provided by research and examples of good practice newly qualified (graduate) staff sometimes had an advantage over some less qualified but more experienced colleagues. This was because of the shift of emphasis in initial training towards understanding the rationale for evidence-based practice. Some departments found particular attention and support needed to be given to those practitioners who did not possess a degree or equivalent qualifications and were less likely to be familiar with research (Brown et al, 2000). Newly qualified health professionals were also likely to be familiar with models of reflective practice. However, the model of the reflective practitioner requires time to be made available for professionals to reflect upon their experience, actions and thinking as a basis for continuing to develop their expertise. Newly qualified staff needed time to reflect with others on their practice at a time when all staff were often feeling stretched by demands on their time in practice.

15.6 Alignment of professional and personal values

Those endeavouring to influence the shape and direction of health care are trying to come to terms with relational and caring constructs, and ethics and values are central to such debates. The newly qualified practitioner has to move towards a position where as an individual he or she is happy that his or her personal values align sufficiently with the professional values broadly espoused by the community of practice to which he or she belongs. For example, physiotherapists doing community work need to believe in the value of patient advocacy as an important component of their work.

For professionals working in health care the job is about more than just technical competence. A distinction can be made between the technical skills required and the need "to develop and sustain therapeutic caring relationships with patients and clients which are conceptualised and practised in an integrated and holistic fashion" (McAleer and Hamill, 1997, p.99). Playle (1995) identifies the shift in the caring professions away from illness-cure models and the objectification of patients towards a more holistic, person-centred approach that "promotes mutual respect, genuineness and joint partnership in the achievement of patient centred goals" (McAleer and Hamill, 1997, p.5). Wright (1994) highlights the value of expressive rather than instrumental care: caring about the patient not just caring for the patient. Expressive caring means professional activities should reflect the value of each individual person, and be imbued with the values of respect, dignity and individuality. Expressive caring contains a more explicit affective dimension compared to instrumental caring in which actions are predetermined in the form of a technique or strategy.

Expressive care for all patients would represent the ideal, but any shifts in practice towards more expressive caring are at least partly dependent upon the personal meanings and the degree of commitment of those newly recruited to the profession. However, Oakley (1993) draws attention to the paradox that the increasing technical competence associated with greater professionalisation may serve to distance practitioners from those for whom they care. Also the policy response of emphasising more person-centred models of care has not always been in step with how to facilitate this in training and implement it in practice.

At the professional level therefore, decisions to opt for particular models of care to underpin practice could affect skill utilisation and development profoundly. For example, if a physiotherapy department encourages an 'empowering' approach to care, where the individual patient takes increasing responsibility for her or his own care, then this can be very time intensive in the early stages, even if it eventually requires fewer interventions. This is because the 'empowering' approach relies upon the establishment of trust, with a focus on support and development, taking time, listening to and dealing with problems, as the individual takes on greater responsibility. The 'control' approach, where the practitioner is much more directive, focuses upon what the client has to do, but with 'ownership' of the process resting with the practitioner, may be used as a means to cope with large numbers of patients. Tensions may arise between these two approaches, and the newly qualified practitioner may require support in this respect, as the controlling approach may initially be easier to accomplish.

Values and meanings need to be discussed in education, training and practice, and individuals should receive support within educational and organisational structures to think about the value frameworks of themselves and others. Some engagement with these issues could take place through discussions associated with reflective practice. The value of explicit discussions about caring and values, not least for the newly qualified practitioner, is that it could lead to staff to arrive at a richer understanding of expressive knowledge, practice and their own self-understanding. By this means it should be possible to facilitate the development of a discourse about feelings, emotions and care.

Newly qualified practitioners also have to come to terms with the personal costs of caring for them as individuals. For example, one unintended consequence of the emphasis upon authenticity of feelings, and that health practitioners should always really care (and give of themselves), is that this could result in many otherwise capable practitioners feeling that they do not live up to the model. It is also by no means clear that unconditional service to others is always the most desirable course of action. The context is important in this respect. Empathy and support may be inhibiting in some circumstances, as they could be disempowering in the sense of restricting patient autonomy and cutting down on opportunities for recovery to be more self-directed. Overall then, those working in health care need to display 'caring' qualities, as well as being technically proficient and being aware that ideas about professional competence and caring are constantly evolving. Ideas of care therefore need to be framed in a particular context and at a given time, but it nevertheless remains important that personal and professional values are in broad alignment.

15.7 Commitment to continuing professional development

In health care minimum levels of continuing professional development (CPD) are often specified as a requirement of professional practice. Standards laid down by professional bodies govern significant aspects of the training, practice and professional development of radiographers and physiotherapists. Hospitals and other health care organisations are therefore obliged to provide a minimum amount of training and support for the CPD of professional staff. This high degree of regulation and highly structured training environment acts to ensure that professional staff is technically well qualified. Besides a general commitment to CPD, there is also an expectation that staff will be trained in the use of new equipment, with technical aspects of, for example, radiography training often being given by the equipment manufacturers. There is access to formal training in association with new treatments and technologies as required throughout their careers for radiographers and physiotherapists.

An important element therefore of the health professionals' status is a commitment after initial training to engage in CPD. Formal CPD could include training through projects, reviews and audits of competence and skill development, giving presentations, one-to-one supervision, and peer review, as well as through attendance at more formal courses. Short courses within departments were available for all staff and higher qualifications such as postgraduate diplomas and Masters degrees were also encouraged for clinical staff. In most cases there was greater demand to participate in further training such as Masters courses than there was funding available. Generally staff undertook postgraduate qualifications on a part time basis and funded at least half of the costs themselves. Departments where staff had attended specialist courses or completed Masters programmes were perceived as offering more opportunities and potentially a higher level of in-house training. This could then be an important factor in external recruitment (Brown et al, 2000).

In this context, however, it should also be remembered that formal education and training provide only a small part of what is learned at work by professional staff (Eraut, Alderton, Cole and Senker, 1999). Even where hospitals had the capacity to provide formal training, there was sometimes a reluctance to release staff when departments were under-strength and working at full stretch and this increased the de facto reliance upon learning through working. This could be effective, but only if the requisite support was available for on the job learning. This too was not always forthcoming. Hence staff at all levels in some departments felt there were times when they were working at the limits of their knowledge and understanding, and that this may have compromised their effectiveness to some degree and resulted in slower patient throughput (Brown et al, 2000).

The importance of CPD is therefore officially recognised by hospitals, but the commitment may be compromised in practice. However, the drive for CPD and further training creates a strong lifelong learning culture within the practitioner community, but this is not always complementary with meeting the full range of demands on services. Budgetary constraints as well as quality and efficiency targets in meeting patient demand sometimes resulted in the 'rationing' of training particularly among intermediate level staff (Brown et al, 2000). All departments had to live with examples of training being squeezed because of more immediate pressures, but the more effective departments did not allow this to become standard practice, rather after cancellations in one period they moved training up their list of priorities for a subsequent period.

Models of clinical governance require particular emphasis to be given to the dissemination of good practice and a commitment to continuing improvement (Department of Health, 1997; NHS Executive, 1999a; 1999b). Professional networks, regional collaboration and formal programmes of continuing professional development were all important in the dissemination of good practice. However, besides such formal commitments most of the departments investigated were acutely aware that newly qualified staff were 'less expert' in some of their judgements than more experienced staff. Some commentators believe the key differences relate to 'generic' competencies based upon personal attributes such as critical thinking, problem solving and analysis (McAleer and Hamill, 1997). The key to developing this type of expertise, however, is the extent to which opportunities are given for these 'generic' competencies to be applied in the particular context of practice. Informal support and more formal continuing professional development can be complementary in this respect.

The amount of underpinning professional knowledge that individuals are expected to master has increased considerably. The move to graduate entry has helped here, but continuing professional development is required, particularly, as in radiography, where the introduction of new technology and innovative techniques can transform practice. Initial training for the first practitioners to use new equipment is usually quite good, but the most effective departments have procedures in place to ensure that such knowledge, and developing protocols learned from experience of the equipment in use, are cascaded to all relevant staff (Brown et al, 2000).

Formal CPD may also play a role in an individual learning additional specialist skills where these were not fully covered initial training. For example, specialist skills were required for work in specialisms, such as mammography, ultrasonography, skeletal reporting and paediatrics in radiography and musculo-skeletal, cardio-respiratory, neurological, paediatrics, rehabilitation, elderly care and community care in physiotherapy. In addition, in some areas, such as paediatric radiography, staff needed to have two years general radiography experience and were only recruited at a senior level. An individual's commitment to CPD, however, should not just involve participation in formal staff development, as practitioners are also expected to engage in their own self-directed learning. As Eraut et al (1998b) point out this should involve individuals in an active role in finding out on their own initiative what they need to know. This could include learning through reading papers, journal articles and case histories.

15.8 Coping with the demands for flexibility, transferability and work intensification in the workplace

The hallmark of successful professional practice is the ability to draw on knowledge, abilities, skills and attitudes used in an integrated, holistic way (Gonczi, 1994). This approach to the performance of professional tasks draws attention to three important features. First, complex professional duties can be performed in a variety of ways. Second, these duties can draw on different combinations of knowledge, skills, abilities and attitudes in effective performance. Third, this approach implies that there is scope for professional judgement, not least in the ability to balance competing demands and the pressures of time. This means that individuals may come up with very different ways of responding to the demands for flexibility, transferability and work intensification in the workplace. Indeed one way forward for the newly qualified and experienced practitioners alike may be to review the different ways individual practitioners seek to tackle their workload as a whole. By this means it should be possible to discuss and share ideas about the most effective ways to tackle a range of problems in practice.

Being able to respond effectively to the demands for flexibility, transferability and work intensification in the workplace requires a collective as well as an individual response. Departments need a sense of shared purpose, and this highlights the social nature of learning and working which should enable practice in the department to be transformed. However, departments as well as individuals are constrained in how they can respond, because of the need to pay attention to institutional performance indicators, which themselves were often explicitly linked to targets set by government. All staff seemed well aware of the need to pay attention to performance targets outlined in departmental plans for service delivery (patient throughput; waiting lists; waiting times and so on). All departments actively reviewed their performance against such targets, and particularly where targets were based upon per capita funding, newly qualified staff could feel under pressure to reach experienced worker standards as quickly as possible.

The most obvious manifestation of work intensification came from the rapidly increasing demand for some radiography and physiotherapy services. Active management at departmental level was required to cope with this increase in demand. Senior staff in some physiotherapy departments spent more time on assessment and education, rather than hands-on practice, as a means to reduce the numbers of people requiring treatment within the hospital. Consideration was sometimes given to the criteria used to ration access to treatment (in relation to who gets referred, average number of treatments and so on). Some departments extended opening hours and introduced more flexible patterns of working, although these goals could sometimes conflict. A balance also had to be negotiated between handling demands for greater efficiency and improved quality.

The consequences of the increasing demand for services for newly qualified staff were both direct and indirect. The direct consequences were reflected in their own increased workload and the indirect consequences came from less time available for some senior staff to devote to training because of the increased time they spent on departmental management responsibilities. For these reasons caseload management and time management have become much more important at the individual level and newly qualified staff in particular may require support to do this effectively. It may also be that the increasing drive for efficiency and performance within health care systems limit the time practitioners have for activities that convey caring rather than just competence.

What is particularly apparent here is that support for the learning of newly qualified radiographers and physiotherapists at work needs to be placed in the broader context of work in their departments (or across departments) as a whole. Using an activity theory perspective, the focus of learning in the department as a whole should alternate between socialisation of staff and framing of new approaches to developments at a departmental level, involving the continuing switching between the internalisation and externalisation functions of learning (Engeström, 1992).

At a departmental level Brown et al (2000) identified several key factors that had enabled departments to battle successfully with the considerable constraints and challenges they faced. These were:

- Proactive rather than reactive management;
- Recognition of the benefits of investing in training;

- Willingness to evolve new models of service including developing collaborative arrangements with related service providers;
- Willingness of staff to work as part of a team and appreciate the different roles and challenges confronting other team members;
- Recognition of the centrality of learning through work for newly qualified staff and paying particular attention to the allocation of work and supporting these individuals (Brown et al, 2000, p.32).

15.9 Concluding discussion

From the foregoing discussion it should be clear that the role played by 'VET professionals' (tutors and trainers) in support of the continuing learning of health care practitioners is partly dependent upon the extent to which peers and more experienced colleagues, who are not 'VET professionals', actively support less experienced colleagues. The relationship between the two types of support should ideally be complementary, but while one group of traditional 'VET professionals' (trainers) have a role to play, perhaps of far greater significance is the support offered by more experienced colleagues. Some of these colleagues may have some formal VET responsibility for the supervision and development of more junior staff, but others do not. The issue here therefore is whether all health care professionals, even those acting principally as practitioners, should be supported in how to offer effective support to the learning of others at work. In this context it may be that the label 'VET professional' is itself unhelpful, because it emphasises that others are not 'VET professionals' even though they play a critical role in supporting learning of the newly qualified. This is unfortunate since their degree of expertise can greatly influence how quickly the newly qualified themselves become experienced practitioners with acknowledged expertise. The key focus should be upon how to facilitate learning, and the role of increasing professionalism of those with significant formal support responsibilities should be weighed against the value of making the support of those playing a more informal role more effective. How best to support the learning of newly qualified therefore needs to be informed by a contextualised understanding of what it is that the newly qualified have to learn in an environment characterised by flexibility, transferability and work intensification.

The context is important because different configurations of staff may radically change the opportunities for different forms of learning. For example, those departments that regularly recruit newly qualified staff (because of high staff turnover coupled with a lack of experienced applicants) will probably need to have in place more formal systems of mentoring, supervision or other support. This will be required in order that the less experienced have opportunities to discuss and practise thinking about complex cases handled by their more experienced colleagues. This may be less vital in those departments where there is a more even balance of more and less experienced staff and as a consequence where there may be more informal opportunities for such discussions to take place. The newly qualified need to practise using their professional judgement, not least in the ability to balance competing demands and the pressures of time. Active reflection and review on different ways practitioners seek to tackle their workload as a whole may be one means by which it is possible for practitioners to discuss and share ideas about the most effective ways to tackle a range of problems in practice.

Traditionally the focus of the continuing development of professional competence in the health sector has been upon skills, methods and techniques. The professional skills of developing and implementing therapeutic plans and negotiating client goals continue to be required. However, the organisational (and administrative) competencies necessary to successful performance in the organisation; and the social-communicative competencies relating to the department, team or professional group's practical environment are becoming even more important than they were in the past. These, however, may receive comparatively little attention either in formal training or informally during learning while working. This is despite work intensification and the sheer volume of work to be completed resulting in organisational or departmental difficulties becoming more intense. Both radiographers and physiotherapists have to learn to deal with complexity, contradictions and uncertainty. This in turn means that the organisational and social-communicative aspects of professional performance become more significant, with a consequent emphasis upon planning, acceptance of responsibility, independent action and social skills. Clinical diagnosis and monitoring remain at the heart of professional expertise, but effective management of a caseload as a whole, as well as of individual cases, has become more important.

One answer to the task of supporting the learning of newly qualified professionals is therefore to make teaching, coaching and helping others learn a central component of the professional expertise of health care professionals. That is, rather than looking to the development of a separate cardre of VET professionals it may be more productive to make the key VET role of facilitating learning an integral part of the continuing professional development of all health care professionals. By this means it should be possible meet the considerable challenges to supporting the learning of newly qualified radiographers and physiotherapists working in National Health Service (NHS) hospitals outlined in this chapter.

References

Benner, P. (1982). Issues in competency-based testing. *Nursing Outlook*, 30, (May), 303-309.

Brown, A., Green, A., Pitcher, J., & Simm, C. (2000). *Changing professional identities in the UK National Health Service: a study of the skill implications of changes in the patterns of work of radiographers and physiotherapists*. Paper presented to the European Forum for Research in Vocational Education and Training, North Wales, 29th June – July 2nd 2000.

Department of Health (1997). *The new NHS: modern, dependable*. Cmnd 3807, London: HMSO.

Engeström, Y. (1992). *Interactive expertise: studies in distributed working intelligence*. Research Bulletin 83, Helsinki: University of Helsinki Department of Education.

Eraut, M. (1994). *Developing professional knowledge and competence*. London: Falmer.

Eraut, M. (2000). Non-formal learning and tacit knowledge in professional work. *British Journal of Educational Psychology*, 70, (1), 113-136.

Eraut, M., Alderton, J., Cole, G., & Senker, P. (1998a). *Development of knowledge and skills in employment*. Research Report 5, Falmer: University of Sussex Institute of Education.

Eraut, M., Alderton, J., Cole, G., & Senker, P. (1998b). Learning from other people at work. In F. Coffield (Ed.), *Learning at work*. Bristol: The Policy Press.

Eraut, M., Alderton, J., Cole, G., & Senker, P. (1999). The impact of the manager on in workplace. In F. Coffield (Ed.), *Speaking truth to power: research and policy on lifelong learning*. Bristol: The Policy Press.

Gonczi, A. (1994). Competence-based assessment in the professions in Australia. *Assessment in Education*, 1, (1), 27-44.

Gray, J. (1997). *Evidence-based health care: how to make health policy and management decisions*. London: Churchill-Livingstone.

Greenhalgh, T. (1997). *How to read a paper: the basis of evidence-based medicine*. London: BMJ Publications.

Lave, J., & Wenger, E. (1991). *Situated learning: legitimate peripheral participation*. Cambridge: Cambridge University Press.

McAleer, J., & Hamill, C. (1997). *The assessment of higher order competence development in nurse education*. Newtownabbey: University of Ulster.

Morrison, P. (1992). *Professional caring in practice: a psychological analysis*. Aldershot: Avebury.

NHS Executive (1999a). *A first class service: quality in the new NHS*. Health Service Circular 1999/033, Wetherby: Department of Health.

NHS Executive (1999b). *Clinical governance: quality in the new NHS*. Health Service Circular 1999/065, Wetherby: Department of Health.

Oakley, A. (1993). *Essays on women, medicine and health*. Edinburgh: Edinburgh University Press.

Playle, J. (1995). Humanism and positivism in nursing; contradictions and conflicts. *Journal of Advanced Nursing*, 23, 979-984.

Sackett, D., Richardson, W., Rosenberg, W., & Haynes, R. (1997). *Evidence-based medicine: health care: how to practise and teach evidence-based medicine*. London: Churchill-Livingstone.

Webb, G. (1996). *Understanding staff development*. Buckingham: Society for Research in Higher Education and the Open University Press.

Wright, S. (1994). *The foundations of nursing – the values and essential concepts for nursing practice*. London: The European Nursing Development Agency.

CHAPTER 16

The practices of a new VET profession

PHIL HODKINSON

IN DIFFERENT WAYS, THE CHAPTERS IN THIS SECTION focus on the nature of a new VET professionalism in the EU, and its potential role in promoting flexibility, transferability and mobility. As the authors have made clear, the nature of this new professionalism is problematic. It is emerging from the changing practices of VET providers, in complex and varied contexts. The other contributors have presented detailed, carefully articulated analyses of trends in current practices. Here, I attempt to complement this scholarship by approaching the issues in a different way. I take as my starting point, the fictional creation of a new, overarching and unified VET profession across the member states of the EU. I believe this to be an unlikely scenario, at least in the immediate future. However, its adoption as an artifice enables me to explore some of the possible workings of VET professionals, and their role in promoting flexibility, transferability and mobility in the workforce. To do that, I emphasise two aspects of professional activity: it situatedness and its relational nature. I start by assuming that a new VET profession has been established, bridging those practitioners primarily located in educational settings, and those in human resource development, across the member countries of the EU.

16.1 The beginnings of the new profession

This new profession has come about, following the strong leadership of the EU and its member state governments. They provided the legal and financial structures to facilitate the birth, supported by many influential organisations, representing employers, trades unions, training organisations, parts of the educational systems in member states and, not least, organisations representing those who eventually entered the new profession. A majority of those eligible to become members of the new profession had joined, through a combination of individual subscription, and the affiliation of existing professional bodies to which they already belonged. In the period of optimism and excitement following the successful launch, the new profession faced three major challenges:

1. To partially integrate their different constituent parts, in order to consolidate professional identity
2. To establish enough influence with other players, to raise the status and quality of VET provision
3. To identify ways in which their influence and provision could help improve the flexibility, mobility and transferability of the workforce who engaged with that VET provision.

These problems are inter-related. For example, the first would be much easier to achieve if success could be demonstrated for the second and third. However, for

W. J. Nijhof et al. (eds.), Shaping Flexibility in Vocational Education and Training, 259-268.

simplicity, I examine the nature of these three challenges separately, in ways that make more explicit the links between them.

16.2 Integration into a partly unified profession

Within the field of VET, much research attention has recently been placed upon workplace learning. Two closely related bodies of theorising are currently fashionable: situated learning (Brown, Collins and Duguid, 1989; Lave and Wenger, 1991; Wenger, 1998) and activity theory (Engeström, 2001). It is illuminating to apply these theories to the new VET profession, for one of the key determinants of a profession is the work its members do. Furthermore, one of the markers of high status professions, like lawyers and doctors, is the ways in which they restrict access to professional work to those they deign to admit as members.

From the perspective of situated cognition theorists, the new VET profession would only have a reality once a strong community of practice had become established. That is, members needed to develop shared understandings, procedures and ways of working that confirmed their similarities with each other, and marked out boundaries between members and others. In other words, the profession had to develop legitimate forms of participation, both peripheral and more central. However, such community practices take time to develop, for they are not primarily determined by explicit statements, structures or procedures, but through partly subjective and partly tacit inter-relationships between context, concept (or tool) and activity (Brown et al., 1989). In other words, the new professional leadership will not determine legitimate participation or those who brought the profession into being, but by the evolution of shared and accepted practices.

The legitimate practices of this new profession can only evolve from those within the existing communities of practice from which the new professionals had been drawn. For communities of practice are essentially cultural entities, whose history exerts a strong and significant influence upon their present existence. This alerts us to a paradox at the heart of the new profession, for some of the very reasons why its creation was thought to be desirable present it with its biggest starting problem. For the new members are culturally and historically diverse. There are many dimensions to their fragmentation, but I have space to detail only three: they are located within different national contexts and traditions; they are located within different occupational sectors; and they are divided between predominantly educational, training and human resource development backgrounds (Heikkinen, Chapter 12, this volume).

National contexts are significant, for there are well-documented differences in VET tradition and practice across EU member states (Skilbeck, Connell, Lowe and Tait, 1994; other chapters in this volume). The new VET professionals have identities and practices deeply located within their own national systems. For example, those working in England inhabit a world of frequent policy and funding changes for VET (Brown and Keep, 1999). The occupational sectors that practitioners work with is also significant. Many of the new VET professionals have firm roots within a particular industry and, despite the undoubted influence of globalisation, there remain significant differences between say, the steel and metals sector, retaining and the burgeoning cultural and media industries. These differences influence the ways in which VET is provided in the various sectors, and much of the detail about what is learned. They are also significant issues in the identity of the VET professionals themselves. The final division, between educational VET providers, trainers and those located within human resources, has been fully explored elsewhere in this section.

Though this fragmentation of working contexts and traditions presented a major obstacle to the establishment of the new profession, it also presented it with a major opportunity. This is because these three divisions in the profession cut across each other, in ways that can help undermine the significance of any one taken alone. Many of the new VET professionals were positioned differently against the three dimensions, giving overlapping identities. Take, for example, an English VET professional in the steel industry, who is a Trades Union learning representative[1]. S/he has three overlapping reference groups within the new profession: other Trades Union officials with responsibility for learning; other VET workers in the steel industry across Europe, and other English VET professionals, working, for example, with National Vocational Qualifications, the Trades Union learning fund, individual learning accounts, and other uniquely English traditions, systems and procedures.

A key strategy for the new VET profession, therefore, was to work to sustain and enhance the tensions between these multiple communities of practice, rather than promoting one at the expense of the others. For if a VET professional saw any one of the three as the only important community of significant others, s/he would have no incentive to see her/himself as part of a wider VET professional community. Being a Trades Unionist, for example, would be enough. For most of the new professionals, one dimension seemed more important than the others. For example, many industrial trainers saw their location within a particular sector or even firm as their prime professional location, and saw little connection with HRD specialists or educational practitioners in other sectors or other countries. Alternatively, many full-time college tutors saw their membership of an educational profession as more significant than either national identity or their work in VET more generally, at least, those in England did. It was when the single individual allegiance was dominant, that the new profession faced its greatest challenge. The strategy was to play up the significance of the weaker two dimensions, without seeming to challenge the validity of the dominant one.

To enhance this integrative process, the new profession embarked upon strategies to bring members from different communities of practice together. This included a major attempt to promote horizontal learning (Engeström, 2001). EU funding was used to set up well resourced, intensive international workshops. These drew upon both research and practical knowledge to help groups of members with over-lapping interests to better understand each other's activities, and to construct areas of mutual understanding and interests, in a context that minimised perceived threats to territory or valued positions.

---

[1] In the last few years, the promotion of learning has become one of the main activities of Trades Unions in the UK. Many workplaces now have Union officials, called learning representatives, whose prime role is to promote learning for their local members.

16.3 Influencing other players

At the same time as working to establish a multi-dimensional professional identity rooted in the newly developing community of practice, the new VET profession worked to extend its influence with other significant organisations. To explain how this happened and why it was important, I now draw on some of the theorising of Pierre Bourdieu.

Rather than communities of practice, Bourdieu refers to fields (Bourdieu and Wacquant, 1992). The new VET professionals existed in such a field, and one that was exceedingly varied, complex and multi-faceted. This field can be defined as the area where VET professional activity takes place. Within that field, there were many different players: as well as the various sorts of VET professional, there were employers, Trades Unions, managers, workers, governments (local, regional and national), guidance providers, numerous agencies and pressure groups, the EU and its various offices, and international organisations, such as the World Bank and UNESCO. The field was vast, because VET, with its growing focus on flexibility, transferability and mobility, was locked into an increasingly globalised system of work, employment and productivity. This field operates simultaneously on several different, interlocking levels: global, national, regional and local (including single firms).

At all levels, the field is made up of unequal power relations. These unequal power relations influence the extent to which players, be they individuals, groups or institutions, can succeed in the field. This happens in three ways. Firstly, the various players are positioned differently in the field, and those different positions affect their ability to influence what goes on. Thus, the national leaders of a professional body with interests in VET, such as the Chartered Institute of Personnel and Development (CIPD) in the UK, was better positioned to influence the field than, say, a professional management trainer, working in the financial services industry. However, though well positioned in the new VET profession, the CIPD's position in the field as a whole was arguably less favourable than that of national governments or major employers. Secondly, different players have different resources and opportunities to do well. They possess, in Bourdieu's terms, greater or lesser amounts of capital - cultural, social and economic. These forms of capital can be accumulated or lost, and can be converted, one to another, as when economic capital can be used to buy influence and access to social networks (social capital). Of course, position and capital are linked. Capital can help establish a strong position, and a strong position brings with it increased capital. However, unequal power relations, and unequal possession of or access to capital, have an even more significant impact. For they are also used to determine the rules of the game within the field: indeed, to influence what counts as valuable capital itself. It is, thus, important to recognise that the success of the new VET profession depended more upon the actions of others, than those of itself and its members. This was particularly true because of the relative marginality of VET activity in the employment field, and in certain national systems.

To illustrate this point, it is necessary to simplify the complex relations involved, by focussing on two players with far more influence than the professionals themselves. Firstly, there were the employers. For employers, singly and collectively, exert massive influence over the careers and working practices of their employees: the workers who are the clients of the VET professionals. They also, of course, exert a major influence over the VET professionals themselves, who are also either employed or contracted by them. Currently, employer involvement in and commitment to high quality VET is widely divergent and varied. For every employer investing in the high skills route to success (Ashton and Green, 1996) there are others who are not. The problem is greater in some countries than others, and also varies from sector to sector. In the UK at least, the increasing proportion of small and medium sized businesses, who often lack an identified training or human resource development section, is a major source of concern. Valkeavaara, Poell and Chivers, in Chapter 14, describe the relative marginalisation of HRD and VET professionals in many organisations. The influence of employers, and of their employment, recruitment and working practices, continued to exert a large, even dominating influence, on the activities, goals, status and identity of the new VET professionals, of all types.

The second example is government, at regional, national and EU levels. The influence of such government on the field is also difficult to exaggerate, and it takes at least three forms. Firstly, much VET provision is located in the public sector. This means that large parts of the VET profession are under the direct control of governments and government agencies. In England, for example, this is the case for VET professionals employed in the health service (Brown, this volume) and in Further Education (FE) colleges. Policies and practices of the new Department for Education and Skills (DfES), and the newly created Learning and Skills Council, which has been given responsibility for most VET funding, directly influence the work of the latter. Over the past few years, several major changes to the conditions of work of FE teachers, vocational and others. There are new conditions of service, major external curriculum changes, a reduction of career hierarchies, reduced pay relative to other groups, an increase in part-time and temporary contracts, a new external inspection system, and, most recently, pressure for the rapid development of a fully qualified teaching workforce. These changes have major consequences for the nature of tutor professionalism in the sector (Ainley and Bailey, 1997; Gleeson and Shain, 1999), and such government influences are significant for the new profession, across Europe.

A second type of governmental influence is over the funding and regulation of much worker and would-be worker learning, within the VET system. These funding and regulatory structures, be they European, national or regional in origin, have a major influence upon the nature of the VET field. They strongly influence, even determine, significant boundaries of activity, creating incentives for and barriers against certain types of practice. The EU is particularly influential in this way, though its funding of a wide range of project activities, each with fairly tight prescriptions of objectives, locations that qualify for funding, procedures of eligibility and fixed timescales.

Thirdly, governments can exert greater or lesser influence on the employment practices of other employers over which they have jurisdiction. The levels of influence and control vary significantly across the EU, but even in the England, where is it arguably relatively low (Brown and Keep, 1999), the impact is significant. For example, the likely introduction of legislation to give Trades Union Learning Representatives similar status to that already enjoyed by their health and safely equivalents will have great significance for VET. Similarly, the current refusal, in England, to take the issue of paid educational leave for workers seriously will be negatively significant, through what it fails to promote or facilitate in the VET arena.

16.4 Proactivity by VET professionals within the field

This sort of analysis, demonstrating that the new VET profession was not the most powerful player in the field, is, fortunately, only part of the story. For, as Bourdieu also shows, all players in a field exert some influence, and VET professionals, be they newly formed or otherwise, are no exception. This point lay at the heart of the case for the creation of the new profession. For, at least in theory, the new, powerful VET profession can work more effectively for the development of the field, in ways that are likely to enhance flexibility, transferability and mobility of a better-educated and trained workforce. The activities of the new professionals themselves impact upon the field at all levels. Within particular localised institutional settings, individual VET professionals, working alone or with small numbers of colleagues, can make significant differences to practices and, sometimes, to policies or strategies. These differences can be achieved deliberately – through intentionally working to change policy and practices, or tacitly, through the largely unconscious practising of their VET activities, and through their interactions with other people whom they come in contact with. Often, their impact is not directly identifiable, let alone measurable, a point I return to later, but it is no less real, for that.

At wider regional, national and international levels, their impact could also be felt. This may be partly the unwitting accumulation of large numbers of localised, small scale activities, making up the evolving practices of the community/ies to which they belong. It could also be a more deliberative and organised impact, through pressure groups and organisations with which they have influence. The hope, upon its creation, was that the new EU-wide VET profession would fulfil both roles: exerting influence at national and international policy making tables, and through its mutually constitutive practices, reforming and strengthening local activity.

However, any influencing and changing of the field, by the new VET professionals, can only be understood and judged in relation to those influences and changes brought about by others. Expressed in another way, the work of the new profession was political, in all senses of the word. At regional, national and EU levels, the profession had to engage in Politics. This entailed the identification of potential allies and/or opponents, and strategic decisions about which battles to fight, and which goals to strive for. At local levels, their work was micro-political, as it always has been.

As the new VET professional body attempted to exert influence in this complex field, two things became rapidly apparent. Firstly, different strategies and approaches had to be adopted in different parts of the field. Existing relationships were built upon, always looking for ways to increase the status and influence of the profession. Secondly, the new profession had to accept widely varying levels of success and influence, in different parts of the field. These processes were also far from smooth. There were negotiations, agreements, partnerships, but also arguments, conflict and disputation. In some contexts, localised horizontal learning proved possible. In others, it did not.

It is here, that the inter-relationship between the three problems, identified early this chapter, became apparent. For the political influence of the new VET professionals partly depended upon how others saw the value of their work. Where other players accepted the view that flexibility, transferability and mobility were significantly important objectives to permit the transfer of resources to their achievement, and also accepted and recognised the significance of the work of VET professionals in bringing them about, much was achieved, quite quickly. For, in a relational field, influence follows success, provided the success is recognised as legitimate and important in the field. What is more, increasing influence meant that the new profession had more of a say in determining what counts as success in the field. Unfortunately, in other parts of the field, the context and relationships were not so supportive, and much less was achieved. Furthermore, the dominant audit culture (Power, 1997) presented the new VET profession with a particularly intractable problem, in relation to the promotion of greater flexibility, mobility and transferability, which I turn to next.

16.5 Struggles and tensions in an audit culture

The third challenge facing the new profession: identifying ways of enhancing flexibility, transferability and mobility, raised a central issue of professional identity: who determines what counts as success, and, almost more important, in the current social and political context, how can such success be measured and demonstrated?

The problem was central to the dominant audit culture (Power, 1997), in employment, government policy and, at least in the UK, public service practices. The dominant view was that nothing could be successfully managed, unless it could be accurately measured and monitored. Thus, increasing emphasis was placed on measures such as productivity, quality control, sales targets etc. From this perspective, the effectiveness of the new VET profession must also be measured. How much impact has it had? Does it give value for money? Performance indicators and targets were set for the activity of the profession. Indeed, some were built into the proposals for its creation. These varied from context to context, and also in the level of detailed prescription. Predictably, many UK contexts had measures that were based on short-term achievements, rather than building for long-term influence. However, right across the EU, the culture of short-term funded projects continued, each having to demonstrate that it was different from what had been done before, and with its own ring-fenced targets to meet.

However, there were two fundamental problems with this approach, which I have written about elsewhere (Hodkinson and Hodkinson, 2001). Firstly, an impressively large number of studies demonstrates that the effects of work-based learning are almost impossible to measure (Harris, 2000). This is because too many other factors, beyond work-based learning itself, impact upon whatever performance indicators are selected. Working practices influence and are influenced by learning, but it is impossible to determine which is significant at any particular time. This meant that those VET professionals working predominantly in the workplace found it very difficult to demonstrate the measurable value of their work. There was no clear link between their activity and either the productivity of the firm, or the mobility of the workforce.

When translated to the level of individual or group professional activity, the second problem became apparent. When VET professionals were set performance indicators to achieve, as part of the audit culture, these indicators often introduced distortions into the system. I can best illustrate this point with a couple of examples of English educational practice. In Further Education, current inspection and funding regimes assume that the success of a VET (or other) course is partly determined by the percentage of students who complete the course and pass the qualification. But recent research (Hodkinson and Bloomer, 2001) shows that the causes of non-completion are complex, and often lie outside the knowledge and control of college tutors – for example in the wider lived circumstances of the students. This means that completion rates are only partly influenced by the activities of the VET professional. Often, if a course is popular, the easiest way to improve completion rates is to exclude students who are likely to face problems - not the policy intention at all. Alternatively, many individual student successes, achieved in difficult social contexts, were over-looked, because the overall statistics for the course concerned looked poor.

The inspection of VET systems, where many of the new professionals worked, also caused problems. For example, it became common practice to monitor courses by conducting an annual review of what went well or badly, with planned ways to improve the course. But the VET inspectors became accustomed to examining these annual reviews, in order to check the health of the course and the efficiency of the course team. Immediately, the construction of the review documents became a matter of presentation. Now, staff could only admit to problems that they could solve, and deeper difficulties were no longer analysed or described. Quality control and audit became partially detached from actual changes in the learning experiences of students.

Often, the growing audit culture was seen as anti-professional, for it attempted to exert increasing external control over what professionals did, giving less and less room for individual responsibility and initiative. A key challenge for the new VET profession, therefore, was the preservation of professional space within this audit culture.

A recent study of professionalism in the UK pointed to a constructive, if problematic, way forward. Stronach, Corbin, McNamara, Stark and Warne (2001) identified constructive tensions in the professional identities of primary school teachers and nurses, between what they termed the 'economy of performance' and 'ecology of practice'. Economy of performance is essentially externally derived, and sees professionalism through metaphors such as measurement, effectiveness and improvement. Ecology of practice is more locally grounded, developing through personal views of professional identity, which appear to be similar to some of the aspects Lave and Wenger (1991) describe in relation to communities of practice. Stronach et al. claim that tensions between economy of performance and ecology of practice form an essential element of professionalism: excess in either leads to deep problems. Too much ecology of practice, and we risk self-indulgent and self-serving professionalism, where only professionals can determine what professionals should do. In the current audit age, and especially for a new low status profession such as that of VET, such an excess seems well beyond the bounds of possibility. Too much economy of performance threatens the existence of key elements of professionalism, such as discretionary judgement, moral engagement, and collaboration (Hargreaves and Goodson, 1996). There were clear signs of this happening within parts of the new VET profession, for too much of what counts within VET was imposed upon the professionals from outside – primarily by employers and governments.

However, Stronach et al (2001) helped point the way for the (micro) political activities of the new VET profession. For they argued that, ultimately, excessive external specification and measurement would fail. This is because the variability, complexity and partly context-specific nature of teaching/training practices can never be adequately captured by performance measures. Those working on the ground will always be confronted by contradictions between universal specifications and the realities of their partly idiosyncratic lives. If this was true of teaching and nursing, it proved even more so of VET practice. The variations between existing communities of practice, and the widely divergent contexts in which those communities operate, meant that any externally driven, universalising system of rigidly applied performance measures or specified procedures, of the 'one-size-fits-all' variety, would simply ensure that the new VET profession never fully came into being. A key role, for the new professional body, was to help sustain the tensions between economies of performance and ecologies of practice. They strived to achieve this, partly by playing off one dominant pressure group against another, and by looking for every opportunity to sustain and promote spaces where their members could exercise their own professional judgements. For it was in this balance that the survival and effectiveness of the new profession would ultimately rest, and, consequently, its ability to help enhance flexibility, mobility and transferability in the workforce.

16.6 Conclusion

This analysis implicitly reinforces the view that the imminent creation of a new VET professional body is unlikely. However, the sorts of processes, problems and possibilities described remain broadly the same for VET professionals, working in their existing fragmented communities of practice. The central points can be expressed very simply: VET professionals and practitioners have some influence over their own futures, but less than many other more powerful players. Furthermore, their impact upon flexibility, transferability and mobility depends as much upon the actions of others, as it does upon the actions of he professionals themselves. Enhanced professionalism, therefore, is one potentially valuable avenue to explore, in improving VET provision with the aim of enhancing flexibility, transferability and mobility. It is not, and cannot be, some sort of universal panacea.

References

Ainley, P., & Bailey, B. (1997). *The Business of Learning: Staff and Student Experiences of Further Education in the 1990s*. London: Cassell.
Ashton, D.N., & Green, F. (1996). *Education, Training and the Global Economy*. Cheltenham: Edward Elgar.
Bourdieu, P., & Wacquant, L.J.D. (1992). *An Invitation to Reflexive Sociology*. Cambridge: Polity Press.
Brown, A., & Keep, E. (1999). *Review of vocational education and training research in the United Kingdom*. Luxemborg: Office for Official Publications of the European Communities.

Brown, J.S., Collins, A., & Duguid, P. (1989). *Situated Cognition and the Culture of Learning Educational Researcher, 18* (1) 32-42.

Engeström, Y. (2001). Expansive Learning at Work: towards an activity-theoretical reconceptualisation. *Journal of Education and Work, 14* (1) 133 – 156.

Gleeson, D., & Shain, F. (1999). Managing ambiguity: between markets and managerialism – a case study of 'middle' managers in further education'. *Sociological Review, 47* (3) 461 – 490.

Hargreaves, A., & Goodson, I. (1996). Teachers' professional lives: aspirations and actualities. In A. Hargreaves & I. Goodson (Eds.) *Teachers' Professional Lives.* London: Falmer.

Harris, H. (2000). *Defining the Future or Reliving the Past? Unions, Employers, and the Challenge of Workplace Learning.* Columbus OH: ERIC Clearinghouse on Adult, Career and Vocational Education.

Hodkinson P., & Bloomer, M. (2001). Dropping Out of Further Education: complex causes and simplistic policy assumptions. *Research Papers in Education, 16* (2) 117-140.

Hodkinson, P., & Hodkinson, H. (2001). *Problems Measuring Learning and Attainment in the Workplace.* Paper presented at the SKOPE/Working to Learn joint seminar, University of Warwick, March 22nd.

Lave, J., & Wenger, E. (1991). *Situated Learning.* Cambridge: Cambridge University Press.

Power, M. (1997). *The Audit Society: rituals of verification.* Oxford: Oxford University Press.

Skilbeck, M., Connell, H., Lowe, N., & Tait, K. (1994). *The Vocational Quest: New Directions in Education and Training.* London: Routledge.

Stronach, I., Corbin, B., McNamara, O., Stark, S., & Warne, T. (2001). *Towards an uncertain politics of professionalism: teacher and nurse identities in flux.* Paper given in a seminar in the Lifelong Learning Institute, University of Leeds, 11th June.

Wenger, E. (1998). *Communities of Practice: learning, meaning and identity.* Cambridge: Cambridge   University   Press.

Index